THE UNIVERSE
ENCYCLOPAEDIA
OF
NATURAL HISTORY

Drawn by Jaˢ Stewart — Engraved by Chaˢ Lawrie

HUMMING BIRDS AMONG TROPICAL FLOWERS

Selasphorus floresii. 1. Male. 2. Female. 3. Euphrusa eximia.
4. Heliathrix purpureiceps. 5. ORCHID. *Stanhopea ecornuta.*

BLACKIE & SON. LONDON. GLASGOW & EDINBURGH.

THE UNIVERSE

ENCYCLOPAEDIA
OF
NATURAL HISTORY

F.A. POUCHET

ILLUSTRATED BY 270 ENGRAVINGS
FROM DRAWINGS BY A. FAGUET, MESNEL AND BAYARD

BHAVANA BOOKS & PRINTS
NEW DELHI

First Reprint in India 2001

ISBN 81-86505-22-9

Published by Bhavana Books & Prints
A-38/2, Mayapuri, Phase I,
New Delhi-110064
Printed at Print Perfect, New Delhi

PREFACE.

My sole object in writing this work was to inspire and extend to the utmost of my power a taste for natural science.

It is not a learned treatise, but a simple elementary study, conceived with the idea of inducing the reader to seek in other works for more extensive and more profound knowledge.

I should feel pleased were this study to be looked upon as the peristyle of the temple in which lie hidden the mysterious splendours of Nature, and if it were the means of inspiring some with a desire to penetrate into the sanctuary itself, and uplift the veil which conceals them.

By the title which I have adopted, my intention was merely to indicate that I had gathered from creation at large, often contrasting the smallest of its productions with the mightiest.

I have gleaned everywhere, to show that Nature everywhere affords matter for interesting observations. The animal and the vegetable worlds, the earth and the heavens, appear by turns upon the scene.

Those who are interested by this compendious series of sketches and of pictures, will find more complete details in the lengthy notes placed at the end of the volume.[1] I know that it would require the learning of a Humboldt and the pen of a Michelet to execute in a

[1] In this translation, the notes referred to, so far as retained, are placed at the bottom of the pages to which they belong.—Tr.

perfect manner the task I have essayed; but, nevertheless, I have resolved to attempt it. I shall do my best to attain success, and wish with all my heart that others may do better.

Whoever aspires to the title of a philosopher has, in the present day, a double mission to perform—to discover and to popularize; he should labour on the one hand for the advancement, on the other for the diffusion, of science. The zoologists and botanists who shed the greatest lustre on our modern epoch, have shown, by the publication of their contributions on natural history, that they appreciate this sacred mission. I have here only imitated them in a somewhat more extended manner, and hope I shall be pardoned for following such an example.

It was in sight of the sea, on the magnificent beach of Treport, that I wrote this book as a relaxation during a vacation; and notwithstanding its elementary character, I thought it only right to place my name on its title-page.

One of my learned colleagues at the Academy of Sciences lately brought out a similar work, but under a fictitious name. The next day everybody knew who the author was. Besides, if a work is not worthy of bearing the author's name, it is not fit to see the light; and when an author consents to publish, it is because he believes his work to be useful, and therefore he ought not to be afraid of placing his name upon it. Hence I have done so.

Natural history is conveyed to the mind by a succession of pictures, and I have therefore in this work endeavoured to represent pictorially as many objects as possible.

The Publisher, who has shrunk from no outlay, has for this purpose placed at my disposal artists of the highest merit, in whose co-operation I have been very fortunate. I have especially to thank M. Faguet, assistant naturalist at the Sorbonne, who, being at once an accomplished botanist and an excellent draughtsman, has given quite a special character to the drawings of the plants; also M. Mesnel, who has drawn the zoological illustrations with much taste; and lastly M. Emile Bayard, to whose pencil we owe some charming landscapes.

F. A. POUCHET.

MUSEUM OF NATURAL HISTORY, ROUEN,
1st *November*, 1871.

TABLE OF CONTENTS.

THE ANIMAL KINGDOM.

BOOK I.

BOOK II.

BOOK III.

BOOK IV.

BOOK V.

BOOK VI.

BOOK VII.

THE VEGETABLE KINGDOM.

BOOK I.

BOOK II.

LIST OF THE ENGRAVINGS.

THE

ANIMAL KINGDOM.

"Savez-vous comment s'ouvre et grandit la semence,
Comment, herbe au printemps, elle est moisson l'été?
Comment au fond du nid de l'hirondelle agile
L'instinct s'épanouit en maternel amour,
Et comment, sous l'abri de la coque fragile,
S'anime un germe ailé qui doit éclore un jour?"

FRÉD. DESCHAMPS.

Know ye how opens out the seed, and how the plant up-grows,
How, soft and green in sweet spring-tide, 'tis ripe ere summer's close?
How, in the downy covert of the swift-winged swallow's nest,
Instinct to mother-love expands in the gentle creature's breast;
And how, beneath the shelter of the frail, translucent shell,
A wingèd germ takes life one day to quit its narrow cell?

BOOK I.

THE INVISIBLE WORLD.

OUR imagination, says Bonnet, one of the most zealous expounders of natural history, is equally confounded by what is infinitely great as by what is infinitely small.

In fact, the phenomena of creation astound us, whether we raise our eyes to investigate the mechanism of the heavens, or bend them downwards to examine the tiniest creatures of this lower realm.

Immensity is everywhere. It stands revealed in the azure dome of heaven, where glows a perfect dust of stars, and in the living atom too minute to display to us the marvels of its organization.

"Whoever," says an illustrious orator, "contemplates this spectacle with the eye of imagination, feels the littleness of man compared to the greatness of the universe." But although it is true that in presence of the immensity of space and the eternal duration of time, a feeling of humility overpowers us; although each step that man takes in his path, and every wrinkle that furrows his brow, reveals his utter feebleness; yet the mind within, that divine emanation, supports him on his journey by showing him both his power and his lofty origin.

If, at the very outset of our studies, we cast a glance upon the universe in general, we are astonished at its vastness, and have to confess that merely human attempts to explain its origin fall far behind the sublimity of its proportions.

For instance, the Chinese accounts of creation represent the first organizer of chaos under the form of a feeble old man, enervated and tottering, called Pan-Kou-Ché, surrounded by confused masses of rock, and holding a chisel in one hand and a hammer in the other. He toils painfully at his work, and, covered with perspiration, carves out the crust of the globe, at the same time that he clears a path through a wilderness of rocky masses.

One shudders at the feebleness of the workman when compared with the immensity of the task. Well nigh lost amidst enormous masses of shattered stone, which surround him on every side and encumber the picture, he is scarcely seen—a pigmy executing a herculean task.

On the other hand, the people of the North, looking upon their own rugged land, thought that some god in his terrible anger had broken up the surface of it, and gathered the débris into heaps. To the children of Scandinavia this deity was not a palsied and infirm old man; they required a divinity endowed with their own savage energy. In their eyes it was the god of tempests; the redoubtable and gigantic Thor, who, armed with a mighty hammer, and suspended over the abyss, with furious blows broke up the crust of the earth, and fashioned the rocks and mountains with the splinters. Here we see a conception far before that of the feeble old Pan-Kou-Ché; manly vigour is substituted for the impotence of old age. Thor shows like a revolted giant, raging and shattering everything that falls within his reach.

But to us, accustomed to bow before an all-powerful Creator, such images appear very puerile. Instead of these old men and giants laboriously occupied in hammering out the globe, we trace everywhere the invisible hand of God. In one place, with a delicacy which passes all conception, it fashions and animates the insect with the breath of life; in another, expanding itself to vast dimensions, it guides and governs the worlds scattered through space, convulses or annihilates them. It is at such times that with direful throes mountains are heaved up and abysses open on our globe; and upon these gigantic ruins, as upon each grain of sand, the philosopher finds written a grand page of natural theology.

In fact, every crumbling peak displays to our view the remains of generations buried by the revolutions of the globe. Their numbers, their size, their new and strange forms astonish us; but we cannot doubt the evidence, for these inanimate remains, of which the earth has faithfully kept the impress, are so many medals struck by the Creator and spared by the hand of time, to reveal to us the world's eventful history.

If we investigate the active forces of our planet, we soon perceive that their power is boundless. When they are unchained within its bowels, the whole surface of the earth is shaken. At one time they raise up the Alps and Himalayas, with their summits towering into the region of the clouds. At another, almost cleaving the globe from pole to pole, the Andes and America rise from the bosom of the sea; then the startled waves, tumultuously pouring over the ancient world, produce one of the more recent catastrophes, the great deluge. Thus the supreme Power decreed!

When, after having viewed the imposing phenomena which are taking place on the surface of the earth, we look down upon its tiniest inhabitants, we see revealed, in unexpected magnificence, the wisdom of Providence; ere long the spectacle of immensity in what is infinitely little, astonishes us no less than the immeasurable power displayed in the grand scenes of creation. Animate life recalls to mind the ancient doctrine of pantheism, according to which every molecule of created matter was imbued with a portion of the all-pervading deity; so life reveals itself everywhere: armed with the microscope the eye discovers traces of it in every interstice of matter.

Fontenelle, the learned secretary of the Academy, used to inveigh against the ancient verbose scholasticism, which he rightly called the philosophy of *words.* He would have had the intellect occupied solely with facts—with the philosophy of *things.* We are about to prove ourselves followers of his precepts by restricting ourselves to the results of observation.

Nothing gives a more brilliant idea of the universal diffusion of life throughout space, than the prodigious number of organisms which we meet everywhere and in all bodies. The demonstration of this fact is one of the most recent and magnificent conquests achieved by science.

We owe it to the microscope, discovered about a century and a half ago. This instrument at once displayed to men objects so new, striking, and unexpected, that it was everywhere admitted to have opened up a new world, by conferring, as it were, upon us an additional sense wherewith to investigate the invisible.

When we read the works of naturalists, and see them penetrating so deeply into the most recondite secrets of the anatomy and habits of beings, the very existence of which the eye could not lead us to suspect, we are apt to ask if the pride of genius has not led it beyond the simple realities of nature; and hence, for a long time, the statements of microscopists were, by some obstructive minds, regarded as fables. But when we see their instruments, and observe the remarkable precision with which they are constructed, we at once conclude that, however marvellous their investigations appear, there has been no self-deception in their case.

The microscope was discovered in Holland about the same time by two men of science, Leuwenhoeck and Hartzoeker, who each maintained that the priority of invention belonged to himself. The former was, however, really the father of microscopy; the latter was essentially a natural philosopher. The discussions between them were often bitter and unseemly. Leuwenhoeck lived isolated and solitary; he did not want any person to penetrate into his secrets; his wife and daughter alone were initiated into them, and his door remained closely shut against his young and turbulent rival.

Stung by this affront, the latter revenged himself to the utmost of his power, and assailed his antagonist sharply, declaring that his discoveries, published for the most part in a low and servile style, were absolutely chimerical. Insult followed hostility, and at last Hartzoeker resolved to stick at no means, and determined at all hazards to pry into the labours of his rival. By the aid of the chief magistrate of Leyden, he introduced himself under a feigned name to Leuwenhoeck, in order to pirate his labours; but the old microscopist, recognizing him, very speedily showed him the door.

Leuwenhoeck's discoveries are really wonderful when compared with his means of investigation; the acute observation of the philosopher transcended the power of his instruments, and even now we ask how he can have guessed at so many truths, which they could not have revealed to him.

In fact, the illustrious Dutchman never possessed an instrument to be compared in point of perfection to those which we use now-a-days; he only employed simple lenses which he made himself; it was with instruments like these that he made his most important discoveries. Any one can verify this assertion in the museum of the Royal Society of London, to which on his death-bed he bequeathed those magnifying glasses that had gained him so much glory.

Leuwenhoeck's most powerful lenses did not magnify more than sixty diameters, whereas we now possess achromatic microscopes which magnify twelve to fifteen hundred diameters.

It was recently stated in some of the scientific journals, that two London opticians had succeeded in constructing lenses of 7500 diameters, equal to an enlargement of the surface of 56,000,000 times. It was added that, notwithstanding such an extraordinary result, everything was seen with great clearness.

Even the measurement of the most minute microscopic details has acquired a degree of precision surpassing everything that could be imagined. There are glass micrometers in which each millimetre[1] is divided into 500 parts, or lines, of such tenuity, that the most practised eye cannot make them out. This is effected by means of an instrument of extreme delicacy, which only works in the dead of night, when there is nothing to disturb it or impede the accuracy of its tracings. For this purpose the workman himself does not enter his work-room; a piece of

[1] Equal to ·039371 inch.

mechanism, moved by clock-work, at a suitable hour sets the machine in movement. The invisible divisions of the glass plate are engraved by means of an excessively fine diamond point, which is found to be totally worn out when its work is accomplished.

But the means of investigation at the disposal of the microscopist do not end here. In observations of extreme delicacy micrometers are called into requisition which are constructed with an ingenious mechanism capable of dividing a millimetre (say $\frac{1}{25}$th of an inch) into 10,000 parts by moving spiders' threads with the aid of a simple screw. The investigator also utilizes in a thousand ways both simple and polarized light, as well as chemical re-agents; and as these last, owing to the vapours they disengage, injure the glasses and dull their surface, those who work with the microscope, in order to avoid the inconvenience thus occasioned, employ particular instruments, the lenses of which are placed below the objects to be magnified.

After this demonstration of the resources at its command, will any one accuse micrography of giving rise to those vain illusions with which those who do not enter upon the investigation it requires with a proper degree of patience, are pleased to reproach it? Perchance! for this science has never ceased to recall the interminable discussions which overhung its cradle. The dispute between Leuwenhoeck and Hartzoeker is not yet allayed.

CHAPTER I.

MICROSCOPIC ANIMALCULES.

The animalcules which compose the microscopic world have for a long time been known by the name of Infusoria, but the term ought to be abandoned, as many of these creatures do not live in infusions, but, on the contrary, inhabit the sea and fresh-water. It would therefore be better to substitute the names Microzoa and Protozoa;[1] the former meaning little animals, the latter the obscure beginnings of animal organization. The latter name is extensively used in England.

For a long time the anatomy of these invisible beings appeared a perfect mystery, and men despaired of ever comprehending it. Baron

[1] Names derived from the Greek words *mikron zōon*, little animal, and *prōton zōon*, first animal.

Gleichen, having steeped carmine in water containing some of these animalcules, was quite astonished to see them fill themselves with colouring matter. But this important fact passed unnoticed. Buffon and Lamarck still continued to look upon them simply as little masses of animated gelatine.

A French naturalist, Dujardin, reared up a complete theory on these data. According to him the substance of the animalcule represents a sort of spongy tissue, capable of hollowing itself out into accidental cavities, which admit food and expel it by means of an outlet which opens for this purpose in the surface of the body. A strange hypothesis, according to which the Microzoon hollows out for itself stomachs in its own substance and of its own free-will!

1. Various Infusoria or Microzoa.

It is difficult to believe that such a theory held sway in France long after the publication of Ehrenberg's magnificent work on the *Infusoria*, in which the learned Prussian naturalist demonstrated, for the first time, that these creatures, notwithstanding their extreme minuteness, possess in some cases a surprisingly complicated internal organization.

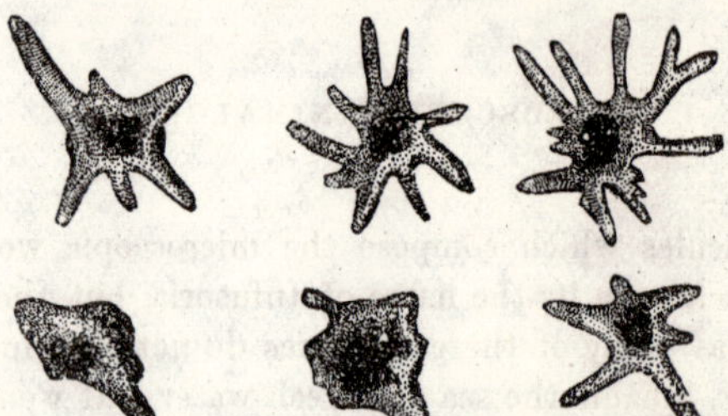

2. Successive forms assumed by the Proteus.

Their form is, as a rule, fixed, yet some of them change their shape at will, and present to the eyes of the astonished observers so many different aspects, that at the expiration of five minutes they cannot be recognized. At one moment they are globular or three-cornered; an instant after they are seen taking on the appearance of a star. Accordingly, these creatures, with their deceptive changes of form, have received the name of Protei, from the famous sea-god of antiquity, who by his wonderful metamorphoses was enabled to elude attempts to catch him.

Some animalcules of this class surround themselves with self-produced feet like living roots, the arrangement of which they are seen

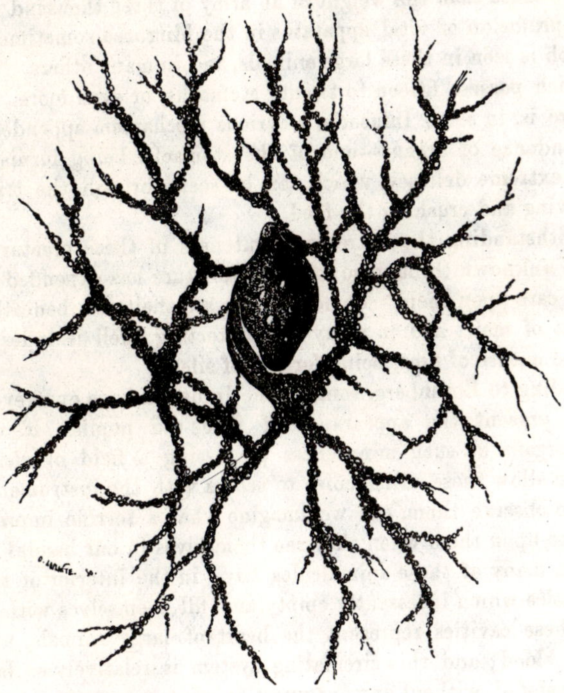

3. Wagener's Lieberkuhnia—*Lieberkuhnia Wageneri* (Claparède).

varying in a thousand ways. Sometimes they extend them to an immense length, sometimes they withdraw them entirely. They spread them out separately, join them together, or entwine them like the locks of a Gorgon.

The microscopic world also has its extremes. There is as wide a distance between the size of its tiniest representative the Monad, and that of one of its largest the hooded Colpodos, as there is between a beetle and an elephant.

Nothing is more marvellous than the organization of these invisible beings, and if attentive observations had not placed the facts beyond doubt, people might have been tempted to think that the accounts given by naturalists were pieces of romance or else barefaced lies.

A single Microzoon has, so to speak, no weight; placed in the most sensitive balance it does not impart to it the slightest oscillation. The whale, on the other hand, attains a length of 100 feet and a weight of 200 tons—more than the weight of an army of three thousand men; and yet, the profusion of vital apparatus in the Microzoa sometimes exceeds that which is seen in these large animals, and in many others. There are some which possess fifteen to twenty stomachs, or even more. In addition there is, in some Infusoria, a curious mechanism appended to this superabundance of organs—one of the stomachs being furnished with teeth of extreme delicacy, which can be seen through the transparent body moving and crushing the food.

Notwithstanding the extreme minuteness of these creatures, which remained unknown through so many ages, nature has expended the most watchful care upon them. Some of them are sheltered beneath a calcareous coat of mail; and in many the protecting shell is indestructible, and of the nature of flint, being formed of silex.

According to Ehrenberg, some of the Infusoria have even eyes, which at times present the appearance of flame-red pupils. If we could suppose organs of such minuteness possessing a field of vision large enough to allow these animalcules to see us with the instruments which we use to observe them, can we imagine what a terrific impression we must make upon them when they see themselves in our hands?

Lastly, many of these animalcules have, in the interior of the body, large cavities which incessantly empty and fill themselves with coloured fluid. These cavities represent the heart of large animals, and their fluid the blood; and this circulating system is relatively so large that it may be stated, without any exaggeration, that some microscopic beings have hearts fifty times as large and as strong in proportion as that of the horse or ox.

If the wonderful organic perfection of those living corpuscles surpass all our preconceived ideas, their perpetual activity affords ground for no less astonishment. The life of all animals is made up of alternate action and repose, of movement which wastes the forces, and sleep which repairs them; but the Infusoria are strangers to anything of the kind; their life is an emblem of incessant agitation. Ehrenberg, who observed them at all hours of the night, always found them in movement, and accordingly concluded that they had neither rest nor sleep! Even the plant, exhausted by the performance of the functions of vegetable life, sleeps at the close of day; the animalcule, notwithstanding its prodigious activity, does not.

Struck with the fact, Owen has conjectured that this extraordinary activity might be due to the enormous development of the digestive system in the Infusoria, seeing that a man, a lion, or a tiger has only one stomach, an ox or a camel four or five, whilst invisible Microzoa have sometimes a hundred!

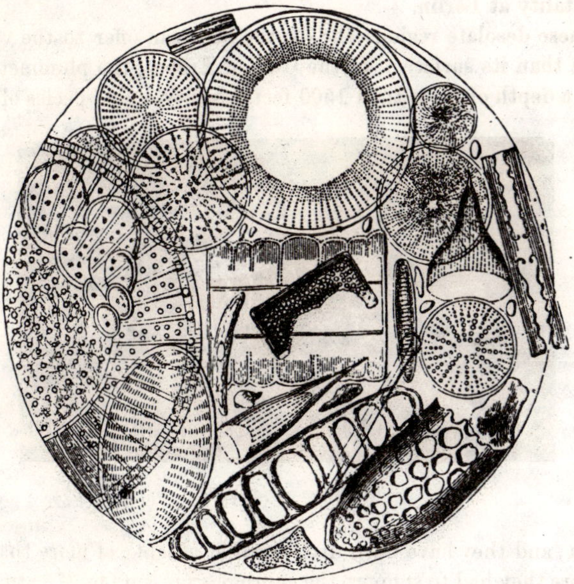

4. Infusoria procured by Sir James Ross from the bottom of the Antarctic Ocean, as seen with the microscope.

In proportion as science has been perfected the horizon of life has been enlarged, and a microscopic world, full of animated existence, has been revealed in every spot to which investigation has been able to reach. The Polar ices, the elevated regions of the atmosphere, and the gloomy depths of ocean, are peopled with living organisms; and everywhere their prodigious concentration astonishes us as much as the infinite variety of their forms.

If the beautiful discoveries of Ehrenberg did not prove the fact, who would believe that these tiny creatures, so minute as to be invisible, possess more vital resistance than the most vigorous animals? Where the severity of the climate kills the most robust of the vegetable world, where a few scattered animals pick up a precarious subsistence, the delicate organism of the Microzoa suffers no injury from the most terrible cold that is experienced. More than fifty species of animalcules with silicious carapaces were discovered by Captain Sir James Ross on the rounded masses of ice which float in the Polar Seas at the seventy-eighth degree of south latitude. Some of those which this navigator collected in the vicinity of Victoria Land, in spite of distance and storms, arrived full of vitality at Berlin.

In these desolate regions the depths of ocean offer to the view even more life than its surface. In the Gulf of Erebus, the plummet brought up, from a depth of more than 1500 feet, seventy-eight species of silicious

5. *Medusa campanularia.*

Microzoa; and they have been discovered at a depth of more than 12,000 feet, where they had to support the enormous pressure of 375 atmospheres —a pressure capable of bursting a cannon, but which the gelatinous body of a microscopic animal resists in some marvellous way.

These living corpuscles, which swarm in the transparent regions of the ocean, abound equally in the muddy waters of our rivers and ponds, and without being aware of it we daily swallow myriads of them in the fluids we drink. If with the aid of the microscope we were to scrutinize everything that a single drop of water sometimes contains, there would be seen enough to frighten many people.

Every one who has sailed at night upon the sea, or passed along its shores, is acquainted with the phenomenon of phosphorescence, which for a long time puzzled the sagacity of the learned. It was attributed to very different causes, but is now known to depend upon the presence of a multitude of animals. Sometimes, when of small extent, it is caused by fish traversing the waves like a flaming arrow; at other times it is owing to the presence of Medusæ, the brilliant disks of which are seen calm and motionless in the depths of the waters; or to the

6. The Hydrostatic Physophora—*Physophora muzonema.*

Physophora, trailing behind them their tresses all spangled with stars like those of Berenice in the firmament. Certain molluscs too, though enveloped in their shells, are nevertheless phosphorescent. Even Pliny remarked that the mouths of persons who had eaten Pholades were quite luminous.

This phenomenon, however, is most frequently seen in places where the sea is in movement; every wave then rolls with luminous foam against the prow of the ship, and the billows gleam like the starry sky. These myriads of phosphorescent particles, which make the sea sparkle, are only Microzoa of extreme minuteness, but of which the size is increased a hundred-fold by their splendour.

The ocean produces these animalcules in almost every part. Each bed of it, says Humboldt, is peopled with them at depths which exceed the height of the greatest mountain chains, and under the influence of certain meteorological changes we see them rise to the surface of its watery expanse, where they form immense luminous furrows in the wake of the ships.

7. The Miliary Noctiluca, highly magnified—*Noctiluca miliaria.*

The Miliary Noctiluca is one of those which play the greatest part in the phosphorescence of the ocean. Seen with the aid of a powerful microscope, this minute animalcule looks like a tiny sphere of diaphanous jelly, bestrewn with luminous points, and carrying a thin filiform appendage, which some naturalists look upon as a sucker.

Water presents another peculiarity equally strange, and for a long time inexplicable. At times it takes on a blood-red tint, which in every age has startled and alarmed the vulgar.

From the remotest times men speculated upon the cause of this phenomenon, which had so much of the marvellous about it, and it was only explained on some strange hypothesis or other. But since the discovery of the microscope it has been thoroughly investigated, and naturalists have shown that the redness of the water depends upon the presence of extremely small plants and animals, which, under the influence of certain atmospheric conditions, multiply in such abundance, that the mind can hardly realize the marvellous rapidity with which they spring into existence.

A Belgian savant, M. Morren, after collecting together nearly all that had been written on the subject of red water from the days of Moses up to our own, gives a list of twenty-two species of animals, and almost as many plants, capable of communicating this blood colour.

When Ehrenberg planted his tent by the shore of the Red Sea, near the town of Tor, not far from Mount Sinai, he had the rare good fortune to behold this sea tinged with the blood-red colour to which, from the remotest antiquity, it has owed its name. At this very time its waves deposited on the shore a gelatinous matter of a beautiful purple colour, which the great Prussian naturalist recognized as being composed of a single microscopic marine plant, the Red Trichodesmia, the sole cause of this celebrated phenomenon.

Water is not the sole domain of microscopic animalcules. They are met with in the earth, in masses which contain them in such enormous numbers as to exceed all powers of calculation. Certain species, so extremely minute as not to equal the forty-five thousandth part of an inch, form in some damp places living beds beneath the soil which are often several yards in thickness.

8. The Red Trichodesmia (*Trichodesmia rubra*), seen under the microscope.

In North America these animal strata are found as much as twenty feet thick, and among the heaths of Luneburg there are some more than forty feet in thickness. The city of Berlin is built upon one of these beds of animalcules, which is even more than three times the size of the last mentioned. Everything here strikes us with wonder. The microscopic creatures of which we are speaking are so minute that 10,000 could be ranged on the length of an inch, and the weight of each is scarcely the millionth part of a milligramme (·0154 grain), for it has been calculated that it requires 1,111,500,000 to weigh a gramme.[1]

Such a soil is naturally wanting in stability. This was seen in the capital of Prussia, where it became necessary, in constructing new buildings, to sink the foundations very deep, several houses having subsided on account of the unstable ground beneath them. In many other places these puny animalcules swarm by myriads of myriads, and form deposits of great size on the superficial strata of the globe. In his remarkable

[1] A gramme is equal to 15·4440 grains. These enormous masses of Infusoria are accounted for by supposing that they are reproduced with miraculous rapidity by way of subdivision. One of these animalcules divides into two; each of these quickly divides into two others; in this way four individuals are speedily formed, then eight, then sixteen, &c. This phenomenon takes place with such incredible rapidity, that, according to Ehrenberg, one of the organisms spoken of above can produce a million descendants in twenty-four hours, and in four days about 140 billions; that is to say, nearly two cubic feet of the ground on which part of Berlin stands.

work on the earth, M. Elisée Reclus states, that in the harbour of Wismar the mud is composed to the extent of a third part or even a half of living species heaped together in incalculable multitudes, at the rate of perhaps a million cubic yards in a century.

A traveller exploring an elevated mountain is sometimes struck by a singular phenomenon, namely, the red colour of the snow. This fact, of which Aristotle, the prince of naturalists, long ago took notice, is due to

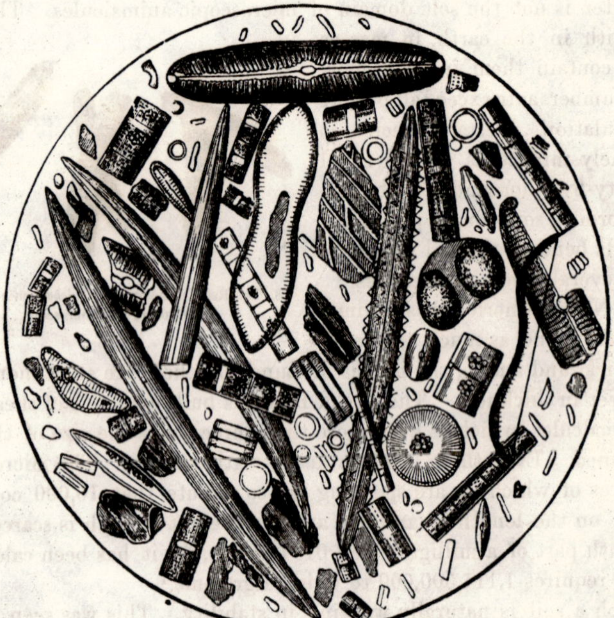

9. Infusoria and Living Diatomaceæ from the Strata under Berlin, as seen with the microscope.

the presence of microscopic organisms; and it is a remarkable circumstance that the same creature, the *Discerœa nivalis*, seems to produce it everywhere; on the icy summits of the Alps and on the snows of the farthest Polar regions to which man has penetrated; for red snow is met with even in these frozen realms.

The pantheists supposed life to be disseminated through all the interstices of matter. These microscopic animalcules recall this theory; as they often abound where we might least expect to find them. Although our enlightened age has destroyed the hypothesis of panspermism, which held that every particle of creation contained germs or living organisms, yet we must admit that though these impalpable metaphysical germs existed only in the imagination, there are nevertheless Microzoa that float hither and thither on the bosom of the atmosphere, notwithstanding it appears to us so transparent and pure.

The invisible organisms that people the air constitute, according to Humboldt, quite a special fauna. But irrespective of these meteoric Infusoria, the existence of which, according to this illustrious philosopher, cannot be doubted, the atmosphere carries an immense quantity of ordinary animalcules, both alive and dead, which its currents take up and transport to all parts of the globe. Sometimes they abound to such an extent in the air as to intercept the light and suffocate travellers.

Ehrenberg, on analyzing a shower of fine dust which, at a distance of 380 miles from the coast of Africa, enveloped vessels in a thick fog, found eighteen species of silica-plated animalcules.

But microscopic life does not invade air, earth, and water only. It is met with again full of vigour and vitality in the interior of animals and plants. No organ, however vigorous or well protected, can elude it. Not only do animalcules pour into every cavity of the animal which is in communication with the outer world, but they are met with in parts closely sealed up from the air. The complete system of arteries and veins by which the circulation of the blood is effected, though closed from the outer world at every point, nevertheless at times contains Microzoa mixed with the blood globules, apparently living quite at their ease in the midst of the incessant flow of the blood. Supposing that this traverses its circuit every day more than 2800 times, and that, not taking account of the capillary ramifications or the bending of the vessels, this circuit is only four or five metres in length, even then the animalcules are borne on a current which carries them daily three leagues—a fearful journey for such frail organisms!

Man himself does not imagine that, despite his pride, a race of invisible beings incessantly devours, and sometimes ends by destroying him. Vibriones, resembling imperceptible tiny eels, are constantly discovered in his intestines. His mouth is always inhabited by myriads of animalcules, the microscopic sepulchre of which is represented by the tartar that loosens our teeth; for, in many cases, it is formed of nothing else but the incrustations of their calcareous skeletons.

Intestinal worms, not larger than the head of a pin, gathering in colonies in the head of the sheep, occasion certain death. They are the cause of that complaint known in our country districts as *staggers*, or more generally as *turn-sick*, because when they are attacked by it they turn round perpetually. Innumerable legions of another worm, still smaller, invade all our fleshy structures, and sometimes multiply in them to such

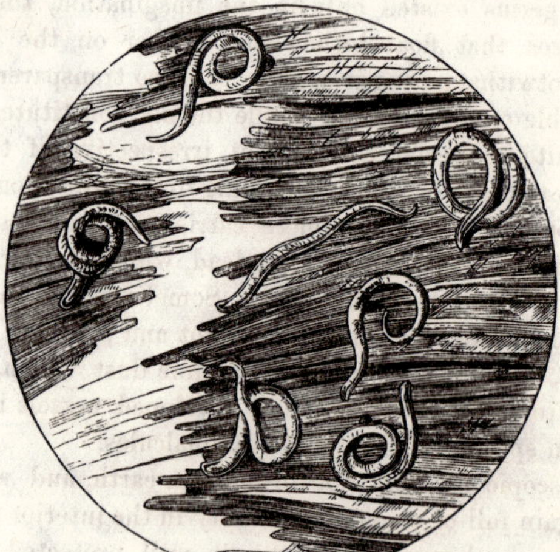

10. Trichinæ gnawing a Muscle, magnified two hundred diameters.

an extent, that as many as twenty-five have been counted in one of the muscles of the ear which does not exceed a grain of millet in size.[1]

11. Female Trichina depositing her young, magnified six hundred diameters.

This worm, which has been a great deal spoken about of late years, is the *Trichina spiralis*. The pig is its favourite abode; but it is sometimes seen in man, especially where, as in Germany, ham and sausages are eaten raw. Once introduced within the frame by means of the food, the Trichinæ multiply in the intestines, and their little ones invade the muscles to such an extent, that as many as six or eight have been discovered in each segment seen in the field of the microscope. A frightful death is the result: we are devoured still living by these imperceptible worms, and no human power can arrest their work.

Thus the dominion of the Microzoa has no bounds, but immensity itself.

[1] I allude here to the *Trichina spiralis*, a little microscopic worm, twisted spirally, which has occasioned numerous fatal accidents in some parts of Germany. Physiologists know that it is propagated by the use of the flesh of animals infected by it. In certain countries,

CHAPTER II.

THE ANTEDILUVIAN INFUSORIA.

The prodigious abundance of the Infusoria during certain geological periods is one of the most extraordinary facts that the study of nature offers. Although, according to the computations of Ehrenberg, there are sometimes more than a million of these animals in a cubic inch of chalk, yet they swarmed in such numbers, and were so miraculously prolific, at the era of this formation, that, in spite of their extreme minuteness, some stratified rocks, entirely made up of their calcareous shells, constitute at the present time mountains which take an important place in the mineral crust of the globe.

Again, microscopists have recently made known a wholly unexpected fact. They have shown that some silicious rocks, known by the name of tripolis, and which to all appearance were homogeneous, are almost exclusively composed of the skeletons of several species of Infusoria belonging to the family of Bacillaria. These skeletons have so faithfully preserved the form of the animals from which they were generated, that men have been enabled to compare them with our living species, and recognize that they had the closest analogy with these.

This remarkable discovery is due to Ehrenberg. He communicated it to Al. Brongniart on the occasion of a journey the latter made to Berlin. This unexpected revelation so excited the illustrious mineralogist that he wrote the following words to the Academy of Sciences:—"I have seen all these marvels. I have compared them with the beautiful drawings of living species made by M. Ehrenberg, and I can no longer retain the slightest doubt."

Thus it is demonstrated that rocks which belong to the most ancient epochs of life on our globe, and which sometimes contain strata of vast magnitude, are only so many graveyards of the Infusoria. The mind grows bewildered in trying to find out in what mysterious way these many invisible animalcules could be accumulated to form such extraordinary heaps of corpses.

where there is a suspicion that it is introduced within the system by the use of raw pork as food, the authorities have already begun to interdict the use of the latter article. This is the case in some parts of Prussia.]

The city of Richmond, in North America, is the centre of one of these districts, where, according to the beautiful saying of Shelley, every grain of dust was once endued with life. The deposit of microscopic skeletons attains a depth of several hundred yards. If as many human mummies were laid one upon another they would form a mountain the height of which would almost equal a semi-diameter of the earth! (W. de Fonvielle).

It is very easy to verify these statements. The reader has only to

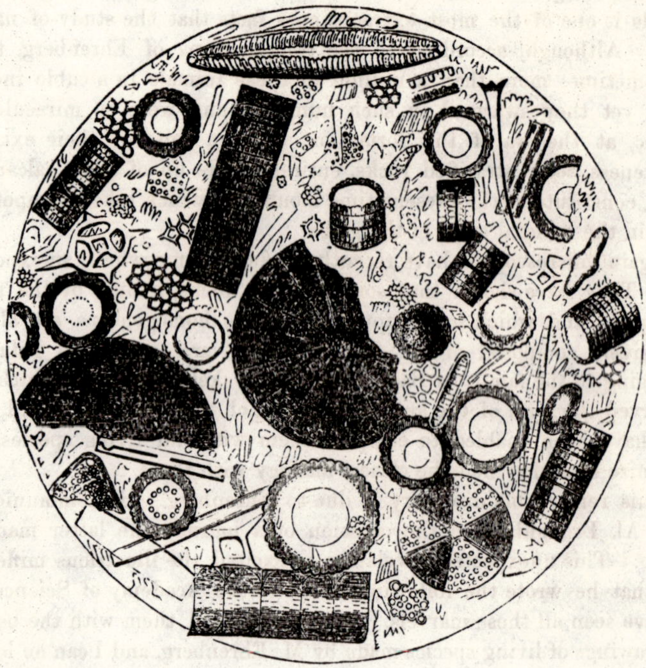

12. Infusoria in Tripoli, from Richmond, N. America, as seen with the microscope.

scrape with a knife the surface of a morsel of one of these tripolis, to let the dust fall on a plate of glass, and to examine it with the microscope after having mixed it with a little water. He will be astonished to see nothing but carapaces of animalcules.

The confirmation of what we have said is chiefly met with in the tripoli of Bilin in Bohemia, and in those of the Isle of France.

The learned Schleiden calculated that a cubic inch of the former contains, in round numbers, forty-one millions of animalcules, and as the schists of Bilin extend over a surface of not less than eight to ten square leagues, and are from two to fifteen feet thick, what an amount of vital activity there must have been in this region to produce such a mass of imperceptible skeletons!

Some tripolis of a red colour are employed in house-painting; others serve for cleaning our plate, dish-covers, &c. A few years ago people little thought that the rose-colour with which we decorate our dwellings was due to the skeletons of invisible animalcules, and that it was they which, from their silicious nature, enabled us to give a beautiful polish to so many articles of copper. It is with the osseous structures of myriads of animals that we scour our cooking utensils?

Not only do the Infusoria enter into the composition of the porous

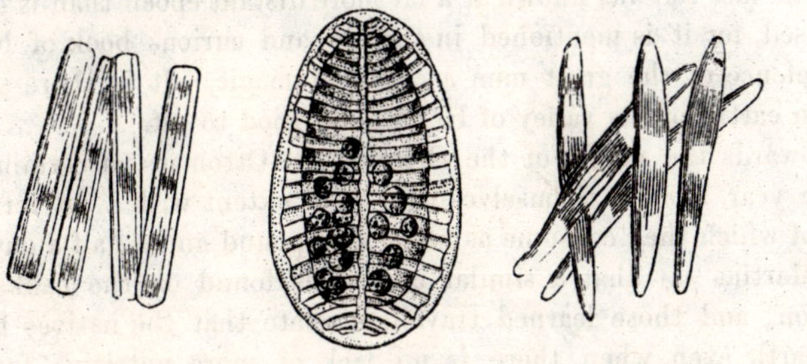

13. Skeletons of Silicious Infusoria, seen under the microscope.

rocks, but we meet with them even in the most compact that are known, such as the silex, which forms our hardest pebbles and gun-flints. Mr. White, in a memoir read before the Microscopical Society of London, described twelve species in the flint of the chalk.

The miraculous abundance of this once living dust in the ancient epochs of our globe is fully shown in the colouring of certain rocks. According to Marcel de Serre, rock-salt, which is sometimes tinged with red, owes its tint to the microscopic animals which lived in the waters wherein it was formed. This savant also tells us that cornelians owe their beautiful red colour to the presence of Infusoria, a fact irrefragably proved by an inspection of some of these stones embedded in which the skeletons of different animalcules can be discovered.

CHAPTER III.

FOSSIL MEAL AND THE EARTH-EATERS.

In several parts of the world the dearth of sources of food compels men to nourish themselves with certain kinds of earth which actually possess a nutritive power.

Travellers are too unanimous on this point to allow of our doubting it. The fact too was known at a far more distant epoch than is generally supposed, for it is mentioned in the old and curious book of Naudé in the defence of the great men accused of magic. It is there said that certain earths of the valley of Hebron are good to eat.

Towards the mouth of the Orinoco, the Ottomacs, at certain seasons of the year, nourish themselves to a great extent with a fat ferruginous clay, of which they consume as much as a pound and a half a day. Spix and Martius say that a similar custom is found on the banks of the Amazon; and those learned travellers relate that the natives there eat this earth even when there is no lack of more nutritive food. We know also that an edible clay is sold in the markets of Bolivia; and lastly, Gliddon assures us that there are a tolerably large number of earth-eating tribes in North America, mentioning in particular the negroes spread through the forests of Carolina and Florida.

Naturalists, struck with these accounts, were eager to make out the composition of these edible earths, and to their astonishment discovered that some of them were nothing else than different kinds of tripolis, or clays, containing a considerable number of fresh-water Infusoria or microscopic shells. It is clear therefore that these alimentary rocks owe their nutritive properties to animal matter which they have retained, and that it is this which renders them of any value as food.

But the revolutions of the earth have not stopped here; they have now and then produced a perfect fossilized animal meal. Nothing more is required than to make it into bread. In fact, it is well known, that in times of dearth, the Laplanders nourish themselves with a white mineral dust, which they substitute for cereal products. Retzius, who examined this meal, found that it is composed of nineteen species of Infusoria, analogous to those which now live in the neighbourhood of Berlin; and the learned professor has even shown that this skeleton dust, which is spread equally through Finland and Sweden, owes its nutritive qualities to a certain amount of animal substance which chemical analysis detected after so many, many ages!

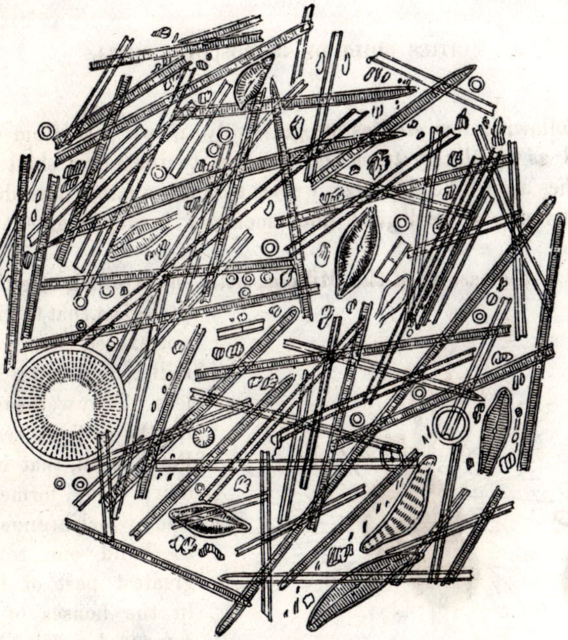

14. Microscopic view of Infusoria in Mountain-meal of Ebsdorf.[1]

Thus modern science throws her vivid light upon a crowd of facts which till our day remained hidden in darkness.

[1] In Europe the most celebrated deposits of mountain-meal are those of Lapland, of Degernä and Lollhagysyön in Sweden, of Ebsdorf in the Lunenburg Heath, and of Santafiora in Tuscany. Smaller deposits are found in Greece, Hungary, Bohemia, France, and elsewhere. I myself discovered one in 1846 at Loulé in South Portugal. Many of these accumulations of mountain-meal are of great importance to man, being mixed with common meal and used as food, though the substance possesses no conceivable alimentary properties. In Europe it is only the mountain-meal of Lapland and Sweden that is so used. Of the mountain-meal of Lollhagysyön, for example, there are every year many hundred waggon-loads consumed. Many of these deposits are especially interesting on this account, that their upper beds consist of diatoms that are still living. To this class belong the deposit not far from Ebsdorf in the Lunenburg Heath, which is about 30 feet in thickness, and according to Ehrenberg, is composed of some thirty different species of diatoms. The prevailing species is, however, *Synedra acuta*, whose hard coverings appear in the form

CHAPTER IV.

CITIES BUILT OF MICROSCOPIC SHELLS

In following our studies progressively, if we pass from organisms so small as absolutely to escape the eye, to those the shell of which approaches a pin's head in size, we see that these latter have determined the occurrence of geological phenomena of immense extent and importance.

This is the case with the Miliolæ, little shells which owe their name to the fact that their size does not exceed that of a grain of millet, and indeed is often less. They were so numerous in the ancient seas of the Paris basin, that in settling down they formed mountains, which are now quarried to build our towns: the greatest part of the stone in the houses of Paris is composed simply of the carapaces of these molluscs agglomerated and closely cemented together; so that one may say without hyperbole that our splendid capital is built of microscopic shells.

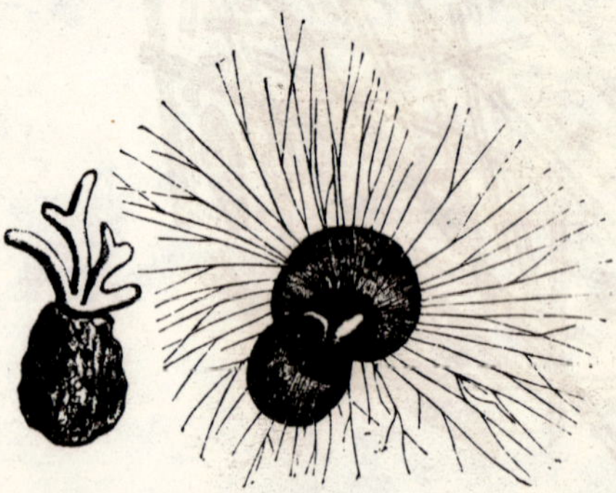

15. Magnified Miliola with its Capillary Appendages projected.

An observation by M. Defrance will give an idea of the minuteness of the Stone Miliola, the species which principally constitutes the coarse limestone used in building. He has computed that a box with a capacity of a cubic line would contain as many as ninety-six!

What a mystery envelops the life of these fragile shells, which, in spite of their insignificant size, have played such a great part in the geologic phenomena of the tertiary epoch! Nature here reveals her

of long ladder-like bodies. Next to it the most conspicuous are *Pinnularia inæqualis* (the crooked, ship formed bodies, marked with cross-lines), and *Gallionella varians* (the large round discs).—Willkomm, *Die Wunder des Mikroskops.*

infinite power by regaining, through prodigious fecundity, what she loses in bulk. Hence, as Lamarck has said, the vestiges of some microscopic creatures have had more influence upon the crust of the globe than those of such huge animals as elephants, rhinoceroses, and whales.

We have seen certain invisible organisms and microscopic shells

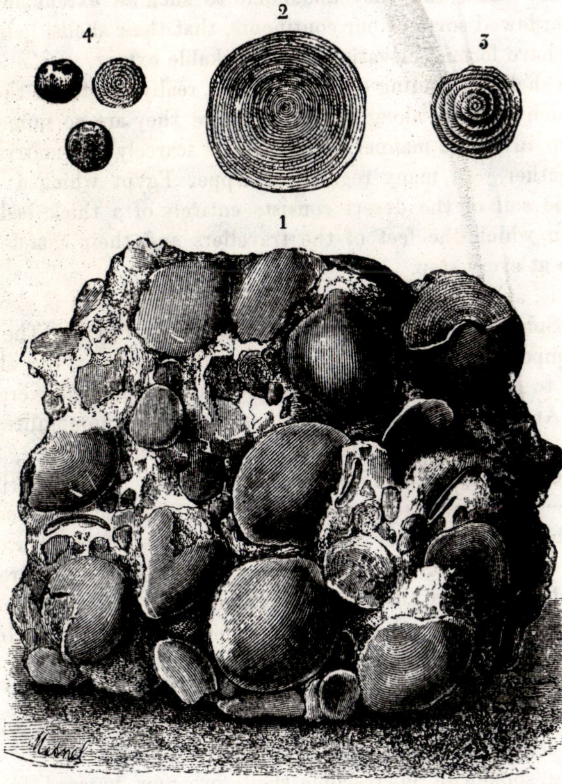

16. 1, Rock of the Arabian Chain formed by agglomerated Nummulites used for building the Pyramids of Egypt; 2, 3, Interior View of Nummulites; 4, Nummulites from the Libyan Chain, of which the Sphinx is exclusively composed.

produce great stratified rocks. If we now examine other molluscs of the same group as the latter, but somewhat larger, the nummulites, we are still more astonished at the vast phenomena to which they have given rise. These phenomena include the formation of long and lofty chains of mountains.

These nummulites receive their name from their flattened discoidal form, which resembles that of a piece of money, in Latin *nummulus*. Many of these shells are very small; others attain the size of a lentil, a seed which they often resemble exactly.

The nummulites then have played a great part at different geological epochs. They are met with in prodigious quantities in the secondary and tertiary beds, and they abounded to such an extent in the seas which overflowed some of our continents, that their shells, being heaped together, have formed elevations of remarkable extent.

These shells, extending over a vast area, really constitute the Arabian chain which extends along the Nile; there they are so numerous, and heaped up in such a manner, that there is scarcely any matrix to bind them together. In many regions of Upper Egypt which I have traversed, the soil of the desert consists entirely of a thick bed of nummulites, in which the feet of the travellers and their camels slip and sink deep at every step.

Paris is, as we have said, built solely of shells; this is also the case with the Sphinx and the celebrated Pyramids of Egypt. The immense blocks composing the latter, neither the transportation nor the raising of which to such a vast height has been well explained, were brought from the Arabian chain, and are composed solely of nummulites. Many of these exactly resemble lentils in their form and size, and this coincidence has given rise to strange mistakes. Time, wearing down the surface of these gigantic monuments, has gathered enormous masses at their bases, where they impede the footsteps of the traveller. In the time of Strabo it was maintained that these were the remains of seeds used as food by the ancient workmen, who had abandoned them, and which had fossilized by the action of time. But the Greek geographer refuted this vulgar tradition, and in his description of Egypt he classes the nummulites among the petrifactions, calling to mind that in his own country, Pontus, there were hills full of tuff stones similar to lentils.

Having spoken of microscopic shells, we now proceed to speak of some colossal ones.

One of these in particular has acquired a certain celebrity on account of its size and the peculiar use to which it has been put. It is the gigantic Tridacna, commonly known as the "holy-water pot," because it is sometimes employed in our churches to contain the consecrated water. But those which we see are far from giving us an idea of the animal. The great Tridacnæ, which can only be detached from the rocks by cutting the fibrous mass that fastens them with an axe, sometimes weigh more than five hundred pounds. In the archipelago of the

17. View of the Sphinx and the Great Pyramid of Egypt.—From a photograph.

Molucca Islands these conchological giants are not rare. The natives eat them like our oysters, to which they are analogous, and the flesh of one is a sufficient meal for twenty people. Their thick valves, which are sometimes five feet long, serve as troughs for the inhabitants, presented by nature ready cut and polished, and which, according to Péron, they often use for feeding pigs and other animals. Sometimes also they convert them into baths for their children.

18. Gigantic Tridacna, used in the Moluccas as a Bathing-tub.

Some of those fossil shells, so well known under the name of ammonites, were of even more gigantic proportions. Buffon speaks of one, the diameter of which was equal to that of a carriage-wheel, and which was used for a millstone.

Finally, if the abysses of the sea do not harbour the monsters with which the imagination of some chroniclers has peopled them, we certainly sometimes discover in the ocean molluscs of prodigious dimensions, the fleshy mass of which is not less than from sixteen to twenty feet in length, without reckoning the arms which crown the head. Such was the cuttle-fish (*Sepia*) which the steamer *Alecton* met in 1861 between Madeira and the Canary Islands. Its weight was estimated at 4414 lbs. avoirdupois, but the crew could not attack it vigorously enough to capture it, as Captain Bouyer was afraid it might upset the boats, by clasping them in its formidable limbs armed with suckers. This encounter strongly impressed the captain, and led him to end his narrative with these words:—

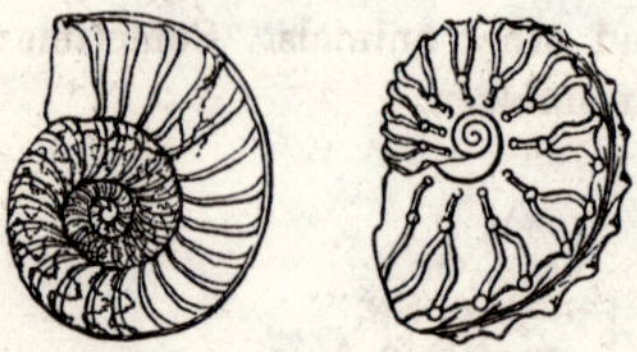

19. Fossil Ammonites.

"Now, that I have seen this strange animal with my own eyes I can no longer refuse credence to the tales of navigators. I suspect the sea has not yet told all it has to tell, and holds in reserve some remnants of its perished races; or that, in its ever-active crucible, it still elaborates unheard-of forms, with which it may appal the mariner, and supply a theme for mysterious legends of the ocean."

CHAPTER V.

THE MONAD.

What a mysterious abyss is expressed by this single word *monad!* This first expression of creative power is only revealed to us by the microscope, and we still only perceive it as a mass, for the individual monads often escape our sight. The extreme minuteness of the monad seems to point it out as an element of the most hidden phenomena of life. How often have philosophers looked upon animal life of the highest order as being merely the representative of an agglomeration of monads!

These minute beings were looked upon by Buffon and some other naturalists as organic molecules, the agglomeration of which, presided over by fixed laws, contributed to the formation of plants and animals. After the time of the immortal overseer of the Jardin du Roi, Oken upheld the same opinion, maintaining that large animals were aggregates of monads; an idea which, as the reader will perceive, seems to be only a repetition of the famous hypothesis of atoms which we owe to Leucippus; which, after having flourished in antiquity, is seen shedding its latest gleams of light upon the writings of Kepler and Descartes.[1]

These monads, which are simply living atoms, are so extremely small, that they can only be seen by the help of the greatest magnifying power. They are met with in all kinds of animal and vegetable infusions, and their number is often so prodigious, that they all seem to touch each other in the drop of liquid in which they move; it is astonishing to see that they do not stifle one another. A single drop sometimes contains more of them than there are inhabitants on the globe.

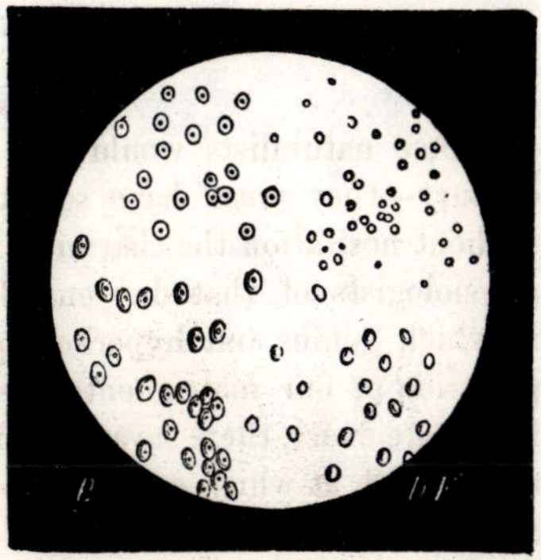

20. Monads.

These animalcules are often mere shells, and show no internal organization; but in some of them Ehrenberg remarked a number of stomachs like little elongated sacks, opening into a common mouth. In others a long movable filament is seen.

We need not remark here that these animalcules, which are complex creatures, have no connection with the imperceptible monads that played so great a part in philosophy from Epicurus down to Leibnitz, and which the latter, in his *Monadology*, defined as a simple substance which has neither extent, figure, nor capability of being divided; representing only the atoms of nature or the elements of things.

[1] The supporters of the famous atomic system, which played such a great part in both ancient and modern philosophy, maintained that the ceaseless production of planets and of all the living creatures on them was due to the fortuitous concourse of atoms. Leucippus, and even more, Epicurus, brought this system into vogue. Though defended by Kepler, Descartes, and Gassendi, modern science has completely overthrown it.

CHAPTER VI.

RESURRECTIONS—THE PHŒNIX AND PALINGENESIS.

Some naturalists would fain transport themselves back to the last century—they must have something of the marvellous. They accept without hesitation the charming little histories with which the rhetorical physiologists of that day embellished their epistolary correspondence, in which genius and hyperbole predominated by turns. Now that the precision of our instruments has rendered our observations a hundred-fold more exact, these savants still obstinately persist in carrying us back to an epoch at which experiment had barely escaped from its swaddling clothes.

Some believe, with the Abbés Spallanzani and Fontana, that mummies can be resuscitated!

To others the legend of the phœnix is still a reality: they believe that certain Infusoria are incombustible.

The following experiment was made at Paris. A zoologist placed on the bulb of a thermometer some earth containing a certain number of little microscopic animals called tardigrades, on account of the extreme slowness and awkwardness of their gait. The instrument was then thrust into a stove, and when the mercury rose from 293° to 306° Fahr. the thermometer was withdrawn. Afterwards, by using proper measures, the animalcules which were found on the bulb were brought back to life.

All present concluded from this experiment that the tardigrades were almost incombustible, and that they miraculously resisted a temperature as high as 306° Fahr.[1]

The miracle of these modern children of the furnace has lessened in proportion as it has been more studied, just as the stature of the Patagonians has diminished since men have seen more of them.

The tardigrades had, it is true, been plunged into a stove heated from

[1] The experiments of which we are speaking here were made in 1841, in the presence of Messrs. de Jussieu, Dumas, Milne-Edwards, and Quatrefages.

It has been clearly shown in the present day that they were entirely erroneous, for the Biological Society, in their celebrated experiments, never saw a single tardigrade resuscitated after being subjected to a temperature of only 212° Fahr.

293° to 306° Fahr. But if they issued from it alive it was because their bodies had never in reality been subjected to this burning heat, which would have been enough to coagulate their fluids and dry up all the sources of life. The thermometer, being extremely sensitive, quickly took on the temperature of the medium into which it had been plunged, but the earth which lay upon it, being a bad conductor of heat, never reached this temperature by a long way. This is the explanation of what appeared so marvellous.

We sometimes see at our fairs fire-proof conjurors, but everybody knows that our power of resisting fire is very limited. Physiologists cite the statement of M. Berger, who saw a man remain seven minutes in a stove heated to 228° Fahr., that is to say, who supported a heat 16° Fahr. higher than if he had been plunged into a tub of boiling water. A young girl mentioned by another savant resisted for ten minutes a heat of 294° Fahr. I witnessed a still more extraordinary feat. During one of my visits to England, I saw a man walk for several minutes in a long tunnel of fire, which looked like the most formidable flaming furnace one can imagine.[1]

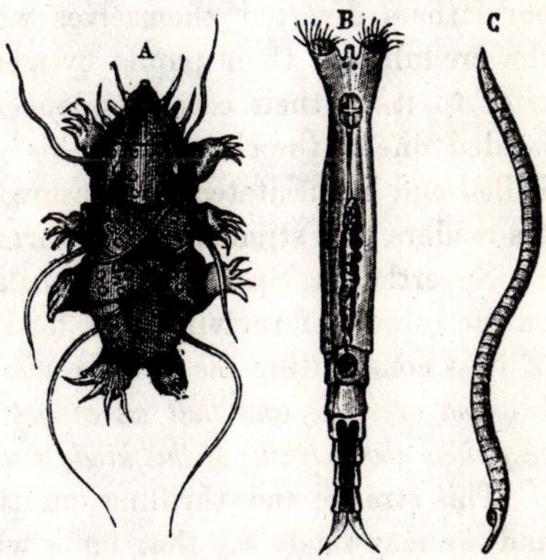

21. Animals alleged to be capable of Resuscitation. A, Tardigrade; B, Rotifer; C, Anguillula.

The case of the tardigrades was similar in the famous experiment. Like the persons we have spoken of, if they issued living from their stove at 306° Fahr. it was because its heat had never reached them, or it would infallibly have burned them.

[1] The person mentioned above performed his experiments publicly at London, in Cremorne Gardens. He walked quietly through a long tunnel of fire, arranged in the form of a cross, and having an opening at the end of each of its arms. This tunnel, formed of a solid trellis work of iron, the roof of which rose a little above the head of the performer, was covered with a heap of resinous wood. The human salamander began his promenade beneath this at the time when the whole affair was a complete furnace, the flames of which rose to a considerable height, and the heat of which compelled us to keep at a considerable distance from it.

The garments of this incombustible being seemed to be of coarse cloth, and at the time when he entered the furnace they showed a vermilion red. But when he came out for the first time I was surprised to see that they had become as white as snow. The head of the experimenter was protected by a thick helmet furnished with glass eyes, and he seemed to carry in the folds of his dress an apparatus for yielding fresh air, by means of which he breathed in the midst of a combustion so intense that one entirely lost sight of him.

Garments skilfully prepared preserve the conjurors from the fatal heat, to which they only expose themselves in appearance; in the case of the tardigrades the earth took the place of the clothes. As the learned Ehrenberg said, with great reason, sand and moss guarantee animalcules as completely against desiccation as a thick woollen mantle protects the Arab from the burning heat of the sun.

This brief account will suffice to overthrow completely the incombustibility of the tardigrades; reason rejects, and experiment condemns it.

But some have displayed even a greater fondness for resurrections, which would indeed be still more marvellous.

This phenomenon was the great attraction of an entire generation; our fathers diverted themselves with it, and learned men played on the credulity of their pupils by means of it. Spallanzani and Bonnet refer to it in their correspondence again and again: the former even headed one of the chapters in his great work "Animals which can be Killed and Resuscitated at Pleasure," a title which did not fail to attract his readers, and stimulate their curiosity to the highest pitch.

Nevertheless, Spallanzani seems at times to have had serious doubts on the subject of revivification, for in one part of his writings he speaks of it as constituting *the most paradoxical truth that the history of the animal kingdom offers us, and that we cannot manifest too much dread of, or be too suspicious about, truths of this kind;* a very sensible remark.

This strange and thrilling question aroused men's passions strongly, and we may safely say that for a whole century it kept up a desperate war in the very heart of the scientific world. Illustrious names figured in both camps, and a full peace has not yet been signed.

At first there was a great rage in favour of the resurrectionists. The Abbé Spallanzani, who resolutely moved in the van, braving the purgatory and thunders of the Vatican, made numerous proselytes, and experimented openly. On the contrary Fontana, one of his adherents, was more timid, and with great reason recoiled before the consequences which must naturally follow resurrection. He only experimented in darkness and concealment, with some confidential friends who went to Florence. "He dare not write upon the subject," said the intellectual Dupaty, "he fears being excommunicated. All the power of the grand-duke could not save him."

In fact, materialism rears its head behind these resurrections. Is not the restoration of life to a dead being, by making it imbibe a little water, subordinating existence to chemico-physical powers? Is it not the greatest height of heresy that it would be possible to profess?

The revolting paradox upheld by Spallanzani did not allow his conscience to be quite at rest, and he, a prey to doubt and remorse, seems as if he wanted to justify himself. "An animal," he says, and the illustrious abbé never spoke with more reason, "which revives after death, and revives as often as one will, is a phenomenon so unheard of that it appears improbable and paradoxical; it confuses all our ideas of animal life."

Ancient credulity was wiser than modern science. Pliny said that the phœnix only revived once; our modern palingenesists maintain that they can repeat the revival of the Rotifera as often as they like!

Three classes of animalcules have especially acquired celebrity in the annals of the resurrectionists. These are first of all the Rotifera, after them the Tardigrades, and then the Anguillulæ of our roofs.

The first are really very curious microscopic animals. They are recognized at the first glance by two structures like discs, which they protrude in front of their bodies, and the ciliated borders of which closely resemble little toothed wheels in movement. From this they are called Rotifera or "wheel-bearing animals." They live in great numbers in the mosses which fasten themselves to the old tiles on our roofs. There their existence is subjected to a host of changes. When it is damp and the soil is steeped with water, rendered tepid by the warmth, the Rotifera are active and lively, running about everywhere to seek their food. But when a powerful sun heats the roof and dries the mosses, they remain shrivelled up so long as this state of things lasts, contracting themselves like a ball, and remain in this condition, perfectly inanimate, till the rain revives them.

This kind of life, by compelling the animals to rest for a considerable while contracted and motionless, has induced the belief that they die at such times. This impression was strengthened by the fact, that so soon as ever they are placed in a drop of water, they swell, recover animation, and again take on an active existence. This very simple fact the believers in palingenesis looked upon as a resurrection. But this pretended revival is only the same phenomenon as is exhibited by the snail, which, when placed in a dry spot, buries itself in its shell till a little moisture is imparted to it.

It has been maintained that the rotifer when shrivelled up is absolutely devoid of moisture, but this is not the case. When it is thoroughly dried it never recovers.

The prestige of these resurrections was doomed to vanish in the laboratory of the museum of natural history at Rouen. Many of my pupils joined with me in bringing back science to rational views.

Professor Pennetier, by his memorable labours, proved that the Anguillulæ do not revive. M. Tinel did the same with the Tardigrades, and I myself as far as regards the Rotifers.[1]

However, although faith in palingenesis has faded before exact experiment, we must admit that the Rotifera possess an extraordinary, and almost prodigious, vital power of resistance. In mould which has been kept two or three years, they can be seen lengthening and recovering animation when they are placed in contact with a few drops of water.

Many other animals exhibit a vitality not less remarkable than that of the Rotifera. However, as they are too large to impose upon us in this way, it is not averred that they resuscitate, but that they can go several years without eating. Sundry molluscs of the snail tribe hold this position, owing to the facility with which they bury and shelter themselves in their shells.

Pupæ, left forgotten in a box, have remained there four years, clinging to the walls in all the immobility of death, and have been released from their torpor and recalled to life by giving them a little nourishment. But the resurrectionists take care not to give these facts, of which an ample supply may be found in the works of naturalists, for fear of compromising their system.

The alleged facts regarding the resurrection of the Rotifera are of the

[1] Dr. Pennetier, in a series of valuable observations, has proved the complete absurdity of resurrections in general. In his special experiments upon the Anguillulæ he noticed, that so far from supporting complete desiccation, they succumbed at a heat of 158° Fahr. M. Tinel, professor of physiology at the Medical School of Rouen, disproved the revival of the tardigrades by showing that these animals perish at a temperature below 177° Fahr., and consequently long before they reached complete desiccation. Lastly, we ourselves, in a long series of experiments, demonstrated that the resurrection of the rotifers does not take place at all, and that they are only resuscitated when they were not dead. Desiccation carried to 194° Fahr. infallibly kills them.

In consequence of our experiments, the Biological Society also undertook a series in order to verify the exactness of our assertions. Every time they conducted the experiments with the precision which we first introduced into science, it was found that not one animalcule could be revived. It is true that *in one experiment* the members of this society succeeded in bringing a few rotifers to life again, after having exposed them for several minutes to a temperature of 212° Fahr., a temperature which had been regarded as sufficient to produce complete desiccation of these animalcules. But in this solitary case they only attained this result by violating the rigorous mode of experiment which I look upon as an indispensable element, for they caused a sudden rise in the thermometer of 72° Fahr.

The charge I make against M. Broca, the learned author of a report on this subject, is that of not having plainly said, as he ought to have done, that the tardigrades, which he never saw resist a heat of 212° Fahr., and the Anguillulæ, which perish at a much lower temperature, ought to be struck out of the list of animals which can be resuscitated. The rotifers do not resist a temperature of 212° Fahr. any better when the experiment is conducted in such a way that they are really subjected to this heat same cast. If they revive after a long starvation, it is because they were no more dead than the molluscs in question. Encased, like them, in their envelope, and perhaps even more effectually, their life in this contracted state is only supported by their organs still retaining sufficient fluid to prevent existence from being extinguished. When they are really dry and dead, not even a semblance of resurrection is possible. To resuscitate a mummy is a threefold absurdity—physical, physiological, and metaphysical.

Physical, because those who have seen a mummy could never imagine that tissues so ruined by desiccation can recover their appearance and properties under the influence of moisture.

Physiological, because organs so changed could not take on their functions again.

And finally metaphysical, because if a small quantity of water could restore to a mummy all the intangible springs of life, it would be the coping-stone of the most incomprehensible materialism. The phœnix only lives as a myth, and the dead no longer issue from their tombs at the voice of Elijah.

Very naturally those physiologists who, in imitation of Dujardin, have likened microscopic animalcules to morsels of living gelatine, hailed the doctrine of palingenesis, or resuscitation from death.

But on the other hand, those men who have made themselves illustrious by their immortal labours with the microscope, such as Ehrenberg and Diesing, reduced this hypothesis to nullity. The former, in a communication to me, with one stroke of his pen characterized the error of the philosophers whom we are opposing. "*They only resuscitate*," he said, "*animals which are not dead.*"

But although belief in revivification has vanished in the presence of reason and experiment, it must be admitted that there were a host of extraordinary circumstances, which were quite calculated to mislead men's minds very easily indeed.

It is true we are, in our day, obliged to erase the charming romance of palingenesis, with which our forefathers amused themselves. Still we must say that, although the Rotifera cannot be resuscitated when they are once dead, their tenacity of life is one of the most extraordinary phenomena. Their resistance to cold is something marvellous, and we don't even know where it stops; the lowest temperature that we can obtain in our laboratories does not seem to have any effect upon them. I have seen these animals defy a cold which would kill a man a hundred times over. Rotifera placed in an apparatus where the temperature was —40° Fahr. issued from it full of vitality.

The natural history of the Rotifera is a marvel from beginning to end. I have sometimes removed them quickly from the freezing apparatus and thrown them into a stove heated to 176° Fahr. When they emerged from this, on being immersed in water they were seen to recover their animation and run about full of life. In this twofold test and formidable transition from cold to heat, these minute animals passed rapidly through a change of 216° Fahr. without being in the least inconvenienced by it.

An ox could not bear with impunity what imperceptible animalcules endure.[1]

CHAPTER VII.

THE SPONGE AND THE FLINT.

These two names seem to form an antithesis, but not so absolutely in natural history as might be supposed, for sometimes one of these bodies is derived from the other. But what connection can there be between our soft and flexible sponges and the hard flint from which the steel draws sparks? Let us see.

From Aristotle down to our days men have never known to what kingdom the sponges should be relegated. At the present time some naturalists consider them as vegetables; others, on the contrary, rank them among the animals. There is even a third opinion, which views them as belonging to both kingdoms at the same time.

Every sponge is composed of a mass, to all appearance gelatinous, supported by an inextricable network of horny filaments, or more rarely by a calcareous or silicious framework.

[1] M. Broca remarks as follows on one of my experiments on this extraordinary vital tenacity:—"Of all the tests to which these revivable animals have been subjected, the above is certainly the most astounding. Before this beautiful experiment was performed by M. Pouchet, we had only a very indistinct idea as to the power of resistance possessed by the tardigrades and rotifers, and it is almost incredible that, when so suddenly heated, in an instantaneous rise, indeed, of almost 180° Fahr., the sudden dilatation of the tissues did not produce rupture of them. But we cannot resist the evidence, and we are bound to say that M. Pouchet has discovered one of the most extraordinary properties of the rotifers and tardigrades."—Broca, *Études sur lès Animaux Ressuscitants.* Paris, 1860, p. 59. Since that date I have succeeded in suddenly raising the temperature of the pseudo-resuscitating animalcules 216° Fahr.

Sponges are the lowest stage of animal life, lower even than the monad. It is true they present very distinct forms to our view, but nothing in them displays the individuality of their architects. They are confounded together in one glairy mass, the undulations of which are almost insensible; while the monad is clearly defined and endowed with an active locomotion.

The vitality of the sponges is indeed of so doubtful a kind, that they have only been classed in the animal kingdom in consequence of deductions drawn from certain phenomena they exhibit. Of organs there is no trace.

Sponges are the most truly manifold in form of any animals; they are met with of all shapes, all sizes, and all colours.

Some branch out like trees; many resemble a funnel or a trumpet; others are divided into lobes like great fingers; for instance, the *Neptune's Glove;* and there are some which are known by the name of *sea-muffs* and *sea-tapers*, on account of their form.

A certain variety produces great masses, which grow from three to six feet high on the submarine rocks. They have a narrow stalk, which at a certain height expands considerably, and gives the structure the appearance of a cup, symmetrically hollowed out and exactly like an immense drinking goblet. To such a colossal vase the imagination of the sailor could only give one name, that of the redoubtable god of the sea; this living vase is the *Cup of Neptune!*

I never see one of these gigantic sponges without humbling myself before the wisdom of Providence. This truly monumental structure is erected solely by myriads of Polypi, fragile animals shrunk within their holes, and only half issuing in order to plunge their imperceptible arms into the waves. And who directs and guides the invisible hands of these Polypi, separated from one another, and often a yard apart, so as to give their works such harmonious symmetry? Who, when the narrow stalk is finished, tells its population that from henceforth they must widen it? Who tells them when the time is come for hollowing the vase, and when it is the season for thinning its edges and adorning the exterior with elegant ribs? And lastly, what supreme inspiration teaches a multitude of workmen, so scattered and all caged in their little cells, that they must mould the cup in all its artistic proportions!

I can understand the bee building her cell; I can understand her foresight, and how a work can be arranged where all the workmen can see, communicate with, and comprehend each other; but I admit that all seems to me incomprehensible in the architectural work of Neptune's Cup. My mind is overwhelmed and confounded. This magnificent construction is the noblest challenge one can offer the school of materialism. Do the physico-chemical sciences explain how these animals communicate

22. Neptune's Cup—*Raphid phcra patera.*

with each other so as to finish their common habitation, for it is absolutely necessary that all should be governed by one dominant idea? Certainly not. There is nothing but utter feebleness in these presumptuous theories, the audacity of which now-a-days alone makes them successful.

We have placed the flint and sponge together, one of the hardest of our stones with one of the softest of animals, because the one seems in some cases to be only a transformation of the other.

Certain sponges, in lieu of having a soft and horny framework, are composed of little hollows or fibres of flint, and accordingly, so far from showing the flexibility of those we ordinarily use, they are excessively fragile, and the least pressure breaks them like glass.

When this peculiarity is taken into account, the proximity of the sponge to the flint appears less extraordinary, for the detritus of the former would be adequate to produce the other by its condensation. Indeed, some geologists think that the flints of the chalk proceeded, if not entirely, at least in great part, from the Sponges and Infusoria which inhabited the cretaceous seas. The flints of some countries even contain the débris of sponges; remains of sponges are also found in jaspers and agates.[1]

Thus a connection is established between one of the most fragile organisms in creation and one of the hardest rocks—the sponge and the flint.

[1] It is to Mr. Bowerbank that we are indebted for having shown that the flints of different localities contain the remains of sponges. He also demonstrated that the moss-agates of Germany and Sicily owe the peculiarity from which they are named to the presence of sponges.—*Trans. Geol. Soc.* v. 4.

BOOK II.

THE ARCHITECTS OF THE SEA.

When ancient philosophy maintained, with Thales, that everything had issued from the sea, it was by no means far astray.

The sea possesses a fecundity which the earth in no way approaches; every drop is a world teeming with animation. So magnificent is it, that as Columbus said, "the tongue and the hand do not suffice to describe it." Life shows itself everywhere; animates its darkest abysses, and displays itself in profusion on its surface. As we have seen, its fragile representatives are found at a depth of 12,000 feet. Others delight to live only in the midst of the waves, as the swimming fucus or sea-weed, which forms immense meadows that stop the ships.

The largest of these fucus banks is found in the path of mariners sailing from Europe to America, between the Azores, the Canary, and Cape Verd Islands. Mention is already made of it in the Phœnician traditions, where they speak of *a herbose* or *gelatinous sea*, situated beyond the Pillars of Hercules. Aristotle says that the boldest mariners of antiquity, startled at its appearance, durst not cross its boundary.

This immense plan of Algæ, known as the Sargasso Sea, which seems to bind the waves, well-nigh hindered the discovery of America. The progress of the vessels of Columbus being seriously impeded at this spot, the crews became alarmed, and dreading that they would never be able to extricate themselves, mutinied, imperiously demanding that they should be taken back to their native country.

There is one very remarkable phenomenon connected with this bank of floating sea-weed, which is, perhaps, five or six times as large as France, and that is its constant stay in one spot during so many centuries, in spite of the perpetual agitation of the waves, and the great movements of the mass of the ocean. "If," says Maury, "we throw into a vessel filled with water pieces of cork, grains of corn, or any other floating bodies, and communicate a rotatory movement to the water, all these light bodies will collect towards the centre, because the water is less agitated there than elsewhere. It is the same thing with respect to the Atlantic Ocean, only that it is a vessel of larger dimensions. Its waters are set in movement partly by the colossal Gulf Stream which extends from Western India to the confines of the Icy Sea of the north,

23. Sargassum or Swimming Fucus—*Fucus bacciferus.*

partly by the equatorial current which traverses the Atlantic Ocean from America to Africa. The central point of rest is just about where we find the bank of Algæ we have been speaking of. It will thus be understood that these do not necessarily grow where they are found; it is indeed much more probable that they are driven from the storm-beaten shores towards the calm centre of the Atlantic basin."

CHAPTER I.

THE CORAL AND ITS BUILDERS.

Coral, celebrated as early as in the songs of Orpheus, and considered as one of the most precious productions of the sea, has beheld ages roll away without diminishing its reputation. The Gauls and Indians decorated their swords and armour with it; now-a-days it is only employed in female ornaments. In one country the daughters of Nubia load their ebony shoulders with long necklaces of coral, the clear red gleam of which, in another land, brings out in full relief the satiny white necks of the beautiful Circassians.

But it has required twenty centuries of incessant groping in the dark to unveil the mysterious nature of this coral.

It forms a branched stem, of a beautiful red colour, as hard as the most compact rocks, and, like them, capable of taking a fine polish. When it is withdrawn from the sea, of which it inhabits the great depths only, it is, from the arrangement of its branches, precisely like a bush in miniature, and a section of its stem presents concentric layers analogous to those of certain trees. Its branches are covered with a soft rose-coloured bark, and display here and there small holes, in each of which resides one of the builders of the coral. These are so many Polypi, which, when they expand, wear all the appearance of pretty little flowers of a beautiful white colour, with eight divisions spread out like rays, and the borders of which are ornamented with a fringe of cilia or minute hairs.

It was this deceitful appearance which made naturalists so long dubious with regard to the nature of coral.

Its extreme hardness, and the beautiful polish it takes, led some observers to look upon it as a simple mineral.

But the idea which seemed to predominate over all others was that of coral being only a submarine shrub. This was the opinion of Pliny and Dioscorides; and these two great scholars, seeing it was so hard and compact, added that the shrub only made its appearance in this indurated form, because it became suddenly petrified when brought into contact with the air, as it issued from the waves.

The sagacious traveller Tournefort gained in respect to coral no additional knowledge from his wanderings in the East, the native land of this celebrated substance. He also took it to be a plant, and even had it engraved under this heading in one of the plates of his magnificent work. It is there placed in the twenty-second class of the

24. Branched Coral—*Caryophillia ramea.*

vegetable kingdom, in the section which he entitles "*of the marine or fluviatile plants, the flowers and fruits of which are generally unknown.*"

For a moment, but alas only for a moment, the opinion of the French botanist seemed to be confirmed by the most strict observation. In the eighteenth century Count Marsigli announced to the scientific world that he had discovered the flowers of the coral, and that consequently its vegetable nature could no longer be called in question. By placing branches of coral in sea-water, immediately after they had been fished up, the Italian naturalist saw the bud-like protuberances which cover its surface open like so many eight-petaled flowers, formed of elegant white and star-shaped corollas, outlined upon the reddish bark of the stems. Marsigli doubted no longer; these were the flowers of the paradoxical shrub; he had solved the problem left unsettled by Tournefort. In his joy, when announcing his discovery to the assembled Academy of Sciences, to whom he had forwarded his specimens, he wrote to the president, "I send you some branches of coral covered with white flowers. This discovery has made me pass for almost a sorcerer in the country; no person, not even the fishermen, having seen anything similar."

25. Red Coral, magnified—*Corallium rubrum.*
A, Polypi; B, Ciliated Ovule; C, Larva.

The illustrious and learned assembly was convinced, but its convictions and the repose of Marsigli were only to be of brief duration. Not long after this supposed settlement of the question, Peyssonnel, a French physician, who in 1725 happened to travel along the coast of Barbary, having been present at the coral fishing, and having instituted some lengthy investigations on the subject, discovered, that what had been taken for the flowers of the coral were only so many little animals or Polypi, which were really the builders of the deceptive stony shrub.

Convinced of the exactness of his observations, Peyssonnel in his turn disclosed them to the Academy of Sciences; but the Academy, still fascinated by the coral flowers which the Italian count had sent, gave no heed to the discoveries of the French physician, and showed this in the most delicate manner.

Réaumur, having been commissioned by this learned body to report upon the discovery, thought he ought not, *out of compassion*, as he said, to name the author; and when he acknowledged the receipt of his memoir, wrote to him in a tone of pity and irony. But the position assumed by the sedate and conscientious Barnard de Jussieu was even more unpardonable. He addressed a letter to Peyssonnel, without any silly raillery it is true, which was indeed totally foreign to his character, but quite as discouraging as that of the entomologist. De Jussieu was, however, the more culpable of the two, for the most superficial examination of the so-called coral flowers would have shown him his mistake. All the fundamental parts of the floral apparatus were wanting, but it appears the botanist did not give himself the trouble to look at them.

The affair made a great stir, and it became necessary, *nolens volens*, to unravel it. As soon as it was cleared up, the conclusion universally arrived at was that it was the simple country physician who had been right and the Academy that had been wrong. The coral flowers turned out to be only Polypi, and the stony shrub a place of abode for them, sculptured and fashioned by the tiny animals.

Such are the facts as regards the nature of coral. Let us revert to the second error which tarnishes its history.

It was difficult when the erroneous view with regard to coral was held to understand how so hard a body could be merely vegetable tissue. The fishermen, following the ancient tradition, explained the matter with perfect satisfaction to themselves, and all the world gave credence to what they said. They maintained that this marine shrub, so long as it is under water, is not harder than analogous terrestrial plants, but that it hardens suddenly when brought in contact with the air. This strange opinion was deeply rooted among the common people, and ranked among the best established facts.

However, M. Nicolaï, inspector of fisheries, determined to verify the affair for himself.

He made one of his coral-fishers dive and see what was really the consistence of the coral; the man brought back word that it was as hard in the sea as in the air. But such is the power of prejudice, that M. Nicolaï only half-believed his servant, and finally decided to dive also and satisfy himself as to the facts. He did so, and found out that coral is really just as hard in the midst of the waves as on land.

Thus for two thousand years men continued to doubt and speculate before determining the true nature of coral.

All this time was necessary to prove that it is only the production of a simple marine polyp, and that in the depths of the seas which it inhabits, and from whence the fishermen tear it up with their nets, it is as hard as when it is fashioned into those bracelets and rich necklaces which form such a charming contrast with the white skins of our most attractive women.[1]

[1] The natural history of coral has been completed quite recently by M. Lacaze-Duthiers. This zoologist observed that the individuals scattered over the branches of the polypoid imitate in their sexual disposition an arrangement seen in certain plants. Some are only

CHAPTER II.

ISLAND BUILDERS.

Unseen by human eye, myriads of animals, more numerous than the cloud of stars in the Milky Way, labour silently in the depths of the sea, and build up structures the size of which astounds us. Their erections, to which is commonly given the name of coral reefs, are sometimes raised with surprising rapidity, making parts of the ocean unnavigable, which vessels had previously gone through under full sail.

These submarine banks are nothing but agglomerations of the calcareous homes of polyps, constructed by fragile animals not unlike minute flowers, and which inhabit the innumerable little holes wherewith the surface is overspread. But these obscure artisans, as modest as they are laborious, frequently conceal themselves from the eye; to see them we must have recourse to the magnifying-glass.

It is principally in the South Sea and the Red Sea that the constructions of these Polypi abound. At the approaches to the Maldive Islands they form extraordinary masses, of not less extent than the Alps, according to the accounts of travellers. The American traveller Dana states that the larger coral islands of the Pacific are at present 290 in number, with a total area of 20,000 square miles—an enormous work, equal perhaps to an eighth part of the surface of all the other islands of this vast sea.

After having described the methods by which the Polypi raise their dangerous reefs so fatal to mariners, Owen thus sums up as to the immensity of their labours. "The prodigious extent of the combined and unintermitting labours of these little world-architects, must be witnessed in order to be adequately conceived. They have built up a barrier reef along the shores of New Caledonia for a length of 400 miles; and another which runs along the north-east coast of Australia 1000 miles in extent." This represents, adds the illustrious zoologist, a mass compared with which the walls of Babylon and the Pyramids of Egypt are but children's toys. And these edifices of the Polypi have

males; others carry only female organs; lastly there are some which bear both sexes at the same time and are hermaphrodite. The eggs of the coral are spherical and of a milk-white colour, and very soon after they have issued from the body of the mother move about actively and seek out a favourable site to plant themselves upon.

been reared in the midst of the ocean waves, and in defiance of tempests which so rapidly annihilate the strongest works constructed by man.

Notwithstanding their extreme minuteness, the Polypi have nevertheless, by their calcareous buildings, brought about important changes on the crust of the terrestrial globe. They have modified it in two ways, by raising the bed of the sea through their ceaseless development, and by forming large calcareous mountains with their débris; in fact, when we examine the layers of which these elevations are composed, we perceive that they are formed entirely of corals and bivalves which swarmed in the ancient oceans of the globe. Ground to dust by the furious waves, these creatures have only here and there left a few traces to attest their presence, and serve as a light to the modern investigators of science. Such is the opinion of Lyell and most modern geologists. In support of this view it has been observed that certain lagoons are filled with a calcareous mud, evidently due to the detritus of the corals, and that so soon as this is dried, it exactly resembles the chalk of our ancient mountains.

To the action of the waves, the chief agent in transforming the coral rocks and bivalves into calcareous strata, there is joined another, much less energetic it is true, but extremely curious. Mr. Darwin relates that all round the coral islands the transparency of the water allows shoals of fish to be seen, principally of the genus Sparus, which feed on the tips of the branching corals, exactly as flocks of sheep browse on the pasturage of our meadows. In their eagerness to feed on the workman, they devour along with him certain parts of his edifice; and as these are quite indigestible, the result is, according to the English savant, that a part of the chalky substance which encumbers the bottom of the sea in the vicinity of the coral reefs comes from the defecations of these fish. When the Spari are dissected, their alimentary canal is often seen filled with pure chalk.

The coral islands generally lie on an upheaval of the bed of the sea. Volcanic action begins the work, and the Polypi finish it; they bring the construction up to the level of the waves. These islands always display a peculiar configuration; they are nearly all circular, and there is a crater-like depression in the middle. This peculiarity seems to be owing to the fact, that the little workmen can support their vital energies better where the water, being agitated, brings them a more ample supply of nourishment. The animals in the centre, being placed under different conditions, are less vigorous and active, and consequently cannot raise their living rampart so fast.

In the Pacific Ocean, where a tolerably large number of those islands are seen, the polyp structures reach the level of the low tides, and after that the great surges raise the middle part, by casting back upon it incessantly the fragments which they tear away from the circumference. When in the lapse of years the island rises above water, the detritus of marine plants raises it still more, and the virgin soil is speedily fecundated by seeds which the winds, birds, and currents carry thither. Soon after man comes to crown the handiwork of nature by raising dwellings on the ruins of those of myriads of unseen beings. Then a king arrives, who sits proudly upon his throne, amidst this mass of skeletons of Polypi abandoned by the sea.

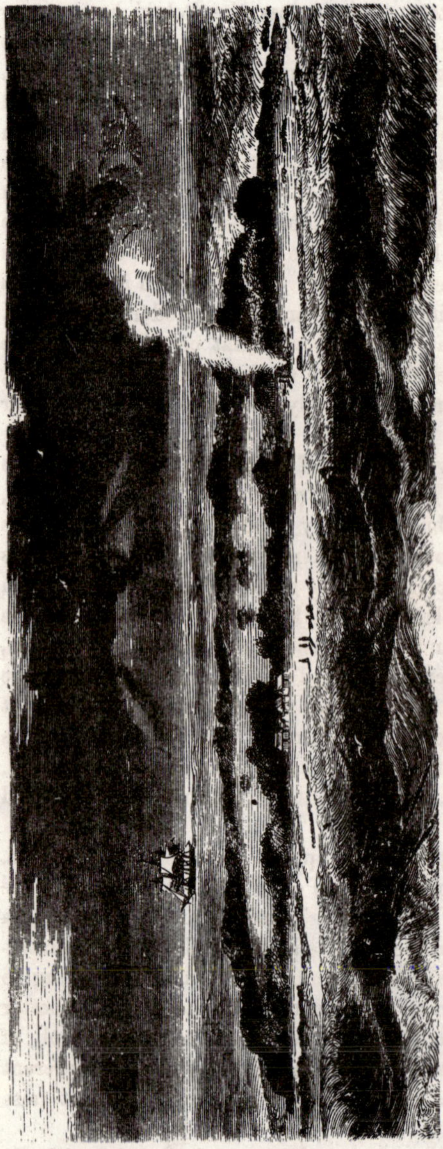

26. Coral Island in the Archipelago of Pometou.

Two of the most celebrated travellers of our epoch, Forster and Péron, think that these coral or madrepore reefs and islands are formed with extraordinary rapidity, and that a few years suffice to materially change the depths of the sea, and strew with dangerous rocks and impassable barriers tracts of the ocean in which, but a little while previously, navigators sailed in safety. These new lands sometimes spring up with such celerity as to baffle all nautical science. One of the straits in the approaches to Australia, which a few years ago only possessed twenty-six madrepore islands, at present displays a hundred and fifty.

Geologists themselves have dwelt upon the power of these *builders of worlds*, as our illustrous Michelet calls them, which recast and changed the surface of the globe at certain antediluvian periods. At that time they swarmed in the immense seas which rolled their tumultuous waves over almost all the lands now covered by our fields and peaceful abodes. Some countries in Europe display remarkably large banks; ancient Germany and its sombre forests rest on a vast cemetery of corals and madrepores.

If the Polypi, being so extremely small as they are, astonish us by the mighty fortresses with which they fetter the ocean, we must admit that they are equally worthy of our admiration when we look upon the task intrusted to them in the midst of their watery solitudes. Their nourishment only consists of the imperceptible débris of animals scattered on every side in the waves, and hence, as Buckland says, they have an important mission to fulfil in the harmony of nature. It is to them that she has confided the office of cleansing the waters of the sea, and purging them of all those very slight impurities which escape the voracious fish. Here, then, we find another reason for humbling ourselves before the wisdom of Providence!

Ellis, when he completed his history of the Polypi, overwhelmed with astonishment at all the magnificence which had been unrolled before his eyes during his long and incessant labours, laid down his pen, and humbling himself profoundly, addressed a hymn to the glory of Him who created so many marvels.[1]

In the countries where they abound, those living reef-builders, though often mischievous, as some slight compensation, render certain services to man. Their structures sometimes form thick and very compact layers, which are made use of as building stone. Forskal, who explored the

[1] After having sacrificed many long years to the very difficult study of the Polypi, Ellis, when laying down his pen, could not refrain, as we have said, from addressing a hymn to the Creator of so many marvels. "In the researches to which I devoted myself," says the English naturalist, "scenes altogether new were unrolled before my eyes, arousing in me a feeling of admiration and astonishment at the diversity and extent of life scattered through the universe. If then such sentiments were excited in me by the facts which I have related, and by these marvels of animated nature where its existence was not even suspected, then without doubt minds more learned, and endowed with a greater power of penetration, will find, at some future day, new facts to be recognized, and new proofs to be revealed, if that were necessary, of one unique will, one omnipotence, which created, and which now preserves the 'great whole' in all its beauty and perfection."

shores of the Red Sea, says that the inhabitants of Suez and Djeddah carry off masses of madrepore as much as twenty-five feet long, and that they build all their houses with them. My learned friend, P. E. Botta, told me that in certain villages in the Sandwich Islands the dwellings are built solely of such materials.

Thus man constructs his abodes with the handiwork of these petty architects, the Polypi.

Each species has its own separate mission and form. Near our reef-builders live other polyps, which, instead of encrusting the rocks, display themselves on their surface like a vegetable forest, the petrified branches of which brave the fury of the billows. Some have so exactly the same physiognomy as our plants, that the old botanists without hesitation classed them among the productions of their domain. Others spread out in vast cup-shaped forms, one rising above the other; as may be seen in the " Car of Neptune," the ruler of the seas.

CHAPTER III.

STONE-BORERS AND WOOD-BORERS.

We have just seen how invisible architects make the depths of ocean bristle with forests of coral or layers of madrepore; we have now to busy ourselves about workmen of another class: the true miners, who build nothing, but instead hollow out for themselves vaults in the submerged rocks. Their ceaseless, and as yet inexplicable, toil enables them to pierce deeply into the most compact stones. We are astonished, in splitting marble, to find living shells in the midst of blocks which the chisel of the sculptor cuts with difficulty.

The most renowned of the stone-borers we are acquainted with, the Pholades, ordinarily scoop out their abodes in the calcareous rocks of our shores. They are thin, white shells, their valves being elegantly ornamented with projecting lamellæ or symmetrically arranged points. Their two ends are opened wide. From one issue the respiratory and nutritive tubes, which lengthen themselves out from the bottom of the cavity inhabited by the mollusc, in order to pump up the sea-water with its myriads of animalcules. From the other, still more open, proceeds the foot, a thick, powerful, living sole, intended to play a great part in the life of the solitary animal.

There are pholas-hunters just as there are prawn-fishers. The former can be distinguished with singular facility at a very great distance, owing to the brilliant whiteness of their clothes. This is not due to their being really of this colour, but to a cement formed by the moist chips from the rocks, which cover the bodies of this peculiar class of men, and which fly off as they cleave the rocks with powerful blows of the pickaxe, in

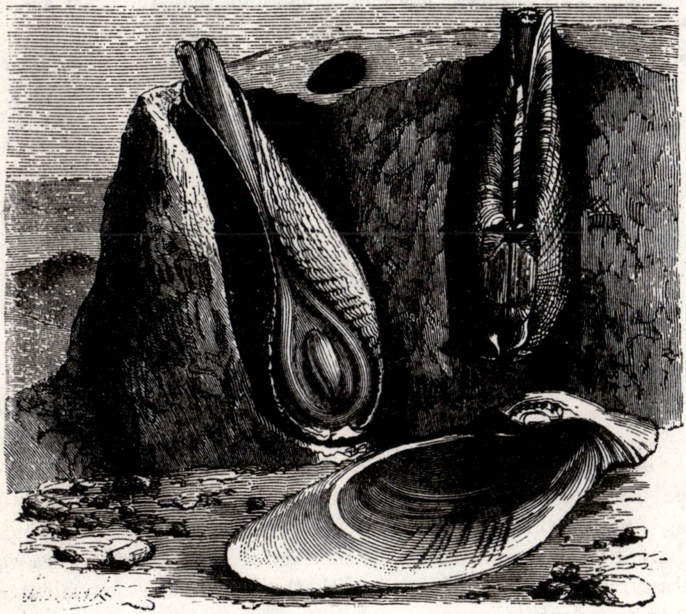

27. Dactyloid Pholades in their holes—*Pholas dactylus.*

order to find in their depths the molluscs, which they sell to the fishermen.

When, after overcoming the obstacles presented by a rocky and slippery ground, we reach the neighbourhood of the laborious workman, and, having induced him to pause from his work, so that our clothes may not be soiled by the chips radiating from his hatchet, we examine the pholads lying here and there among the broken stones, we return quite convinced that there exist shell-fish which gnaw stone—a fact which many people doubted not long ago. But another problem remains to be solved, and that is to know how these animals execute a task which seems so much beyond their powers.

Some naturalists have fancied that the Pholades are only a kind of living files, mechanically boring their habitations by rasping the rock with the aid of the sharp points on their shells. But this opinion is quite untenable, for before they could pierce the hard stone these delicate projections themselves would be completely worn away.[1]

Other naturalists think these molluscs make use of some chemical process, and hollow out their abodes by distilling an acid which acts upon the stone. This theory is not more admissible than the other, for it is certain that, the calcareous outer skeleton of the animal being of a composition analogous to that of the rock, it would itself be the first victim of the corroding agent, and would be dissolved long before the hole was formed.

It is, however, clear that among the Pholades living in the calcareous

28. Stone-eating Modiolus, *Modiolus lithophagus.*—From nature.

rocks of our shores, the strongly made foot undertakes the task in question. By its ceaseless movements this fleshy sole, little by little, wears away the rock which the water has softened. In fact, the rock, which is so hard in its dry state, is on the contrary very soft when the sea-water has saturated it, and rubbing it with the finger for a few minutes is enough to indent it deeply.

But though the problem may be considered solved so far as regards the Lithophagi, that is to say, the eaters of stone which live in the soft limestone, there seem to be some doubts as to those found in our most compact marbles, for it is evident that the movement of the foot would not suffice to pierce so unyielding a body.

One of these marble-cutters has acquired a great celebrity in the annals of geology, from its having attacked the temple of Jupiter Serapis at Pozzuoli, on the border of the Mediterranean, and almost on a level with its waves.

[1] As to the pholads of our shores, I have proved the fact by demonstrating that all the interior of the hole, on a level with the shell, is covered with a layer of mud, which would prevent the action of the sharp points upon the irregularities of the stone.

29. Ruins of the Temple of Jupiter Serapis, on the shores of the Bay of Baiæ.
From a photograph.

It is a Modiolus which has cut numerous excavations in the beautiful columns of this sanctuary, and has even gnawed them in an unsightly manner for the space of about three feet at a height of six to seven feet above the fore-court. Philosophers suppose that at some epoch, of which history makes no mention, this celebrated temple had sunk in the sea, owing to one of those movements in the soil so common in volcanic countries, that it was then invaded by the stone-eating molluscs, and that afterwards, being raised by a contrary movement like a scene on the stage, the monument, rising like magic from the bosom of the waves, reappeared in the air, displaying to our astonished eyes the destruction effected by the animals which had gnawed it during its stay below the waters.

But the labour of the mollusc, and the double movement of the famous temple, will perhaps long remain enveloped in mystery, albeit Schleiden relates, that an old monk from a convent in the neighbourhood stated that in his youth he had gathered grapes near the monument, in a spot where now the boats of the fishermen are rocked on the waves.[1]

The sea owns yet other workmen, but they dread the hard stone and only attack wood. As to them, all the world knows them and sees their doings. They are the sea-worms, only too zealous at their work, which make such deadly havoc with our dikes and ships.

These enemies of our naval works are the Teredoes or ship-worms (*Teredo navalis*), worm-like molluscs which live constantly in the interior of wood submerged in the waves, and are perpetually gnawing it, and hollowing out numerous tortuous galleries. We know exactly what their tools are, being nothing more than the cutting edge of the little shell which is projected in front of the long and soft body of the animal.

The ravages of the Teredo are terrible. In a short space of time they reduce the strongest beams to a state of fragile sponge. In 1731 these molluscs well nigh occasioned the submersion of Holland, having devoured the greatest part of the Zealand dikes. They are a complete pest, which we cannot check when we like.

These animals incessantly assail the framework of our strongest ships,

[1] I have twice visited this celebrated temple, and the more I have examined it the more difficult has the problem appeared to solve. Three of its gnawed columns of beautiful cepola marble are still standing, the others are levelled with the ground; but the base is so perfectly horizontal that it is hard to understand how it can have been engulfed and magically raised up again, while still preserving its level, and without the whole of the columns being overturned. On the other hand, it seems as if it could scarcely have served for a marine fish-pond, or a sacred bath, as I at first thought.

and by perforating their timbers place them in danger and threaten them with instant shipwreck. It is solely to preserve vessels from these

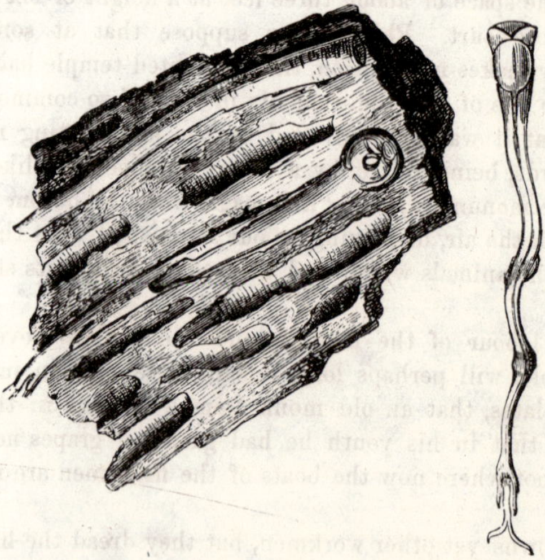

30. Teredo or Ship-worm, and Fragment of Wood devoured by others.

terrible wood-devourers that all vessels going on long voyages are copper-bottomed.

These then are the fragile molluscs which ravage our naval structures; later on we shall speak of the insects which pitilessly consume our dwellings.

CHAPTER IV.

MOUNTAIN BUILDERS.

Torn from the depths of the crust of the earth, and forcibly upheaved above the clouds by a formidable power, the lofty mountain systems of the globe, such as the Alps and the Cordilleras, astonish us by their mass and their elevation. But there are others which, though less gigantic, have quite as marvellous an origin, although of a different kind; these are the mountains of shells.

The exuberance of life in the ancient oceans surpassed everything that we can imagine; our modern seas give us no idea of it. The molluscs lived at that time in such serried and compact masses, that their remains have produced by their accumulation deep strata and lofty eminences.

The phenomena which prevailed when these were generated exhibit a threefold modification.

Sometimes seas, the calmness of which rivalled their fecundity, had their beds slowly raised, the cemeteries of their innumerable inhabitants being in this way raised also. The shells, quietly deposited there one upon another, show no trace of erosion. After so many thousands of years we find them still ornamented with their most delicate projections, with their almost imperceptible striæ. What do I say? There are some which still reflect the colours that decorated them in the first days of creation, long before the work was finished!

In other places, swarming in the midst of a boundless ocean tumultuously agitated, the shells, ground by its furious waves, and precipitated in the form of impalpable dust, also formed mountains.[1]

However extraordinary such an origin may seem, we yet cannot doubt it; in fact, in certain localities we pass by insensible transitions from rocks wholly composed of entire shells heaped up, to strata in which they are more or less finely ground down.

Other calcareous prominences have a still more extraordinary origin, being formed solely of microscopic beings, which although of extreme minuteness have miraculously braved the destructive action of time. I am not speaking here of one of those ingenious theories which formerly science was so fond of adopting. The microscope proves, with a precision that cannot be contested, the truth of what we advance. Ehrenberg has even given excellent figures of all these marvels in his *Geological Micrography.*[2]

Thus, then, when we speak metaphorically of the bones of our globe, so long as the name is applied to the mountains of coarse limestone, we are right. If it cannot be looked at as the skeleton of our sphere, it can at least as that of innumerable myriads which formerly peopled it.

The geological chalk formations, which here and there rise in long chains of mountains, are due to similar agglomerations of animalcules

[1] To these crushed shells, which compose the principal part of the grains of calcareous strata, are joined also, as Lyell points out, the shattered remains of a vast number of polyp-dwellings.

[2] There can be no doubt on this point. In his *Geological Micrography,* Ehrenberg has given plates representing numerous fossils from the chalk. They are so crowded together that they touch each other. Sir Charles Lyell also, in his *Geology,* observes that certain calcareous strata are composed of small fragments of shells and coral.

with calcareous shells, and in spite of the size of the layers, are nevertheless composed entirely of the débris of microscopic Foraminifera. It is they that encircle England with the immense rampart of beautiful white to which it owes its ancient name of Albion. In Russia, near the Volga, in the north of France, in Denmark, Sweden, Greece, Sicily, Africa, and Arabia, many chalk hills have a similar origin.

The imagination is scared when it tries to realize the power of organic life which produced such masses by the simple agglomeration

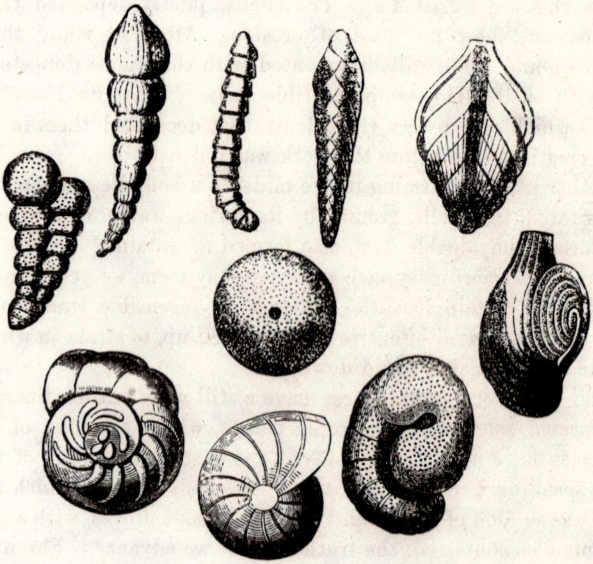

31. Shells of Molluscs. Foraminifera greatly enlarged.[1]

of creatures almost invisible. In fact, their minuteness is such that Schleiden maintains that a single visiting card, when it is covered with a white layer of chalk, represents a zoological cabinet containing nearly 100,000 shells of animals.

In a hill in the environs of Dover, after long preliminary workings, a mine containing about 181 cwts. of powder was sprung in the year 1843. When it was ignited by means of the electric battery, it tore up, almost without any noise, the sides of an imposing mass of chalk, the

[1] The sand of every sea-shore is so full of Foraminifera that it may be said to be one-half composed of them. In a single ounce of sea-sand from the Antilles, 4,000,000 individuals may be counted.—*Chenu.*

débris of which, computed at about 1,000,000 tons, was precipitated into the sea, spreading itself in a layer twenty feet thick over an extent of fifteen acres.

Against what were these formidable engines of war employed? Against what was this gigantic effort of the human mind projected? Simply the piled-up skeletons of little animalcules which the finger would crush by thousands!

The shells of the microscopic molluscs which compose mountains

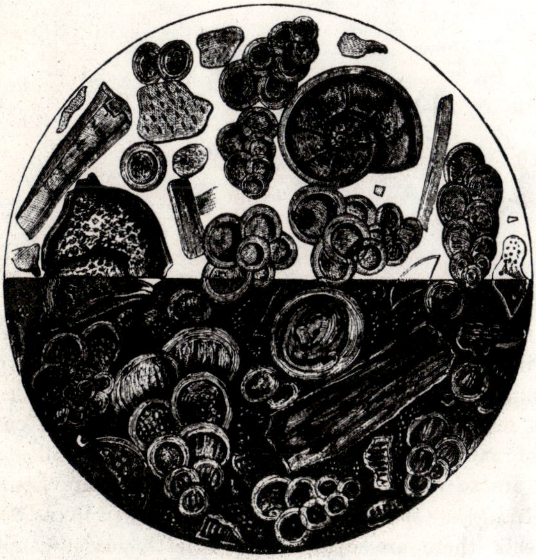

32. Chalk of Meudon, seen with the microscope.

are only formed of carbonate of lime, and are so extremely small that it has been calculated it would require about 10,000,000 to make a pound of chalk, and that there are more than 150,000,000 in a cubic yard. Favoured by their inconceivable fecundity, these animalcules filled up the cretaceous seas, and by accumulating in layers at their bottoms their skeletons have formed the great masses of chalk strata of which, at the present time, some mountains are composed. Sometimes they are solely constituted of little shells still entire, as is seen in the rocks of Sicily and the chalk of Meudon, when submitted to the microscope. Sometimes the weight of the new superimposed layers has reduced those at the base to a fine powder, and then we find only a soft thin clay.

To sum up then:

The layers of our calcareous mountains may be of three kinds: One composed of entire shells piled up; the second are formed of shells crushed fine; and, finally, there are some the bulk of which is only made up of microscopic shells.

The formation of the first surprises, that of the latter confounds, us.

BOOK III.

INSECTS.

To a marvellous delicacy of organization these animals join a still more marvellous intelligence. The perfection of their microscopic tools would lead us to suppose them capable of executing works of boundless variety; and this is indeed the case. These minute creatures often build up structures of an elegance and size that far surpass all expectation. These, too, are so varied that Réaumur, and after him Rennie, in his admirable *Architecture of Insects*, grouped the workmen in castes. Indeed, among insects there are evidently architects, masons, upholsterers, paper-makers, joiners, paste-board makers, and hydraulic engineers. Others dislike work, and are veritable pirates, always engaged in war and pillage.

We find also in this class extremes of size and strength. One gigantic beetle, such as for instance the Goliath, may exceed the size of some of the humming-birds, which he would pitilessly strangle in his claws if he caught them in his path; while another insect may be so small, so calculated to escape notice, that we only discover it by the aid of the magnifying-glass.

The insect class displays in every part a harmonious organization, which at the first glance distinguishes it from all others. Nevertheless, it is perhaps the section of the animal kingdom in which we observe the greatest diversity of form; some insects indeed display at times such anomalies that we can only make them out by their fundamental characteristics. There are even frequently extreme differences between the male and the female.

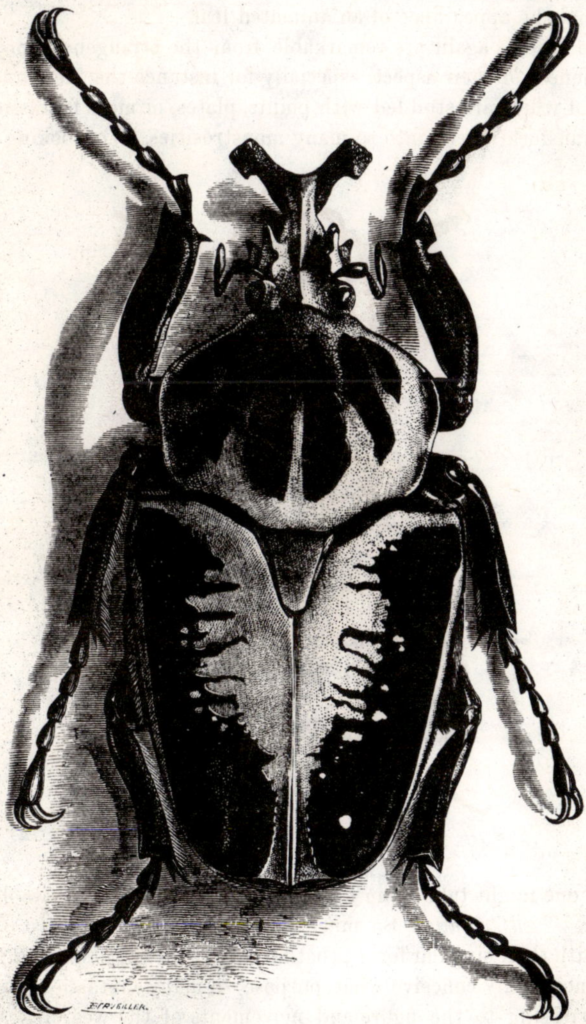

33. Goliath of Drury—*Goliathus giganteus* (natural size).

Some insects possess such an abnormal exterior that they exactly resemble leaves of trees, having the same venation and colouring; when they are at rest we might take them for leaves, and even the greedy bird is deceived by them. This is the case with some Mormolycæ. In them it is the wings that are transformed into green membranes, which give the animal the appearance of an animated leaf.

Some insects again are remarkable from the strangeness, not to say grotesqueness of their aspect, especially for instance the Membraceæ, the corslets of which are studded with points, plates, or most fantastic knobs, which transform them into so many monstrosities. On looking at some

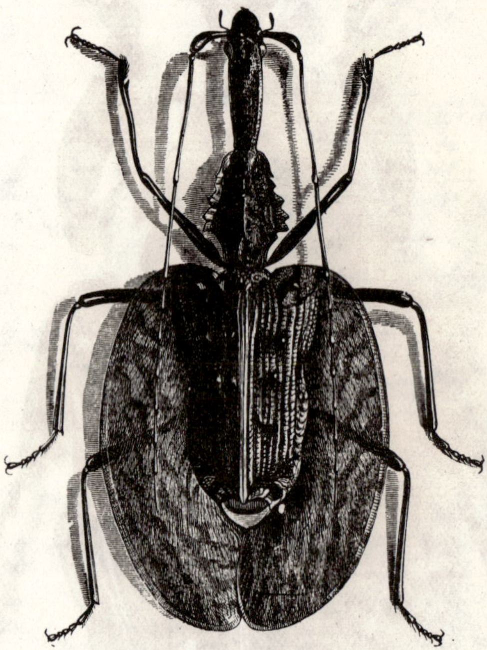

34. The Mormolyce phyllodes (natural size).

of them one might take them for insects in masquerade, veritable sports of nature—*lusus naturæ*. So much was the old entomologist Geoffroy struck with their singular forms, that he gave them the name of *little devils*. One cannot really conceive what purpose so many fantastic appendages, so embarrassing to the figure and movements of the wearers, can serve among these fragile tribes, for they are all of the smallest dimensions.

If anything in insects surpasses the diversity of forms, it is the prodigious variety of colouring. Their mantles gleam with the richest hues in nature. Their splendour can only be compared to that of jewels and metals. The purest gold and silver, the sapphire and the emerald, gleam on their wings and corsages; their tints mingle together, melt abruptly, or imperceptibly shade into each other.

Some groups are more particularly remarkable for the richness of their vestments, as for instance the Buprestidæ, which owe their French surname of "Richards" (millionaires) to their metallic lustre; such are

35. Various Membraceæ, much magnified. "Little Devils" of Geoffroy.

also the Curculios, which gleam like precious stones, and which, like the preceding, are used instead of them in India and China, where they are made into trinkets for women, such as pins and ear-drops.

Among the brilliant genera we find also the Cetoniæ, of which the wing-cases are often variegated with the most beautiful velvety tints; and lastly, the Carabi and the Calosomæ, all glittering with gold.

As the great Linnæus said, Nature takes no leaps (*Natura non facit saltum*), and among insects she proceeds, as elsewhere, by insensible transitions.

We are accustomed to recognize a butterfly only by its ample wings, nevertheless naturalists have discovered many species of this order which are wingless. But although we see some individuals of this group

36. *Buprestis imperialis.*

37. *Cetonia Cervus.*

deprived of these organs, others exhibit the vestiges of them to show the gradation.

Thus, for instance, though the female of the *Phalæna nuda* (a kind of

38. *Phalæna hyemalis*, male and female.

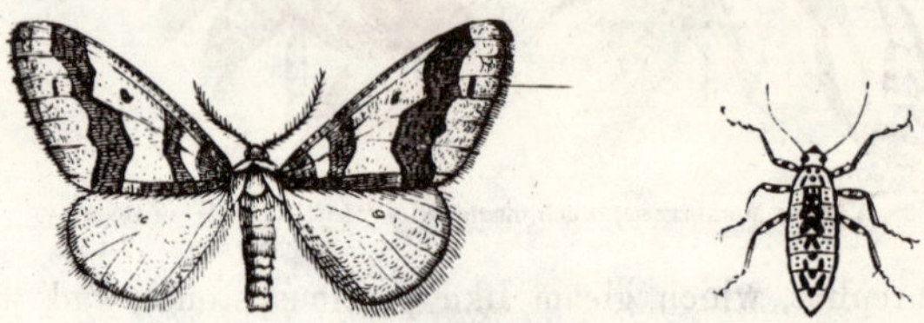

39. *Phalæna nuda*, male and female.

moth) is entirely deprived of wings, we find by the side of it the *Phalæna hyemalis*, the female of which possesses rudimentary ones, thus forming a transition to the other species of an order, the members of which have four very large wings.

In the same manner when we examine the lower members of the order of flies or Diptera, we find the same modifications here also.

Certain flies (*Stenopteryx*) which never fly, and remain all their lives adherent to the feathers of the swallow, have nevertheless vestiges

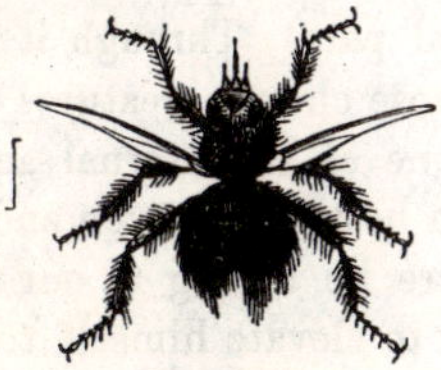

40. Stenopteryx of the Swallow—*Stenopteryx hirundinis.*

41. Melophagus of the Sheep—*Melophagus ovis.*

of wings, quite unsuited to flight; whilst others (*Melophagus*), still more degraded, have none at all, and pass their lives clinging to the wool of the sheep.

CHAPTER I.

MARVELS OF INSECT ORGANIZATION.

The torch of anatomy has shed a flood of light upon the organization of the inferior animals, and the microscope, by allowing us to pry into the most intricate structural details, has unfolded before our eyes a field as vast as it was unexpected. But we must acknowledge, that if the investigation of the infinitely small has acquired such an advanced degree of certainty, this result is due to men who have often devoted all their lives to the task.

An advocate of Maestricht, Lyonet, passed nearly all his life in studying a caterpillar which gnaws the wood of the willow, and produced on this insect one of the most splendid monuments of human patience.

Goedart, a Dutch painter, spent twenty of his best years in watching the metamorphoses of insects—a most interesting spectacle for him who looks at it with the eye of religion. Hence, in the midst of the most brilliant parties (into which affliction makes its way despite both pomp and gold) he felt tempted to exclaim, "Ah! let me rather see a butterfly born. In his puniest creatures God reveals his power and majesty; you, in your splendid fêtes, often display only your weakness and misery!"

Anatomically and physiologically speaking, the human mechanism seems rude and coarse when we compare it with the exquisite delicacy revealed in the organism of certain animals. But in us the intellect, the real sceptre of the universe, predominates over the apparent imperfection of the material part. Through it man alone approaches those chosen creatures who shine near the throne of the eternal and form a bond of union between heaven and earth; if in his structure he belong to our sphere, he seems already to elevate himself towards the supreme Essence by the splendour of his genius.

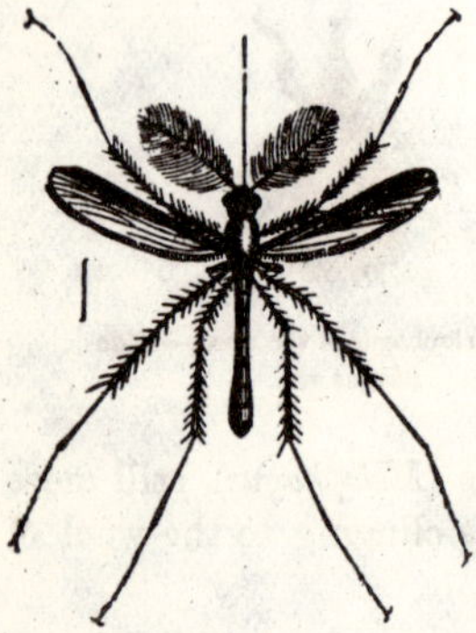

42. Mosquito, highly magnified—*Culex*[1] (Linn.)

A grand and philosophic truth, which a glance at the organization of insects will instantly demonstrate.

In her slightest sketches nature knows how to unite power to an exquisite fineness of mechanism; the first glance at insects proves this, and thus so soon as their interesting history is displayed before us, we feel no longer tempted to treat

[1] There are many species of gnats, distinguished by the generic name *Culex*, but all having a similar conformation and similar habits. The species found in foreign countries are generally known as mosquitoes; but mosquitoes and gnats are the same thing.

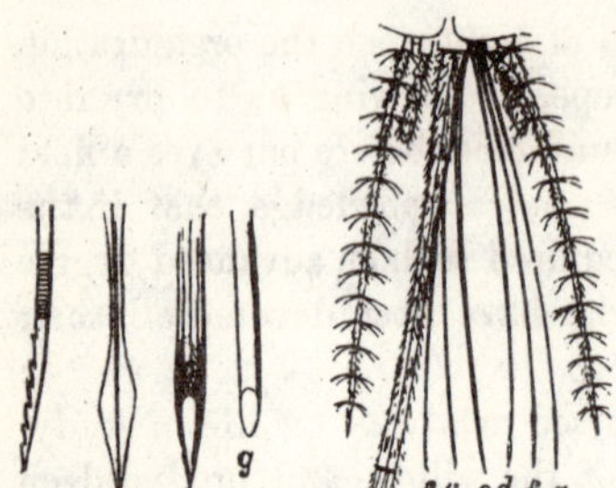

43. Organs of the Mouth of Gnat.

The weapon with which the gnat makes its attack is a long and slender proboscis, which projects from the mouth like a very fine bristle, appearing to the naked eye quite simple. Under the magnifying power of the microscope, however, it is seen to be a flexible sheath (*i*) inclosing six distinct pieces, two of which are cutting blades or lancets (*g*), two notched like a saw with reverted teeth (*f*), a tubular canal (*e*), and the central one an excessively acute point, which is also tubular (*d*). When the attack is made, the gnat brings the tip of the organ within its sheath to press upon the skin, into which it presently enters, the sheath remaining without and bending into an angle as the lancets descend. When the weapon has penetrated to its base—a distance of one-sixth of an inch or more—the lancets move laterally, and thus cut the flesh on either side, promoting the flow of blood from the superficial vessels; at the same moment a highly irritative fluid is poured into the wound, which has the effect of diluting the blood, and thus of rendering it more capable of flowing up the slender central tube into the throat of the insect. It then sucks, if undisturbed, till its stomach is filled to repletion, leaving a painful tumour accompanied with an intolerable itching. It is the female gnat alone which is noxious; the male, whose proboscis is feathered, has no power of sucking blood.—*Gosse.*

them with the disdain that poets have shown. A simple butterfly, a single fly, humbles the pride of man, and in spite of all he can do levels his forests, devours his crops, and reduces him to despair.

Simple little two-winged flies, gnats and mosquitoes, the puny appearance of which would never lead one to dread aggression from such a quarter, are nevertheless enemies of the most inconvenient kind to our species. In some countries, where they swarm by myriads on all sides, man is forced to succumb to their hostility, and only avoids their attacks by adapting his abode and manner of living to the emergency. At the time when the mosquitoes are most prevalent in Senegal, the negroes, notwithstanding the constraint of such a kind of life, remain constantly enveloped in the midst of thick smoke. For this purpose they set up regular roosts formed of branches, and suspended above masses of wood which burn perpetually beneath them. Squatted on these they receive their friends during the day, and at night, heated from below and smoked on all sides, they stretch themselves on them in order to sleep.

Some savage races only free themselves from the onslaughts of this accursed brood by smearing their bodies with a filthy coating of grease; and it is to protect himself against them that the miserable Laplander condemns himself to be smoked all day long in his dark hut. The companions of the astronomer Maupertuis were so tormented by the stings of the mosquitoes during their travels in Lapland, that to free themselves from them they had recourse to the extreme measure of covering their faces with tar.

An ordinary-looking fly inhabiting Africa is still more formidable; it disputes the soil with us foot by foot; there is a struggle between man and it as to which shall have possession. Where it lives it prevents him from carrying on agriculture, and limits his explorations; he can only become master of the soil when he has exterminated it. This fly, generally called *tsetse* by the natives, is shaped like our common species, and seems to all appearance equally inoffensive, but its mouth secretes a venom the activity of which by far surpasses that of the most poisonous serpents. A few stings of the *tsetse* are enough to kill the strongest ox in a short time; and yet if we attempted to ascertain the weight of its poison apparatus by means of the most delicate balance, we should perhaps find the calculation impossible on account of its smallness.

It is an inexplicable anomaly that this fly, which inevitably kills certain animals, does not injure others. It selects all its victims from our cattle; the goat and the ass alone defy its sting. Nor do its attacks produce any effect upon man and wild animals. But what is still more singular, this dipterous insect kills the adult animal, but sucks the blood of its offspring without doing any mischief. The tsetse quickly poisons the full-grown ox, but produces no effect upon the calf. Livingstone says that during his wanderings his children were frequently stung by it, without ever suffering in the least degree; in fact, they paid no attention to it; whilst the deadly fly killed forty-three oxen in spite of the strictest watch.

The tsetse infests both banks of the Zambesi, and moves only to a short distance from them; it catches its victims as they make the passage, and darts upon them with the speed of an arrow. Dr. Livingstone says that at the time he travelled in this region these flies sometimes buzzed

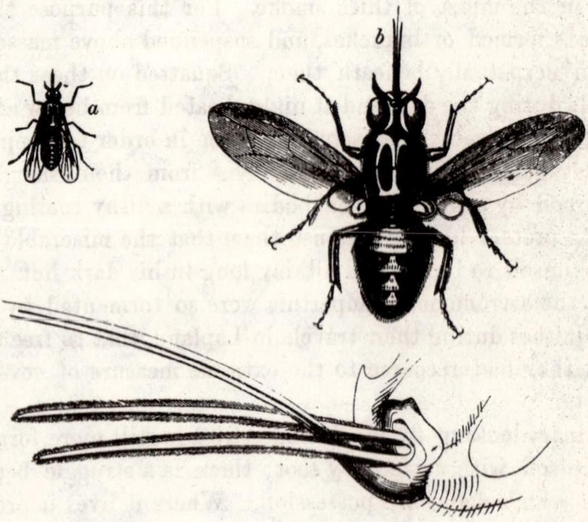

44. The Tsetse Fly. *a*, Natural size; *b*, magnified; *c*, proboscis magnified.

round his head and those of his fellow-travellers as thick as a swarm of bees. They were often stung all over, as were also their asses, but without either themselves or their beasts of burden experiencing any troublesome result. The sting of this blood-sucker being fatal to our domestic animals, the ox, horse, sheep, and dog, in the countries it devastates, the goat and ass make up the sum total of agricultural cattle.

The victims know their executioner; and when the hum of one of these flies rings in the ears of the cattle they fly, struck with fright, in every direction.

Such pests as these not only paralyze agriculture, but place a limit to the explorations of man. Deprived of his beasts of burden and his food, he cannot pass through the country of the redoubtable fly; and if by chance he can brave the danger, it is only by taking advantage of the time of its repose. Whenever one is obliged to send flocks of sheep or herds of cattle across countries infested by the tsetse, the natives choose cold moonlight nights, knowing that at such times the insect, sunk in sleep, will not sting the cattle.

The domestic fly, inoffensive in our dwellings, torments without ceasing those who travel in hot countries. There it is dreaded more than the hyæna and jackal, and we can only guard against it by having a crowd of slaves about us. In some of the villages of Upper Egypt I have sometimes seen in their mothers' arms, children at the breast, whose faces were covered by such dense swarms of flies that the insects looked like crawling black masks.[1] All were hard at work with their probosces, the delicate anatomy of which surpasses everything one can imagine.

With us it is quite an exceptional occurrence for the house-fly to attack man. Nevertheless, the meat-fly sometimes mistakes persons sunk in the degrading sleep of drunkenness for dead bodies. When they awake the active offspring of their assailant are already gnawing their palpitating flesh, and making their way under the skin of their cheeks and skull: a horrible infliction, which is certain to end fatally.

But it is especially in our forests and fields that insects leave such lamentable marks of their passage. Their legions descend in frightful numbers on certain plants and trees. According to Ratzeburg the pine-tree alone serves as a refuge for more than 400 species, the greater part of which are hurtful to it; and Charles Müller tells us that the oak extends its hospitality to upwards of 200 insects which are united to it by their parasitic existence.

[1] I am not speaking at all hyperbolically here. The children I mention had their faces literally covered with a layer of flies, which only allowed their eyes to be seen.

Some years ago one of our great surgeons, Jules Cloquet, published an account of a drunken man who, having fallen asleep in the open air near Paris, was carried to one of the hospitals in that city with legions of blow-flies developed in his nose and ears, from whence they had hollowed out paths between the skull and the hairy scalp. The irritation and suppuration which they set up speedily occasioned the death of this person. A case of death from this cause is also mentioned by Kirby and Spence.

In saying that an insect often causes the death of a man, we have only stated a sad truth. The sucking Diptera, such as the gad-fly, the fly, and gnat, after sating themselves with the fluids of a corpse in a state of putrefaction, attack man, introducing the germs of death by means of their lips tainted with pestilential humours. The sting of these insects frequently produces gangrenous affections, and especially malignant pustule, under which the patients succumb. Several cases have been seen in the London hospitals of serious disease from irritation set up by the *Musca carnaria*.—See *Dict. des Sc. Méd.* t. xlvi., p. 258.

Certain velvet-winged Phalenæ, notwithstanding that they seem so harmless as they fly by night, in a short space of time devastate the most magnificent forests of Coniferæ, and open out extensive clearings in their sombre shades more quickly than the axe of the woodman.

In some regions of Europe a little yellow fly streaked with black,

45. The Pyralis of the Vine in its different stages—*Pyralis strigulalis.*

the *Chlorops lineata*, alarms the farmer by attacking the grain crops. Linnæus says that in Sweden this fly, unassisted, destroys more than the fifth part of the barley crops, equivalent at least to 100,000 tons. In central France this insect sometimes devours half the ears of corn in our fields.[1] Another, the olive-tree Dacus, is the cause of our losing

[1] The *Chlorops lineata*, a fly the name of which indicates its yellow colours barred with black, makes such havoc in the wheat fields, that those who have followed up its history

every year 3,000,000 olives. Finally, a butterfly, the Pyralis of the vine, carries despair into all our wine countries, which have now for a long time vainly implored the aid of science.

When trees attacked by dense swarms of insects do not sink under their fangs, they escape with singular deformities.[1]

The sting of an extremely small insect, the woolly aphis (*Aphis lanigera*), which, when on the branches, would elude the eye were it not enveloped in a tuft of white wool, covers our apple-trees with numerous excrescences, and these often end by killing it.

The wounds inflicted by insects also give rise to those tufts of deformed, closely-set branches, which appear in the tops of the pine-trees, and to which the German foresters give the name of *witches' brooms;* strange-looking bunches, which the superstitious wood-cutters of the Hartz fear to touch less they should be struck by a thunderbolt, for they believe these growths attract the lightning. They therefore call them also *thunder-bushes.*[2]

In the domain of the infinitely little the physiological phenomena astonish us no less than the extreme slightness of the motive organs! A single comparison will demonstrate this.

When we communicate an elevating movement to our arms, and suddenly bring them back to the body, a second of time will scarcely suffice for the act; but, according to the experiments of Herschel, some insects vibrate their wings several hundred times in this short period!

M. Cagniard-Latour affirms that a gnat vibrates its wings 500 times in a second.

Mr. Nicholson goes still further; he asserts that the vibrations of the wing of the common fly are as many as 600 in a second, since it passes through space at the rate of six feet in this time. But this observer adds, that for rapid flight we must multiply this number by six, which means that in a second, or the time we require to execute a single movement of one of our members, the fly with its wing can

maintain that it would soon annihilate this cereal altogether if its increase in numbers were not checked by different causes. Another insect undertakes this task, and carries it out to a considerable extent; this is *Alysia Olivieri*, which perforates the eggs of the Chlorops with its ovipositor, in order to secure a shelter for its own offspring.

[1] In the magnificent plates of Ratzeburg's work on the insects of the forest, may be seen a representation of a forest quite deformed by the attacks of the pine-twister.—*Hylophthires et leurs Ennemis.* Leipzig, 1842.

[2] Schacht, who has described the witch-brooms at full length, seems to attribute them to the stings of insects, which determine an exuberant flow of vital powers to the part where they have been inflicted. He says that these brooms, when they are covered with leaves, look, if seen at a distance, like a great mistletoe.—Schacht, *Les Arbres.* Bruxelles, 1862, p. 140.

perform 3600. The mind is stupified at such calculations, and yet they are of unimpeachable accuracy! This marvellous rapidity of movement in the wings of insects explains the astonishing ease with which they fly. As M. Blanchard says, "In our days the railway traveller, carried at full speed, often amuses himself by watching from the window the movements of the gnats that flit about with incomparable ease. These puny flies, notwithstanding the agitation of the air, dart back-

46. Sphinx Galii sipping up Honey.

wards and forwards, wheel, rise, sink, and continue their gyrations for hours at a time, as if they were there to show us that the greatest speed we can attain is trifling compared to the power of their delicate wings."

After this we are no longer astonished at the activity shown by some butterflies, such as the sphinx, when they rifle the flowers of our gardens. They flit from one to the other with the speed of an arrow, and, like the humming-birds, they hang motionless before the corolla, plunging their long tongues to the bottom in order to sip the nectar, whilst their wings are agitated by movements which the eye cannot follow!

The delicacy of these aërial oars is not less remarkable than their movements.

However gently we take hold of the wing of a butterfly, our fingers never leave it without having some particles adhering, which seem only a fine dust, the source of the magnificent colouring of the insect. But when this dust is submitted to microscopic examination, the observer is surprised to see that each of these grains represents a little flattened plate, lengthened out and of a delicate and complicated structure, which reflects the most magical colours. One of its extremities is generally toothed more or less deeply, whilst the other displays only a little

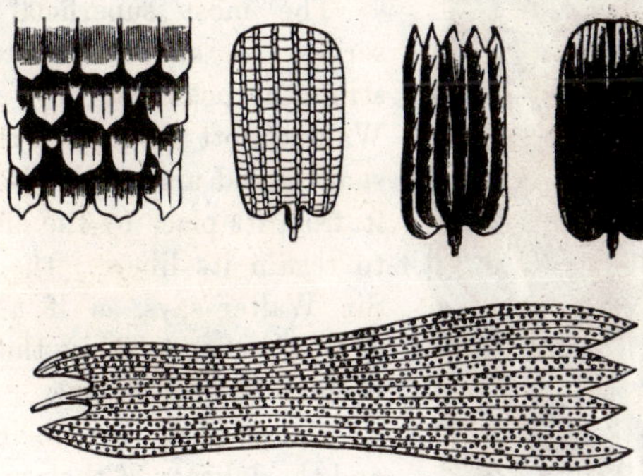

47. Scales from the Wings of different Butterflies, seen with the microscope.

pedicle by which each imperceptible scale is attached to the transparent membrane of the wing.

If a portion of this be now examined by the aid of a low magnifying power, it will be seen that all the scales are arranged with admirable symmetry, one above the other like the tiles on a roof, and as they are of uniform shape and often of very varied colours, the surface of the wing closely resembles a mosaic of marvellous fineness, not like that of our artists, but like the result of divine art.

Our varied movements are executed by the aid of voluminous fleshy muscles attached to the skeleton. In respect to these the insect possesses both a numerical and a dynamical superiority over the human race. Anatomists calculate that there are only 370 of these muscles in man, whilst the patient Lyonet discovered more than 4000 in a single caterpillar.

Insects equally surpass us in respect to strength. A man of average physical powers cannot move without difficulty a weight of fourty-four pounds, placed horizontally. As he himself weighs from 150 to 200 pounds, he only moves in so doing a mass the weight of which does not equal a third of that of his body. If we subject a mole-cricket to the same test, the results are quite extraordinary. This creature, which only weighs about sixty-two grains, can with its two large hands move a weight of about three pounds five ounces, which means that it displays a strength 375 times exceeding its own weight!

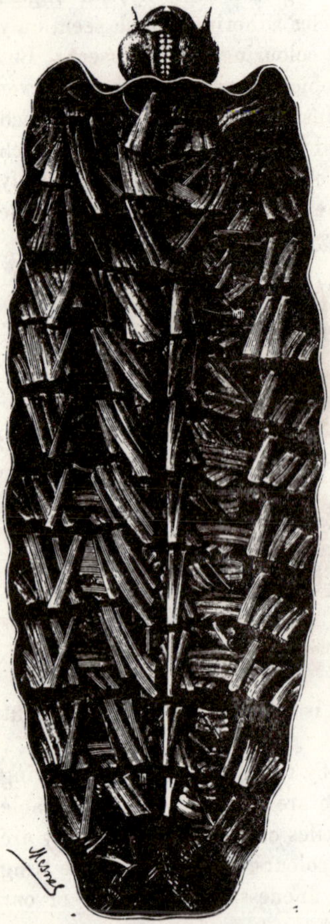

48. Muscular Apparatus of the Willow-eating Caterpillar—*Cossus ligniperda.*

The most superficial observation serves to show the extraordinary strength possessed by insects. Sir Walter Scott has related that a garden-snail placed under a candlestick moved it from its place by the efforts it made to regain its liberty; the same thing, Sir Walter says, as if a prisoner in Newgate were to shake the prison walls by his efforts to escape.

Notwithstanding their minuteness and the delicacy of their anatomy, some other insects also exhibit a comparative strength which astonishes us. Although it is almost puerile to speak of the flea, still we may take it for an instance, as it is unfortunately known everywhere. M. de Fonvielle, in his interesting work on the *Invisible World*, maintains that it can raise itself from the ground to a height equal to two hundred times its stature. At this rate, he says, a man would only make a joke of jumping over the towers of Notre-Dame and the heights of Montmartre; and a prison would be an impossibility unless the walls were built more than a quarter of a mile in height.

If we can scarcely believe in the prodigious movements of the wing of insects, and its mosaic of jewelry their feet, though less agile and less adorned, are yet equally worthy of our attention. Those of the working-bee are perfect master-pieces; they exhibit at one and the same time a basket, a brush, and a pair of pincers. The brush is an article of extreme fineness, the hairs of which, arranged in symmetrical rows, are only to be seen with the microscope; with this brush, of fairy delicacy, the bee continually brushes her velvet robe to remove the pollen dust with which it becomes loaded whilst she is rifling the flowers and sucking up the nectar. Another article, which is hollowed like a spoon, receives all the gleanings which the insect carries to the hive; it is a basket for provisions. Finally, by opening them one upon another, by means of a hinge, those two pieces become a pair of pincers, which render important service in the construction of the combs,

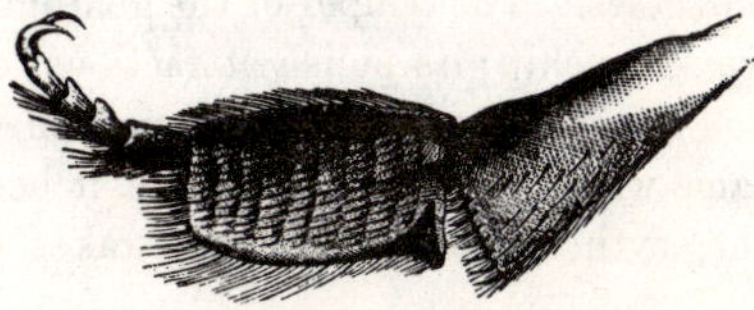

49. Brush and Pincers of the Common Bee.

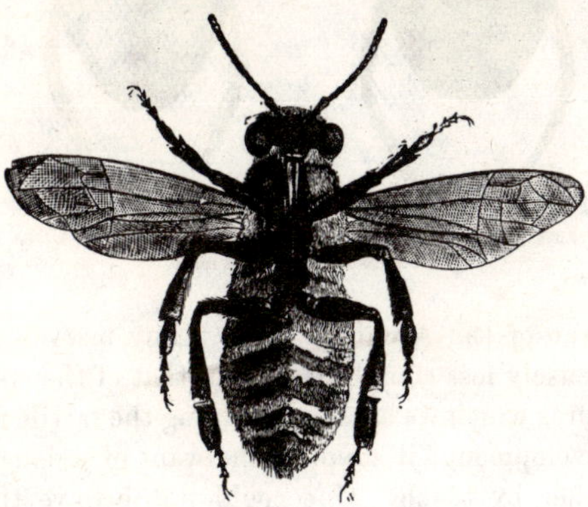

50. Bee seen from below with its Ventral Segments of Wax.

and it is with them that the bee lays hold of the semicircles of wax below its abdomen, and carries them to its mouth.

In some aquatic insects each foot is transformed into a delicate oar, as is seen in the Dytiscus, in which it is flattened out and bordered with cilia or delicate hairs, so that a larger surface may strike the water. Others, like the flies, have at the extremities of their limbs a kind of small notched lamellæ, which allow them to adhere to glass and the most polished bodies.

How rough and coarse the works of man appear by the side of those of nature! Compare the instruments which the insect uses for its work with those which we employ. Behold its saws, its rakes, its brushes, its chisels; compare them with ours, and you will at once admit that the tools fabricated by man are all immeasurably inferior to what the insect possesses. The scalpel of the anatomist seems to have an edge of delicate workmanship; its polish attracts us; examine it with the microscope, and you are surprised to see it transformed into a coarse saw-blade. It is the same with the point of a needle, it becomes an imperfect awl. Scrutinize the scythes, the darts, or the rakes of an insect, and everything there

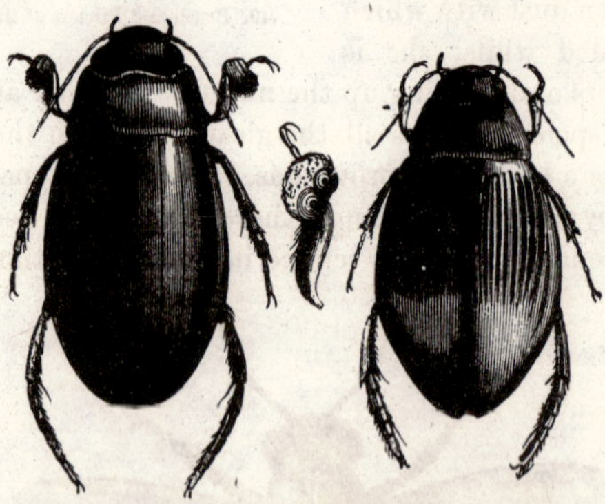

51. Hind Feet, used as Ciliary Oars, in the male and female Dytiscus, and the Prehensile Foot of the male.

reveals the power of the Architect of so many marvels. The claw of the lion is immensely less complicated than that of the spider!

In the creatures which we are now studying the tactile faculty acquires a marvellous development; it supplies the want of a language; the ants talk to each other by touch. One could not believe this if a careful observer had not demonstrated it, and yet the fact is so obvious that any one can at any time verify it. When two of these intelligent insects meet in their career, we see that they touch each other differently with their antennæ, and that after doing this they seem to form some fresh resolution, in consequence of this tactile communication, which Huber calls *antennal language*.

The following experiment, undertaken by this naturalist, gives incontestable evidence in favour of the fact. Having placed a colony of ants in a closed and darkened chamber, he remarked that at first they all scattered in disorder; but he soon noticed that if an individual in the course of his peregrinations discovered an outlet, he returned to the midst of the others; of these he touched a certain number, and after this communication the whole population assembled in regular lines, which marched out under the impulse of one common thought—that of liberty regained.

In all the large animals there are but two eyes; in this respect the smallest insect is infinitely better provided than they are. The ant, the

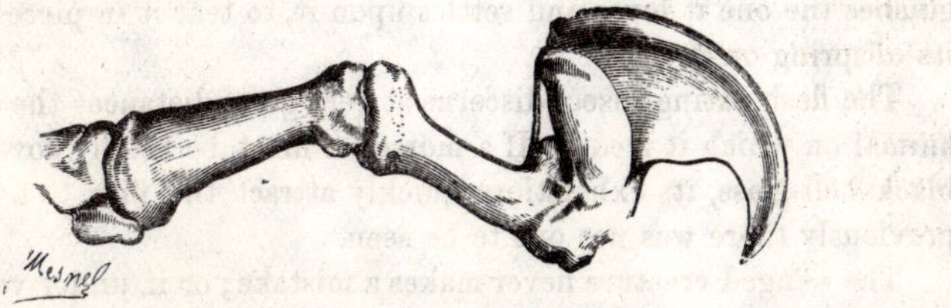

52. Claw of the Lion.

visual apparatus of which is one of the least perfect, possesses fifty. The common fly has 8000, and in certain butterflies as many as 25,000 have been counted. Each of these organs, too, presents, in microscopic proportions, the greater number of the structures which enter into the composition of the globe of our eye. Closely packed together, these eyes make

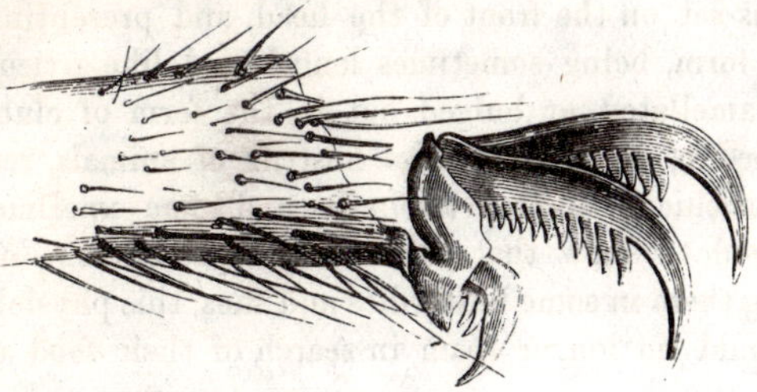

53. Spider's Claw, seen with the microscope.

up for their immobility by their bulk, and this is so great that in some flies the eyes almost cover the head, and even constitute a fourth part of the weight of the body.

This powerful optic apparatus exhibits some curious modifications which reveal the habits of insects.

Those which seek their prey by night have their eyes more deeply set, in order better to absorb the least luminous rays. In the flesh-eating insects they are larger. In some aquatic species the head is furnished with several pairs, some directed upwards, others downward, in such a way, that while swimming on the surface of the water the animal can see at the same time the fish which menaces it from the depths, and the bird which is about to swoop upon it from above. From the former it escapes by flight, and from the latter by diving.[1]

The insect is endowed with an exquisite fineness of smell. The slightest odour is perceived by it at very great distances. In the perfumed air exhaling from the thousand plants of a meadow or garden, it distinguishes the one it loves and settles upon it, to tear it in pieces or deposit its offspring on it.

The flesh-eating insect discerns at very great distances the smell of an animal on which it feeds. If a morsel of meat be totally covered with a black bell-glass, its exhalations quickly attract the flies to a spot where previously there was not one to be seen.

The winged creature never makes a mistake; or if, under very unusual circumstances, it should happen to do so, it would be because there was a perfect identity between the odorous emanations. For instance, the putrid exhalations from the flowers of the Stapelia and Arum attract some insects just as putrid meat would; and these, deceived by a false resemblance, deposit upon the plant their offspring, which must infallibly die of hunger.

But where does a sense so delicate reside? Analogy made Réaumur and De Blainville think it ought to be placed in the antennæ, those little mobile horns set on the front of the head, and presenting the greatest diversity of form, being sometimes lengthened like articulated threads, sometimes lamellated, or bulged out in the form of clubs or bladders. The antennæ do, indeed, like the nostrils of animals, receive the first pair of nerves which issue from the brain; and some experiments conducted by Dugès tend to show that they really represent the organ of smell. After cutting them in some butterflies and flies, this physiologist observed that they could no longer roam in search of their food and the female insect.

But the extreme acuteness of smell manifested by some insects is only obtained by means of organs of marvellous delicacy, and so complicated as to surpass at times all our preconceived ideas. Man and the larger animals have never more than two olfactory cavities; in fishes these are

[1] We speak here of the little whirlwigs, elegant aquatic beetles of extreme brilliancy, which sparkle like diamonds when the sun lights upon them on the surface of the water, where they pirouette constantly with surprising velocity: hence the name whirlwigs. These insects have four groups of eyes in their heads. Of these two are placed below, and give them notice of what is going on in the depths of the water; the two others are turned towards the sky.

reduced to a pair of little sacks scarcely to be seen. In the may-bug odours are perceived by means of microscopic pouches, but instead of being limited to two, these pouches are many thousands in number. Here the infinitely little surpasses the infinitely great; the insect outstrips the elephant.

There must necessarily be organs of hearing in insects, because they are attracted together by certain sounds, and even possess a very varied set of instruments wherewith to produce sounds. But we do not yet know where their auditory apparatus is.[1]

One very extraordinary fact is, that these animals only seem to hear sounds which are serviceable to them, whilst others, whatever be their

54. Diversiform Antennæ.

intensity, do not affect them in any way. The queen-bee, by means of a scarcely perceptible hum, sets all her people in movement, and compels an army of combatants to follow her; but if, on the contrary, fire-arms be discharged quite close to a colony of bees, not one of them stirs; it seems as if the sound was not noticed by them.

The horse has only one stomach, the insect has often three; in the former it occupies only a somewhat limited portion of the body, in the other it sometimes forms almost the entire body—the animal resembles a walking digestive sack. The ravenous activity of many Orthoptera (locusts, &c.) is even aided by great teeth, placed in the interior of the

[1] Latreille seems to think that the auditory organ of insects may be seated at the base of the antennæ, because in certain Orthoptera, there are at this spot traces of the membranes of the tympanum, as is observed in some crustaceans.

In order to omit none of the recent conquests of science, we should also mention that Cuvier and Duméril place the seat of smell at the orifice of those small openings, like button-holes, called stigmata, by which the air enters the trachea. And, in fact, there is here a manifest analogy with the position of the nose, which, in the large animals, is placed at the entrance to the respiratory apparatus.

stomach, which act like a second mouth, and complete the crushing of anything that has escaped the action of the jaws.

In certain caterpillars the digestive power is so great that they swallow every day three or four times their own weight of food. If the elephant and rhinoceros were to feed on this scale, and were as numerous as the others, they would require only a very short time to devour all the vegetation on the globe.

The first period of an insect's life is devoted to development, to nutrition, and frequently it is only during this time that it eats in the gluttonous manner we have just spoken of. When it has reached its full

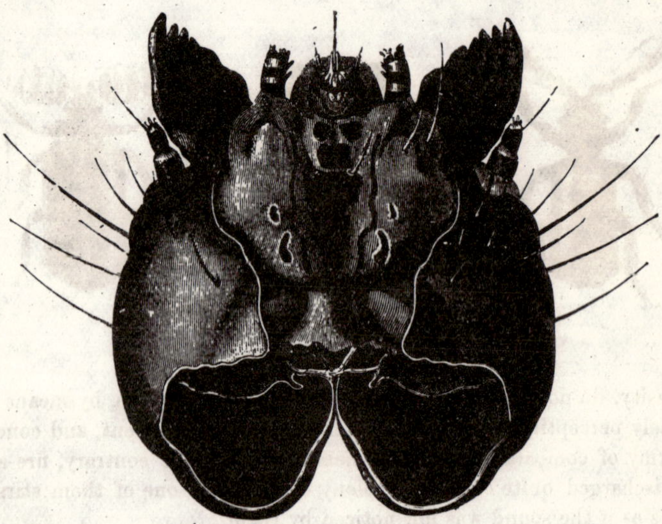

55. Head and Jaws of the Willow-eating Caterpillar.—From Lyonet's Anatomical Treatise.

development it seems to have no other object in its existence than reproduction; sometimes even the alimentary canal is obliterated, and the animal takes no nourishment. The caterpillar, with its destructive jaws, the ruin of our harvests, is transformed into a butterfly, the harmless proboscis of which only imbibes the nectar of flowers.[1] In its last stage the Ephemera lives on love alone; its digestive apparatus has quite disappeared.

Some Hemiptera are, however, all through life extremely abstinent and only feed on the juices of plants. They do not suck them, although generally said to do so; their organization does not allow of such a thing.

[1] See a more special reference to this form of metamorphosis at page 99.

Not having any apparatus for forming a vacuum and sucking up fluids, they draw them off by means of the mouth, which for this purpose is transformed into the most delicate little suction-pump that can be imagined. The lower lip represents a tube terminated in a point, on the upper part of which extends a groove. In this four delicate bristles move like pistons, and in the course of their action to and fro attract the liquids of plants and animals so soon as ever the insect has pierced the envelope with the point of its beak. Thus when the bloodthirsty gnat settles on our skin and gorges itself with our blood, it does not suck the fluid, it pumps it up with pistons of exquisite delicacy.

Our heart, the structure of which is so much admired and so admirable, is nevertheless only a very coarse forcing-pump compared with that of an insect. All the apparatus of the central organ of circulation is limited to two large openings, each furnished with two valves or valvlets, intended to prevent the reflux of the blood; but if, by the aid of the

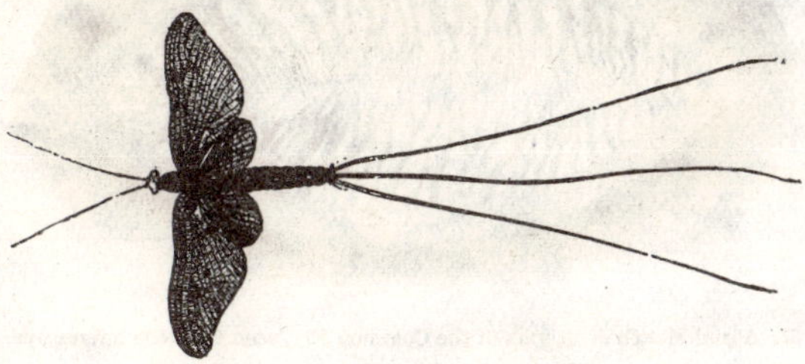

56. Common Ephemera—*Ephemera communis.*

solar microscope, we project the transparent body of an Ephemera upon a huge screen, one is astonished at the magnificent spectacle offered by the movement of the blood. The heart is represented by a long vessel which occupies all the back of the animal, and into which the circulating fluid precipitates itself by eight or ten lateral openings, like small streams converging towards a more impetuous current. As many valves rise and fall to allow entrance to the fluid and hinder its return. In the interior of this lengthened heart larger valvules, to the number of six or eight, are folded back against the wall to let the blood pass forward, and re-open directly afterwards, during each contraction, in order to prevent its flowing backwards. Vessels arranged in loops are distributed to all the members.

The course of the blood in the colossal insect seen upon the screen resembles so many little streams bearing globules more or less crowded together; this is proved by the strictest evidence, and yet who would believe that Cuvier and his school would never credit this phenomenon? Instead of looking, which was so easy, they preferred to deny the circulation in the insect, and to regard its wonderful heart as a simple secreting vessel affected by contractile movements. It is thus that physiological science advances; a hundred battles are requisite to make men admit the most easily verified truth.

With us, as with all the large animals, the air rushes into the respiratory apparatus, without the least check, by a simple and very ample opening; all the impurities in the air may be swallowed, to the defilement of our lungs.

Insects, on the contrary, inspire the atmospheric air through several

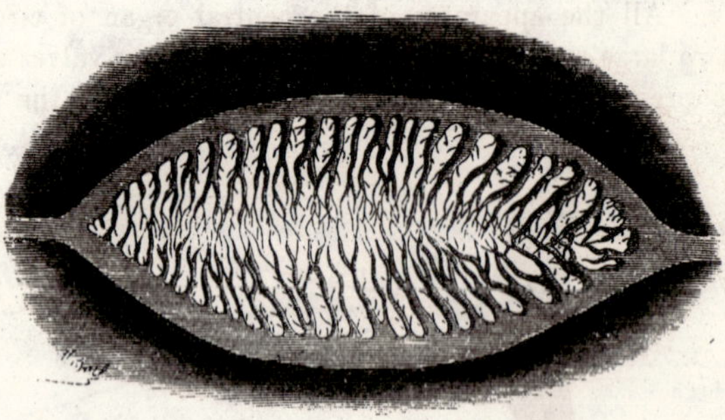

57. Aërial Mouth or Stigma of the Common Fly, seen with the microscope.

orifices, and this is well purified before it is introduced into the organism. For this purpose all their aërial mouths are in some closed with a membrane, which is perforated like a sieve with an immense number of small holes, and so is fitted to arrest the smallest particles floating in the air, and act like a veritable strainer. In others each respiratory opening is obstructed by hairs, which form a kind of net, intended for the same purpose. Without these providential precautions the air-tubes of these animals, often as fine as hairs, would be obstructed every instant by the dust in the midst of which they live.

In the case of insects inhabiting the water, other precautions, not less admirable, prevent the fluid from forcing its way into the air-passages. Sometimes at the entrance of the respiratory organ there is a door, with five or six leaves of the most ingenious mechanism, which the animal opens or shuts at will. It only opens them when it comes to the surface of a pool to breathe; when it plunges into the depths the leaves of this little air-door are closely shut, and the pneumatic channels are effectually defended against the invasion of the liquid, which would disturb the organization. This is seen in the larva of the common gnat, which swarms in our stagnant waters.

In the larger animals the respiratory function is performed by the aid of a distinct, restricted apparatus confined to one region of the body. In the insects it has a much larger field of action. The air diffuses itself everywhere, and after having bathed the internal organs by means of particular vessels, the *tracheæ*, which are easily distinguished by their pearly tint, it reaches the extreme terminations of the feet and the antennæ. For this purpose these are provided with a most remarkable structure. They are composed of a fine cartilaginous lamina, rolled in like the metallic thread in an elastic brace. This arrangement serves to

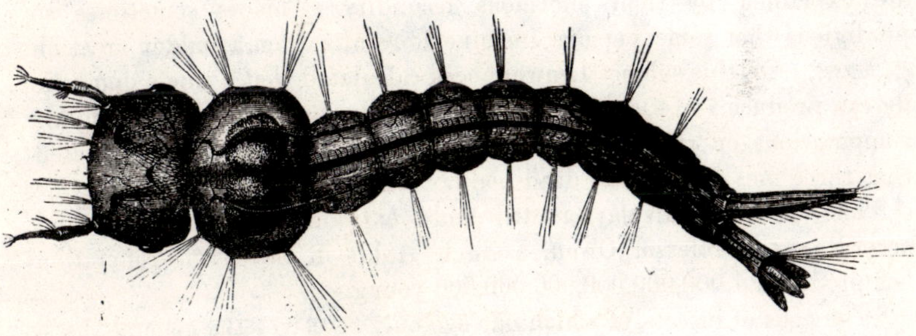

58. Larva of the Common Gnat—*Culex pipiens* (Linn.), seen with the microscope.

keep their walls constantly separated, and to facilitate the free circulation of air through their imperceptible canals.

Every person has seen, and with some disgust too, a white larva with a long tail, which lives in the filthy stagnant waters of our courts and roads, and which is vulgarly called the *rat-tailed maggot.* When I was young this creature inspired me with the same repugnance as it inspires in most people; but since I have examined it by the aid of a lens, and studied its habits, repugnance has given way to admiration. The extraordinary tail to which the animal owes its name is an organ of respiration. It contains two vessels which serve to disseminate the air through all the body of this fly-larva, for such it is. These two air-channels are enveloped by tubes of a different calibre, which fit one into another and move exactly like the tubes of a telescope.

This worm, not having any swimming organ, possesses in this ingenious arrangement a means of constantly opening the orifice of its respiratory apparatus at the surface of the water, whatever may be its level. If the liquid sink in the puddle which it inhabits, all the tubes enter one another like those of a telescope and the aërial tubes wind inside them. If, on the contrary, a violent shower should make the water rise above its bounds, they are all projected outwards, being drawn out as far as possible so that their orifices still reach the surface.

The final intention of nature is so manifest in this circumstance, that if we, in imitation of Réaumur, plunge one of these larvæ into a glass containing only a little water, and the quantity of this be gradually augmented, the insect's tail lengthens in proportion and indeed acquires an extraordinary size, so that, without quitting the spot, the larva may carry on the act of respiration, the aërial tubes opening out on the surface of the fluid.

The ravages of insects, which sometimes occasion such serious panics, are explained by their enormous fecundity. This is sometimes so prodigious that some persons imagine it results from a sudden creation *en masse.* On this subject Leuwenhoeck calculated that a single domestic fly can produce 746,496 young in three months; and Linnæus, basing his computations on the voracity of the hungry offspring of the fly, stated that three flies destroy the dead body of a horse as quickly as a lion.

The Termites display a still more extraordinary fecundity; and according to Professor Owen, a single Aphis in the tenth generation has produced 1,000,000,000,000,000,000 young.

The eggs of insects, of which our eye only perceives the general shape and colour, appear like so many master-pieces of art when the magnifying glass reveals their delicate chisellings and mechanism. They generally approach the form of a sphere or an ovoid. Some butterflies lay cylindrical eggs, and those of the gnat look like charming microscopical amphoræ. There are some, the extremity of which is surmounted by a crown of points; others exactly represent a delicate miniature saucepan, the young inhabitant of which, in order to be born, has only to lift up the lid.

The egg of the louse, which disgusts us so much, presents this curious structure, but in addition its opening is embellished by a little projecting rim, and a groove into which the edge of the cover enters in such a manner as to close it hermetically. A still more ingenious mechanism is seen in some of the wood-bugs. The young insect does not even require to lift the lid; there is within a spring on which this office devolves; at the moment of birth the occupant has only to emerge, and one may say with justice of him, that he does not even take the trouble to be born.

The surface of these eggs is often remarkable on account of the exquisite fineness of the entwining ornamentation. Some are covered

59. The DRONE-FLY, *Eristalis tenax*, and its Larva the Rat-tailed Maggot.

with large ribs which extend from one end to the other; others display only fine lines artistically engraved; others again have the surface covered with a net-work of lace. For them nature has exhausted the riches of her palette; they are dyed with the softest or the most brilliant tints of blue, green, and red; some absolutely resemble mother-of-pearl, and there are some that one might take for so many charming little iridescent pearls.

The sexuality itself of insects offers some curious particulars. There are not only males and females among them, but some of their republics have, in addition, individuals absolutely deprived of sex; these are the neuters, which alone work, and constitute the element of the prosperity and power of the state. Some are true workmen, others valiant soldiers. But these individuals which we recognize by their form or their particular weapons, are in truth only aborted females; the bees themselves know this perfectly, as we shall see.

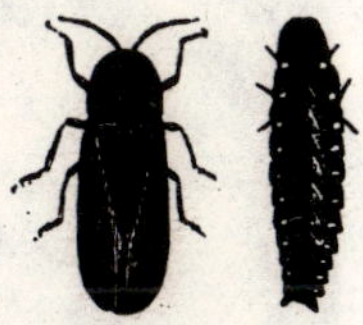

60. Glowworm, male and female —*Lampyris noctiluca.*

To all these marvels of insect life we must yet add the inexplicable phenomenon of the dazzling light which they project into the midst of the darkness, and which sometimes in their flight furrows the air with long streams of fire, sometimes peacefully illuminates the foliage on which they repose.

61. Luminous Beetle of the Antilles —*Elater noctilucus.*

Every person knows the Lampyris, or glow-worm, which in the autumn gives our green turf the appearance of a starry sky. But in tropical America there are phosphorescent insects of far superior splendour. The great lantern-fly can supply the place of a lamp with the bright light with which its monstrous head gleams. Sybille de Mérian relates that at Surinam she sometimes read the newspapers by the aid of a single one of these Hemiptera.[1]

In the West India Islands the phosphorescence of these insects is made daily use of; they employ there a luminous beetle the corselet

[1] As is the case with so many vital phenomena, the phosphorescence of insects is still far from being explained. Sir Humphry Davy and Treviranus attributed it to a substance containing phosphorus, which is secreted from the fluids of the animal, and beams like this substance by means of the oxygen of the air. This would be a true combustion. The

of which becomes dazzling in the gloom. In Cuba the women often inclose several of these Coleoptera in little cages of glass or wood, which they hang up in their rooms, and this living lustre throws out sufficient light to serve to work by. Travellers there also, in a difficult road, light their path in the middle of the night by attaching one of these beetles to each of their feet. The creoles sometimes set them in the curls of their hair, where, like resplendent jewels, they give a most fairy-like aspect to their heads. The negresses at their nocturnal

62. Negro Hut lighted up with Luminous Beetles.

dances scatter these brilliant insects over the robes of lace which nature provides for them, all woven from the bark of the Lagetto. In their rapid and lascivious movements they seemed enveloped in a robe of fire.[1]

presence of phosphoric acid in the atmosphere seems to give a certain amount of authority to this hypothesis. A German anatomist, the celebrated Carus, discovered that the eggs of these animals are themselves luminous—a very curious fact, and of a nature to throw some light upon the question.

[1] Though sometimes called the Great Lantern Firefly, it is quite distinct from the Firefly (*Elater noctilucus*), which belongs to the click-bettles, and is also said to be used by the Indians to work or travel by. As recently, however, as 1858 Dr. J. A. Smith exhibited a specimen of the Fulgora to the Royal Physical Society of Edinburgh, and stated that it

Science has not satisfactorily explained the colouring and secretions found in certain insects; and indeed it has only been moderately successful in the seeking in the outer world for all the elements of the mysterious phenomena of organic life, which will possibly, for a long time, conceal from us the secrets of its constitution.

How does the cochineal insect find in the green juices of the cactus which nourishes it, the magnificent red colour, the carmine, which inflates its whole body?

The musk Cerambyx exhales the most grateful odour of roses;

63. The Sweet-smelling Staphylinus—*Staphylinus olens.*

all round about the willow which it inhabits the air is perfumed with

was still an undecided question among naturalists whether these flies are really luminous; and in the *Zoologist* for 1863 Mr. R. Jeffry of New Grenada says that it gives no light and that he imagines the use of the diaphanous projection on its head, from which it takes its name, is to prevent the insect from knocking against hard substances in the night. The same discrepancy of opinion has been observed with respect to the Chinese candle-beetle (*Hotinus candelarius*), which is said to emit at intervals a brilliant greenish light, and even to have been captured by Count d'Enzenberg in this state; whereas Sir John Bowring, who made such a splendid collection of beetles during his many years' residence in China never saw any luminosity about it. The reader will find these beetles beautifully represented in a coloured engraving in the first volume of *Nature and Art.*—Tr.

the scent, and these emanations betray the insect with fatal certainty to the collectors in pursuit of it. But the leafage of this tree nourishes also stinking bugs. Can the one draw from the same aliment the most marvellous essences, and the other only repulsive and fœtid fluids?

The bee exudes the softening wax from one region of its body, and burning poison from another; can the nectar of flowers furnish the perfumed honey and the most acrid venom?

The Cantharis and the Meloë transmute the harmless juices of our ash-trees and the grass of our meadows into dangerous poisons, and how many persons have fallen victims to these poisonous insects in our country![1] Yet it is the same grass which loads with fat the flesh of our cattle.

And lastly, how does the scented Staphylinus extract from the foul stuff on which it feeds the grateful perfume which exhales from its rings, and covers the fingers of those who touch it?

[1] The *Cantharis officinalis*, so much employed at present for making blisters, is one of the most deadly poisons in the world. It produces death when given in a very small dose, and even the external use of it is not free from danger. The works of writers of every epoch contain lamentable accounts of poisoning produced by this formidable beetle. Pliny relates that Cossinus, a Roman knight, and a favourite of Nero, died after having taken a drink prepared with Cantharides by one of the Egyptian physicians, who were at that time very much sought after in Rome. The writings of Galen and Dioscorides contain similar tales. Among modern authors Orfila and H. Cloquet also quote a number of those cases of poisoning, which are common enough.

Other Coleoptera contain poisons which are no less active than those of the blistering fly, as for instance the Meloës, heavy insects of a deep blue colour, having only rudimentary elytra, and which are found in the grass at the spring of the year. Latreille thinks that it was these that the ancients called Buprestides, and accused of being fatal to oxen when they swallowed them along with the grass of the meadows. According to the same learned author, the criminal use of these insects was so common at that time, that the legislators were obliged to try and check it by proclaiming the Lex Cornelia, which condemned to death any man who poisoned his fellow-man with Meloës.—Latreille, *Cours d'Entomologie*. Paris, 1831, p. 56.

CHAPTER II.

METAMORPHOSES.

Born in one shape the insect dies in another, and the metamorphoses which it undergoes are the most important portion of its life, and the most extraordinary phenomenon in physiology. Organism, functions, all things change: the ugly caterpillar is transformed into a butterfly gleaming with azure and gold, and if this butterfly were restricted to the fresh leaves of which it devoured such quantities in its youth, it would die of inanition; it requires a more delicate nourishment now that it has become adorned with its brilliant wings, and only lives on the nectar of flowers.

The Libellula, or dragon-fly, when it appears in its last dress, assumes different habits. It has passed all its life beneath the water in the condition of an ignoble larva, soiled with mud and filth; but now that the time has come, it aspires to soar into the air. Having mounted on some plant or other, it attaches its aquatic garment to it, and unfolds the brilliant iridescent wings of gauze which bear it away. The metamorphosis is so radical, and its new wants so imperious, that if we attempt to retain the insect a single minute longer in its ancient element it will perish on the spot. It has lived till now in shade and in stagnant water; henceforth it can only breathe the pure air and live in the glowing light.[1]

The grown insect differs so widely from the young, that one cannot in the least recognize the one in the other. The Scarabæus, or sacred beetle, with its emerald elytra, which was worshipped in ancient Egypt, does not in the least resemble the hideous subterranean worm which produces it; a singular metamorphosis, in which, according to M. Goury, the nations on the banks of the Nile beheld the symbol of the transmigration of souls.

Aristotle, whose genius has thrown such a brilliant light upon the

[1] This insect is so little like itself at different stages that any one who did not know its metamorphoses would look upon it as an animal belonging to totally different genera. The nymph of the dragon-fly has been taken by Rondelet for the aquatic Cygala; by Mouffet for the water-flea or grasshopper; and by Redi for the aquatic scorpion. The three different states of certain Acridia have also been described as three different insects.—Lesser, *Théologie des Insectes.* Trad. de Lyonet. Paris, 1745, p. 169.

history of animals, had only a suspicion of their metamorphoses. We must come to the period of the Renaissance, and see Redi begin to trace their history with a steady hand. To the illustrious physician of Florence succeeded Malpighi, the great anatomist, and Goëdart, a simple and excellent observer, who, in a book as rare as it is curious, brought under notice each caterpillar and its butterfly.

At birth the insect is always wingless. The apparatus for flying is only developed at the last stage of its existence—that which is consecrated

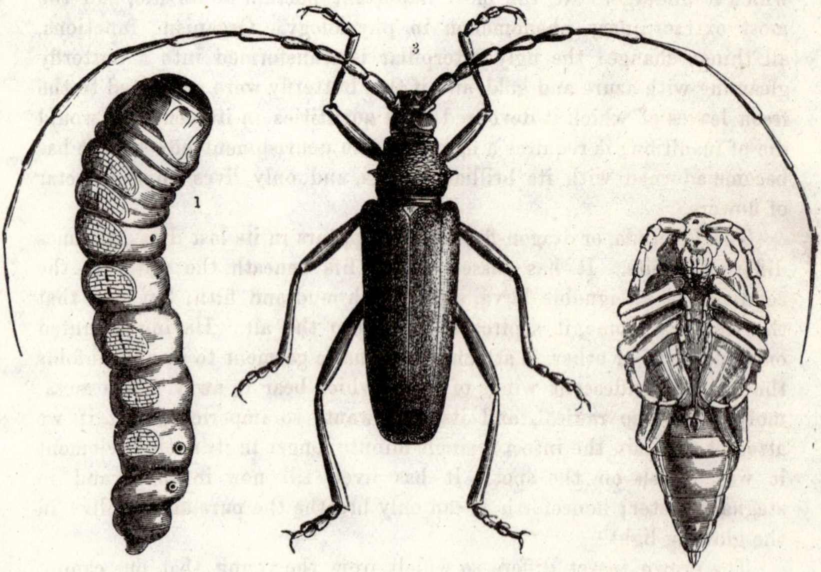

64. The Three States of an Insect, as seen in the Great Capricornis.
1. The Larva or Caterpillar. 2. The Nymph or Chrysalis. 3. The Perfect Insect or Imago.

solely to reproduction. The young creature generally presents itself under the form of a worm, to which Linnæus gave the name of larva or mask, —an ingenious reminder that this worm is only a kind of preliminary disguise beneath which is hidden the brilliant livery of the perfect insect.

This first period of life is given up entirely to development; the larva does nothing but eat and grow. But at a given time its activity ceases, it shrivels up, casts off its skin, takes on a new form, and becomes motionless. It is then that the name of nymph is given to it. This is a mere transitory state, and in this kind of temporary sepulchre

65 Life and Metamorphoses of the Dragon-fly, *Libellula depressa*. A, The Perfect Insect. B, The Insect casting off its worn-out Nymph's Skin. C D, Larvæ and Nymph.

the unfinished existence of the caterpillar is annihilated, and that of the perfect insect begins.

The transfiguration is as complete in the interior as at the surface. At a certain time the whole organism seems resolved into a homogeneous paste, from which springs the new living being. Generally the nymph is only covered with a brown winding-sheet of the most modest kind, it looks like an immovable mummy enveloped in bandages, but sometimes, in imitation of monarchs, it carves out for itself a sarcophagus enriched with gold, and from this is derived the name of chrysalis which is given to it.

At the decisive and final moment, the dawn of a new life, the

66. Emperor Moth.

mummy swathed like Diana of Ephesus awakes from its torpor, becomes full of life, rends its lowly covering, and appears under the form of an insect all glittering with emeralds and sapphires. It is in this last epoch of organization that it is called the perfect insect, the imago, as Linnæus named it in his figurative language.

The birth of the young creature is truly marvellous, for in spite of the unheard-of efforts demanded by the act, it issues from its swaddling-clothes in a state of inconceivable freshness.

The slightest graze rubs off the scales of the butterfly, and yet not one of them is lost when it escapes through the narrow opening of its prison. The Emperor Moth, with its great Argus-eyes upon its robes, emerges from its horny sarcophagus without catching a hair of its velvet wings against it!

Many insects do even more to protect their metamorphosis; they envelop themselves in a mantle of silk which preserves them from the assaults of the rain and cold. In certain butterflies it is evident that this covering is so arranged as to fulfil this double task; a dense

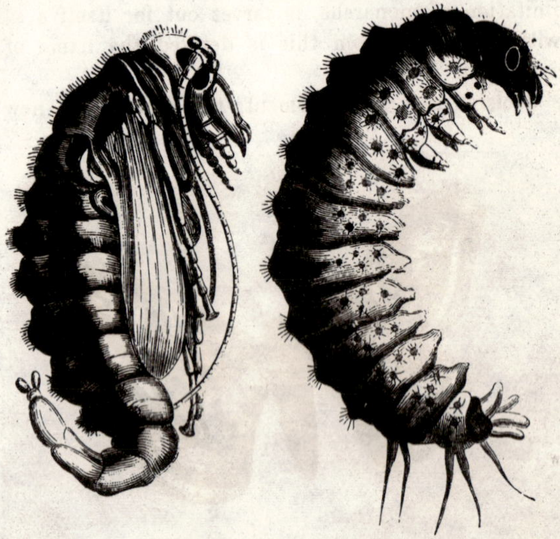

67. Larva and Nymph of the Panorpis, much enlarged, showing in this Fly the passage from one state to another.

external tegument, similar to the straw thatch of our houses in the country, allows the storm to pass over without penetrating; another, internal and softer, defies the cold of winter. Buried at autumn tide in this double shelter, the butterfly securely awaits the coming of spring to be born again.[1]

The magic of these metamorphoses surpasses anything one could imagine; they are so many dramatic scenes, in the last of which arises a creature quite unexpected in appearance.

[1] It is the cocoon or silken covering spun by the bombyx of the mulberry-tree that furnishes our silk, such a well-known source of our industrial wealth. Boyle the chemist relates that a lady, having taken the trouble to unravel a cocoon of silk very carefully, and to measure the thread, found that it was more than 300 English leagues in length.—Boyle, *Subtilty of Effluvia.* Lyonet with much reason thinks there must be some mistake here. He found this thread to be only from 700 to 900 feet long.

The butterfly, which at different stages of existence so little resembles its former self, seems to be born and die three times; but it is only a question of simple development, accomplished in the midst of an apparent torpor during which life only preserves its hidden springs. The caterpillar already contains all the rudiments of the forms which it is to take on in succession. The genius of the anatomist discovers in it three creatures, one encased within the other, the last of which, enveloped in a double winding-sheet, finally throws it off to appear in all its beauty.

Some insects, however, show neither the immobility nor the complete transformation we have been speaking of. The passage from one life to another takes place by means of a successive development. Some even maintain a constantly active existence in every stage. We only recognize the larva by the absence of its wings, and the nymph by its having merely rudimentary ones; this is the case with the wood-bugs and the Forficulæ or earwigs. But generally the perfect insect only reaches the

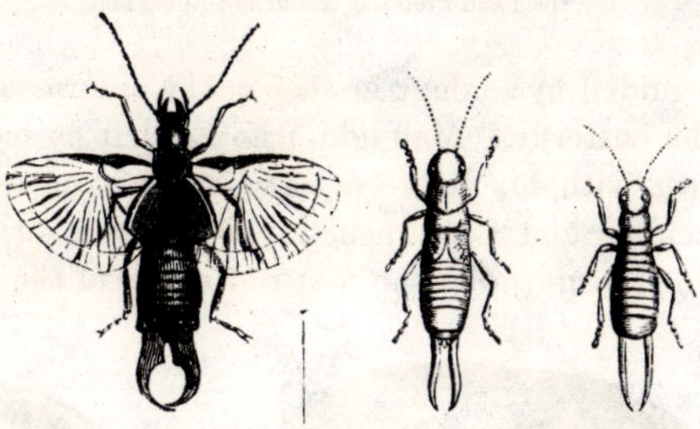

68. Earwig—*Forficula auricularia.* Adult, Nymph, and Larva

term of life after having undergone a total metamorphosis. Its last form is only a brilliant wedding garment, and it almost always expires as soon as ever the torches of Hymen are extinguished. Many an insect, the Ephemera for example, passes several years in its development beneath the mud and water, an unknown and imperfect larva; then it acquires wings and only exists an hour with all the prerogatives of life!

In species which display radical metamorphoses, the two modes of existence having no relation, the organism naturally undergoes an absolute transformation.

The butterfly, which is henceforth to nourish itself with nectar, throws off its voracious caterpillar's head and powerful mandibles, now become useless; an extended proboscis to suck the juice of flowers replaces them. The vigorous feet of the larva—the hooks of which cling so strongly to the leaves—would injure the flowers which the butterfly is henceforth to haunt; he releases himself from them, and exchanges them for long and delicate members which scarcely rest upon the velvet of the petals.

Up to a certain point the genius of the anatomist penetrates the inten-

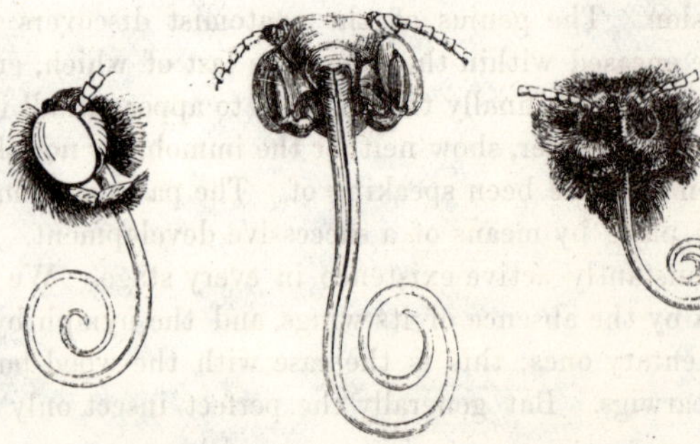

69. Head and Proboscis of different Butterflies.

tions of nature; guided by analogy he sees in the unformed caterpillar the lineaments of the butterfly. Malpighi, who has left us such noble works on the silk-worm, with his lynx-eye saw in the nymph the organs of maternity. Ramdohr and Carus penetrated still further, and succeeded in discovering in the caterpillar the first rudiments of the ovary, in which

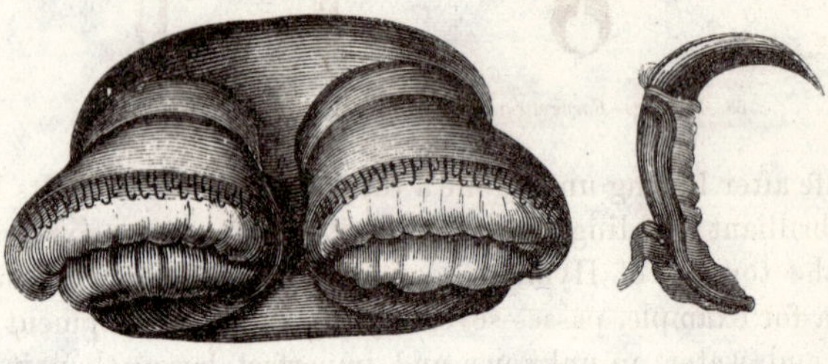

70. Hooked Feet and Nail of the Willow-caterpillar.—From Lyonet.

the eggs are produced. But what unperceived, unexplained marvels still remain! The imago is carefully protected by a series of coverings, of which it successively denudes itself. Then, as befits the last scene of life save one, that which the chrysalis now takes on is thicker, stronger, darker, and less ornamented than all the others, and nevertheless it is beneath this that a divine alchemy scatters its dust of gold and silver upon the elytra of the insect, or enamels them with sapphire and ruby.

When the new creature, bursting the envelope in which it was developed, expands itself in the light, its dazzling robe reflects the brightest sheen of metal or the sparkle of precious stones. No animal, no plant, displays such riches; our most beautiful ornaments cannot compete with them. Hence Lesser was so overcome by admiration as to exclaim in his *Theology of Insects*, "Never was Solomon on his shining throne so magnificently apparelled as one of these fragile creatures!"

In the old chronicles we often read of drops of blood scattered here and there being regarded as a sinister omen, or even of regular showers of blood which carried terror into the minds of our superstitious ancestors. Now-a-days philosophers can clearly explain this phenomenon, which is connected with the metamorphosis of insects.

Gregory of Tours speaks of a shower of blood which fell in the reign of Childebert and spread alarm among the Franks. But the most cele-

71. Great Tortoise-shell Butterfly—*Vanessa polychloros.*

brated is that which took place at Aix during the summer of 1608. It struck the inhabitants of all the country with terror. The walls of the churchyard and those of the houses of the citizens and peasants for half a league round were all spotted with great drops of blood.

An attentive examination of them convinced a savant of that day, M. de Peirese, that all that was told about the subject was pure fable. He could not at first explain this extraordinary phenomenon, but chance revealed the cause clearly. Having inclosed in a box the chrysalis of one of the butterflies which were then showing themselves in great numbers, he was perfectly astonished to see a stain of scarlet-red at the spot where the metamorphosis had taken place!

The philosopher had discovered the cause of the wondrous rains which had struck so many people with stupor. Many butterflies indeed, a few moments after they issue from their chrysalis swathing-clothes, expel a thick coloured fluid which has accumulated in the intestine during their seclusion. It is of a bright red in certain diurnal Lepidoptera, in particular the Vanessæ, and especially among them the great tortoise-shell, to which Réaumur principally ascribes the occurrence.

M. de Peirese farther made out that the shower of blood at Aix had been accompanied by a prodigious swarm of butterflies, of the same species as the one that he had shut up in the box, and in the *Encyclopédie* it is said that his conjectures were confirmed, by their not finding any spots on the roofs, but only on the lower stories of the houses, the places which the butterflies choose for their metamorphoses.[1]

CHAPTER III.

THE INTELLIGENCE OF INSECTS.

Descartes, who paid little attention to insects, only saw in them ingenious machines, living automatons, wound up once only to put their wheels and springs in movement; all that is so marvellous in their existence escaped this brilliant genius. But when Cartesianism had had its day, a few timid philosophers consented to recognize some obscure traces of instinct in these animals.

In proportion, however, as they studied these miniature specimens of creation, men discovered certain elevated faculties and perfect senses, to which succeed comparison and judgment. We even see them accomplish acts the aim of which puzzles us. They act, foreseeing a future the existence of which no really existing picture could have revealed to them.

Everything in the life of the insect astonishes us, not only the prodigious extent and finish of its work, but also the fact of its being impelled to a task the necessity for which cannot have been taught it by tradition.

This butterfly which escapes in spring from its mummy coffin never yet held intercourse with its kin; how can it in autumn display so much provident care for an offspring which it will never see! This delicate care, this deep foresight, cannot even be a reflection of its first impressions! The traces of them must have been effaced during the metamorphoses which so completely transformed it.

Who revealed to this dragon-fly (*Libellula*), born beneath the water, living in gloom and sunk in the mud, that its last country is the brilliant

[1] The *Encyclopédie* of Diderot contains a very good article on these showers of blood.

sky? And when, hurried away by a supreme instinct, it prepares to throw off the ignoble garment of the larva, to drink in the air and light, who points out to it the precise moment at which it ought to tear itself away from the depths of the marsh, adorn itself with its brilliant holiday robe, and launch itself like a bird into the atmosphere?

Gall and Camper, who computed the intelligence of mammals according to the proportion of the brain or the facial angle, would have found something also to observe in insects. It has been remarked, indeed, that the most intelligent among them possess a more centralized nervous system than the others, and a proportionally larger head.

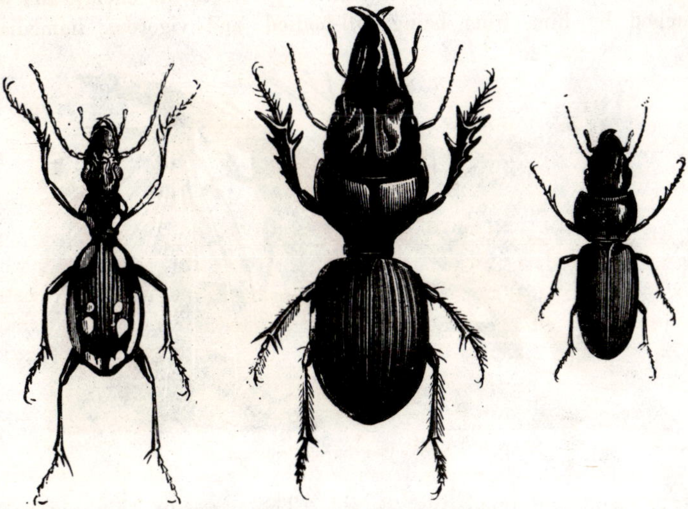

72. Coleoptera of the family of Carabidæ.

This observation has been made by celebrated physiologists in respect to bees and spiders, which assuredly possess more elevated faculties than any other animals of their tribe. Ratzeburg, indeed, in the magnificent plates of his work, represents the brain of the bee in order to give an idea of its bulk.

It is well known that Camper considered that the more acute the facial angle in animals the lower their intelligence. Mr. White, an English naturalist, has made this clearly perceptible by representing the heads of a large series of Vertebrata from man to the crane, the extreme lengthening of the face of which corresponds to its intellectual inferiority. An analogous work might perhaps be executed in respect to insects. At the beginning of the picture would be found the tiger-beetle and the Carabidæ, daring flesh-eating insects of ferocious habits, and with strongly marked heads; at the other end of the scale we should find the long-beaked Curculio, which, from the extreme prolongation of its facial angle and its limited capacity, would correspond perfectly with the crane.

The intelligence of insects rises under certain circumstances to the most finished subtlety; we are surprised to find so much cunning and resource among them. Of this there are abundant instances. A carnivorous animal hungering after living prey, but having a disgust for dead bodies, is on the point of seizing in the water the large shelly larva of a Dytiscus. All at once the latter perceives his enemy, and when touched by him, from being full-bodied and vigorous, immediately

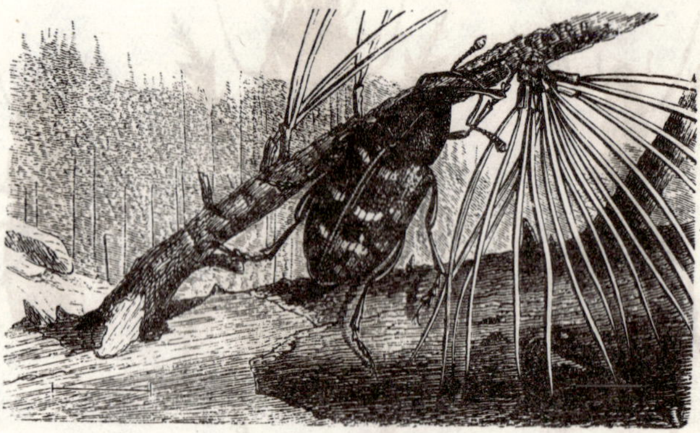

73. The Pine Curculio, enlarged.

becomes soft and repulsively flaccid. The aggressor, thinking he has only a dead animal in his mouth, drops his prey in disgust.

This beetle, having reached its final stage and acquired its horny wing-covers, cannot collapse, and it therefore employs another stratagem. When we take a Dytiscus from one of our marshes, it is scarcely laid hold of before we see a white, milky, repulsively stinking fluid issue from all the pores of its skin, which the most hungry animal could not endure.

As children, we have all been struck with the sight of beetles, which, so soon as we touch them with our fingers, feign death by becoming perfectly motionless, and which, when they are left to themselves, gather their legs together, and very soon scamper off at full speed. Some of them remain so absolutely motionless, that nothing can withdraw them from their determined dissimulation. The borer or death-watch (*Anobium*) will allow itself to be singed or drowned rather than fly when once fear has made it shrink. What I state has been confirmed by experiment. De Geer and Duméril relate, that having thoroughly frightened several Coleoptera of this species, they allowed themselves to be burned without attempting to escape.

Others, in order to evade their enemies, carry deception still further. When young and feeble, they assume for the purpose of deception a repulsive and ragged or foul-smelling covering of spider threads or excrement, though at a later period they die clad in a mantle of purple and gold.

Such is the Lily Crioceris. Its humble larva, soft and timorous, covers its back with its own fetid dejections, in order to disgust the insectivor-

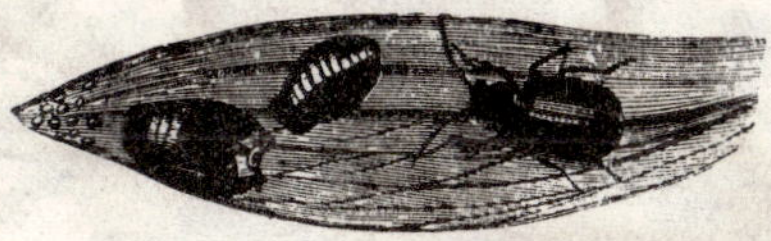

74. Lily Crioceris and its Larva—*Crioceris merdigera* (Leach).

ous birds. Subsequently, freed from this filthy garment, it promenades upon the royal plant in a magnificent carapace of vermilion.[1]

The bombardier beetles are even more ingenious; they alarm their enemies by means of real artillery. These Coleoptera, when threatened, suddenly expel from their intestines a whitish acid vapour, the explosion of which as it issues produces a slight detonation, which carries disorder among the aggressors. This explosion may even be repeated a certain number of times. Hence, when one of these insects is pursued by an enemy, it fires off its artillery anew. The instinct of defence is so inherent in the tribe of bombardiers, that at the sound of a cannon shot from one of them, all the others fire at the same time—there is a running fire along the whole line.[2] The sound produced by these Coleoptera is intense enough to startle those who do not know the ruse. We often

[1] The excrement piled upon the back of the Lily Crioceris forms an enormous and heavy mass compared with the volume of the larva, which it entirely conceals from view. We only see what appear to be little packages of moist defecations, walking upon the leaves of the plant. The worm deposits them on its back as fast as they are produced, and this is done by means of a special organ. The anal orifice, instead of being quite at the end of the body, is placed above in such a manner that each globule of excrement is disposed in its proper place, thus contributing to the increase of the mass in proportion as the animal grows older.

[2] It is, according to Rolander, furnished with an apparatus which enables it to discharge twenty shots in succession. Another less-known species, the small green beetle, *Anchomenus prasinus*, also fires off repeated discharges. It is found near London.—Tr.

see young people who have seized one, let it escape suddenly from their fingers, astonished by this singular attack.[1]

The automatic nature of insects has only been maintained by those who have never observed them; on the contrary, those naturalists who are acquainted with them assign to them decidedly high faculties.

A hemipterous insect, the tricks of which have rendered it celebrated enough, the *Reduvius personatus*, conceals itself under a disguise quite as

75. Calosoma (*Calosoma inquisitor*) pursuing a Bombardier (*Brachinus crepitans*), who is fighting in retreat.

deceptive as that of the Crioceris, but which has the advantage of being infinitely less disgusting. It covers itself with a ragged coat of spider-threads and dust, in order to be less distinguishable from the latter, in the midst of which it hides itself to watch for the passing prey.

Baron Geer, the Réaumur of Sweden, has described the wiles of this insect in a very picturesque manner. "This bug," he says, "in the state of a nymph, or before its wings are developed, possesses a hideous and revolting exterior. At the first look one might take it for one of the ugliest of spiders. What makes it so disagreeable to the sight is its being entirely covered with and enveloped in a grayish matter, which is nothing but the dust one sees in the nooks of an ill-swept room, and which is

[1] The bombardier, called also the Gunner Scarabæus (*Brachinus crepitans*), belongs to the genus Brachinus. It is a little beetle which lives beneath stones. The gaseous fluid which produces the detonation has a pungent odour, is acid, and reddens tincture of litmus. Some entomologists have considered it as analogous to nitric acid, and add that when brought into contact with the skin it produces a yellow stain.

generally mixed with sand and portions of wool or silk, making the feet of the insect clumsy and misshapen, and giving the whole body a very singular look."

The Reduvius, nevertheless, is of a very slender form; but to appreciate this one must give it a brush. In its disguise it moves very slowly as if overloaded by the weight of its accoutrements, in order to take its prey by surprise. But when it has thrown off its garment and acquired its wings, it becomes active, and we then see it gaining its livelihood in open view.

When an enemy little to be dreaded sneaks into a hive of bees, the first sentinels that see it pierce it with their stings, and in the twinkling

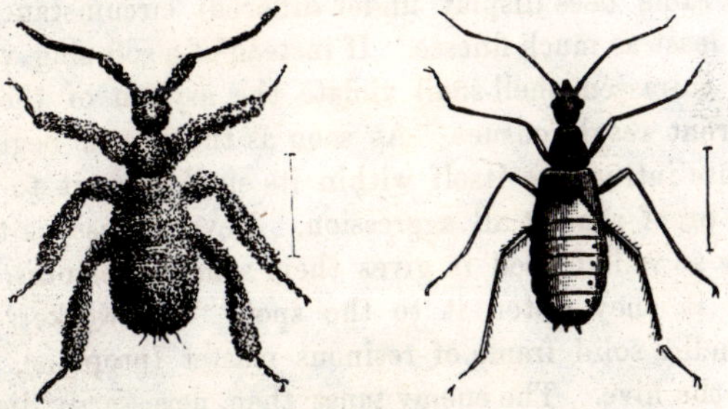

76. Young of the *Reduvius personatus;* the one covered with its tatters of dust and spider-threads, the other freed from these by brushing.

of an eye eject the corpse from the common dwelling. The work is not interrupted by such an event. But if the aggressor be a strong and heavy slug, matters go differently. A general agitation seizes the workers, each one gets ready his weapon, whirls round the invader, and pierces it with his dart. Assailed with fury, wounded on all sides, and poisoned by the venom, the creeping animal dies in violent contortions. But what is to be done with such a weighty foe? The little feet of all the tribe would not suffice to stir the corpse, and the narrow door of the hive would not allow it to pass. Its putrid exhalations would, however, soon infect the colony, and develop the germ of some malady. How are they to escape from this dilemma?

The republic take counsel, and come suddenly to just such a resolution as they would have done if they had thoroughly known one of the arts of ancient Egypt. As under the Pharaohs men embalmed the corpses of animals, either with a religious view or to preserve themselves from their pestilential emanations, so all the bees now set to work to embalm the dead animal, the presence of which is a menace to them.

For this purpose the workers scatter themselves over the country in order to gather the resinous matter (propolis) which clings to the buds, for this is what replaces the essences and aloes used by the undertakers of the Thebaïd. The bees closely envelop the dead body with this in the form of little fillets, and deposit all round it a thick solid layer which preserves it from putrefaction.

After seeing so many ingenious combinations, who would be tempted with Malebranche and the upholders of the scholastic philosophy, to look upon the insect as an automaton, necessarily destined to accomplish only a series of acts adapted to its mechanism? We are here far beyond the flute-player of Vaucanson and his famous mechanical duck, which ate and digested its food in presence of the spectators.

But the same bees display under different circumstances, if not as much art at least as much finesse. If instead of a soft slug, vulnerable on all sides, a cuirassed shell-snail violate the asylum of the republic, a totally different result ensues. As soon as the swarm begins to attack it, the mollusc intrenches itself within its shell, fixes it to the ground, and is then proof against all aggression. Nevertheless, as the presence of an enemy so well fenced in gives them some uneasiness, and as they cannot slay it, they fasten it to the spot. The workers deposit all round its shell a solid frame of resinous matter (propolis), which glues it firmly to the hive. The enemy must then necessarily die in his lair, for all movement, all escape, is henceforth impossible.

Réaumur discovered a snail cemented in this way to the glass of one of his experimental hives, into which it had imprudently penetrated; and I myself have seen another such prisoner in the same condition.

Do not such facts prove a certain foresight? Could blind instinct bring them about, and who could venture to refer them to mere mechanical action?

Some insects have an idea of order and strategy. When they go to the chase or to battle, as we shall see in another chapter, their army advances with a care and prudence we should be far from expecting in such puny creatures; there are leaders, videttes, and reconnoitrers.

But no act of intelligence in insects is equal to that by which the bees create themselves a queen when their own is lost to them. By a singular anomaly in insects it is the females which, though more delicate, take charge of the work; the males do absolutely nothing. But these females have none of the attributes of their sex; they are genuine neuters, in which the nurses have contrived scientifically to make every principle of fecundity abort. These work-women, when in the larval state, have their bee-bread doled out to them with a very sparing hand; in vain do they cry and struggle at the bottom of their cells; the step-mother remains inflexible, and when the nurse thinks the proper moment has arrived, she inexorably incloses the larva, saying, "Thou shalt go no further." And thus the organic development is paralyzed.

But if any accident carry off the queen from a republic of bees, they miraculously know enough of the springs of life to create themselves another. The nurses are aware that the abortion of their fellow-beings is due to their own selfishness, and they now make prodigious efforts to procure themselves a new sovereign. At the edge of one of the combs we see them accumulate ample materials, and construct a vast royal cell forty or fifty times as large and weighty as the others. After that they bear away a simple work-woman from her narrow cell, and place her in this palace. So soon as ever she is installed in her sumptuous abode, the nurses, now full of tenderness, load her with more agreeable and sweeter scented bee-bread, and under the influence of this ambrosia the organs of fecundation appear in the larva, which was only called to the most humble condition; henceforth she is a queen!

Is it possible to carry further the intimate knowledge of one's being and the divine art of modifying its nature?

Maternal instinct also enables the insect to accomplish works which I was about to call herculean; but I must go further and call them more than herculean. This instinct develops a prodigious perseverance and an incomprehensible power.

Linnæus saw one of the flies which attack large cattle (an Œstrus) follow a reindeer a whole day, though dragging its sledge at a gallop over the snow. The ominous fly flew almost continually by its side, watching for the moment when it might introduce one of its eggs beneath the skin!

These creatures, so contemptible as to their size, astonish us by their ingenious tenderness: their maternal foresight is unbounded. Some of them imitate the rabbit, which denudes all its belly to form a soft pillow for its nest of young. They go even further than the mammal; it only deprives itself of a part of its wool, whilst some butterflies, to protect their offspring, tear all the hair off their bodies, and expire so soon as this act of devotion is accomplished. One of the pests of our fir forests, the *Bombyx dispar*, acts in this way. Its nest is composed of a double shelter—a fine down on which the eggs lie, and which covers them closely, and of an external layer formed of dense hairs laid on like the slates of a roof, and forming an impermeable cloth. Thus the young brood are doubly protected: against the severity of winter's cold, and against its destructive rains.

Some kinds of gall-insects, still more devoted to their offspring, immolate themselves in order to protect them. As the enormously distended insect gradually expels its eggs, it heaps them up in a little pile, and when its body is quite cleared out, so that it resembles a hollow bladder, the female straightway covers her progeny with it, attaches the edges round them, and dies directly after; thus forming for them a convex, solid roof, the impermeability of which protects the eggs against the injurious agency of the air and storms. The mother has paid for her

77. Pine Silk-worm Moth (*Bombyx dispar*)—Caterpillar, Chrysalis, and Butterfly male and female.

child-birth with her life, and her young are born under the shelter of her mummified corpse.

Some insects are guided in another way by maternal instinct. Instead of sacrificing themselves, they kill other animals in order to minister to the wants of their hungry offspring. As each species requires a peculiar food, it is only by the aid of various processes that the parents succeed in procuring it for them.

Live prey is imperatively necessary for some larvæ; they require it so soon as they are born, and as the mother cannot fetter it to their cradle, she poisons it. But more ingenious than Locusta, she only administers as much poison as is necessary to stupify or paralyze it, so that the young insect, when it issues from the egg, finds near it the dying insect, which it ends by devouring. This is the case with many of the Sphex species. The fly places one of its eggs at the bottom of a little hole which it makes in the ground; it then goes out to hunt till it discovers a spider or a caterpillar; and so soon as it finds one, it stings it scientifically, and bears it quite paralyzed to its nest.

Finally, having placed its victim close to its egg, the Sphex closes

78. Caterpillar devoured by the Larvæ of Ichneumons, and Caterpillar covered with their Cocoons.

the opening of the subterranean hollow with a little stone, and takes wing, giving it no further heed. Nothing more remains for maternal tenderness to do.

Some ichneumons, or *vibrating flies*, are much more rapacious and bold. The larvæ of some of these, though extremely small, nevertheless attack large caterpillars, fix upon their bodies, and gnaw away till death ensues. The mother, by the aid of her boring instrument, pierces the other's skin in order to insert her eggs beneath it. She lays a pretty large number there, and when the young are hatched, protected by the skin, they begin to eat the fat; it is only towards the close of their existence that they assail the vital organs, for, in order to have always plenty of live flesh to devour, these hungry anatomists take good care not to eat into them at first. Then the caterpillar dies, and the larvæ of the ichneumon issue by numerous openings and spin silky cocoons on the

79. Dung Beetles, or Sacred Scarabæi (*Ateuchus sacer*), making their Balls.

surface of the corpse. These nymphs, swathed in their white winding-sheets of silk, are sometimes so numerous and close together that they entirely conceal their victim.

This extraordinary peculiarity remained for a long time unknown, even to the most celebrated entomologists; they thought at first that these little cocoons which envelop the caterpillar were only the offspring carefully preserved from cold by maternal foresight. It was reserved for the father of microscopy and for one of the most celebrated observers of Italy, Leuwenhoeck and Vallisneri, to shed a flood of light upon this curious fact and establish the truth.

The sacred dung-beetle, which played so important a part in the theogony of the banks of the Nile, also executes most arduous tasks in order to protect its offspring. This beetle only bestows its care upon one egg at a time, but this care is incessant. So soon as it has laid it, the Scarabæus makes its way to the dung of some herbivorous mammal and bears off a small mass, in the centre of which this egg is carefully placed. Afterwards it forms a regular spherical ball with it, the bulk of which exceeds that of its own body. When it is finished the insect takes it with its two hind feet, which are long, crooked, and suited to this work, and rolls it about in every direction, pushing it backwards. By dint of being worked along the sand and fine earth, this ball of excrement, soft

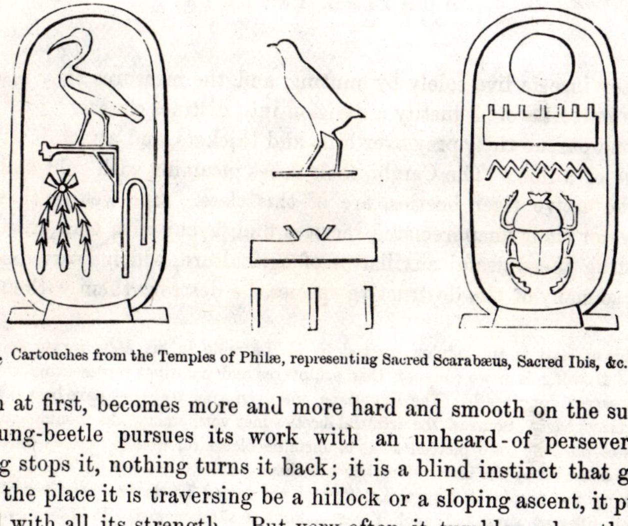

80. Cartouches from the Temples of Philæ, representing Sacred Scarabæus, Sacred Ibis, &c.

enough at first, becomes more and more hard and smooth on the surface. The dung-beetle pursues its work with an unheard-of perseverance; nothing stops it, nothing turns it back; it is a blind instinct that guides it. If the place it is traversing be a hillock or a sloping ascent, it pushes its ball with all its strength. But very often it tumbles, when the ball escapes from its legs and rolls away. The insect then seeks it anxiously, and if some neighbour, without anything to do, has taken possession of it, or if it be lost in the high grass so that it cannot be found again, the beetle forms a new one, and lays another egg.

When the ball is quite finished, well rounded, large and hardened, the beetle, which has dug a hole for this purpose, pushes the ball into it and leaves it to its fate. And thus the arduous work is finished.

It was these remarkable labours which drew the attention of the ancients to the insect. In ancient Egypt, where men marvelled at this prodigious care, the sacred Scarabæus became the symbol of fecundity, and sculpture multiplied to infinity its image on all the monuments of the Pharaohs, from the mouth of the king of rivers to the heart of Nubia.

On the other hand, the perseverance with which the dung-beetle rolls up its ball again, like Sisyphus in the fable, seemed to some to offer a reminiscence of the labours of Isis and Osiris. Hence we see it represented everywhere on the pediments of their temples, having its ball, an emblem of the globe, placed between its legs.[1]

CHAPTER IV.

HUNTING INSECTS.

Many insects live solely by hunting, and the measures they resort to in this pursuit would justify a division into distinct classes.

Some pursue their prey over hills and thickets, and attack it with the courage of a lion. The Carabi, their robes gleaming with gold and blue, and the active tiger beetles, are of this class. And yet neither their beauty nor their unappreciated services find favour with man; instead of protecting these useful auxiliaries of agriculture, which every day annihilate so many of the destructive species, he destroys them without pity.

[1] This at least is the opinion avowed by M. Latreille in his *Mémoire sur les Insectes Sacrés.* Nothing is more common than sculptures and paintings representing the Scarabæus or sacred dung-beetle of the Egyptians, and even some real ones have been discovered in the sarcophagi. Some of the artificial beetles met witn among the monuments on the borders of the Nile were pierced so as to form necklaces for women; others were used as seals, as is shown by the inscriptions beneath them.

Among the people of Egypt the effigy of the sacred beetle has been repeated in a thousand different ways, as though it were a kind of tutelary god. It is seen everywhere carved on their monuments, temples, tombs, and obelisks; there are even some represented on most bas-reliefs, and they are found at the present day sculptured of all dimensions, and in every possible material, from the commonest stones to the most precious metals. There are some of colossal size in the British Museum; they are of granite, and three to four feet long. But for common use they were made of very small dimensions and in prodigious quantities; they are found of marble, porphyry, agate, lapis-lazuli, garnet, and gold.

In my narrative I have conformed to the opinions of French zoologists, but it is probable that when the history of the dung-beetle has been thoroughly studied, we shall not hear that it is in spring, but in autumn or the beginning of winter that they form their balls. Indeed, it was in October that I saw, for the first time, the sacred dung-beetle in the environs of Rome, occupied on the little hills of Tivoli in rolling its balls, and in Upper Egypt I found them at the same task in November. Perhaps also on the borders of the Nile they do not all make use of dung, as in Europe. In the part where I saw them busy forming their balls, the river was bordered by a wide desert, so that it was difficult to see where they could have found dung. Their balls seemed made entirely of Nile mud.

Others, not less ardent in the pursuit of prey, but much more ingenious, stretch out nets or construct insidious snares, into which their victims inevitably plunge.

The life of insects presents some anomalies which are not seen in other animals: totally different habits being met with in species almost physically identical. Thus we have seen that the nymph of our magnificent dragon-fly (*Libellula*) lives in the mud of the marshes; on the other hand the larva of another kind, which resembles it in every respect, one of the Neuroptera, the famous ant-lion, so called on account of the frightful carnage it makes among the ants, delights only in the sand and the burning rays of the sun.

This insidious larva, the most ingenious perhaps that is known, con-

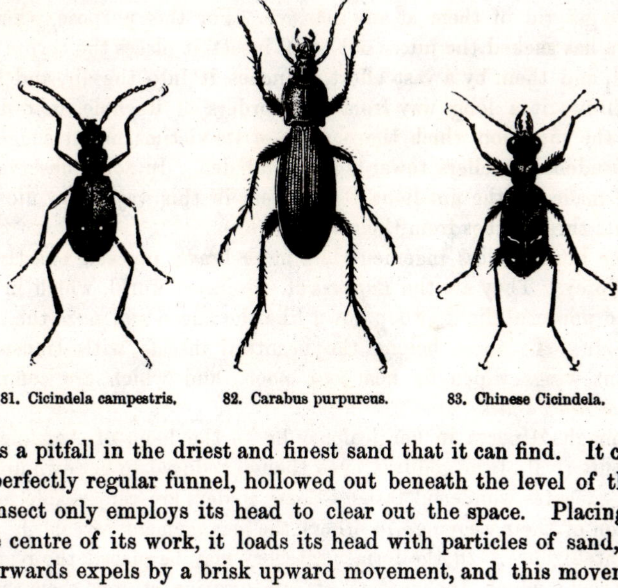

81. Cicindela campestris. 82. Carabus purpureus. 83. Chinese Cicindela.

structs a pitfall in the driest and finest sand that it can find. It consists of a perfectly regular funnel, hollowed out beneath the level of the soil. The insect only employs its head to clear out the space. Placing itself in the centre of its work, it loads its head with particles of sand, which it afterwards expels by a brisk upward movement, and this movement is repeated with such frequency that the particles form an almost continuous jet. When the sides of the funnel are so regular and sloping that they cannot be climbed, the larva buries itself in such a way at the bottom, that we see only the threatening mandibles, which stand open, waiting for an opportunity of being exercised.

So soon as ever an ant stumbles over the edge of the pitfall it is inevitably borne down by the inclined plane of the infernal funnel. In vain does it try to rise again; the sand yields beneath its feet and it rolls with fatal certainty to the bottom, where the terrible jaws of the ant-lion at once seize and despatch it.

Sometimes a larger insect falls into the deadly ambuscade. It resists and tries vigorously to scale the slope again. In the meantime the treacherous ant-lion remains at its post, but dreading (from the bulk of the débris which rolls upon its head) the size of the animal which has thus lost its way, it now takes a direct part in its destruction, and in order to impede its attempts, launches in swift succession masses of sand upon its prey, which accelerate its fall to the bottom of the gulf. Once there it is infallibly lost; the ant-lion, thirsting for blood, shows no mercy.[1]

But if the ant-lion were to keep the remains of its food near it, its pit would soon be converted into an uninhabitable charnel-house; it must therefore get rid of them at any sacrifice. For this purpose, whenever the larva has sucked the juices out of an insect, it places the corpse upon its head, and then, by a vast effort, launches it into the air, and sometimes throws it a long way from the borders of its hole, in order to obviate the suspicion which the corpses of its victims might suggest to the imprudent travellers towards the fatal den. In some observations which I made on the ant-lions I saw them in this way throw flies and large ants three inches from their dwellings.

Other hunters, less ingenious but more brave, proceed exactly like birds of prey. They are the *Raptores* of the insect world, which in their agile and powerful flight swoop down like the falcon and seize their prey in mid-air. To these belong the beautiful insects with transparent iridescent wings which fly near our pools, and which are commonly known as *dragon-flies.*

Although Minerva in her jealousy broke the loom of Arachne, still the obscure rival of the goddess, even though reduced to her own unaided powers, executes wonderful tasks. Some spiders are remarkable for the perfection of their weaving; in others the arrangement reveals the most astute intelligence. In the former category may be placed the regularly circular nets which the spiders of our gardens stretch from branch to branch; in the other the webs of the species which invade our dwellings.

[1] The larva of a fly (*Rhagio vermileo*), not unlike the common flesh-maggot, constructs a funnel-shaped opening like that of the ant-lion. At the bottom of this it lies waiting for grubs which fall into the trap, and on which it feeds. Should they attempt to escape it hurls jets of sand-earth at them, and not unfrequently brings them down again. The ant-lion, though not uncommon in France and Switzerland, has not, I believe, of late years at least, been seen in Britain.—Tr.

84. The Ant-lion (*Myrmeleon formicarius*), and its Pit.

These latter, usually built in the corners of the walls, exhibit a horizontal net soiled with dust, which is in a sense only the basement floor of the carnivorous insect's structure, for it is in the threads irregularly crossed above this that the prey gets entangled and lost. But the most ingenious part of this destructive engine is the lair in which the hunter lies concealed. It is in the form of a circular tunnel, with a double outlet, and serving a double purpose: one outlet is horizontal and opens upon the web: the other is vertical and gives passage below. It is from the former that the spider darts upon its prey; the other fills the office of a trap-door.

The spider takes the greatest care never to leave on its web the carcasses from which it has sucked the blood: such a charnel-house would alarm its living prey. So soon as ever a fly has been immolated, the insect seizes it, drags it to its tunnel, and ejects it by the lower opening. Thus when we look at the part of the floor below, we are astonished at the numbers that have fallen victims to the sanguinary spider. Sometimes also this hidden exit serves for it to escape by when menaced by some serious danger. But this is a very rare case; its special use, its exclusive purpose, is to receive the débris of the spider's repasts; a fact, I believe, not noticed by any observer.

The disgust inspired by the spider is not well founded. No insect possesses more intelligence or a more wonderful structure; its ugliness is forgotten so soon as we look at it without prejudice. The fear with which it petrifies some persons is quite beyond reason. It is true there are spiders the bite of which is as formidable as that of our vipers, but they only inhabit tropical countries. The species found in France and England are almost harmless. The spider found in cellars is the only one the bite of which can be considered as attended with danger, and the results of its bite, although some cases are related in which it has been fatal, are limited to a sharp pain and some swelling and inflammation.

The notorious Tarantula itself, when more closely studied, loses its strange prestige; its bite has ceased to produce the furious dancing mania so much spoken about, even in medical works.[1]

[1] The Tarantula is a large hunting spider, which inhabits a hole it scoops out of the earth, from whence it throws itself upon its prey. It is met with all through Italy, but especially in the neighbourhood of Tarentum, from whence its name comes. It is found along the coasts of the Mediterranean, in Sicily, Barbary, and Provence. This spider was formerly much dreaded, and the symptoms produced by its bite were compared to those of hydrophobia, which procured for it the name of the "mad spider." Old authors maintained that those who were bitten by it fell into a profound stupor or were seized with convulsions, for which music was a sovereign remedy, by inducing them to dance, which they did till

The poison apparatus of spiders is precisely analogous to that of serpents, only that it is of microscopic size. It possesses mobile teeth,

85. The Bird-eating Spider (*Mygale avicularia*) killing a Humming-bird.—From Sibylle de Mérian.

they were exhausted and fell down senseless. Baglivi, though a learned physician, was yet deceived as to the Tarantula disorder, about which he wrote a special treatise, in which we find set down the airs most suited to effect a cure.—Baglivi, *Dissert. de Anat. Morsu et Affectibus Tarentulæ, 1745.*

hollow fangs which distil the poison into the wound, and this is secreted by a peculiar gland, situated in the interior of the palpi attached to the under-jaws, which effect the bite.

In the large tropical species this lethal fluid is so active that it kills in an instant animals of a far superior size, and is often employed against the birds which the spiders seize on the trees. In one of her magnificent plates Sibylle de Mérian, so celebrated for her knowledge and her beautiful paintings from natural history, represents a touching scene; that of a spider, the *Mygale avicularia*, which is killing a humming-bird near its nest.[1]

Some well-known spiders, which are almost as large as the fist, sometimes fasten on chickens and pigeons, seizing them by the throat and killing them instantaneously, drinking their blood at the same time. Hence in Columbia, where these disagreeable guests are common enough, they are called *chicken-spiders*.

CHAPTER V.

SLAVE-MAKERS AND WARLIKE TRIBES.

When we search into the history of insects we are surprised at finding such violent passions in such fragile creatures; hatred animates them; thirst for booty directs them. To gratify these evil propensities they fight bloody battles, and become transformed into land pirates.

Man leads to the battle-field a ponderous troop of animals; insects go single-handed. The 6000 elephants which Porus opposed to the triumphal march of Alexander went forth to fight only when guided by experienced drivers; whilst ants, left to their own resources, fight great battles, and, incredible as it may seem, display a great deal of strategy.

The slave-making instinct is strongly developed in this group. A race of zealous servants is indispensable to their existence, and in order to procure them they act like villainous slave-stealers.

[1] This animal, known in South America as the Abamdiu, or Great Spider, measures an inch across the thorax, and spins a cocoon three inches long and one broad. It is not certain whether it belongs to the hunting or the working spiders. Madame de Mérian's statement, that it attacks the humming-bird, though at one time boldly denied, has been confirmed in Bates's *Naturalist on the Amazon*, and in the paper from which this note is taken.—Termeyer, *Proc. Essex Institute, U. S.*—Tr.

Observers had for a long time remarked that certain ants carry others in their mouths during their peregrinations, but they could not make out for what purpose. It was Pierre Huber who discovered the mystery. These movements are so many raids, which the insects carry out in the interests of their republic—slave-razzias executed by main force. These microscopic filibusters do not go into the markets to sell their captives by auction, but like effeminate sybarites, keep them in order to impose all the household work upon them.

At the head of these daring slave-makers we must put the red ant, or Amazon, the military expeditions of which have been most carefully observed by the naturalists of our epoch. They are so frequent that one may enjoy the sight of them any fine day during the summer season. Huber says that the excursions of these warrior tribes have only one object, that of carrying off the ants, so to speak, in their swaddling clothes, from the midst of a laborious people, and converting them into helots who will work for them.

When the Amazon ant takes the field in order to capture slaves, and especially the miner ants, of which it generally makes use, it goes about its work in a very orderly way. The excursion always begins when night is drawing on. When they have issued from their abode, the Amazons array themselves in serried columns, and their army takes its way to the ants' nest which they are about to spoliate. In vain do the warriors seek to bar the entrance; in spite of all such efforts the others penetrate into the very heart of the place, and pry into all the compartments in order to choose their victims, the larvæ and nymphs. The workers which oppose those raids are simply thrown down; they are not made prisoners, because they would adapt themselves with difficulty to the yoke; the assailants want only young individuals which they can mould to their will. When the place is completely sacked, each conqueror takes a nymph or larva delicately between its teeth and prepares to return. Those who cannot find nymphs or larvæ carry off the mutilated dead bodies of their enemies in order to feed on them. Then the whole army, laden with booty, and sometimes stretching out in a line 130 feet in length, triumphantly regains its city in the same order as at its departure.

So soon as the young ants, torn from their homes, reach the abode of their spoilers, the slaves already there lavish the most attentive care upon them; they give them food, cleanse them, and warm their chilled bodies.

In the slave-making republics conquerors and slaves end by changing places, the former only displaying courage at the moment of conquest. Having stowed away their booty in the nest, the Amazons refresh themselves after battle by the pleasures of laziness; but being soon enervated

86. Return of Ants after a Battle, magnified.

thereby, the spoilers pass under the yoke of those they conquered. Their dependence is so complete, that if, after this, one were to carry off their slaves, privations and inaction would soon destroy the tribe.

These spoilers, so ardent in the chase, revolt against all domestic work; they only understand fighting. Incapable of constructing their abodes or nourishing their young, they leave both these duties to their slaves. Should the tribe be forced to abandon a nest which is too old, or become too small, the slaves decide upon the question, and carry the emigration into effect. The Amazons seem at this time to be sunk in the most disgraceful sloth. Each slave takes in its mandibles one of its degenerate masters, and bears it to the new dwelling, just as a cat carries in its mouth the kitten taken from its cradle.

The ingenious Huber wished to see how far the dependence of the two social classes went; and soon perceived that the chiefs, left to themselves, were quite unable to provide for their wants even in the midst of abundance. This naturalist having inclosed thirty Amazons with a plentiful supply of food, but without any slaves, saw that they fell into a state of the utmost apathy, although he placed the larvæ and nymphs alongside of them in order to stimulate them to work. No work whatever was done, and the recluses would every one have died of hunger rather than eat alone. Many had already died, when it occurred to the Genevese savant to furnish them with a slave. She was scarcely introduced among the dead and dying when she was at work, giving food to the survivors, lavishing her care upon the young larvæ, and constructing shelter for them. She saved the colony.[1]

[1] Mr. Holt (*Science Gossip*, July, 1868) says the ants (probably *Formica fuliginosa*) observed by him seemed to have but very little idea of locality, and that, in their eagerness to obtain water, they fell into a tank in such numbers as to threaten the extinction of the population. Mr. Frederick Ward, too (*Science Gossip*, Aug. 1868), says that, having closely observed some in a glass formicary, he found less order and method in their operations than he expected. They seemed to work night and day: he sometimes turned on the gas suddenly at 2 A.M., and found them as busy as ever; still they did not seem to get on in a workmanlike manner. He frequently noticed an ant come out with a piece of dirt in its forceps, and run about apparently in a state of distraction, as if it did not know what to do with it. Two ants were often seen tugging at the same piece for a long while, which was certainly a waste of time; and a piece of stone was often dragged backward and forward by two ants in their galleries, from a mere spirit of opposition it would seem. Again, an ant might be seen to come out of a gallery with something in its mouth, run about with it and put it down, having apparently lost itself—a proceeding which it terminated by disappearing down another hole. Sometimes, too, they would go on excavating without removing the rubbish till they were nearly blocked in, or till there was only room for one to pass. He admits, however, their sagacity in ejecting the dead bodies of their comrades, and throwing them into a tank; their wonderful industry, and their courage. The species observed by Mr. Ward also seems to have been the *Formica fuliginosa*.—Tr.

Nothing can be more incredible than those facts, and yet they have been verified with the most scrupulous care, both by the great

87. Ant about to milk Aphides, highly magnified.

historian of ants, and more recently in England by Messrs. F. Smith and Darwin.

All kinds of ants do not so easily adapt themselves to slavery. There are some very small ones, such as the yellow ant, which set the Amazons at defiance, and although much weaker, frighten them by a show of boldness: courage supplies the want of strength. Hence the blood-red ant, which is one of the most thorough-going slave-makers we are acquainted with, never attempts to plunder the dwelling of the yellow ant, which fights with fury to defend its home, its family, and its liberty. This is so constantly the case, that Mr. Smith, to his great surprise, found a little tribe of this valiant species under a stone close to a nest of slave-makers. They knew how to make themselves respected there, and even frightened the others by their warlike attitude.

The slave-making tribes are not occupied solely with the capture of helots; they frequently spread out over plants in order to carry off the Aphides. These are their cattle, their milch-cows, their goats; people would never have thought that ants were a pastoral race. They are extremely fond of a sweet liquor which distils from two little teats which the Aphis carries at the extremity of its back. We often find them scattered over the surface of plants sucking this fluid from individuals by turns as they encounter them. At other times, accompanied by their slaves, they carry off the Aphides, and imprison them in their dwelling, in order to milk them at leisure, and there they are nourished exactly like stalled animals. An ant-nest, says Huber, is more or less rich according to the number of Aphides it possesses.

Huber discovered that the ants are so greedy after this sweet liquor, that to procure it more conveniently they make covered ways which lead from their nests to the plants inhabited by these miniature cows. Sometimes they carry their foresight even to a more incredible extent. In order to reap a richer harvest from the Aphides, they leave them on the plants which they habitually feed upon, and with finely-tempered earth build there little stables in which they confine them. The naturalist we have just quoted discovered several of these surprising constructions; the fact is therefore beyond doubt.

Some ants, in place of deriving from other insects this saccharine juice, of which ours seem so fond, find an abundant supply of it in their own bodies. This is seen in the case of the honey-ant. These strange insects, first described by M. Wesmael, inhabit Mexico, living in little subterranean galleries. At a particular time the abdomen of a certain number becomes globular, transparent, and full of a saccharine matter, to such an extent that it equals in size a small cherry. This honey-like secretion being of an exquisite taste, in certain regions where these ants abound the women and children go and dig up their subterranean abodes to collect the insects, which after being deprived of head and thorax, are served up at dessert.

Under certain circumstances the ants fight battles which seem to have no other ground than antipathy between species or tribes.

Ant-battles have had their historian, we might almost say their bard, for the younger Huber has described them with as true poetry as we find in the tales of Homer or the strophes of the Thebaïd.

We can see this in the description of one of these battles taken verbatim from the Genevese savant. It took place between two ant-colonies situated a hundred paces from each other. "I shall not say," exclaims Huber, "what lighted up discord between these two republics, the one as populous as the other; two empires do not possess a greater

88. Honey ant—*Myrmecocyctus Mexicanus.*

number of combatants. The two armies met midway between their respective residences. Their serried columns reached from the field of battle to the nest, and were two feet in width. An immense reserve thus supported the fighting body, where thousands of ants, mounted on the smallest eminences, fought two and two, attacking each other by means of their jaws. Others carried off prisoners, but not without rough struggles, for they knew the cruel fate that awaited them so soon as they should reach the hostile nest.

"The field of battle, which extended over a space of from two to three square feet, was strewed with dead bodies and wounded; it was also covered with venom and exhaled a penetrating odour. Here and there single combats were still maintained. The struggle began between two ants, which locked themselves together with their mandibles, while they raised themselves upon their legs. They quickly grasped each other so tightly that they rolled one over the other in the dust. Generally the two athletes were succoured, and chains were seen of six or eight ants, locked one with another, and dragging the two adversaries in different directions until either one let go, or was carried off by superior strength."

At the approach of night the two armies effected a retreat and re-entered their dwellings. But the next day the carnage began again with still greater fury, and Huber saw the melée extend over a depth of six feet and two feet of frontage. The exasperation of the combatants was so great that not one of them noticed the observer, or dreamed of attacking him.

CHAPTER VI.

ARCHITECTS AND DEVOURERS OF TOWNS.

If we transport ourselves to tropical regions, where nature, more vigorous than in colder climes, multiplies on every side the sources of life, we see insects attacking the possessions of man, and fighting with him foot to foot. They assail his plantations or his dwelling and wage a regular war against him—a cruel and pitiless war—which must at times be decided by the cannon.

This is the case with the warrior-ant in the neighbourhood of the Cape of Good Hope, which has attracted the attention of every traveller by its extraordinary buildings, and the havoc it makes.

These Termites (*Termites bellicosi*), or white ants, as they are frequently though wrongly called,[1] live in republics composed of different sorts of individuals; the males, which have wings; and the workmen, soldiers, and queens, which have none.

The workmen are occupied solely in constructing buildings.

The mission of the soldiers is to defend the colony and maintain order.

Lastly come the females or queens, worshipped by the whole population, which look to them for the continuance of their race. They are only monstrous egg-sacks; mere egg-laying machines of the most astonishing fecundity. When their abdomen is swelled to its utmost extent, it is not less than 2000 times its previous size; they can no longer drag it about with them, and henceforth remain chained to one spot. The laying is so

[1] They do not bel ng to the same order of insects as our ants; which are Hymenoptera, while the Termites are Neuroptera.—Tr.

rapid, that we seem to see a fountain spouting eggs. This receptacle of offspring projects them at the rate of sixty a minute, or 80,000 per diem.

The dimensions and solidity of the nests of the warrior Termes, compared to the weakness of the insect, have always excited the astonishment of travellers. They are sometimes twenty feet in height. Their pyramidal form gives them the look of a colossal sugar-loaf enlarged at the base, and with the flanks broken by little accessory hillocks. When

89. Warrior Termites (*Termes bellicosus*, Smeath.; *Termes fatalis*, Linn.) Soldier, Workman, Male, and Female swollen with Eggs.

one traverses a part where the colonies of Termites abound, one might take them at a distance for an Indian village. The walls of these dwellings are so solid, that the wild cattle climb upon them without crushing them when they place themselves there as sentinels; and the interior contains chambers so large, that a dozen men can find shelter in some of them; the hunters place themselves in them to lie in wait for wild animals.

Besides these extraordinary chambers, we find also in the cities of

90. Village of Warrior Termites.—From the Memoir of Smeathman.

these social republics long galleries as wide as the bore of a large cannon, and which extend as much as three or four feet into the ground.

The monuments of which we are proud are insignificant structures compared to those built by these fragile insects. The nests of the Termites are often 500 times as high as the length of their bodies, and it has therefore been calculated, that if we gave our houses a proportional height, they would be four or five times as high as the pyramids of Egypt.

Other Termites, instead of constructing these astonishing abodes, occupy themselves mischievously in attacking ours, and invade them sometimes from the roof to the foundation; everything then goes to ruin, house and furniture alike. These insidious depredators make their way silently underground, and tunnel long galleries, by means of which they all at once invade our dwellings. Then they penetrate into all the timber-work, and totally destroy the interior of it, only leaving a surface as thin as a wafer. Nothing reveals their hidden havoc to the eye; we see our house, we believe in its real existence, while we possess only a phantom of it—a house of cards, which falls at the first shock. Smeathman, who has left us such an interesting history of these Neuroptera, relates that they sometimes destroy large towns, which have been deserted by their inhabitants.

Mrs. Lee told me that in the districts of Africa where she lived, the Termites take but a very short time to devour an entire dwelling. A staircase of very fair size is eaten in a fortnight; tables, arm-chairs, and chairs in much less. This celebrated traveller assured me that often at Sierra Leone, on returning to one's house after a short absence, only the ghost of the furniture is to be found. The exterior still possesses all its freshness, but the substance is gone, and every piece that is hollowed out falls to powder beneath the hand of any one who touches it, or under the weight of any one who sits down upon it.

Instead of these conical domes ornamented with turrets grouped together in villages in the middle of the plains, some species of this group, such as the tree termite, prefer to suspend their nests amid the large branches of the strongest trees. These aërial masses, mingling with the foliage of the trees, are very striking, for some of them are larger than a hogshead. The nests, which are extremely porous, present inside an inextricable labyrinth of tortuous canals; they are formed of a matrix or compact paste composed of fine particles of wood, gum, and juices of plants.

For some years past two species of this kind have been established in France, and have caused very serious havoc in some of our southern departments; they are the light-shunning termite and the heath termite. Their introduction does not seem to date further back than 1780.

The devouring cohorts of the light-shunning termite have invaded Rochefort, La Rochelle, and Aix, where they have completely undermined a number of houses, and entirely ruined them. At one time these destructive pests set to work to gnaw the prefecture of La Rochelle and

91. Nest of the Tree Termite (*Termes arborum*).—Museum of Rouen.

the archives, without any person suspecting it; wainscotting, pasteboard, papers, were all annihilated without any external sign of this havoc appearing. At present the papers of the bureaux are only preserved by keeping them in zinc boxes.

At Tonnay-Charente the Termites, having gnawed away the supports of a dining-room without its being perceived, the flooring collapsed during a party, and the entertainer and his guests sank through.

In tropical regions certain ants are not less to be dreaded than the voracious Termites. They do not destroy our houses, but they invade the fields and build there enormous nests fifteen to twenty feet high, which look like so many little hills. They multiply to such an extent in certain plantations, that the colonist is obliged to abandon them. Sometimes, however, he resists the invaders, declares a war of extermination against them, and burns their dwellings by the aid of certain combustible materials. Sometimes artillery charged with grape-shot is employed to overthrow the lofty fortresses of these ants, and scatter both the ruins and the architects.

Thus is man obliged to attack an insect with cannon.

Sometimes he resorts to the mine, a step he is compelled to take against certain winged ants in the tropical countries, which sink their nests as much as twenty-five feet in the ground, and these are so compact that they can only be torn up by the aid of powder, and by overturning all the earth round about them. Ch. Müller relates that in Brazil, large districts on the banks of the Parana have been in this way transformed almost into deserts.

CHAPTER VII.

GRAVE-DIGGERS AND MINERS.

Despite that supremacy over all creation which the pride of man attributes to himself, a feeble insect often surpasses him in energy, and in certain cases in intelligence. Leave one of our race entirely to the resources of his own organs, and bid him bury an elephant or rhinoceros; he would spend the best part of his life in trying. His nails would be worn out before the pit for the colossus was finished, and all his strength would be exhausted to no purpose in order to place it there and cover it with earth.

Among the Coleoptera there is one which undertakes to execute an equally herculean task in a few hours.

When a dead mole is abandoned in a field we immediately notice the arrival of a little insect speckled with black and orange, which in three or four hours effectually inters the mammal. And yet its size compared to that of the latter is not greater than that of man in proportion to the elephant.

Go a step further, give one of our species pickaxes and wheelbarrows to break up and carry off the soil, and he will take more weeks to accomplish his task than the burying-beetle, for such is the name of the insect, requires hours.

92. The Burying-beetle —*Necrophorus sepultor.*

It is a maternal instinct that guides and animates the burier. The insect requires a dead mole or some other mammal, to the shelter of which it may intrust its offspring, and it only inters the corpse in order to keep it fresh up to the moment when its hungry larva will issue from the egg.

The insect requires for its progeny a food they will like. If we throw a frog or a bird upon the ground, it will not bury either of them; but throw out a dead mole in a garden where these burying-beetles are perhaps never seen, and one of them, which has scented it afar off, will immediately arrive and inter it.

93. Burying-beetles interring a small Rat.

For this purpose the Necrophorus does not begin by digging a hole, as one might think; it always remains unseen, hidden beneath the corpse which it is burying. The work goes on without being noticed, and consists in throwing up on the sides of the mole the soil which was below it; this manœuvre being continued at the same time beneath all parts of the dead body, it disappears, sinking little by little. And when it has at last arrived below the level of the soil, the sexton has only, in order to hide it from view and finish its work, to throw a few portions of the upturned earth upon the little animal, which is as completely entombed as if it had been placed in a liquid paste.[1]

Thus ends the task which I have several times seen executed with

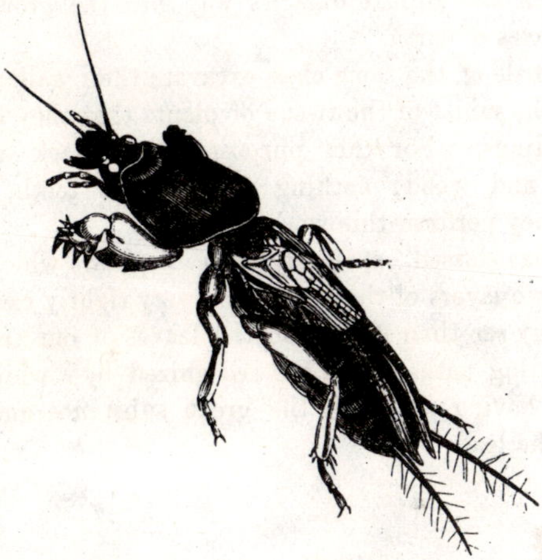

94. Mole-cricket, natural size—*Gryllotalpa vulgaris.*

my own eyes, and which some persons have called in question on account of its being so extraordinary.

Other insects hollow out the ground solely in order to find their food there, and to construct a lodging for their offspring. These are true miners in the strict sense of the word.

Many belong to this category, but there are scarcely any the work of which is so dreaded by the farmer as that of the mole-cricket. In some parts of Germany the alarm which this insect inspires is such, that a popular saying warns the driver of any vehicle to kill without

[1] The English burying-beetle (*Necrophorus Vespillo*), almost, if not quite, identical with that of France, certainly inters birds. Rennie found four hard at work on Putney Heath, burying a dead crow; and M. Gleditsch says that in fifty days four beetles interred four frogs, three small birds, two fishes, one mole, and two grasshoppers; besides the entrails of a fish, and two morsels of the lungs of an ox.—*Act. Acad. Berolin.* 1752.—TR.

pity all those he finds, should he even have to check his team on the slope of a mountain or the edge of a precipice.

This insect, the name of which recalls at the same time its subterranean habits and its family, often causes great havoc in our gardens by hollowing out its galleries, and cutting through the roots of plants which cross its path.[1]

Nature has for this purpose endowed it with formidable weapons. These are its fore-paws, the outspread end of which has the greatest analogy, both as to the form and the way in which the insect uses it, to the large hands of the mole; they act like powerful cutting picks, by means of which the animal digs its way into the ground and throws back the particles of earth.

Other animals of the same class excavate their galleries in a picked soil; it is in the midst of the tissue of plants that they hollow out their tortuous windings. For this purpose they attack indiscriminately leaves, fruit, and wood; nothing resists their teeth, which are the instruments they perform this work by.

Réaumur has classed separately the caterpillars which bore galleries between the two layers of the leaves, and very rightly calls them miners. We can any day see their doings on the leaves of our trees, where they carve out winding paths which are recognized by a white track, caused by the insect having eaten all the green substance and only left the epidermis of the leaf.

CHAPTER VIII.

UPHOLSTERERS AND CARPENTERS.

Despite the proud pre-eminence claimed by man, in how few cases will the work of his hands compare with that of the lowest creatures! Can the thread spun by human means stand comparison with that of the spider? The work of the insect too exhibits a remarkable complication; for fine as it is, it results from the union of many distinct threads. It is produced by four or six teats or spinnerets situated at the extremity of the abdomen, and the silky matter itself issues

[1] Possibly in pursuit of worms and ants, on which it feeds. It eats on an average about three worms a day, sucking out the flesh and leaving the skin entire.—*Science Gossip*, 1867, p. 232. Mr. Gould fed one for several months on ants.—Tr.

by a sieve-like apparatus; each sieve containing, according to Bonnet, more than a thousand holes. As the filaments are projected outwards, they agglutinate together in such a manner that each thread is composed of at least 4000, and sometimes of 6000 fibres, and yet Leuwenhoeck affirms that it is so slender as to require 4,000,000 to make up a silk thread as thick as one of the hairs of one's beard.[1]

The threads of some exotic species possess a much greater power of resistance than we observe in ours. Travellers relate that in equatorial countries spider-webs are seen strong enough to arrest humming-birds as a net would, and it has even been said that a man only breaks them with some difficulty.

The silk of our spiders is always of a dirty gray, but in tropical regions the colour varies to a certain extent. Some of these insects produce different coloured threads, which they interlace with admirable skill. Some are red, others yellow, others again black, and with all these they form a three-coloured fabric.

Industrial art has vainly attempted to utilize the silk of the spider; but that produced by the European species has so little power of resistance that it has never been used to any profit. Entomologists, however, relate that Louis XIV. had a dress made of it for himself, but the want of strength in this newly invented cloth soon disgusted him with his phantasy. But it appears that the webs of some American species possess a sufficient power of resistance to admit of being employed for this purpose. Alcide d'Orbigny had a pair of trousers made of spider-webs, which lasted a very long time.

Some years ago, on a magnificent autumn morning, I was walking in the vast meadows which border the Seine; the sky was azure, and the sun was shining splendidly. What was my astonishment at seeing that the entire surface of the freshly mown grass was covered with a net-work of fabulous delicacy!

The rays of light, gleaming obliquely upon this immense white veil, made the whole surface of it iridescent, and the harmonious regularity of this sheet of silk, which extended further than the eye could see, was only interrupted by the rents made by the grazing cattle, the limbs of which, covered with silky flakes, bore witness to their theft of the delicate gauze. Finally, here and there some of these white filaments, borne by the breeze over the surface of the meadows, floated in the atmosphere and fell upon our dresses.

I had come by accident upon all the phases of a phenomenon, the

[1] Kirby and Spence say that the holes of the threads are so fine and so crowded together, that there are 1000 of them in the space covered by the point of a needle.

mystery of which our savants have long been unable to penetrate. This silky tissue, spread over all the herbage, was the work of myriads of little spiders, beautified by the splendour of the heavens. And these flakes wandering in the air represented fragments of it, being nothing more than the mysterious filaments called by the vulgar *threads of the Virgin.*

These flakes, seen falling from the air in fine autumn days, after having been looked upon as a simple chemical product of the atmosphere, condensed by some special agent, have been made out by Latreille to be only the handiwork of different kinds of spiders, and particularly of the garden-spiders, transported to a distance by the agitation of the winds.[1]

Other spiders, instead of displaying their productions in the form of carpets woven as it were of the mist, which overspread our verdant fields, construct compact and solid hangings, with which they line the insides of their dwellings. The mason-spider (*Mygale cæmentaria*, Latreille), very

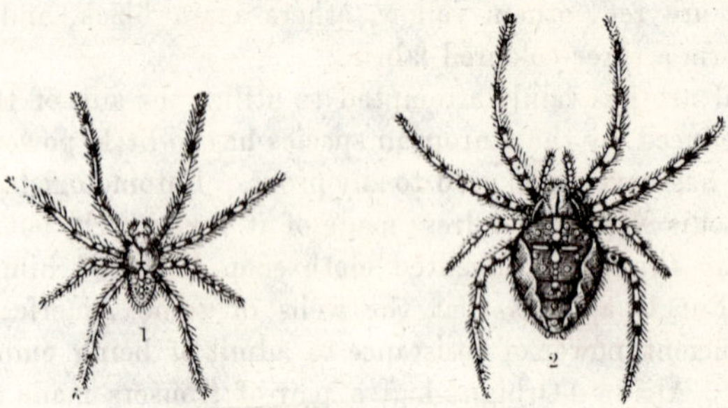

95. Garden-spider (*Epeira diadema*). 1, male; 2, female.

appropriately thus named, occupies itself in this way. It is a true sybarite, which incloses itself in its abode, and there reposes upon soft yielding drapery.

Its habitation consists of a hole several inches deep excavated in the ground and perfectly cylindrical. All the interior is tapestried, and in this part of the work the mason-spider imitates the decorator who places only a coarse material next the wall, and afterwards covers it with rich hangings. The spider also makes use of a double layer; the one, which it fixes upon the rough earthen wall of its subterranean hole, is thick and negligently wrought; the other, which is placed over this, is, on the contrary, woven with its finest silk and skilfully hung.

[1] According to Latreille, these "threads of the Virgin" are principally produced by young spiders belonging to the genera Epeira and Thomisus. Some chemists thought with M. Raspail that they were only aërial albumen precipitated to the earth in the form of flakes.

The entrance to the habitation is closed as hermetically as it can possibly be by a little door or lid, the lower side of which is slightly convex and furnished with a cushion of silk, whilst the upper part is made of the same materials as the soil, in such a manner that when the insect is inclosed within its abode, nothing without reveals its existence. This door itself is a little master-piece of finish and patience. The mason-

96. The Mason-spider—*Mygale cæmentaria* (Latreille), and Interior of its Dwelling.

spider (*Mygale*) possesses the knowledge of the miner, but in no degree that of the joiner or potter; hence it learns from its own resources to barricade its refuge. The solid lid which serves it for this purpose is composed of layers of silk, between each of which is found a layer of earth. When the task is completed, forty alternate layers of silk and earth can be counted, and it is with the first, which extend from the soil to the door, that the little elastic hinge is formed.

When the spider wants to issue forth, it lifts this movable cover, and when it re-enters its underground abode, it shuts up its trap-door close and sleeps in security. But should any noise, any shaking, intimate that an attempt is being made to violate the sanctity of its dwelling its vigilance is awakened in an instant. With one bound it darts to the gate, to which it hooks itself by half its claws, while with the others it clings to the tapestry of its hole. If we now, for curiosity's sake, gently raise the door, a slight resistance is felt, and when it is half open we see the last struggles of the spider and its threatening head; it defends its hearth to the last extremity.[1]

The name of *joiners* is given to those legions of insects which, with their powerful mandibles, cut and divide wood, either to nourish themselves with, or to construct little rooms furnished with partitions, and destined to receive their offspring.

The jet ant (*Formica fuliginosa*), so wonderful as a carver, belongs to the first section of these ingenious joiners. It establishes itself in the holes of our aged trees. There it excavates an elegant and complicated dwelling, consisting of a certain number of stories one above the other, the floors of which are but a little thicker than stout paper, and support long vistas of tiny columns of polished wood; the whole forming a perfect palace through which an animated throng keeps moving about. Other kinds of ants do not disdain to establish themselves in the large timbers of our houses, the stability of which is sometimes thus endangered.

In the second category is found the larva of the goat-moth, a night-moth which sometimes reaches a length of four or five inches, and is thicker than the finger. It gnaws the inside of great trees, and scoops out in their trunks wide and long tortuous galleries, which sometimes suffice to kill them. We see that it works all the more zealously because its labour is to satisfy a want; it lives on wood.

When several of these powerful caterpillars attack an elm at the same time it is ruined very rapidly. This insect has sometimes been seen to utterly destroy large avenues of lofty trees: hence the name of *Cossus ligniperda* (Wood-destroying Cossus) has been given to it. This Cossus is unfortunately common enough in France. Frequently while walking in a

[1] Several species of mason-spiders form nests of this kind. Among these are the *Mygale nidulans* of Walckenaer, and the *Mygale cratiens*, or clay-kneader, of Latreille. A nest supposed to belong to this insect was opened and shut several hundreds of times in presence of different persons without in the least destroying the hinge. One of the most extraordinary spiders is that found by the Rev. Revett Shepherd in the fen ditches of Norfolk, which forms a raft of weeds about three inches in diameter, probably held together by silken cords, on which it floats about for the purpose of seizing drowning insects.—*Kirby and Spence*, Introd. i. 425.—Tr.

97. Goat-moth and Willow-eating Caterpillar—*Cossus ligniperda.*
1, 2. Imago or perfect insect. 3. Pupa. 4. Larva.

plantation of elms we can see on the surface of some of these trees holes from which issues a sort of moist saw-dust. These are the entrances to the hidden tunnels gnawed by the larva of the dreaded moth.

The larva of the Great Capricornis (*Cerambyx heros*), which mines the interior of ancient oaks, and often injures the most beautiful pieces of carpenter's work, has its back cuirassed with solid wrinkled plates,[1] which serve the same purpose as the chimney-sweep's knee-pads, and protect its skin when it climbs its wooden chimneys.

But we find artisans endowed with a very different kind of ingenuity,

98. Carpenter-bee and its Chambers for its Young.

in a certain tribe of bees called carpenter-bees, from their great skill in working wood. They live principally in tropical countries. One kind, however, inhabits our latitudes; it has the look of a great humble-bee of the most beautiful blue colour, and is known by the name of the carpenter-bee, *Megachile Sicula*. Impelled merely by maternal instinct, its work, which consists of as many little chambers as it lays eggs, is a master-piece of skill and foresight. It generally attacks beams, cutting in them, lengthwise, canals which are as much as a dozen inches deep, and more than a third of an inch wide.

[1] See the figure on p. 94.

When one of these great excavations has attained its entire length, the artisan occupies itself in sheltering its offspring in it. For this purpose it divides the groove into as many little chambers as it is about to deposit eggs. Each of these chambers receives one egg only, and before closing it hermetically the bee stores up a mass of honey and pollen which will suffice for all the wants of the larva that is to be born there. After this the skilful carpenter, by means of finely rasped wood agglutinated with its saliva, constructs a slender partition which separates each one from that next to it. In the long excavation which it has hollowed out the insect thus forms a dozen little cells, which are stuffed with alimentary pap.

When the little creature is born, it finds itself sufficiently restricted as to space, but in proportion as its food diminishes, its movements become more free. The aliment has been wisely proportioned to its wants; the life of the larva terminates at the moment when famine is about to set in. The chrysalis rests imprisoned in its little chamber, but when the fly has thrown off its coverings, air and light are absolutely requisite for it. It then gnaws the partitions which intercept its way, and commits itself to the air, soon in its turn to commence labours similar to those its mother executed. Such is its destiny.[1]

[1] The English carpenter-bee is far inferior in skill to this insect, the beautiful violet Xylocopa (*Xylocopa violacea*) of English naturalists, which bores a tunnel twelve times the length of her body without leaving any chips, and fixes her shelves so finely that a number of fragments are as solid as one piece. It can, however, scarcely be said that either of these insects excels the poppy-bee and the rose-leaf cutter either in skill or taste.

The poppy-bee (*Osmia papaveris*, Latreille) excavates a hole three inches deep in the ground, which it smooths, polishes, and then hangs with the flower leaves of the scarlet poppy, laid down with such skill that they are as smooth as glass, although when we cut them with scissors, and take the greatest care with them, it is almost impossible to keep them from wrinkling. The rose-leaf cutter (*Megachile centuncularis*, Latreille) requires circular pieces of rose-leaf to line her nest, so she cuts out the portion she wants as quickly as we could do with scissors and much more neatly. Not to impede her progress she keeps the cut portion between her legs, using her body as a trammel. When she has nearly completed this part of her task, she poises herself on her wings lest the weight of her body should tear off the piece prematurely. Then taking the piece to the cell, she fixes it to the inside, solely *by calculating upon the natural spring of the leaf*, and so adapts the pieces that the *middle of one always overlies a join in the others.* Finally, having stored the cell with pollen and honey, she deposits an egg and covers the opening with three pieces of rose-leaf, so exactly circular that they could not be more accurately drawn with compasses.—Tr.

CHAPTER IX.

CLOTH-CUTTERS AND LEAD-EATERS.

Seamen are great admirers of certain crustaceans which have the singular habit of eating a certain class of proprietors in order to make themselves masters of their domiciles. After having devoured the mollusc which resides in a particular kind of shell, they convert it into an abode, which they drag about everywhere with them, and beneath the roof of which they shelter themselves from their enemies by burying themselves like a soldier in his sentry-box, or a frightened monk in his cell. Hence the names of soldier-crab and hermit-crab which are given to these curious brigands of our shores.

Certain insects which require a shelter are less ferocious and much

99. Larvæ of the Clothes-moth (*Tinea sarcitella*), magnified.

more intelligent in their manners. Too weak to bear the injurious action of the air, their larva knows how to cut out for itself a suit of clothes. Felted with great care, this suit is enlarged in proportion to the growth of the larva, which makes continual additions to it. Should the reader amuse himself with despoiling the worm of its covering it immediately fabricates another. And as its toil is incessant, if we place it upon cloths of different colours, it forms for itself a perfect harlequin's dress made of party-coloured shreds and patches. This insect is the clothes-moth *Tinea sarcitella* (Fabricius), unfortunately too common in our wardrobes, and which, after undergoing its metamorphosis, displays to us a little butterfly of surprising beauty.

100. Clothes moth in its butterfly state, magnified.

Certain aquatic larvæ, not finding the fine cloth dress of the clothes-moth a sufficient protection against fish and frogs, require a stouter envelope, and choose the most varied materials to make it of. They often form an extremely solid sheath by gluing and fitting together little stones.

Sometimes also the Phryganeæ, for so these prudent workmen are named, construct their protecting sheaths of fresh-water shells; finally, at other times they cut up for this purpose slender herbs, and cover their whole body with them in such a manner that at the bottom of a pool

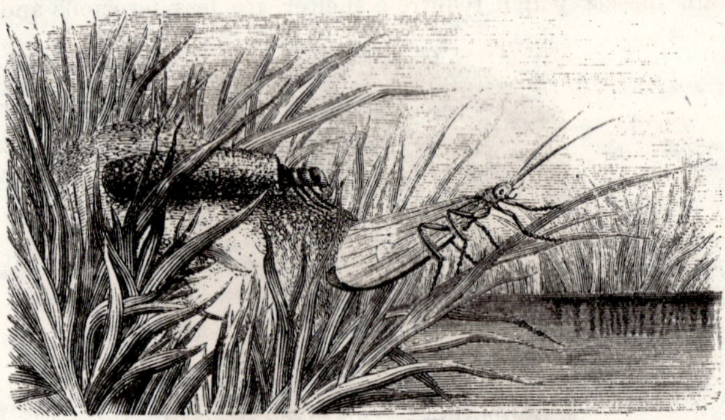

101. Sheath Phryganea—*Phryganea striata* (Linnæus). Larva and Adult Insect.

they look like tiny bottles of hay walking about of themselves, for we do, not perceive the timid inhabitants.

However, the common Phryganea (*Phryganea communis*) seems to give little heed to the nature of the materials it employs, and willingly makes use of all it finds at hand. Having carefully extracted several of its larvæ from their shelly sheaths, and afterwards placed them in vessels of water, the bottom of which was covered solely with little pearls of various colours, I saw them immediately set to work to make a new residence, choosing here and there pearls of the most different hues, in such a way that when the construction was finished, each Phryganea's dress resembled a little case in mosaic, promenading on the walls of my crystal vase.

Other insects, instead of these portable abodes, laboriously hollow out for themselves a refuge in the hardest bodies, even metals. The most extraordinary animal of this kind that is known is a powerful hymenopterous insect, the Giant Sirex, the larva of which, during our expedition to the Crimea, gnawed the balls in the soldiers' cartridges,

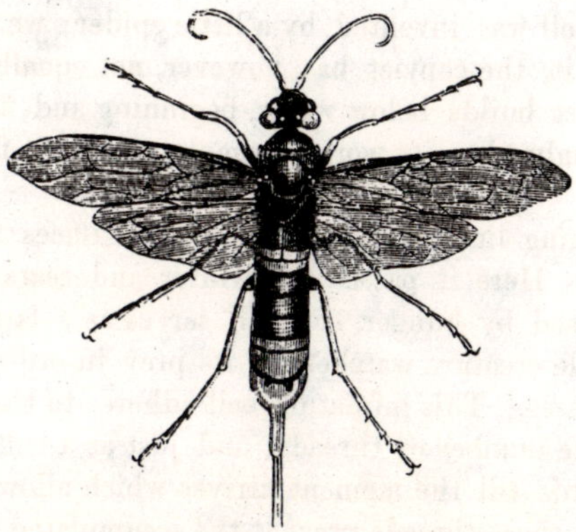

102. Giant irex (*Sirex giganteus*), the Larva of which gnaws Lead.

and bored deep holes in them in which it might find a secure shelter. Marshal Vaillant presented to the Academy of Sciences several balls which had been pierced through in this way by these insects.

Several of these metal-eaters might be mentioned. The larvæ of a Cetonia, as has been known for a considerable time, sometimes pierce the lead coverings of our roofs; and a piece of the gutter of a church, which presented numerous perforations produced by a Callidia, was recently brought to me at the museum at Rouen.

CHAPTER X.

HYDRAULIC ENGINEERS AND MASONS.

The diving-bell was invented by a little spider; we had nothing to do but imitate it; the copyist has, however, not equalled the inventor. In fact, the insect builds below water, beginning and finishing its task there, and it is only when its work is completed that it fills the structure with vital air.

It is a charming little house of silk, which suffices for all the wants of its occupant. Here it passes the winter and rears its young; and when it is pressed by hunger, the bell serves as a lair from which the bloodthirsty little creature watches for its prey in order to throw itself upon it as it passes. This miniature bell adheres to the adjoining grass by a considerable number of threads; and just as a balloon is held back by numerous cords till the moment arrives which allows it to soar into the clouds, so do these threads prevent the accumulated air from carrying off the abode.

These little spiders swim easily, and it is to their entirely aquatic life that they owe their name of naïads (*Naiadeæ*), given them by Walckenaer, their ingenious historian. A layer of air, fixed to the hair of their bodies, and which gives them under water the lustre of a living pearl, materially assists their power of swimming by lightening them. It is by means of this that they succeed in filling their little bell with respirable gas so soon as it is built. For this purpose the spider comes to the surface of the stream, takes a bubble of air under its abdomen, and carries it to its submerged refuge; and it repeats these voyages till the bell is completely filled with air.

Entomologists are acquainted with other hydraulic engineers also, but none of them equal in intelligence the naïads, of which we have just been speaking.

One of our great French Coleoptera, the water-beetle (*Hydrophilus piceus*), whose name is suggestive of its aquatic habits, also builds an impermeable silken retreat under the water, but does not inhabit it, and restricts itself to intrusting its progeny to it. It is simply a shell for its eggs.

In other cases insects build with more solid materials. They employ

103. Aquatic Spider and its Diving-bell.

mortar and paste, and are masons, in the true sense of the term; but, instead of working in our fens, set about their task in the open air, on our elevated monuments, or near the tops of trees.

The Wall Megachile (*Xylocopa*, Fabricius), commonly called the mason-bee, has acquired great celebrity from its nests built of small stones or of mortar which it attaches to houses. They are in the shape of ovoid cells, each capable of containing a hazel-nut. These are so many lodgings to which this fly intrusts its progeny. When after long toil the miniature monument is finished, the mother places one of its eggs inside it, and then retreats by the opening left in the upper part, which it walls up hermetically before taking wing.

The progeny of the bee thus finds itself inclosed alive in a tomb, but maternal tenderness here displays all the resources of the greatest foresight. Before leaving, the Megachile lines the walls with a fine hanging of silk. Thus the larva is sheltered from the night cold, and has not to dread contact with the rough walls of its little chamber. By dint of laborious journeys the mother has contrived to amass in the cradle a sufficient quantity of food for its little one. And when it incloses it in its cell by means of a partition of masonry, it knows that it is provided with sufficient air and nourishment to support it, and that when the moment comes for it to take flight, it will, like its mother, be in possession of working implements to break down the wall within which it is imprisoned.[1]

In those countries where the mason-bees are very rare, their nests are isolated, or there are only a few alongside of each other. They are often met with in the hollows of stones or the flutings of columns. I found some solitary on different monuments in Italy; they were adherent to pillars, and constructed of little stones agglutinated together by a very fine mortar. They were extremely solid.

In Egypt, where the mason-bees are very common, we find in many monuments numerous clusters of their nests. The roofs of some of the ancient subterranean temples are sometimes entirely covered by them. They are so heaped and piled up one upon another, that they hang from the ceilings like the stalactites of our caverns. But these nests are not built with little stones; in imitation of the fellahs of Upper Egypt, the mason-bee constructs its abode with the mud of the Nile.

The ceiling of an apartment in a temple at the island of Philæ, in which I bivouacked for some days, was completely hidden from view by

[1] A species seen in England (*Osmia bicornis*) selects as the material for its nest banks of brown clay, which it moistens with saliva, and moulds into pellets as large as peas. It is supposed that a bee will prepare as many as 140 to 180 of these pellets in a day.—TR.

these nests! While I was lying down, I saw those lizards which attach themselves so adroitly to the slightest asperities on the walls, running about in the midst of them with surprising activity. These were geckoes, which darted on the young bees as they issued from their abodes, or devoured the larvæ when any crack or opening in the nest enabled them to reach them.

104. Paper-making Wasps—*Vespa nidulans.*

But if any insect merit the palm of architecture, it must certainly be awarded to the paper-making wasp (*Vespa nidulans*, Fabricius). It builds abodes much more ingenious than our domestic bee. If the wax-cakes of the latter exhibit cavities of marvellous regularity, the wasp of which we speak

105. Nest of the Paper-making Wasp.

is remarkable for the general arrangement of her building. It is composed of regular stages placed one above another in a species of circular tower. Some of these houses possess as many as fifteen to twenty stages, which all communicate with each other by means of a hole placed in the centre of each. The cavities which shelter the architects are placed on the ceiling of each compartment. The entire building of this fly, which ordinarily hangs to a tree, is composed of a kind of brown paste exactly like cardboard, and from this comes the name by which it is known. But we are totally ignorant of the source from which the insect, an inhabitant of Cayenne, draws its materials.

BOOK IV.

RAVAGERS OF FORESTS.

Under this title the reader naturally expects to see on the stage animals the size of which must be in proportion to their formidable powers of destruction. But it is quite the contrary. It is not the auroch with its shaggy mane, nor the powerful stag, nor the wild boar that ravages or destroys our forests, but tiny insects which cause the death of its aged denizens.

If, when the warm breath of spring drives away the rigour of winter and renews life in the fields, we enter one of the great coniferous woods of Germany, we are astonished at the tumult and activity which prevail in lieu of the silence we went there to seek. Everything is in movement.

Groups of woodmen, foresters, and overseers move about by hundreds, and stretch away like columns of skirmishers; it is a complete army in the field, which opens out wherever there is a large space, and of which the wings are sometimes lost in the windings of the roads, or hidden by the projection of some hillock. This mass of men always moves in order, distributed in troops commanded by experienced leaders. They are all provided with long weapons, which at a distance might be taken for lances.

Elsewhere, again, we find a lengthy train of pioneers regularly posted, and vanishing in the distance; all, animated with feverish activity, are digging up the soil, and making, for many leagues, long trenches of circumvallation, which follow the roads and serve to isolate the different districts of the forest from one another.

Or if the excursion be made by night, another spectacle awaits us. The whole forest seems on fire. In every part are burning great trees, erect and isolated, like huge threatening torches, the flame of which rises to the clouds and casts a baleful glare on all around. A few foresters, standing in silence, contemplate the progress of the conflagration, and watch its ravages. Lastly, at other times, as a final resource, the entire forest is given up a prey to the flames, and whirlwinds of fire, menacing and dreadful, spread on every side; a woody region, lately fertile, is entirely devoured by fire, and only an immense mountain of charcoal and ashes remains of all this mass of wealth.

We ask against what formidable enemy such an army of men has been directed? Whom are they going to attack with their rods which they brandish on all sides? What redoubtable aggressors are the others attempting to stay the march of, by means of the long trenches they are digging? Why these frightful fires in the middle of the night? Why this general conflagration?

This formidable enemy is at times only a single insect, but it threatens everything with its destructive tooth, and men prefer decimating the forest to losing it entirely.

One is struck dumb with amazement at seeing so many and so vigorous efforts directed solely against the progeny of a simple butterfly; but its caterpillars sometimes multiply to such an extent that it is necessary to exterminate them utterly in order to preserve the forest from ruin. In one part the woodmen and their families, who are called out *en masse*, are occupied in crushing these destructive creatures upon the trees. In another the others are cutting off the infected districts by ditches, in order to check the invasion of the caterpillars, which, when they have devoured everything in one place, proceed in immense bands to invade the healthy localities.

But in spite of so much labour, man is sometimes vanquished by the insect, and there only remains one last resource—that of setting fire to the forest and burning the invaders.

All this war of extermination, of which we have just given a succinct account, is directed against only a small number of our enemies, as for the most part they are able to keep out of the power of the cultivator, and their formidable army defies our weakness.

These extensive operations are undertaken especially against certain night-moths, for it is among the simple moths that we find insects which are to be classed among the most destructive ravagers of the forests. They are attacked in their three different phases. Their caterpillars are crushed as they climb the trees. When after devouring a complete section of the wood, they pour forth in serried columns to attack a sound part, they fall into trenches hollowed out by the pioneers, and when they fill these, they are stifled in a heap by covering them over with earth. The great fires lighted at night are directed against the moths themselves. The glare attracts them, and they are soon scorched by the flame in consequence of going too near it.

The Pine Bombyx enjoys the evil prerogative of being placed in the

106. Pine Bombyx or Phalæna—*Phalæna Bombyx pini* (Linnæus). Larva, Cocoons, and Butterfly.—From Ratzeburg.

front rank of the enemies of our forests. Of all insects it is the most injurious to the tree of which it bears the name. It especially attacks wood of from sixty to eighty years old, and many examples are known of forests at this age being totally destroyed by these caterpillars, which the German wood-growers call "pine spinners," on account of the numerous cocoons with which they cover the leaves of this tree.

The foresters equally dread another moth, commonly called the monk or nun, on account of its robe being laced with black and white like that of certain devotees. It is all the more fatal because its caterpillar attacks not only the coniferous forests, but in addition all forest trees, such as the birch, oak, beech, &c. The perfect insects are met with in autumn, and sometimes in such abundance that at a distance one might take them for snow-flakes drifting about. The regular exterminations of which we have previously spoken are also directed against this insect.

Among those insects, the progeny of which devastates our woods, we should mention also the Pine-eating Phalæna. Its caterpillars, which sometimes multiply to an extraordinary extent, make great havoc in the pine forests. They are particularly to be dreaded, because they show themselves very early, and devour the young shoots. The same means are taken to stop their ravages as with the others; their invasion is checked by trenches, and in some places by herds of pigs which eat them in heaps. For this purpose the pigs are led to the forests towards the month of August, a time at which they seize the caterpillars as they descend from the trees in order to hybernate under the moss or earth.

Other insects, in lieu of attacking stems or leaves, attach themselves to the buds. One of them produces great havoc by gnawing those of the pine. Its caterpillar, which is very small, being introduced beneath the scales of the bud, gnaws a part of it in such a way that the stalk, warped at the very core, loses its straightness, twists, and becomes deformed. We can see from a distance when these artisans have assailed a part of a wood, by the strange aspect which the tops of the trees present. All the terminal buds are more or less bent and contorted, instead of possessing their normal direction. It is to this result that the species owes its name of pine-twister, by which the foresters generally designate it.

Some destroyers, instead of this openly declared war, carry on their assaults silently and in the shade; these are concealed enemies, which nothing can track out, and we have frequently no suspicion of their presence till they have slain their victim. Some live on wood, and hollow out ample tortuous galleries in it, which very speedily modify the organism of the tree so profoundly, that the strongest succumb to it. Others work between the bark and the sap-wood, using up materials that offer less resistance to their teeth.

In the former category must be placed the Cossi, those skilful

107. Pine eating Phalæna (*Phalæna Bombyx pinivora*), the progeny of which devastates forests.—Ratzeburg.

carpenters of which we have already made mention. In the second category may be ranked the numerous legion of insects which ornament the surface of wood in a deplorable manner with chisellings that roughly resemble printing, writing with chalk, or in short-hand. Each species invariably draws the same design, so that we can always discover who our enemy is by his work without seeing him.

Almost all these labourers are beetles of very small size, belonging to the genera Bostrichus and Hylesinus. Their teeth, with deadly quickness, cut numerous galleries between the wood and the bark, so that both portions of the tree are assailed at the same time. These tiny ravagers are often not more than about the sixth of an inch long, and hence, as

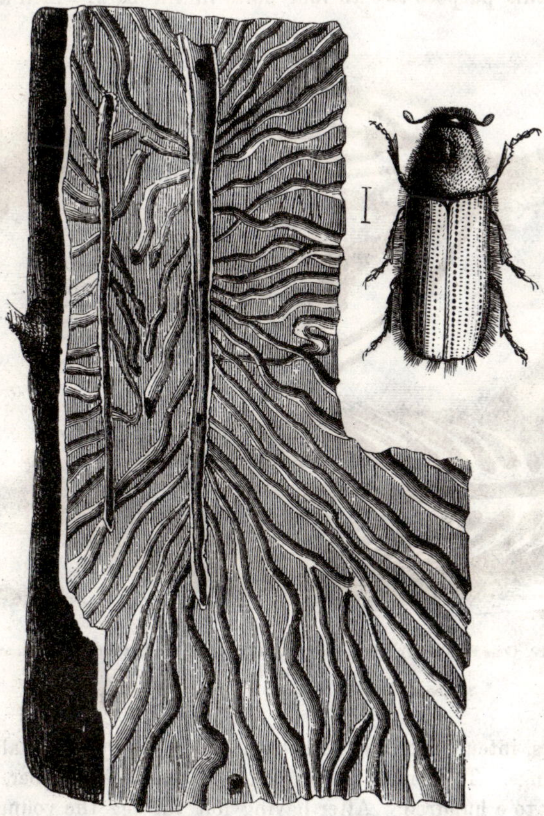

108. Nuptial Chamber of the Pine Hylesinus, of natural size, and the Insect enlarged.

their bodies are slender in proportion, they only require a very narrow trench to promenade in at their ease. Nevertheless, as each insect reproduces its species very rapidly, the number of galleries hollowed out by a single family sometimes covers a large part of the surface of a tree, and if the species multiplies round about it the result of its work is to detach the entire bark, which falls to dust.

The attentive observations of foresters have shown that nearly always a pair of typographer beetles enter the tree together by perforating the bark, and this first task accomplished, they hollow out at this spot a central gallery, which is nothing more or less than a nuptial chamber for the pair. Here, resolved to make their lives as agreeable as possible, they pierce for this purpose two to four holes in the bark, which are simply

109. Cone Pyralis—*Tortrix Strobiliana.* Caterpillar and Butterfly, enlarged and of natural size.
Section of Fir Cone, to display the work of the Caterpillar.

ventilators, intended to air the little chamber, and possibly also to light the windings. The female lays her eggs all along the chamber, producing from fifty to a hundred. After having left the egg the young larvæ, in order to nourish themselves, excavate all the little galleries which branch out from the whole length of the central gallery. It is towards the extremity of these that they undergo their metamorphosis, and when their arrival at the state of the perfect insect takes place, and the desire to breathe the pure air comes upon them, they bore through the bark, and scatter themselves abroad.

Of all these wood-cutters, the Typographer Bostrichus is regarded by M. Ratzeburg as the most dangerous. He says that it ravages the forests of fir-trees in such a manner, that often not a single tree escapes its attacks. It is doubtless in order to give an idea of the extent of its depredations that this naturalist has bestowed on such a little insect the alarming name of the "great pine-gnawer." Next to it must also be placed the Curved-tooth Bostrichus and the Pine Hylesinus, which are almost identical with it in their habits.

Each organ has its enemy. That our apples and plums are gnawed and injured by worms is no wonder, as their soft tissue admits of such mischief being done with the greatest ease; but fruits so hard and well protected as those of the Coniferæ would seem as if they ought to be safe from such attacks. This, however, is certainly not the case. The progeny of certain very small butterflies, that of the Cone Pyralis in particular, delight in gnawing and destroying the strong scales of these cones. They hollow out galleries in their axis, and from thence spread out between the scales.

BOOK V.

PROTECTORS OF AGRICULTURE.

Along with these innumerable legions of enemies, the devouring fangs of which, ever active, injure or even ruin agriculture, there has been created a valiant army which alone is capable of checking their ravages. But too often man, unthinkingly or through ignorance, destroys these auxiliaries sent by Providence, and only seeks to recall them when he has exterminated them. To-day he sets a price upon their heads; to-morrow he would buy them back at their weight in gold.

All the pleasant guests of our groves have been alternately thus treated. The titmouse, the black-cap, the nightingale, the blackbird, and many others, destroy swarms of all these caterpillars that ruin us, and they are more skilful than we are in discovering the hidden retreats of these pests. Among our auxiliaries we should have to name nearly all the small birds in our woods. And yet how often has the weapon of the sportsman destroyed these charming and active workers! It is only quite lately that we have checked his ravages and protected their broods.

If some destructive insects eat our crops, their natural exterminators again are found among the carnivorous mammals and birds.

At the head of these protectors of agriculture must be placed, at the present day, the mole, the habits of which have been for a long time misunderstood.

Far from being hurtful to the products of the earth, it is one of

110. Common European Mole—*Talpa europæa* (Linnæus).

their most effective guardians; occupied from morn to night in devouring all the enemies of their roots, it never attacks a root itself.

The food of the mole is composed of cockchafer grubs, of mole-crickets, and insects of all kinds. A naturalist has calculated that a mole devours annually 20,000 grubs. But the animal on which it declares war most savagely of all is the earth-worm. It is so voracious that it must eat every six hours. No animal is so favoured in its carnivorous instincts as the mole; forty-four teeth studded with points never cease working from morning to night. It requires nourishment to such an extent, that if deprived of food for a day it dies of inanition. It is a perfect eating machine, gulping down every day an enormous quantity of food, so that

M. De la Blanchère was right in saying, that "if we could magnify the mole to the size of the elephant, we should be face to face with the most terrific brute the world ever brought forth."[1]

Had the fact not been attested by a savant like E. Geoffroy Saint-Hilaire, no one would believe that the mole, an underground animal *par excellence*, though buried beneath the soil, nevertheless catches birds in order to devour them. The crafty mammal executes this bird-catching manœuvre by moving its muzzle slightly on the surface of its mole-hill. The bird thinks it is a little worm stirring, and swoops down to seize it, but finds only the hungry gullet of the earth-digger, which engulfs it in an instant.

The structure of the workman is wonderfully adapted to its kind of life; its fore-limbs present two broad cutting shovels, moved by a muscular apparatus so powerful that it alone weighs almost as much as the rest of the body. Its muzzle, a movable snout, first pierces the soil, and its paws clear the earth away in proportion as it is loosened. Aided by such organs the mole cuts out its underground tunnels with prodigious velocity; it is a living auger, a perfect earth-borer.

This animal devours its prey with such voracity, that when this is of some size, as a rat or bird for instance, the mole penetrates in some sort into the entrails of it, the head and fore-feet being so thrust in that one cannot see them. The carnivorous animal bores its victim as if it were boring the earth.

The mole never gnaws roots; I have opened hundreds without finding one in their stomachs, which, on the contrary, were always gorged with grubs of the may-bug and earth-worms. This insect-eater is therefore one of our best friends; this is well known where agriculture is intrusted to experienced hands. In such places, and in some vineyards devastated by the above-mentioned grubs, men buy moles in order to consign to them the destruction of these formidable enemies.[2]

[1] In Switzerland M. Weber experimented upon two moles. Such was their voracity that in nine days they had eaten 341 white-worms, 193 earth-worms, 25 caterpillars, and a mouse, both the bones and skin of which they swallowed. When he restricted them to a vegetable diet they died of hunger. Messrs. Dugès and Flourens have proved that they perish if kept for a day without food.

[2] All those authors who have recently written upon agriculture, or have interested themselves about the mole, such as Ratzeburg, Joigneaux, and De la Blanchère, consider this animal as of great service to farm husbandry. Ratzeburg, *Hylophthires;* Joigneaux, *Le Livre de la Ferme*, 1866; De la Blanchère, *Les Trois Règnes de la Nature*, 1866; "La Taupe," p. 134. Many more errors than we have mentioned have been circulated about the mole. Aristotle and all those who copied from him, not being able to perceive its eyes, believed that it cannot see. Its eyes, deeply hidden by hairs, are, it is true, unsuited for good vision, but it is evident that the mole can see with them. Le Court, the chief of the

Another very useful mammal, respecting which men have been as much deceived as about the other, is the hedgehog.

The hedgehog, represented everywhere as a pilferer of our orchards, carrying off apples and pears on its spines to eat them in its retreat, on the contrary never touches any fruit. It is an active flesh-eater, which only feeds on worms, snails, and rodent animals injurious to our dwellings. Far from devastating our gardens, it protects them. This is well known in some countries—Astrachan, for instance, where it is substituted for the cat in the town houses.

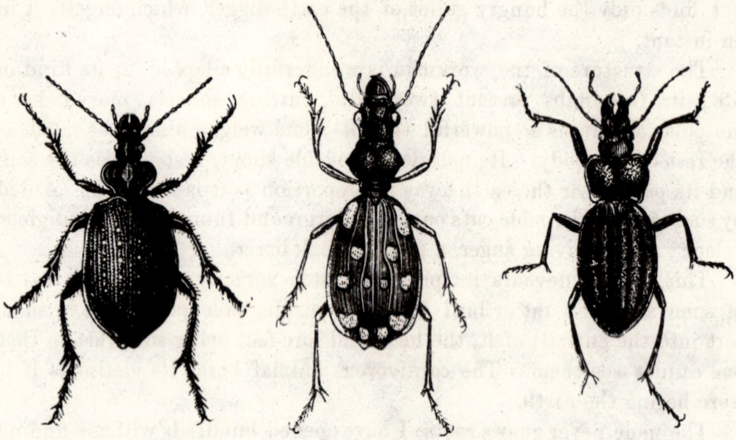

Flesh-eating Coleoptera of the family Carabidæ.
111. *Calosoma sycophanta.* 112. *Anthia duodecimpunctata.* 113. *Carabus gryphæus.*

To these auxiliaries of notable activity must be added an ample host of smaller ones; the work of which, however, when multiplied by numbers, amounts to a large figure. They are found as a providential compensation in that class of insects which causes us such damage. These benefactors —lost, unrecognized in the midst of the enemy—belong principally to

mole-catchers in France, even says that he has seen it swim across rivers guided only by its sight.

The existence of the mole is a series of paradoxes. The cleanliness of its fur, for instance, is wonderful; though it is always buried in the earth or the mud which invades its subterranean dwelling, yet, when we withdraw it, its coat is beautifully fresh, unsoiled with spot or dust. This silky robe has often tempted those in search of new frivolities. Some ladies of the court of Louis XV., having a fancy to match it with the patches, rouge, and paint with which they covered their faces, conceived the whim of having eyebrows of it; whilst the courtiers of this prince collected masses of moleskin to have their dresses made of them. But all they got was dress of a costly kind and of a very disagreeable smell, so that the fashion soon died out.

the ravenous-jawed Carabidæ family;[1] they are in especial the Calosomæ, the Cicindelæ, and the Carabi, all gleaming with purple and gold, which, full of valour, courageously throw themselves upon all insects that pass

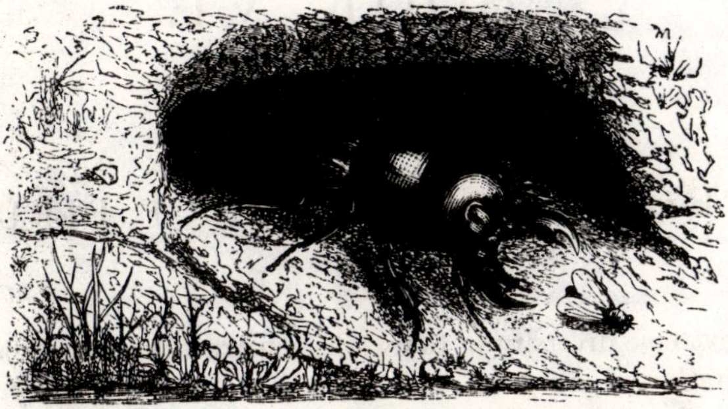

114. Giant Scarites (*Scarites lævigatus*) in its Lurking-place.

within reach. In another place we find the insidious Scarites concealed in their underground dwellings, and entrapping their prey as it passes.

Instead of pitilessly destroying these beneficent Coleoptera, as is generally done when we see them in our gardens and fields, one ought to protect them; for they devour *en masse* the caterpillars which ruin them.

[1] Thousands of insects called *Carabidæ*, varying greatly in size, from half a line to an inch in length, may be found under stones and clods in fields, meadows, and gardens, where they secrete themselves by day, and sally forth at night to feed upon other insects, worms, larvæ, &c., which come to the surface at that period, either to feed or to migrate; they are consequently eminently serviceable in reducing the ranks of noxious animals. During a drought they retire into cracks in the earth and to the most humid spots, and evidently enjoy the refreshing rains which succeed. I have seen the large *Carabus glabratus* in mountainous districts running about immediately after a thunderstorm, each having a tolerably large earth-worm in its mouth; others, as the splendid *Calosoma sycophanta*, live entirely upon caterpillars in trees; and there is one which well deserves notice from its feeding upon the wire-worms. It is called *Steropus madidus*, from its inhabiting wet and damp localities. It is a very active insect; it prowls about at night, and is admirably adapted to its predacious mode of life.—*Farm Insects*, by John Curtis, F.L.S.

BOOK VI.

THE ARCHITECTURE OF BIRDS.

The extreme diversity in the works constructed by birds has excited the admiration of every one. These animals vary to infinity the forms, style, and materials which they employ. It is therefore possible to divide them into as many classes as there are kinds of work. Some are carpenters; others weave; some build; and we find among them navvies, masons, and miners; blacksmiths alone are wanting.

Alongside of our gigantic monuments, such as St. Peter's at Rome and the pyramids of the Pharaohs, the nest of the bird is only a point in space; but the work suddenly expands before our eyes when we compare the weakness of the workman with the magnitude of his task; for some of our aërial architects, in order to build their dwellings, amass more earth in proportion in one season than a man would heap up in his whole life.

Their nests lend animation to every part of the world. Some, like the eagle and vulture, only build them on the shattered mountain tops, on the naked and arid rocks; others, more delicate, such as some of the humming-birds, let them wave at the will of the zephyr, and content themselves with suspending them at the end of a palm-tree leaf which just touches a sheet of water. Some birds only build in the depth of caverns, or in the midst of ruins never trodden by the foot of man; to escape all notice is with them an imperious necessity. On the contrary, there are some which like to be near us. Quite assured of the affection we feel for them, and full of confidence, they enter our dwellings as if they belonged to the household, and in spite of the noise and uproar about them, sleep peacefully in the cradle they have hung there.

The swallows seem to know instinctively that no person would dare to do them harm. Almost all the other species flee us; they alone install themselves securely near us: they are our guests.

A chimney-swallow, the nest of which is preserved in the Rouen

115. Nest of the Common Magpie—*Corvus pica* (Linnæus).
From the Rouen Museum.

Museum, built its nest in the centre of a foundry belonging to an esteemed friend of mine, in the vault of a forge in full work, without being alarmed either at the fierceness of the fire, the torrents of smoke, or the continual clang of the hammers.

In the bird maternal love becomes ingenious in the highest degree. Although the quail and the partridge, like too confident mothers, deposit

116. The King Penguin—*Aptenodytes patagonica* (Gmelin).

their young uncovered on the ground, and expose them to the rapacity of every carnivorous animal that passes, other species take infinite precautions to defend them. The king-fisher hollows out a deep and winding underground passage to shelter its young. The magpie, to protect its little ones, constructs a regular casemated citadel, into which it enters, and from which it issues merely by a narrow passage. Only that in lieu of wood work and earth, the nest is covered with closely interlaced branches, which also defend it against the eagles and falcons, the brigands of the air.

Among the different tribes of the air, only one species, a singular one in all respects, almost as much fish as bird, evades the general law, and does not commit its offspring to any kind of nest: it is the Patagonian penguin, which lives amid ice, rocks, and waves, and of which the wings are quite unfitted for flying. But we must admit that the love displayed by the parents for their brood makes one at once forgive their idleness and stupidity.

Like the kangaroos, those mammals of Australia which conceal their little ones in a ventral sack, the female penguin constantly carries her solitary egg in a pouch formed by a fold of the skin of the abdomen, and it is held so fast in this, that she leaps or sometimes rolls from rock to rock without letting it fall. It is well for her she does so, for should such a mishap befall her, the male bird chastises her without pity. This egg is even concealed with so much care by the mother, that to get possession of it, it is necessary to engage in a regular battle with her. The male also mixes himself up in the affair; at his mate's call of anger he rushes to the spot, and throws himself upon the ravisher with a fury which only ceases when he sinks under his assailant's club.

CHAPTER I.

GIANTS AND PIGMIES.

Nature presents everywhere the most opposite extremes. Birds have also their pigmies and their giants, their idlers and indefatigable workers. Their habits display, side by side, imbecility and intelligence, solitude and family life.

Often in the tropical regions, where the sun darts his fiercest rays, we may see flitting over the flowers brilliant birds, which sweep rapidly past like a spark of topaz or ruby; these are the humming-birds, living diamonds, slighter than some insects, and which often become the prey of huge spiders.

The giant of this group scarcely attains the size of a sparrow, and the smallest hardly surpasses in size a humble-bee. Hence, to the humming-birds, as they are commonly called, each speck of creation is a world. A simple leaf suffices for the gambols of a whole family; a flower is the

117. MOA, or Gigantic Dinornis (*D. giganteus*) restored; and APTERYX (*A. Mantelli*).

perfumed throne on which the nuptials are accomplished, and the petals of its corolla spread out to form a velvet canopy which hides their chaste loves.

Were we to compare the size of different birds, we should arrive at wonderful results. Lacépède, who doubtless could not boast of being as exact as Archimedes, calculated that it would require a thousand millions of shrew-mice to equal a whale in weight. If that were true, we should also have to pile up some millions of humming-birds to weigh against the heavy ostrich.

We have just spoken of the ostrich, but it again is only a bird of insignificant size compared with two ornithological marvels, the recent discovery of which we owe to the illustrious zoologists Prof. Owen and Isidore Geoffroy Saint-Hilaire.

One of them, the gigantic Dinornis of New Zealand, a part of the skeleton of which is in the Museum of the London College of Surgeons, was eighteen feet high. The bone of a man's leg is only a slender spindle compared to that of this colossal bird.

The disappearance of this huge bird dates from no very distant epoch, and everything attests that the first inhabitants of New Zealand were perfectly acquainted with it. The ancient legends of the island tell us that at the time of its discovery it was full of birds of appalling size. There are also ancient poems there in which the father teaches his son how to hunt the Moa, the name belonging of old to this species; in these are described the ceremonies which took place when one had been killed. They feasted on the flesh and eggs, while the feathers served to adorn the arms of the vanquishers. Some hills are yet strewed with the bones of the Dinornis, the remains of these great feasts of the hunters.

Another colossal bird, the Epiornis, which formerly lived in Madagascar, must have been of even greater size. One of its eggs, which is now in the museum at Paris, is six times as large as that of the ostrich, and it has been calculated that to fill the cavity would require 12,000 humming-birds' eggs. Its shell, about two twenty-fifths of an inch thick, could only be broken by a blow with a hammer. What strength then must the beak of the young bird have possessed to be able to make a hole in it!

What differences also in strength are found in birds!

When fleeing before the hunter, whose Arab steed comes ever closer and closer, the alarmed and furious ostrich presses its toes into the ground and tears up the soil of the desert, leaving deep marks beneath each footstep, while it launches afar behind it a cloud of sand and pebbles. When, on the contrary, a flock of humming-birds, attracted by the expanded and floating flowers of the Victoria Regia, play and gleam round them like a casket of topazes and rubies struck by the rays of the sun, neither the smooth surface of the lake nor the beautiful flowers are in the least degree disturbed. And when one of these winged diamonds perches itself upon a petal of their virgin corolla, it does not even stir it. Again, when the fragile bird takes flight, its tiny claw has not injured the velvet softness of the flower. It might have lighted upon one of the twigs of the modest sensitive plant without this taking any alarm.

The secretary-bird, on the contrary—a powerful bird of prey belonging to Africa, incessantly occupied in combating reptiles—with one blow of its wing stuns a tortoise or a threatening serpent. The swan, with the

118 Comparative Dimensions of Birds' Eggs. 1, That of the Epiornis. 2, Of the Ostrich. 3, Of the Hen. 4, Of the Humming-bird.

same member, can break a man's leg, or, as has been sometimes seen, dash him headlong into the water. The bearded vulture (*Gypaëtus barbatus*), some zoologists tell us, attacks the hunters unawares in the dangerous passes of the Alps, and occasionally gives them a great deal of trouble. And the eagle in its bold flight carries children through the fields of air, and crushes them in the mountain precipices.[1]

[1] An instance of this kind took place in the Valais in 1838. A little girl, five years old, called Marie Delex, was playing with one of her companions on a mossy slope of the mountain, when all at once an eagle swooped down upon her and carried her away in spite of the cries and presence of her young friend. Some peasants, hearing the screams, hastened to the spot, but sought in vain for the child, for they found nothing but one of her shoes on the edge of a precipice. The child, however, was not carried to the eagle's nest, where only two eaglets were seen, surrounded by heaps of goat and sheep bones. It was not till two months after this that a shepherd discovered the corpse of Marie Delex, frightfully mutilated, and lying upon a rock half a league from where she had been borne off.

119. Nest of the Saw-beaked Humming-bird—*Petasophora serrirostris.*—From Gould.

If we examine the form which our winged architects give to their nuptial couches, or the materials of which they build them, we see that they vary infinitely. Some birds, like the eagles and goshawks, which build their eyries in the midst of solitude and rocks, only employ in their construction rough fragments of stick heaped up in disorder; others make use of leaves and moss, which they arrange with skill. But such materials are still too coarse for the delicate bodies of the sparkling army of humming-birds. They, as for example the saw-beaked humming-bird, often construct for themselves a charming little downy cup of cotton, wherein to shelter their emeralds without sullying the lustre of them. Other species of the same group, which also make use of soft pillows, garnish the outside of their nests with fragments of lichens, doubtless to hide it better from the animals of prey that live in the midst of the foliage. This is the case with the mango humming-bird—the black plastron humming-bird of Buffon.

CHAPTER II.

THE INSTINCT OF CHEMISTRY.—MOUNTAIN BUILDERS AND GLEANERS.

Some birds attract attention by the size of their constructions, and by the innate notions which they seem to have of certain chemical phenomena which we see them make exactly the right use of.

An earthen mound in an English garden astonishes us by its dimensions, and the labour which it demands. Many hands and much time have been occupied with it, and yet if we compare the work with the means of him who orders it to be formed, this mass of earth seems but a small matter. A bird, the Mound-building Megapodius, accomplishes by itself a task a thousand times greater.

It has the carriage and size of a partridge, and its modest brown robe recalls the sombre colours of almost all the birds of its country, Australia, that land of zoölogical marvels, but its labours and its intelligence soon make us forget the inattractive aspect of the workman.

The nidification of this species is a truly herculean work, and one would not credit it were it not attested by the most authentic evidence.

The immense structure built by the Megapodius rests on the ground. The bird begins by getting together a thick bed of leaves, branches, and plants: then it heaps up earth and stones, and strews them round about in such a way as to form an enormous crater-like tumulus, concave in the middle; the place where alone the materials first collected remain uncovered. One of these nests, the dimensions of which are given by the illustrious ornithologist Gould, was fourteen feet high, and presented a

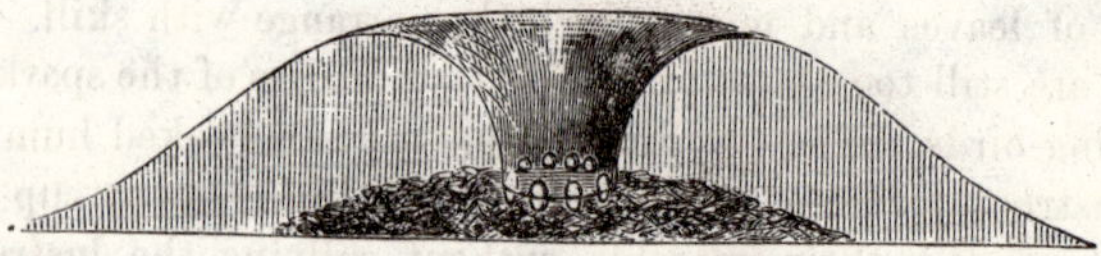

120. Nest of the Mound-building Megapodius, vertical section.—From Gould.

circumference of a hundred and fifty feet. Compared to the size of the bird, the dimensions of such a mountain are almost prodigious, and we ask how, with its beak and claws only for pickaxe and entire means of transport, it contrives to get together such a mass of materials! The

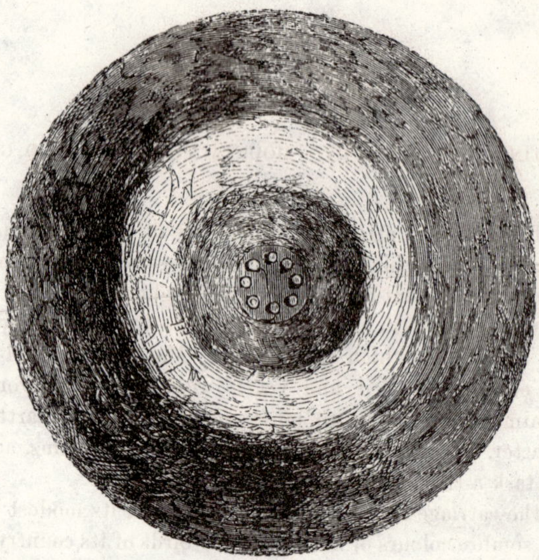

121. Nest of the Mound-building Megapodius, seen from above.—From Gould.

celebrated tumulus of Achilles, and that of Patroclus, assuredly demanded less labour.

Were we to try to establish a comparison between the work of the Megapodius and that which a man could execute, we should really be astonished at the results. The comparative size of the animal being very

122 Australian Landscape, with Nest of the Mound-building Megapodius—*M. tumulus* (Gould).

difficult to arrive at on account of the variety of its attitudes, if then we take the weight as a standard, we find that a Megapodius weighing rather above 2 lbs. sometimes raises its mound more than 10 feet in height;[1] now as a man weighs on an average about 130 lbs., he must, in order to build a structure corresponding to the nest of the bird, accumulate a mountain of earth which would be almost double the height and bulk of the great pyramid of Egypt!

The mighty task completed, the female bird confides its eggs to it. She usually lays eight, which she disposes in a circle in the centre of the nest among the herbs and leaves which lie heaped up at this spot. They are placed at exactly equal distances from each other and in a vertical position. When the laying is completed the Megapodius abandons its master-piece and its offspring, Providence having revealed to it that henceforth it is no longer useful to them.

Endowed with a marvellous chemical instinct, this bird only collects such a mass of vegetable matter, that it may commit the hatching of its eggs to the fermentation produced among the collected plants. It is in fact on the heat so engendered that the bird relies for supplying her place; the mother thus substituting a chemical process for her own cares.

Réaumur proposed to leave the incubation of our hens' eggs to the heat of dung, but they were poisoned by its mephitic vapours. The Megapodius, more judicious than the celebrated academician, employs the fermentation of grass and leaves, which is not attended by the same inconvenience.

Everything in the history of this animal is extraordinary. Instead of being born naked, or covered with down, and of issuing from the egg incapable of procuring its subsistence, the young Megapodius when it breaks its shell is already provided with feathers fitted for flight. It is scarcely free ere it aspires to seek the light and air, throws off the leaves which surround and stifle it, mounts on the crest of its tumulus, dries its yet moist wings in the sun, and tests them by a few flaps. Lastly, quickly becoming confident in its strength and fortune, and having cast a disturbed and inquisitive look upon the surrounding country, the feeble bird takes its flight into the atmosphere and quits its cradle for ever; it knows how to nourish itself as soon as it is born!

Another Australian bird possesses the same instinctive foresight as that of which we have been speaking; but, instead of building mounds,

[1] One measured by Mr. Jukes was 150 feet in circumference, the slope of the sides 18 to 24 feet, and the perpendicular height 10 or 12 feet. The eggs are as large as those of a swan, and are considered a great delicacy.

it is a sturdy gleaner. The *Talegalla Lathami*, for so it is called, is of the size and has the look of a fowl, and builds its nest with grass which it gleans in the fields, and of which it gathers an enormous heap, comparable, indeed, to the cocks which our hay-makers form in the meadows. But it is not with its beak, it is with its claws that it works. By means of one of them it collects a little bottle of hay, which it grasps in its toes; this it carries to its nest, hopping along upon the other foot. When, as a result of innumerable journeys, the heap has grown large enough, the female lays its eggs in it. Knowing as well as we do that hay heats by drying, it relies upon the warmth for the incubation of its brood, which it abandons immediately after laying. The young Talegallas are born as completely feathered as the Megapodii, and just as able to shift for themselves when they issue from the egg. Hence, a few minutes after having scattered about the hay which surrounds them, they take flight.

A little rodent of the Siberian Alps, the Lagomys, the size of which does not equal that of a rabbit, accumulates similar heaps of hay as much as five feet high and eight feet in diameter. The Tartars frequently appropriate the fruits of its labour in order to feed their horses. Some day perhaps man will in the same way make use of the nests of the Talegallas, which are even more laborious gleaners.

CHAPTER III.

WORK AND THE FAMILY.

The whole tribe of wrens and titmice make us forget their tiny size in the skilful finish of their work, and the delightful love which reigns in every family; their households are sometimes a perfect marvel to witness.

Among these charming guests of our thickets we may refer to the common wren, which builds a nest similar to a little underground house. Then comes the long-tailed titmouse, the globular abode of which does not exceed the size of the fist, and which is made of moss and lichen. The mother enters by an excessively narrow opening, and often nourishes ten or twelve little ones. It is quite inexplicable how so numerous a family can be crowded into such an extremely little chamber. One would think they must be stifled; but the young birds, heaped one upon another, are only so much the more thoroughly warmed, and the whole brood live happy and gay in their tiny little bed.

In respect to the elegance of its construction the penduline titmouse astonishes the observer still more. Its nest, suspended to the branch of a tree, has exactly the shape of a chemist's retort, only that instead of

123. Nest of the Penduline Titmouse—*Parus pendulinus* (Latham).—From the Rouen Museum.

being manufactured of such hard material, nothing enters into the composition of it but fine moss and down. The opening is carefully woven, not one vegetable fibre protrudes beyond the other!

Who can describe in what a marvellous manner the bird, while still on the wing, approaches its nest, enters and issues by an opening which seems to have scarcely the diameter of its body, and without ever deranging a fibre?

124. Nest of the Cape Titmouse (*Parus capensis*).—From Sonnerat.

The huts of some savages remain constantly open; their limited capacity has not yet taught them to invent the protecting door. Spiders are more ingenious. There are some which, as we have seen, understand how

125. Nest of a Community of the African Social Grossbeaks—*Loxia socia* (Latham).

to secure themselves in their subterranean abodes by a skilfully constructed door. Some birds take analogous precautions.

In his work on the *Birds of India*, Mr. Jerdon details the curious domestic arrangements of some species of the genus Homrain of French naturalists, the males of which, at the time of laying, imprison the female in her nest. They close the entrance to it by means of a thick wall of mud, leaving only a small hole by which the hen breathes and protrudes her beak to receive her food. To this, indeed, her too stern spouse brings every moment some morsel for her to peck at, for to his praise be it said that though he is barbarous enough to immure her, he feeds her with the most tender solicitude. This enforced retirement only ceases with the termination of the hatching, when the pair break the prison-door.

In his voyage to India Sonnerat speaks of a Cape titmouse, the nest of which, shaped like a bottle and made of cotton, merits notice. Whilst the female is hatching inside, the male, a most watchful sentinel, remains outside, resting in a pouch made for the purpose, fixed to one side of the neck of the nest. But when his mate moves off and he wishes to follow her, he beats the opening of the nest violently with his wing, and succeeds in closing it, in order to protect his young from enemies.

In respect to ingenuity of construction developed by the love of family and work, there is nothing that can be compared to the doings of the sociable grossbeak. This little Cape bird, of the size and appearance of our sparrow, lives in numerous societies, all the members of which unite to form an immense city, built upon a tree, having the appearance of a gigantic umbrella, of which the trunk of the tree is the handle. There are sometimes more than 300 separate compartments, which means that it is inhabited by more than 600 birds. This nest is so heavy, that Levaillant, who brought one away during his travels in Africa, was obliged to employ a waggon and several men to remove it. When they are seen at a distance in the landscape, we might think we were looking at huge roofs suspended to the trunks or branches of the trees scattered about, and round which a multitude of birds are playing.

We have said that amongst the winged tribes specimens of almost all the industrial arts are found. One would scarcely expect to find seamstresses among them, for the beak of the bird seems ill-adapted enough for needle-work, and yet some of these animals produce work exactly analogous. I do not here in any way allude to the weaver-birds, the nests of which, made of fine grass and known to all the world, represent an inextricable net-work; but to the tailor-bird, a charming exotic species, which takes two very long lanceolated leaves and sews the edges of them together by means of flexible grass instead of thread. After this the female fills the little sack which they form with cotton, and deposits her pretty young ones upon this downy bed, which is gently rocked by the least breath of wind. This nest, which is extremely rare, but of which I saw some specimens in the British Museum, is a real masterpiece of ingenuity.

126. Tailor-bird and Nest.—*Sylvia sutoria* (Latham).—From the British Museum.

The oriole of our climate executes an analogous task. Its nest resembles a circular concave cup, and is formed of a mass of plants finely interlaced. The bird always suspends it from the bifurcation of two branches of a tree. For this purpose it chooses those which lie horizontally, and always stitches its airy abode by means of a round stitch, done not with grass, but with a piece of string or a thread-end, which it has

127. Nest of the Golden Oriole—*Oriolus galbula* (Linnæus).—From the Rouen Museum.

stolen from some neighbouring factory or dwelling, so that one might feel inclined to ask what it did before pack-thread and spinning were invented.

CHAPTER IV.

IDLERS AND ASSASSINS.

It would seem that in the bird activity and intelligence are in inverse proportion to size. The idlers and freebooters of the air generally belong to the most robust tribes.

The wren lovingly hatches its charming little family beneath a dome of moss and down, constructed with delicacy and ingenuity, and often sheltered by the eaves of our roofs; a perfect mattressed sphere, which the mother scarcely dares to quit, so much does she love her brood.

The ostrich, a living emblem of force united to indolence, does not give itself the trouble to construct a nest at all. After having simply scattered the sand by means of its feet, it deposits its eggs upon the place, and commits their incubation to the burning sun of the desert. It only sits upon them in cold and damp nights; and, as if even this maternal effort were too great a strain upon her tenderness, several mothers are seen dividing among them the cares of a doubtful parentage, for it seems certain that several ostriches lay their eggs together in the same excavation in the sand. Levaillant watched a whole night in a thicket in order to observe the manœuvres of these birds, and saw four females betake themselves to the same heap of eggs; "they relieved each other in succession," says this traveller.[1] The male is equally called upon to make up for the indolence of his mate; he sits upon the eggs also: a nurse of the opposite sex.

The long-eared owls (*Strix bubo*, Linn.), and the great owls (*Strix otus*, Linn.), are scarcely more interested in their nidification. Almost all these nocturnal idlers simply deposit their eggs upon the dust which time has accumulated in the nooks of rocks or caverns; others install themselves in ruined chateaux or churches; some content themselves with the holes afforded by the decaying trunks of aged trees. The

[1] The traveller Levaillant counted as many as thirty-eight eggs in an ostrich's nest, which leads to the inference that several females were concerned in laying them. His observations and those of Sparmann prove that the males take upon themselves the duty of incubation. Both these travellers surprised males on the nests; and the latter of the two saw as many traces of the one sex as of the other at these places, showing that they are equally frequented by males and females.

barn-owl (*Strix flammea*, Linn.), a little less careless, before laying, covers with a thin layer of moss the bare stone of the obscure vault in the depths of which she rears a brood that dread the light.

128. Nest of the Common Wren—*Troglodytes Europæus* (Cuvier).

The birds of the tribe to which quails, partridges, and hens belong, are all very clumsy workmen, contenting themselves with exposing their broods on miserable litter, or on the arid soil itself. The beautiful doves themselves scarcely take more care of their progeny. Their nests, negligently placed on the boughs, consist of a platform of loosely laid twigs, without moss or down, in which the egg, exposed to the air on all sides, seems every instant in danger of falling. It is the handiwork of a

129. Nest of the Barn-owl—*Strix flammea* (Linnæus).—From the Rouen Museum.

thoughtless beauty, whose couch seems as if it would be more likely to freeze than warm her young family.

We find more extent but not more intelligence in the buildings executed by the great carnivorous birds, such as the eagles, goshawks,

130. Nest of the Goshawk—*Astur palumbarius* (Bonaparte).
From the Rouen Museum.

and falcons—the lords of the air. Fierce and solitary, the former perch their nests in the midst of the most horrible precipices, without dreading either the roar of the cataract or the crash of the avalanche. The bulk of the work and the mass of the materials employed are in proportion to the strength of the architect. The eyry of the eagle is a heap of great branches of trees carelessly flung together, forming a thick rude mattress, twelve to fifteen feet in circumference. This nest serves the couple which build it for their whole lives, but its size increases with years, because the bones of all the animals brought thither by the parents and devoured by the hungry family, are heaped up round it in such a manner, that at a certain lapse of time the eyry of one of these robbers becomes a pestilential charnel-house.

The nests built by the goshawk display even less skill: it employs only little faggots, and yet its nest is four feet in circumference.

Some of our idlers, resolved to do no work at all, become nothing more nor less than thieves; others, more courageous, are regular brigands. The latter attack face to face the enemy they want to devour; or throw their victim from the window in order to take possession of its domicile.

To this legion belong the voracious butcher-birds of our woods, which slaughter so many little birds and spit their bodies on the thorns of our thickets.

In the ranks of the most obstinate thieves we must place the sparrow. Linnæus and Gmelin relate as an established fact, that before the return of the swallows, a sparrow will sometimes take possession of the dwelling deserted by the travellers. Here it installs itself, and when the legitimate proprietors return, threatens to cut them open with its powerful bill. The plundered swallows call their companions in the vicinity to their help. Then begins the siege of the place; some retain the enemy a prisoner, whilst others occupy themselves in walling up the doorway with quantities of pellets of earth, and in a very short time the usurper, closely imprisoned in the nest he has invaded, dies of asphyxia.[1]

But of all these winged spoilers the most cruel is the cuckoo. The mode in which it proceeds is as follows:—

This idle and savage inhabitant of our woods does not care either to

[1] Although this story has been accepted as authentic by Gmelin, the laborious commentator on Linnæus, as well as by several French savants, Spallanzani, in his *Mémoires sur les Hirondelles,* regards it as doubtful. "It is true," he says, "that sparrows not unfrequently take possession of the nests before the arrival of the swallows. But the legitimate masters at once make a stir, going to and fro about the sparrows, picking quarrels with them, and ending by making them give up possession."—Spallanzani, *Voyages dans les Deux Siciles.* Paris, an viii. t. 6, p. 22.

build a nest, to hatch its eggs, or to feed its young. By means of trickery it hands over this necessary task to other birds, and it is always upon species of the smallest size that it imposes the charge from which it frees itself.

The most illustrious naturalists, both of antiquity and modern times, had already remarked that the cuckoo makes itself master of a strange nest, the legitimate proprietors of which are sacrificed for the benefit of the invader's progeny. But it is only recently that these odious wiles have been clearly unveiled.

Nature, niggardly with regard to the cuckoo, has only allotted it two eggs. Here, however, a wise foresight may be recognized, for in order to rear its two little ones, a good number of others are barbarously sacrificed.

It is the nest of the golden-crested or common wren that this bird selects for the accomplishment of its designs, and it only deposits one egg in it.

Here a curious problem presents itself. The nests of these charming visitors of our groves are too narrow to admit of a bird so large as the cuckoo either entering one, or resting upon it in order to lay; how then did it manage to introduce its progeny? Levaillant quite despaired of being able to penetrate this mystery, when chance furnished him with an opportunity of doing so. The celebrated traveller, having killed a female golden cuckoo in Africa, found in its gullet an unbroken egg which he recognized as that of the bird itself, and his negro assured him that frequently, when killing these cuckoos on the wing, he had seen the eggs fall from their mouths.

A modest savant, M. Florent Prevost, to whom we owe extensive and interesting observations, has discovered that the same thing takes place with respect to our common cuckoo. He has noticed that the female lays her egg on the ground, and then takes it in her beak, places it in her gullet, and deposits it in the nest of the insectivorous species of which she makes choice.

Pliny relates at length, that when the young cuckoo is in the midst of the little family of the titmouse, the latter seeing it so strong and handsome, sacrifices, from a sentiment of maternal vanity, all her other little ones to it, and allows it to devour them before her eyes, falling herself a prey to it in the end.

Such is the fiction. Let us abandon it for the reality, which is no less extraordinary, and which was revealed to us by a man of deathless fame—Jenner, the discoverer of vaccination.

It is not the mother but the young cuckoo that undertakes the assassination. The great physician describes the process in the *Philosophical Transactions* as follows:—"The young cuckoo, a few hours after its birth, tries by the aid of its rump and wings to glide beneath

131. Cuckoo killing Golden-crested Wrens.

the little bird whose cradle it shares, and to get the latter upon its back, where it keeps it by raising its wings. It then works itself backward to the edge of the nest, raises itself up for an instant, then making an effort, expels its load from the nest. After this feat it rests for a few moments, as if to assure itself of the success of its attempt."

The spoiler displays frightful perseverance in accomplishing its work of destruction, it toils at it incessantly and ejects everything from its cradle. Colonel Montague saw a young cuckoo, with indefatigable perseverance, for four whole days continue to expel a newly hatched swallow, which he took care to replace each time beside it; after this period it lived on the best of terms with its little companion.

Now as the brood of each wren numbers about ten, it results that, to rear its progeny, the cuckoo sacrifices every year a score of young birds. This is the reason why it has drawn down upon itself general dislike, and has, in Germany, with good ground, become the symbol of ingratitude.

According to the authors of the *General Dictionary of the Sciences*, the female cuckoo sometimes takes upon herself the task of massacring the little ones which are already hatched at the time when she deposits her eggs in the nests.

CHAPTER V.

ARCHITECTURE INTENDED FOR ENJOYMENT.

Maternal love, as we have seen, works prodigies, and neglects nothing requisite for the welfare and protection of the family. But we come now to birds which devote time and labour merely to luxury and pleasure, and which, instead of ingeniously contrived nests, build elegant groves intended only for enjoyment—for promenades, tender pastimes, and love-meetings.

The most skilful of these builders of bowers, of these ornithological Le Nostres, is the Spotted Chlamydera, or bower-bird, which is very like our partridge. It may, however, be distinguished at the first view by its deep-coloured plumage, set off by clear spots and a pretty rose-tinted collar.

The couple proceed in an orderly way to build their arbour. They usually set it up in an exposed place, to enjoy the sun and heat better. Their first care is to make a pavement of rounded shells of tolerably equal size; when the surface and thickness of this are sufficiently forward, they begin planting a little avenue of branches. For this purpose they are seen bringing in from the fields fine shoots of trees about the same size,

132. Nuptial Arbour of the Spotted Bower-birds -- *Chlamydera maculata.*—From Gould.

the thick ends of which they thrust firmly in between the interstices of the pebbles. The birds arrange these branches in two parallel rows, making them all bend one towards another, so as to resemble a miniature avenue. This improvised plantation is about a yard long, and of such breadth that the two lovers can amuse themselves, or promenade side by side beneath the shelter of its shade.

So soon as ever the arbour is finished, the amorous couple think about embellishing it. For this purpose they wander through the country in every direction, and appropriate every brilliant object they meet with in order to decorate the entrance. Gleaming mother-of-pearl shells are special objects of predilection; hence the outlets of the bower are provided with a thick shining layer of them.

If these novel decorators find any beautiful birds' feathers in the fields, they collect and hang them up like flowers to the dry twig-ends of their abodes. One thing is quite certain; every brightly coloured or shining object on which the sun has accidentally cast its rays is immediately carried off. Mr. Gould even told me that, in the districts where these birds build, if a traveller chance to lose his watch, his knife, or seal, it is useless to look in the place where they have been dropped: they are certain to have been carried off by the bower-birds of the district, and are always to be found in the nearest of their bowers.

The discovery of this arbour of love being quite an unexpected fact in ornithology, Mr. Gould was afraid that his narrative might be received in Europe with suspicion; he was accordingly anxious to bring proofs for it. For this purpose, having carried away one of these promenades, or "runs," he contrived, by dint of infinite care, to transport it to the British Museum, where it can now be admired.

So soon as people became acquainted with the work itself they wanted to make trial of the workmen. One of these rustic architects was brought alive to the Zoological Gardens at London. It was placed in a large room surrounded by all the materials necessary for its edifice, but the poor bird made a very sorry affair of it; the air and sun of its country were wanting, and, above all, it had no companion. Its spirit was gone. When I saw it, to plant a few branches irregularly in a heap of stones and earth which it had collected was as much as it could do.

CHAPTER VI.

NAVAL ARCHITECTURE.

Many very inexact statements have been made about the naval architecture of certain birds. Fiction has dethroned truth, and yet the latter is infinitely more interesting than the tales which have been substituted for it.

One of the most hardy inhabitants of our fens, the water-hen (*Fulica chloropus*), awakens surprise by the form and elegance of the nest which she plants sometimes near the edge of the water, sometimes on its surface. In the former case these nests are so many little altars raised above the ground, and covered over by an arbour of reeds, the bent leaves of which form an elegant little vault of verdure above the brood. In other cases, floating on the surface of some pond and almost totally concealed from sight by a hedge of young reeds, they have the entrance, by a peculiarity met with nowhere else, adorned with a long train of reeds, sloping from the edge of the nest into the water, and forming a kind of ladder by which the family are enabled to mount to their resting-place, after swimming home.

It has often been repeated in old works on natural history that the reed warbler (*Motacilla arundinacea*) fixes its nest, which is of interlaced grasses, to the reeds, and that the elegant cradle, filled with the young, floats on the surface of our streams, rising or falling along with the supporting plants according as the water rises or falls, but always swimming on the surface and preserving the young from shipwreck.

This is not correct, however. The nest of the warbler displays an ingenious structure, and that is all. It is formed of tangled grass, and is always fixed near the top of three stems of the common reed. It is in this that the pretty little female hatches her eggs in security. But its nest neither rises nor falls upon the tripod of plants which it binds closely together, and if it did it would not float, being quite permeable by water, so that the brood would be drowned.

The ancient authors, both poets and historians, have often celebrated other floating nests, viz. those of the Halcyon, the bird that delighted to live in the midst of the waves, rocked with its nestlings in the floating cradle which it intrusted to the sea. In their charming fables they relate

133. Nest of the Reed Warbler—*Motacilla arundinacea* (Gmelin).

From the Rouen Museum.

134. **Floating Nests of the Little Grebe**—*Colymbus minor* (Gmelin).—From an original sketch by M. Nourry of Elbœuf.

that it was towards the setting of the Pleiades that the bird of the storm built it. Then the murmur of the waves ceased, and the winds grew silent, in order that the work of God might be accomplished on a tranquil sea. These were the beautiful days which in the East occur at the winter solstice, and which the pilots called "the days of the Halcyon."

"These nests," says Pliny, "are worthy of admiration; they have the shape of a ball and resemble a large sponge. They cannot be cut with iron, but a violent shock shivers them." Plutarch believed that they were composed only of fish-bones interlaced; but it appears that the philosopher mistook the carapaces of the sea-urchin which are often brought ashore by the waves for the nests of the Halcyon.

Though it is now well known that the Halcyon of antiquity, which is nothing more than our kingfisher, does not commit a floating nest to the sea, the ardent ornithologists who study the habits of the dwellers in our fens have discovered some species, the marvellous nidification of which outstrips even that fabled to be practised by the Halcyon.

This is the case with the nest of the little grebe. This swimming bird hatches its young upon a regular raft. It is a mass of strong stems of aquatic plants closely united together, and as these contain a considerable amount of air in their ample and numerous cells, and as, in addition, they set free gases during the process of rotting, these aëriform fluids, imprisoned by the plants, make the nest lighter than water. It is found floating in lonely spots where the tall rushes and great reeds grow. There, in her improvised craft, the female, upborne on her watery bed, tranquilly broods on her offspring. But if any intruder happen to discover her, if anything threaten her safety, the wild bird plunges one of her feet into the water, and makes use of it as a paddle with which she transports her dwelling to a distance. The little sailor guides her frail skiff whither she likes, sometimes dragging along a perfect sheet of water-plants with her. The whole structure looks like a little floating island carried away by the labour of the grebe which moves in the centre of a mass of verdure.

Thus the truth is more extraordinary than fiction.[1]

[1] All the details related here as to the little grebe (*Colymbus minor*) were given me by M. Nourry, director of the museum of natural history at Elbœuf. The sketch representing the nests of this bird was also executed by this distinguished ornithologist, who often lived in the midst of the forests in order to study the manners of birds unobserved.

CHAPTER VII.

MINERS AND MASONS.

Every traveller who approaches the shores of the southern seas is struck by the sight of the innumerable flocks of penguins which swarm upon them.

Birds in their radical organization, they are quite fish in their habits. Their wings, transformed into fins, render them unfit for flight, and their feet are only suited for swimming. Hence, not being able to rise in the air, or escape by running, they stumble and fall to the ground at every step they take when they are trying to escape from some aggressor. The sailors calculate upon their falling, when they wish to kill them, and often make a complete massacre of them. But matters are quite different when the penguins gain the water, their favourite element. They precipitate themselves into it from the tops of rocks ten to fifteen feet above the waves, and having reached the sea, dive and swim with a swiftness which mocks that of the largest fish, and utterly confounds the smaller ones—their habitual prey.

Seated on their tails, and always in an upright position on the shore, these birds, scattered about in innumerable bands, with their white bellies and their black cowls and cloaks, recall the costume of certain religious bodies; a fact which has made sailors often compare them to a procession of penitents.

Excellent swimmers, but bad walkers, penguins, not being able to build either in trees or on the sea, have been obliged to content themselves with the shore. Of too limited a capacity to weave a nest, they are satisfied, being simply miners, with scooping out a hole in the ground.

It is generally on desert islands covered with grass that these animals establish their subterranean abodes. They hollow these out by means of their beak and feet just beneath the ground, and make them sometimes as much as three feet deep. The interior by its form gives one the idea of an oven, of which the narrow and depressed entrance well represents the door. From every cavern proceeds a concealed road, carried through the tall grass and covered by the tops of it. It is by these tortuous and shady paths that the birds pass from their nests to the shore.

135. Nests of the Red Flamingo—*Phœnicopterus ruber* (Cuvier).

These subterranean works have multiplied to such an extent in some localities, that it often happens that the sailors sink in when walking. The penguin, disturbed by this unexpected invasion, throws itself upon the imprudent mortal who has broken into its abode, and frequently the visitor cannot withdraw his leg till he has received some smart wounds from the sharp blows of its beak. More than one mariner has left a portion of his trousers behind him.

The tribe of masons is very numerous, and these winged architects employ very various materials in their edifices. Many, like the ancient Germans, construct their buildings only with earth or clay. Others make use of plants after having worked them into a pulp like mortar or mastic.

The most powerful, but at the same time the clumsiest, of all our race of masons is the flamingo, the rude constructions of which we pardon for the sake of its splendid plumage, tinted with rose colour and brilliant red. This great wader, gorgeous troops of which enjoy themselves on the shores of hot countries, usually builds its nest not far from the sea, and arranges it in a very peculiar way, as its monstrously long legs would not adapt themselves to the ordinary style of nest-building.

Flamingoes place their nests upon the ground, and build them solely of coarsely tempered mud. These nests are very curiously shaped, being like a narrow, lengthened cone, and are about 20 inches in height; their truncated summit presents a concavity, at the bottom of which the female deposits two or three white eggs. In order to hatch them she places her abdomen over them, and allows her legs to hang down on both sides of the raised cone which forms her edifice.

Our visitants the swallows are more skilful builders than the flamingoes. The little nuptial chambers which they construct beneath the cornices of our windows, or in the pointed arches of our churches, are made of pure earth, which they pick out bit by bit on the bank of the river. Who knows in the course of how many journeys?

The Salanganes or esculent swallows, which inhabit China and the neighbouring islands, build nests which resemble so many little bowls, which they affix by thousands to inaccessible rocks, or in sombre caverns, as if to hide their chaste loves from every gaze.

These nests are formed of a dirty white substance, which seems exactly analogous to isinglass reduced to filaments agglutinated to one another; this singular appearance has made people ascribe them to the most diverse sources. They seemed so odd to Kæmpfer that he would not believe in them; the celebrated explorer of Japan insisted that they were made artificially from the flesh of various Polypi.

M. Poivre, who to the title of Governor of the Isle of France, united another which conferred far higher renown upon him—that of a distinguished philosopher, was the first who cleared up the history of the Salanganes, and gathered some of their nests with his own hands; but he was mistaken in supposing that these swallows built them of fish-spawn, an opinion which long prevailed.

It was M. Lamouroux who, first of all, in 1821 gave us an exact account of the composition of these extraordinary nests. He found out

136. Edible Nests of the Salangane—*Hirundo esculenta* (Latham).

that the birds build them of various marine plants which they gather in the waves, belonging chiefly to the genera Gelidium and Sphærococcus. These the swallows bear away from the surface, while skimming over the billows, gulp down, and afterwards disgorge, mixed with their digestive fluids, which render them glutinous and facilitate the building of the maternal homes.

The gathering of these nests is dangerous, because the swallows often place them in the depths of inaccessible caverns, into which it is

137. Nests of the Party-coloured Wren—*Regulus omnicolor* (Vieillot).
From the Rouen Museum.

necessary to slide by a rope, or descend by means of long bamboo-ladders. The Chinese, who make a business of collecting them, only begin after they have secured the protection of the gods by certain preliminary sacrifices, and perfumed the entrance to the caverns with benzoin or other odoriferous substances.

The nests of these swallows have acquired great celebrity on account of the use to which they are put in China for food. There they are an indispensable ornament of every grand repast. Their price is very high, so that persons who own caverns frequented by these swallows derive considerable revenues from them. Broken up into little morsels, they take the place of rice or tapioca in soup, and their taste greatly resembles that of the latter.[1]

But the most charming of our aërial masons is assuredly the party-coloured wren, crowned with its brilliant crest of gold. Its nests resemble so many wide-mouthed extinguishers reversed, and glued by one side to the stems of reeds. These little breeding-cups are composed of bits of grass pasted together with mud and saliva, forming a thin wall almost as hard as cardboard—a transition step to the nests of the esculent swallow.

There are also workers which employ mixed materials, and which we do not know how to classify. Among these is the common thrush. Externally its beautiful nest is formed entirely of tufts of moss, as if it were to be a luxurious structure; internally it is lined with a compact coating of earth, on which the brood lie naked, as if the parents dreaded the effect which the heat of down would have upon them. This bird is therefore only half a mason, and its nest is a perfect architectural anomaly in the class to which the bird belongs; since in this class the parents usually deposit their progeny on a soft and warm bed of down, while it places them on a surface cold and quite bare.

We have, at the beginning of this chapter, seen that there is a web-footed bird which hollows out a kind of oven under the soil, in which incubation takes place. An American sparrow is still more ingenious; it builds one. It is a regular mason, and hence the name of *oven-builder*

[1] These birds are found in great abundance in all parts of the Eastern Archipelago, and also on the continent of India; the nests are collected in large quantities, and constitute an important article of commerce with China. The prices paid for these nests in the Canton market vary greatly according to the quality: those of the best and purest sort fetch the enormous price of 3500 Spanish dollars (=4*s.* 6*d.* each) per pecul, or about 25 dollars per pound; the second quality brings 2800 Spanish dollars per pecul, and the third not more than 1600 dollars. In some parts of China, however, as much as 40 dollars has been paid for a catty of birds' nests, or rather more than one pound and a quarter.—*Goodrich.*

has naturally been given to it. It is a more robust workman than the swallow. It is astonishing what a number of journeys it must make to

138. Burrowing-owl—*Strix cunicularia* (Ch. Bonaparte), and Section of its Burrow.

carry to the tops of the trees the tempered, almost pure, earth of which its family-dwelling is composed. The oven-bird is the size of a quail. Its hemispherical nests, placed in the bifurcation of large branches of trees, are more than eight inches in diameter, and weigh from three to four pounds. Even if such a building cannot be compared in point of labour to that of the Megàpodius, it is nevertheless remarkable for its compact masonry and for its opening being exactly similar to the mouth of a baker's oven.

Prince Charles Bonaparte has made us acquainted with a charming and curious little owl, which ought also to be placed in the category we are speaking of. It is a revolted child which disdains all the traditions of its family, and which; in spite of an owl's nocturnal livery, deserts the ancient ruin and the obscurity of the cave, to hunt in full day and by a bright light which would blind its comrades. This species abounds in the Mississippi regions, where it shelters itself in subterranean abodes several yards in depth, the entrance to which is crowned by a mound of earth. It is called the burrowing-owl (*Strix cunicularia*); nevertheless it does not strictly merit the appellation, for it is often simply a spoiler, installing itself in the villages of the marmots or prairie-dogs, which it probably drives away. What is certain is that, according to this illustrious ornithologist, the two animals do not live together, but when menaced by a common danger the marmot and owl squat at the bottom of the same hiding hole, where they are sometimes found surrounded by the most unexpected guests: in the midst of a company of toads, rattlesnakes, and lizards!

CHAPTER VIII.

WEAVERS.

Many birds construct for their nests a kind of canvas, composed of grasses twisted together in a very compact manner, resembling a coarse cloth woven upon the loom of some primitive tribe. These are in truth weavers who work up vegetable fibre like wool or cotton, possessing only their beaks for shuttles, and using them with great activity in order to interlace the fine stems of the grasses, and form a sort of textile fabric, very thick and very difficult to tear. The tissue, notwithstanding its complicated character, is made very rapidly, the workman passing and repassing its beak with extreme swiftness through its substance, so as densely to interlace all the fibres. One never tires contemplating the dexterity it displays. These winged workers construct different kinds of dwellings. Some consist of a sort of purse, having in the interior a little pannier affixed to its sides, in which the female places her brood. In this case the entrance is frequently situated at the lower part, which represents a kind of wide-mouthed funnel, by which the wedded pair enter and leave the family mansion: this is the fashion adopted by some Troopials. Others are simply long and wide sacks with one or more openings, suspended to the branches of trees.

139. Nest of the *Fondia erythrops* (Bonaparte).—From the Rouen Museum.

On this account the name of weavers has been given to a tribe of sparrows remarkable for the perfection of their work, but other birds imitate their industry although they belong to different families.

Some weavers, less skilful, content themselves with twisting grass rudely together, and forming a little cup of it, in which the female lies deeply ensconced. It is in this that she carefully hatches her eggs. The *Fondia erythrops* builds one of these nests of imperfect tissue.

140. Nest of a Troopial.—From the Rouen Museum.

The Cassicans and the Baltimore-bird deserve to be mentioned in the first rank among another kind of workmen, on account of the large bag-

141. Nest of the Baltimore-bird—*Icterus Baltimore.*

shaped nests which they hang to the trees, and in which they rear their young.

The nests of the Crested Cassican (*C. cristatus*) are built of dry grass, and resemble very long sacks bulging out at the base, having an entrance in the form of a slit of considerable length, situated above and placed laterally in such a manner that the rain runs over the edges and cannot penetrate into the interior of this vast family domicile. These nests are sometimes more than two yards long. They are fastened to the branches of trees, and from a distance look like strange fruits of enormous size. Thus when the birds are numerous in a district, and they build a great number of nests, these, suspended in the midst of the foliage of the trees, impart to the intertropical landscape an aspect very peculiar, and indeed unique.

The nests of the Baltimore-bird are shorter and formed of delicately twisted down; here we have an artisan that works more elegantly than the other, and requires a warmer and more luxurious bed. Its buildings have the aspect of coarsely knitted sacks of wool attached to the branches by a large surface, and having a wide and rounded opening.

BOOK VII.

THE MIGRATIONS OF ANIMALS.

Many animals, impelled by imperious demands, or by an instinctive irresistible force, quit their habitual residence at a certain time, and direct their way to distant regions. Such migrations, the object of which eludes our observation, are noticed in nearly all classes of the animal kingdom. Usually they are seen to take place periodically, but at other times they only occur, as it were, accidentally, and all at once astonish the inhabitants of the countries which are the theatre of them, and into which the unexpected invaders carry sometimes devastation, famine, and death.

At other times it is violence that compels legions of animals to quit the place where they had established themselves. In the countries where man does not decimate them, they swarm in such abundance, and are so crowded together, that one can scarcely understand how they exist; their numbers are alarming. The pictures that Livingstone has drawn of the exuberance of game in wild districts of Central Africa, and in particular on the banks of the Zambesi, suffice to give us an idea of the fecundity of nature. But this very fecundity is fatal to the weak tribes; the stronger ones, getting the upper hand, drive them away or annihilate them. They have no choice left, and thus forced migrations arise.

Civilization proceeds in the same manner. Animals disappear as it advances. It drives them back, or utterly destroys them. Many large species which found shelter in the former forests of Gaul, the aurochs and others, have vanished from our land. We only find now the crumbling bones of these wild mammals which our sturdy forefathers hunted.

When animals perform their journeys annually we observe an amount of order and foresight which are not seen in erratic migrations. During these latter the whole colony sometimes expires, overcome by the elements or hunger; not a single individual ever sees again the country which the tribe quitted in innumerable columns. In the former, on the contrary, instructed by an experience from which all profit, the journey is performed with a degree of order that fills us with astonishment.

The arrangement observed by wild geese in traversing the air, when they are making their way to a distant country, shows that they possess a certain power of mental combination. They are placed one behind the other in two long oblique lines, which form an acute angle in front, the most suitable form for cleaving the air. And as the individual placed at the head of the phalanx exerts himself more than the others to open the path, he is observed, so soon as he finds himself fatigued, to drop behind and take the last place, while another succeeds to his.

I thought there was perhaps more poetry than truth in what the old naturalists have related on this head, but having, on the banks of the Nile, frequently seen flocks of geese traverse the air on their route to Nubia, I was enabled to verify the accuracy of their narrations.

I have also observed, that when these travellers, worn out with fatigue, rested at different places on the banks of the river, there were placed all around the dense crowd of sleeping birds motionless sentinels, which, with watchful ear and keen look-out, carefully scanned the neighbourhood, and gave the alarm to the whole camp so soon as an enemy approached. Our hunters tried to surprise them, but always in vain. Long before they were within gun-shot, these vigilant sentries were seen to raise their necks, watch those approaching, hesitate a few moments, beating their wings, and then with a low cry take wing, when all the troop of emigrants followed.

Nevertheless, it is probable that the ancient Egyptians, more skilful than we are, succeeded in capturing these travelling bands. In fact, among the paintings or hieroglyphs on the monuments of the Pharaohs, we frequently find represented wild goose-fowling with the net, and people carrying these birds in panniers to market for sale. Lepsius, in his beautiful work on Egypt, has reproduced some of these fowling scenes from the paintings and bass-reliefs of Beni-Hassan and the great pyramids of Gizeh.

Some insects, when they remove from their dwellings, observe a degree of order which is no less remarkable. One species of the order Lepidoptera has become celebrated on account of the law which its larvæ

142. Catching Wild Geese, from a painting in the Subterranean Temples of Beni-Hassan.—Lepsius, "Monuments of Egypt and Ethiopia."

constantly follow during their peregrinations. When the troop issues from the lair or sack in which the whole family have been sheltered in a mass, one caterpillar marches at the head; then come two; after that three; next four abreast, the squadrons always augmenting and marching regularly one after the other. Their files, which sometimes stretch out for a length of thirty to forty feet, in this way make numerous windings over the downs and roads, imitating the order of a procession in movement. This has procured for the butterfly which gives birth to this dangerous cohort the name of Processionary Bombyx. When they are encountered, it is necessary to let them alone, for neither man nor animal can disturb their march, or even approach them without being severely punished for it. The hairs which cover these caterpillars become detached during their evolutions and float all about the army; it is extremely dangerous to inhale them, for when any enter the lungs an obstinate and distressing cough immediately ensues, which goes to the verge of suffocation.

An irresistible desire to change their locality or country is usually seen only in animals in the full flush of strength. Nevertheless, it is also observed in certain young creatures just hatched. This takes place in spring among the eels. The progeny of this fish, the life-history of which is not yet fully unravelled, pass up our rivers at this time in such compact swarms that all the travellers seem to touch each other; anything like numbering them would be impossible.

Near the steep banks of the Seine these young eels form a band quite a yard wide which sometimes takes more than a week to pass the neighbourhood of Rouen, and after that time these millions of animals suddenly disappear without leaving any trace. Whence does this animated milky way reach us, and what becomes of this diaphanous and scarcely developed brood? This is as yet an impenetrable secret.[1]

Our commercial relations with distant countries also favour the migrations of certain animals, but still not to such an extent as one might be tempted to think. Transported to a strange climate, they mostly die: the cold freezes some, the heat suffocates others. It is not uncommon to see in European ports some serpent or spider from tropical countries, which our ships have disembarked along with their cargoes of dyewoods. But stupified by the want of sunshine these exiles soon die, regretting their happier country.

[1] According to M. Coste a single pound of the fry contains about 1800 little eels. This progeny, looking like thread-worms, inspires some persons with disgust. In some countries they are fished for by torch-light and used for food. In Caen, where this takes place, the fry is sold in the markets and streets in large buckets. Its price varies according to the yield of the fishery; generally it is sold at about a franc a quart. It is eaten in different ways, prepared with white sauce, fried, and even made into patés.

CHAPTER I.

MIGRATIONS OF MAMMALS.

Generally speaking, heavy and bulky mammals are not prone to quit their haunts; travelling is difficult to them, and being sufficiently powerful not to fear any enemy, they rest peacefully quartered in spots where suitable food is found. This is the case with the great aquatic herbivorous animals, which require two essential conditions in one and the same place—food and water. Where these exist they found a colony.

Such are the Hippopotami which are found living in numerous and peaceful families in the rivers of Central Africa. There, giving themselves up to all the happiness of a tranquil life, some bathe or play amid the tall herbage; whilst the mothers tenderly carry their little ones on their backs at the surface of the water.

The numerous tribe of kangaroos are equally attached to their native soil. Their disproportionately long hind-legs, it is true, enable them to leap with great agility, but their fore-feet are too small to allow of long journeys. And besides this, the virgin soil of Australia always provides them with abundant nourishment in the midst of its lofty herbage.

The most remarkable thing is that those mammals which seem endowed with the greatest facilities for moving from place to place, are precisely those which lead the most restricted life in this respect. We mean the bats, which, although they possess wings large enough, are never known to quit the site they have chosen. Thus the Nycteris of Upper Egypt, which can make itself exceedingly buoyant by filling with air certain pouches under its skin, scarcely quits the sombre windings of the pyramids and temples of ancient Egypt, where it sometimes swarms in such numbers as to extinguish, when flitting about, the torches carried by the travellers.

But some mammals, though placed in circumstances much less favourable than other animals, nevertheless effect migrations, the magnitude of which, and the intelligence they display, awaken astonishment and admiration.

Nothing presents a more imposing spectacle than the immense troops of bisons which traverse the savannahs of Louisiana. When the time appointed by the decree of Providence arrives, one of these savage mammals constitutes himself chief of the emigrating troop. His roars resound through the vales of the Meschacebé, and he soon gathers round him a formidable troop, ready to follow him across the wilderness. "When the moment arrives," says Chateaubriand, "the leader, shaking his mane, which hangs from every part over his eyes and curving horns, salutes the setting sun by lowering his head and lifting up his back like a mountain; at the same time a dull sound, the signal of departure, issues from his deep chest, and then all at once he plunges into the foaming waves,

143. Nycteris of Upper Egypt—*Nycteris Geoffroyi* (Desmarest).

followed by the multitude of heifers and bulls which roar lovingly after him."

The migrations of the squirrels which fill with life the forests of old Scandinavia, if less noisy, are marked by more ingenuity.

Whilst the formidable bisons overturn everything that lies in their way, colonies of squirrels, timid and silent, run a thousand risks in order to establish themselves far from their natal soil. Travellers assure us that, in America and Lapland, when a river checks their passage, each member of the wandering family transforms some fragment of wood or bark into a raft, displays its large tail to the wind, by way of sail, and the little living flotilla, carried by the breath of the zephyr, thus reaches the opposite bank.[1]

These pretty mammals of Lapland, the lemmings, which are not much larger than mice, accomplish still more extraordinary and daring migrations. At a certain period of the year these adventurers, urged by a mysterious instinct, descend from the mountains in troops so numerous that over considerable spaces of country the face of the land is absolutely covered by the compact moving army. Always advancing without halt or pause, no obstacle checks them; neither rivers, lakes, nor arms of the sea; a hundred enemies decimate them, a hundred dangers threaten them, but nothing stays their course; the long living lines formed by their troops advance just the same towards the spot they fatally wish to reach.

Astonished at the sudden irruption of these innumerable legions of rodents which devastate everything in their path, the rude inhabitants

144. Lemming—*Myodes lemmus.*

of the North believe that this plague falls from heaven. It is particularly when a premature winter produces a dearth in the high-lying districts that the lemmings reach the lower lands.

These emigrants are all animated with an amount of courage one

[1] Linnæus himself seems to believe in this remarkable migration of squirrels. Regnard observed the fact during his travels in Lapland. "When it is necessary," he says, "to pass some lake or river, as happens at every step in Lapland, these little animals take the bark of a pine or birch tree, which they drag to the brink of the water; they then set themselves upon it and abandon themselves to the mercy of the wind, erecting their tails like sails. Sometimes the wind, becoming too strong, overturns both the ship and the pilot. This shipwreck, which very often overwhelms 3000 or 4000 vessels, generally brings an extraordinary influx of wealth to those Laplanders who find the remains on the shore, and who, if the little animals have not been too long on the sand, make use of them for food, &c. Many of these animals make a successful voyage and arrive safe in harbour, provided the wind be favourable and not strong enough to raise any waves, which need not be violent in order to engulf these little craft. This singular performance might be considered as a fable if I had not witnessed it myself."—Regnard, *Voyage en Lapponie.* Paris, 1820, p. 202.

would not expect to find in such puny creatures. They advance in a straight line, climb rocks, pass rivers by swimming, and defend themselves against every one who attacks them. Even man himself, when he bars their way, does not alarm them, and they will bite his stick with their feeble teeth.

When the departure coincides with the birth of the young, maternal love effects prodigies; each mother takes a little one in her mouth and carries another on her back.

But so much courage, energy, and perseverance generally end only in disasters. The emigrants leave behind them a long line of corpses; very few ever see their mountains again. Many become the prey of foxes, fish, and carnivorous birds; others perish in the midst of the waves, or are decimated by hunger and fatigue; sometimes even death mows them down in such prodigious numbers that the very air is infected with them.

CHAPTER II.

MIGRATIONS OF BIRDS.

No animals display so much power and instinct in their distant excursions as birds; their migrations are really something marvellous. It is only by the aid of accurate instruments and knotty calculations that the sailor trusts himself upon the sea; whereas our winged travellers, without guide or compass, and without ever losing their way, transport themselves from the polar circle to the tropical regions. The cranes pass the summer on the stormy strands of Scandinavia and the winter amid the ruins of the palaces of the Pharaohs.

The mechanism of birds is admirably suited to aid their rapid flight. Their aërial oars, moved by muscles of extraordinary power, easily adapt themselves to all the hazards of their peregrinations through the elevated regions of air. There are birds, as the swallow, for instance, to which flight is so easy that they seem to make a sport of it. A passive force further assists their suspension in the plains of the atmosphere; air, rarefied by the warmth of the body, penetrates into all its cavities and even to the interior of the bones. Rendered thus specifically lighter, like Montgolfier balloons filled with warm gas, they float without effort amid the clouds. Such is the daring flight of the condors which launch themselves from the frozen summits of the Andes towards the sky, and soon disappear from sight, without one's being able to explain how they can breathe so rarefied an atmosphere.

The bird, though endowed with such a slight frame, nevertheless

145. Crane's Nest on an Egyptian Monument.

surpasses in strength the ponderous engines which glide along our rail roads. Its vessels and fibres, notwithstanding their wonderful delicacy, work and resist more energetically than our heavy wheel-work and cast-

146. The Condor or Great Vulture of the Andes—*Vultur gryphus* (Linnæus).

iron tubes; in the one is seen the finger of God, in the other only the genius of man! Launched like an arrow into space, the bird, playing the while, silently clears twenty leagues an hour. A locomotive going at high pressure, enveloped in fire and smoke, attains the same speed only by consuming heaps of coke and water amid the infernal uproar of its wheels and pistons.

According to Sir Hans Sloane, the sea-mews which nestle on the rocks of Barbadoes take every day a journey over the sea of 130 leagues, to amuse themselves and seek for food on a distant island. The animal thus casts in the shade the results of man's ingenuity.

On their adventurous excursions birds follow their track unerringly, guided by sensations of an unknown nature and of extreme delicacy, among which sight and smell play a great part. Historians relate that after the battle of Pharsalia, the putrid emanations from the dead heaped upon the ground attracted the vultures from Asia and Africa, which came thither to make their repast. It is certain, according to Humboldt, that if a horse or cow be killed in the most solitary passes of the Cordilleras where one might think not even condors could exist, several of these sordid carnivorous birds, attracted by the stench, are soon seen arriving in order to gorge themselves with the putrefied flesh.

The migrations of certain birds are understood; we know from whence they start, where they halt, and where they end their journey. Thus, for instance, in autumn, bands of quails which are emigrating, constantly arrive exhausted at the island of Malta, where they meet with fatal hospitality. They are taken in swarms in the streets of the town and on the roads, and as the inhabitants cannot consume the whole of this living harvest, it is sent to distant markets. The deck of the ship in which I left the harbour was laden with them.

The mysterious emigration of the swallows has particularly occupied the attention of observers. Men could not make out what became of these charming visitors when they suddenly disappeared, and not long ago the strangest suppositions were indulged in on this head.

As these birds in autumn seek their insect prey in the fens, and seem to plunge into them, it was for a long time believed that they buried themselves in the mud, to issue again with the return of the spring warmth, which reanimated them after a six months' asphyxia. Olaus Magnus, a northern naturalist, more erudite than observing, was the first who propagated this fable, going so far as to maintain that the Norwegian fishermen often take in their nets a great number of swallows along with the fish. It was even asserted that if the poor birds, all soiled with mud, soaked with water, and stupified with cold, were exposed to the heat of a stove, they were seen to become speedily dry and return to life.

Linnæus, Buffon, and even Cuvier believed such stories! Ought we to consider this as a reproach to them, when we see that some physiologists of our own time obstinately maintain that certain animals can be reanimated?[1]

As the swallows have for a long time concealed their winter residence, it became the subject of all sorts of conjectures. Some naturalists maintained that, instead of emigrating to distant regions, they hid themselves and became torpid in the depths of some cave, just as the bats do. One of the most reliable of these men, Larrey the surgeon, mentions having discovered in the neighbourhood of Maurienne a grotto, the roof of which was lined with a mass of swallows which kept themselves attached to it like a swarm of bees.

But the experiments of Spallanzani have destroyed all these false creeds. The learned abbé found that the swallows which he tried to throw into a state of hybernation in an ice-house, did not become torpid, but died.

Adanson has taught us that the swallows betake themselves to the Senegal during the cold season. Those which are scattered through our country unite together at autumn on the shores of the Mediterranean, and when an irresistible desire impels them to depart, cross this sea in numerous troops. Thus then in summer the swallow builds its nest under the sumptuous cornices of our palaces, and in winter inhabits the huts of Senegambia.[2]

1 The idea that swallows winter in the mud of our marshes was so popular, that a German academy thought it advisable to examine whether there was any foundation for the opinion or not. This learned body accordingly proposed to give their weight in silver for all the swallows brought out of the water, but the prize was never claimed. The most astonishing part of the matter is to find Cuvier believing in such a fable. In his *Règne Animal* he says, "It appears certain that swallows become torpid during winter, and even that they pass this season at the bottom of the water in the marshes."—Cuvier, *Règne Animal*. Paris, 1829, t. i. p. 396.

2 Mr. Charles Buxton, who has paid great attention to the acclimatization of birds, and who appears to have succeeded wonderfully with his experiments at Northrepps Hall, in the woods round which live, winter and summer, African parrots, Bengal parroquets, and Philippine Island lories, &c., lately read a paper on this subject at a meeting of the British Association, in which he stated his reasons for believing that the migration of birds "depends altogether on food, and not the fear of cold. Even the delicate little long-tailed titmouse, and still more delicate little golden-crested wren, remain with us the whole winter without appearing to suffer."

[This power of resisting cold Mr. Buxton attributes to the impermeable covering of down below the feathers of birds, and possibly to their having a greater supply of heat than other animals.—Tr.]

147. The Ariel Swallow (*Hirundo Ariel*).—From Gould.

All do not attain the goal of their pilgrimage. The waves engulf those who have reckoned too much upon their strength, unless some propitious rock or ship happen to be at hand to lend them refuge. During one of my voyages across the Mediterranean, some strayed swallows happened, when we were mid-way between the two coasts, to fall totally exhausted on the deck of the frigate which was carrying me towards Africa. Everyone on board, soldiers and sailors, overwhelmed them with attentions, which they received without exhibiting signs of fear. When they had at last recovered from their fatigues, they recommenced their journey towards the high regions of Senegal, and perchance rested beneath the cabins of savages long ere we had greeted the ports of Algeria.

But after long and perilous journeys these charming visitors of our dwellings return each year with touching fidelity to find their old domicile again. If the rains and winds have injured it, the architects quickly repair it before making it witness of their loves. Spallanzani has even noticed that the feathered couples become strongly attached to their particular nests. Having fixed party-coloured ribbons to the feet of some of them, he recognized them the year after, when they came to take possession again. He saw them return thus for eighteen successive summers. How many among us never enjoy such a long tenancy!

Another species of the same group, the ariel swallow, fondly returns to its republic, formed of agglomerated nests, and more ingeniously constructed than those of our swallows. These nests resemble so many wide-necked bottles hung by the bottom in inaccessible places.

Less remarkable for the instinct which guides them than for the innumerable multitudes composing their armies, the passenger pigeons (*Columba migratoria*) traverse the forests of America in such compact masses that they absolutely intercept the rays of the sun, and cast a long track of shadows on the ground. Their compact columns extend over such a space that the eye cannot take in the full extent of it. It has been calculated that it is often sixty leagues in length. The passing of these columns sometimes lasts three hours, and as these birds travel at the rate of nearly twenty leagues an hour, their army must necessarily extend over fifty to sixty leagues of sky.

This immense host never travels by night; so soon as darkness overtakes them, they precipitate themselves breathless and exhausted upon the nearest forest, there to rest from their fatigues. Their legions alight in such numbers upon the trees that the great branches yield or break beneath their weight. Soon, however, all the invaders are composed to sleep.

But scarcely are the pigeons installed there than all the able-bodied people in the country hasten to the spot, and make a complete carnage of them. The well-sustained noise and firing do not in the least interrupt the sleep of these harassed travellers. The victims fall; the women and children pick them up, or even kill with sticks those pigeons which have perched within their reach. The yield is so abundant, that, not being able to consume in the locality all the birds which are killed, they are often obliged to salt and pack them in barrels, so that they may be kept or sent to a distance.

148. The Passenger Pigeon—*Columba migratoria.*

The cold of winter drives most animals from the Polar regions, and compels them to withdraw to countries more favoured by the sun. The penguins of the Cape alone seem to evade this universal law. These bird-fish, being intrepid swimmers, are most at home in the midst of the ices or the roaring waves. They only haunt the shores of Africa in order to scoop out their nests, hatch their eggs, and rear their young. When the young have become sufficiently robust to support the fatigues of the journey, all these swimmers, mysteriously obeying an instinct of which the Creator alone knows the aim, suddenly disappear from the African

149. Family of Sparkling-tailed Humming-birds—*Typhœna Duponti* (Gould).

shores, and seek during six months of winter the frightful regions of the south pole, condemned to incessant struggles amid tempests and ice. But at the return of spring the penguins reappear in numerous troops, and cover anew the banks now smiling with verdure, grouping themselves in long processions, seemingly occupied only in revelling in light and love. In contrast to these pictures of the wandering life of certain birds may be placed those in which, notwithstanding the strength of their wings, these tenants of the air live almost entirely at home, only flitting round the environs of the site which nourishes them and sees their birth. Whilst in their daring flight some of the wading birds cleave their way through the clouds and sweep a whole hemisphere, a little family of humming-birds have only a rose-bush for their universe. Like an elegant vase ornamented with lichens, the humming-bird's downy nest of cotton is balanced on the extremity of the most slender branches of the plant, whilst these aërial diamonds make prey of the insects which the flowers attract, or drink the pearls of dew which their petals distil. This is, for instance, the life of the sparkling-tailed humming-bird (*Typhæna Duponti*) —a charming family of which we here give as an illustration, taken from the splendid plates of Gould, the prince of modern ornithologists, both by his scientific knowledge and the magnificence of his works.

In the same manner the humming-birds, robed in changing green, which attract and charm all eyes, the "emeralds of Brazil" (*Chlorostilbon prasinus*), as they are commonly called, set up their family nests upon the slender pendent stems of the creepers, from the vicinity of which they rarely move. Rocked by the zephyr, the female broods tranquilly on her eggs while her lord flits amorously near her; here are spent all the happy days of the gentle pair.

CHAPTER III.

MIGRATIONS OF REPTILES AND FISHES—SHOWERS OF FROGS.

Reptiles scarcely ever carry out migrations on such a scale as to astonish one, either by the number of travellers or by the space over which they extend, but there is one fact in their history which has given rise to long debates, and that is *the showers of toads and frogs*, which in reality mean *compulsory migrations.*

Mention is made of these in very remote times, but later writers generally believed that the assertions of the authors who related them were inventions. Modern observations have at last demonstrated the actual existence of this phenomenon, which is explained now-a-days in a very rational manner.

These showers of frogs must have been common enough in ancient Greece, seeing that Aristotle gives them a particular name. Alluding to the prevailing idea of his time, which supposed them to come from heaven, he called them *messengers of Jupiter*.

Two carefully observed instances in modern times have especially wrought conviction among the learned.

The first was attested by a whole company of our soldiers, who, during the revolution, were on a march towards the north of France. In the open country they were assailed by a shower of little toads, which were dashed in their faces, falling with torrents of water. Astonished at such an unwonted attack, and desirous of satisfying themselves as to whether this living shower came from above, the soldiers spread out their handkerchiefs on a level with their heads, and found they were covered directly. After the storm, the astonishment was general when the soldiers saw this unexpected brood leaping about in the folds of their cocked hats.

The second well-attested shower of toads fell in 1834, in the town of Ham, when the streets, roofs, and gutters were immediately filled with a great quantity of these young animals.

As far back as the epoch of the Renaissance, a celebrated physician, Cardan, who brought out so many strange hypotheses, nevertheless hit upon the truth in respect to this phenomenon. He supposed that the showers of frogs were to be attributed to water-spouts which carried these animals off from the mountains, and let them fall at some distance, when they burst. Recently, when this phenomenon gave rise to such great discussion in the Academy of Sciences, the wise and learned Duméril leaned to this opinion. He supposed that the water-spouts, passing over the fens, pumped up the water as well as all it contained and carried it off to be deposited at a distance.

In support of this very rational hypothesis, Arago mentioned that whirlwinds often bear away from the sea masses of water, which they let fall in the form of rain six or seven leagues from the shore. Hailstones, much larger than little toads, are completely suspended for a certain time in the clouds.

It is, however, maintained, that if this opinion were correct, showers of fish ought also to fall. In reply to this objection several instances of such a fact have been cited. Authors mention showers of sticklebacks, certainly among the smallest of their kind, which live in the pools and streams of our country districts. These fish, pumped up along with the water of some fen by the suction of a water-spout, have been seen to fall in heaps at great distances from the place whence they were lifted.

Thus modern science has established the reality of a phenomenon advanced by antiquity, and the strangeness of which caused men for a long time to doubt it.[1]

Among the fish there are some the migrations of which have acquired great celebrity, especially those of the herring. It is thought that the

150. Stickleback in its Nest—*Gasterosteus trachurus.*

northern seas ought to be considered as the favourite residence of their

[1] Among the writers of antiquity who mention showers of frogs we may mention Ælian, on whose back one fell as he was travelling from Naples to Puzzuoli.

The showers of fish which have been the subject of discussion were made up of very small species, which, like frogs, sometimes swarm to an extraordinary extent in the fens, so much so that cart-loads of them are taken away to manure the ground and feed the cattle with. Those naturalists who, like Messrs. Defrance and H. Cloquet, maintained that showers of toads ought to be ranked among popular errors, thought that these batrachians, which sometimes appear in such multitudes after a heavy shower that it is impossible to set one's foot down without crushing some of them, were made up of the young which had lain hidden in the clefts of the dry ground, and had been driven out by the rain.

innumerable cohorts, and that it is from thence that the long bands start which annually bear to Europe so much food, and give such an impulse to maritime commerce. Their extreme fecundity alone explains how these fish subsist in spite of the enormous consumption of them during so many ages. When their wandering masses issue from the Polar seas, they are said to divide into two columns. One of these advances towards Iceland, and skirts the shore of America; the other takes an opposite direction along the broken shores of Norway, and furnishes a branch to the Baltic, whilst the mass spreads out on the coasts of France and Great Britain. The route is so regular that some authors have ventured to trace it out on the geographical charts which accompany their works.[1]

The fishermen recognize the presence of the shoals of herrings at a distance during the daytime by the clouds of birds of prey which accompany them, devouring all those which approach the surface of the waves, and at night by the long luminous track which stretches over the surface of the sea as far as the migration extends.

The tunny and mackerel also perform similar voyages.

[1] We do not wish to call in question an opinion which is widely spread among fishermen, but we must say that these migrations are very doubtful. Two of the most celebrated ichthyologists of our epoch, Bloch and Noël, deny these extraordinary migrations of the herring. It is supposed, perhaps on better grounds, that this fish always haunts the places where it is seen only at a certain period of the year, but that it lives at the deepest parts of the sea, and only comes to the surface at the period of reproduction, and for a short time.

Fishing in these shoals of herring began at a very remote period. In the chronicles of the monastery of Evesham, which date from the beginning of the eighth century, we find them already mentioned. Different documents show that in the eleventh century men pursued this calling in France. At one time the principal source of the wealth and maritime power of Holland lay in the herring fishery. This nation was so sensible of the fact, that a statue was reared to Buckalz, who taught the art of salting this fish, and whose memory was honoured by a visit which Charles V. paid to his tomb. At the time when this fishery was most flourishing, the Batavian republic sent yearly 2000 ships to it, and employed more than 400,000 souls in equipping the fleet and in the fish-trade. The Dutch estimated the advantages it brought them so highly, that they expressed their feelings in a popular proverb; *Amsterdam,* they used to say, *is built upon herring-heads.* A prodigious quantity of these fish is taken every year for the use of Europe alone. To the north of Bergen from 500,000 to 600,000 barrels are caught yearly, equivalent to more than 300 million fish. As many as 659,000 tons of herrings are caught off Norway in a single season, the export of which brings to the country £400,000.

[In 1873 there were caught off the coast of Scotland and cured 939,233 barrels of herrings; and as each barrel contains 700 fish, the number of herrings taken and cured would amount to above 657 millions.—Tr.]

CHAPTER IV.

MIGRATIONS OF INSECTS.

The greatest depredators on our globe are not the huge bisons, the roar of which shakes the desert, nor the winged invaders which devastate our forests; they are the puny insects which the wrath of Jehovah disperses over the earth to make manifest his power.

Such is the wandering locust (*Acridium peregrinum*), one of the most terrible scourges of agriculture. In Africa and Asia it appears in such masses, that when they are seen advancing at a distance they resemble immense black clouds which intercept the solar rays and plunge the country in the most profound darkness. A formidable sound, which Forskal compares to that of a cataract, announces the arrival of these redoubtable insects. When they alight upon the ground they form a living sheet more than a foot thick, and when, worn out by fatigue, they pile themselves upon the trees, the branches bend and break under their weight. The entire track of these devouring insects seems to have been wasted by a fire; not a trace of verdure is seen on it.

Human skill is inadequate to exorcise this pest. In vain do armies and peoples rise *en masse* to arrest these terrible devastators. All efforts fail. And if death overtake these famished guests, their corpses, heaped up on the soil, exhale pestilential vapours; mortality succeeds to ruin, and men perish by thousands.

These terrible emigrations have been observed in all epochs of history. Moses teaches us that at the voice of the Eternal locusts covered all the land of Egypt, devoured the crops, and even invaded the palaces of the Pharaohs. Pliny says that in Africa some countries have even been depopulated by their ravages. The alarm they occasion drew from St. Jerome these words, "What is there stronger and more terrible than locusts? All human industry cannot withstand them. God alone regulates their march."

Modern history has had only too often to register these disastrous visitations. One of them, which obscured the sun like a hurricane, checked the passage of Charles XII.'s army when he was crossing Bessarabia, and compelled him to arrest his march.[1]

[1] The historian of Charles XII. speaks in the following terms of the invasion of locusts

In every age man has attempted to repel these formidable invasions. In ancient times severe laws ordained the massacre of the wandering insects. In the island of Lemnos, each private person was compelled to bring to the magistrate a certain number of measures of locusts as annual

151. Migrating Locust—*Acridium peregrinum*.

tribute. Pliny relates that in Cyrenaica the law even compelled the people to make an exterminating war upon them three days per year. Any citizen who refused was punished as a deserter.

which arrested the march of this monarch's army.—"A horrible swarm of locusts arose generally each day before noon on the side towards the sea; first in little waves, and then in clouds which darkened the air and made it so sombre and thick, that all over this vast plain the sun appeared entirely eclipsed. These insects did not fly near the ground, but kept at about the same height as we see the swallows, till they saw a field upon which they could alight. We often met them on the way, when they rose up with a sound like that of a tempest. Subsequently they fell upon us like a storm, threw themselves upon the very plain where we were, and without any apparent dread of being crushed by the hoofs of the horses, they rose from the ground and so covered our bodies and faces that we could not see before us till we had passed the place where they were. Wherever these locusts rested they made frightful havoc, devouring every green thing to the very roots, so that, instead of the beautiful verdure with which the country was formerly covered, only a dry and sandy land could be seen. No one would have believed that so small an animal could cross the

The old naturalist maintains, that in Syria the Roman legions were sometimes employed for this purpose. A similar course has been adopted on various occasions in modern times.

M. Virey tells us that in Transylvania recourse was had to soldiers for the same purpose. Entire regiments collected locusts, and 1500 men were occupied solely in crushing, burning, and burying the living harvest. This happened in 1780, but the year following the pest reappeared, and its ravages assumed such proportions, that in order to combat it, they were obliged to call out the entire population. Notwithstanding this, a large number of districts were utterly ruined.

Ibrahim Pacha more recently employed his whole army in crushing one of their armies and destroying the pestilential remains. The great captain braved the hottest sun while stimulating the zeal of his soldiers by his presence.[1]

Other insects are less remarkable for their number than for the order which regulates their migrations; they act as prudently as an army in the field. An intelligent leader seems to direct all their movements, as may be seen in the excursions of the travelling termite. When a body

sea, if experience had not so often convinced those poor people of the fact; yet, after having passed a small arm of the Euxine Sea, these insects traverse great provinces, where they destroy everything they meet with, and even gnaw the doors of the houses."—*Histoire Militaire de Charles XII.*, t. iv. p. 160.

[1] But although the migrating locust must be considered one of the greatest scourges to agriculture, it still renders certain services to man. From the remotest antiquity he has used it for food, and this practice is kept up in many parts of Asia and Africa, where quantities are consumed. In the Bible days the Jews doubtless ate it extensively, seeing that Moses mentions four species, the use of which was permitted by law.

[Among the ancient Assyrians the locust was also an article of food. On the sculptures from Kouyunjik now in the British Museum, men are represented bearing dried locusts fastened on sticks. The annexed engraving shows the hands of one of them with the sticks of locusts.]

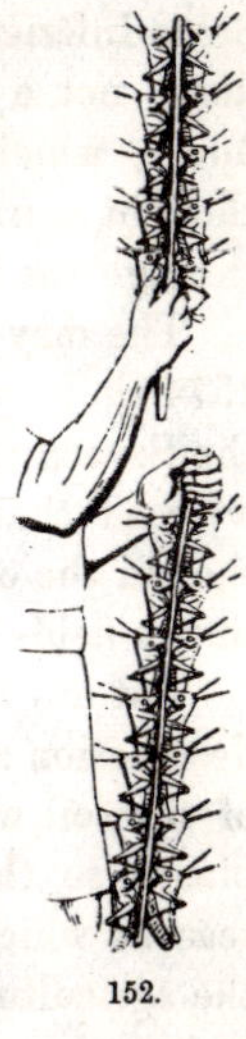
152.

There are countries where enormous quantities of locusts are still eaten. In the markets of Bagdad they compete with meat. In Arabia they are dried, ground, and substituted for flour in the preparation of bread. In 1693, Germany being desolated by an invasion of these insects, some of the inhabitants ate them, and were unanimous in the opinion that their flesh is analogous to that of crayfish, and of a very agreeable flavour.

At the present time the Bushmen, one of the most degraded of the human races, living in a country which is utterly naked, the greatest part of them never having seen a tree, people who have neither huts nor dress, subsist almost entirely on locusts. These insects, which Livingstone even considers as a benefit conferred by Providence, and the exquisite taste of which he praises, are their favourite food.

of these insects undertakes a distant journey, they advance in a straight line, and all the workers march in columns of ten to fifteen individuals, as compactly as a flock of sheep. During this time those termites that are armed with strong mandibles, and play the part of soldiers, spread themselves out like reconnoitrers on each side of the main body, in order to guard it against every attack. Should a plant more elevated than the others lie in the way of the emigrants, the soldiers may be seen climbing to the highest leaves, and resting suspended there like so many sentries charged with the office of watching the route. Should any danger arise, these soldiers, by striking the leaves with their feet, produce a clicking noise; a signal that agitates the entire army, which replies by hissing, and immediately after redoubles its pace with fresh ardour.

In juxtaposition with these emigrating insects, we ought to mention those which, without executing adventurous journeys, suddenly appear in compact masses and become for a time the scourge of our fields.

One of these voracious depredators is the may-bug, so common in France. In his magnificent work on the enemies of woodland culture, M. Ratzeburg does not hesitate to represent it as *the most terrible destroyer of our plantations.* The annals of agriculture abound with melancholy details of the ravages caused by this insect. It is sometimes seen to devour in a very short time all the foliage of a vast extent of forest. I was enabled to observe one of these devastations in a wood in the department of the Seine-Inférieure. All the trees had been utterly despoiled of their verdure; not a leaf, strictly speaking, hung on one of them; and in this forest, which we traversed in the middle of summer, we might have thought ourselves in mid-winter, had not the burning sun, striking through the bare branches, scorched us with his rays.

The may-bugs often quit the forests in order to attack the fields. In 1574 they swarmed so on the coasts of England, that when they fell into the Severn they clogged the wheels of the mills. In a chronicle of 1688 we read that these insects multiplied so fearfully that year in Ireland, that in the county of Galway the air was obscured, and they swarmed so in the fields that it was difficult to make a path through them.

But its larvæ, which the French peasants call *mans*, cause far more destruction among the forests and crops. They live beneath the surface of the soil where it is difficult to track them, and gnaw the roots of the plants, so that they sometimes totally devastate rich fields. In those seasons which favour their multiplication they become a fearful pest to the agriculturist. Normandy, which is often ravaged by their devouring legions, has at different times begged of the government to take some measures that would arrest this invasion. In 1866 these larvæ were so abundant in several cantons in the department of Seine-Inférieure that they absolutely annihilated whole fields of beet-root and colza. In one canton alone there was collected in a fortnight enough of these worms to fill completely a railway train of thirty-two carriages.

Some insects, even those of the smallest size, devastate and devour our crops of all kinds; wherever they appear, no human power can stay their ravages. According to M. Guérin-Méneville, they annually consume a large portion of the harvests of France, sometimes as much as a fourth,

153. Common May-bug—*Melolontha vulgaris*, Male, Female, Larva, and Nymph.
A most terrible destroyer of plantations.

which means that they cause destruction to the value of 500 millions of francs (£20,000,000).

The frightful rapidity with which some insects multiply, and the enormous consumption which they occasion, notwithstanding their minute size, demonstrate the unfortunate exactness of these figures. An experimenter having inclosed a dozen male and a dozen female weevils in a box of wheat, found that these minute beetles, which are only about the tenth of an inch long, had at the close of six months brought forth an innumerable progeny, and had with their assistance eaten thirty-three pounds avoirdupois of the grain in which they were inclosed. It has accordingly been calculated that this little weevil[1] alone devours more than 300,000 bushels of wheat in the granaries of Europe.

In respect to their migrations the crustaceans have been little studied; we only know that some animals of this class, of strange habits, perform some very singular journeys; these are the large crabs called land-crabs. Formed like their congeners to respire water by means of branchiæ or gills, they yet live on land, and are met with in compact bands on the

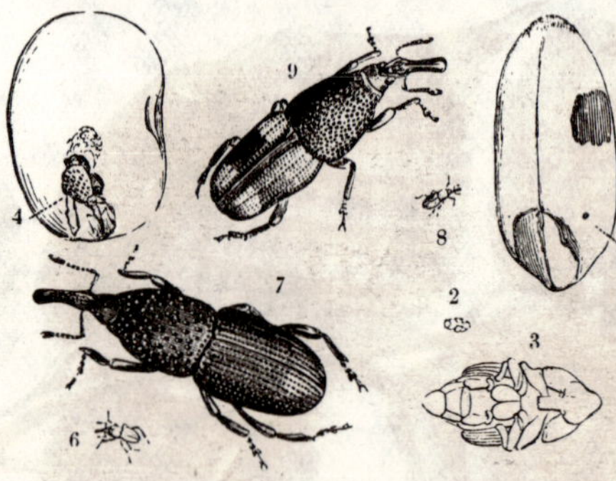

154. Corn-weevil. 1, Grain of wheat, showing the punctured hole; and 5, the exit of the perfect Weevil. 2, Pupa (natural size); 3, magnified. 4, Grain of Indian Corn, with Weevil inside. 6 and 7, Corn-weevil (*Calandra granaria*), natural size and magnified. 8 and 9, Rice-weevil (*C. oryzæ*), natural size and magnified.

mountains and in the forests of Brazil, where they dwell in holes. But each year these animals make a pilgrimage to the sea in order to deposit

[1] The one most injurious to the farmer is the *Calandra granaria*, or "corn-weevil," which lives in stored grain, whether it be wheat, barley, oats, maize, or rice. Early in the spring, as soon as the weather is warm enough—for being natives of southern regions they do not like cold—the beetles pair, and as soon as the female is impregnated she buries herself in the heap of corn, makes a puncture through the skin of one of the grains, and there deposits her eggs, one only in each grain. The hole is not perpendicular to the surface, but runs obliquely, or even parallel to it, and the small aperture is closed by her excrement. The eggs, then, are safe even if the grain be moved about. The maggots soon hatch and feed upon the contents of the grain, until the husk alone is left, which lasts them until they have arrived at maturity and changed to pupæ. In about six to eight weeks from the time of impregnation the perfect weevil is produced, which eats its way through the husk, and is then ready to propagate its species. In five months a pair of weevils have been known to produce 6045 individuals, each of which required for its cradle a grain of the farmer's crop. Owing to the workmanlike manner in which the female deposits her eggs, it is very difficult to detect their presence in the grain, which is generally not discovered until the perfect animals are seen walking over the heap, when the empty husks are readily picked out. The specific gravity being much lighter than sound grains, they may always be discovered if placed in a basin of water—the sound grains sinking, and these floating on the surface.—*Our Farm Crops*, by John Wilson, F.R.S.E.

their young there, and this act performed they return to their favourite haunts.

As it is necessary during this long and double journey to breathe either water or at least moist air, nature has provided for every emergency. The *tourlourous*, for these crabs are popularly known by that name, possess for this purpose, above the branchiæ, a kind of sacks which serve

155. Labyrinthine Cavity or Water-reservoir of the Anabas.

as reservoirs of liquid. When one of these crustaceans wants to travel, its first step is to take in a stock of water by completely filling these sacks. During its march the liquid falls drop by drop upon the respiratory organs, and moistens the vessels. The branchiæ being thus constantly wetted, the aquatic animal can live in air and move about, in

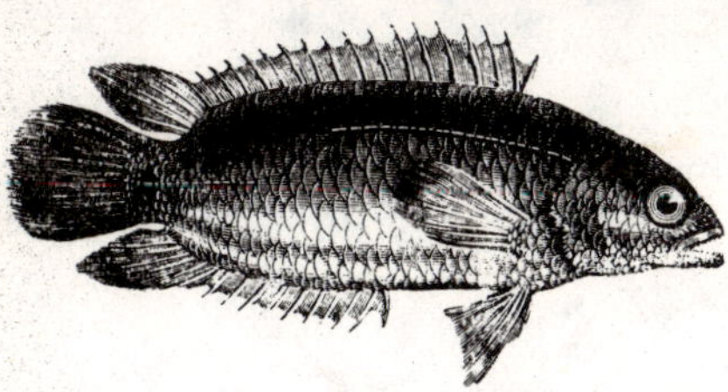

156. The Anabas or Climbing Perch—*Perca scandens.*

spite of the dryness and heat. Like a locomotive in action, it carries with it its supply of water, and has only to feed itself.

A singular fish, the anabas or climbing perch (*Perca scandens*), displays an organization exactly analogous to that of the crab we have just spoken of. It fills with water a labyrinthiform cavity which is also situated above its branchiæ. Then, after having taken this precaution, the prudent fish boldly issues from the waves and leads the life of an inhabitant of air. It climbs the banks and rocks by means of its spiny fins, taking care, during its vagabond course, to moisten its respiratory apparatus little by little with the liquid wherewith it filled the cells in its head. It has even been said that the anabas has been seen climbing a tree, making use of the cracks in the trunk, and drawings have often been made representing this circumstance.

THE

VEGETABLE KINGDOM.

Ruhige Pflanzenwelt, in deiner kunstreichen Stille vernehme ich das Wandeln der Gottheit; deine verdienstlose Trefflichkeit trägt meinen forschenden Geist hinauf zu dem höchsten Verstande; aus deinem ruhigen Spiegel strahlt mir sein göttliches Bild.—Schiller, *Der Menschenfeind*, scene vii.

Peaceful plant-world, in thy well-ordered stillness I perceive the hand of the Deity; thy un-earned excellence bears my inquiring spirit up to the highest Intelligence; from thy placid mirror His divine form beams upon me.—Schiller, *The Misanthrope*, scene vii.

THE

VEGETABLE KINGDOM.

INTRODUCTION.

In the harmony of the spheres everything is in a state of mobility and perpetual transmutation. The heavens are tenanted with new nebulæ, and old stars disappear in the abyss of immensity. On the earth new generations of animals and plants arise, while the scythe of time mows down those which but lately flourished there. On the one hand, the mass of animated matter visibly reveals its vitality; whilst, on the other side, its occult forces hide themselves and act only in the most hidden recesses of the organism. But all is carried away by the supreme power of life—that inexplicable and unfathomable mystery!

We behold animals which at a certain season, and at a given moment, display themselves in irresistible power, or disappear, providentially guided by an unknown force. Sometimes it seems as if a ray of light attracted them whilst darkness drives them away; at other times it is the reverse.

When night begins to spread its sombre shades over the earth, legions of twilight-loving moths flit heavily near their haunts. whilst the bat, issuing from its ruins, shakes its membranous wings and launches itself in pursuit of these insects. Some delicate molluscs rise towards dawn to the surface of the sea, and sink beneath its waves so soon as ever the sun gilds its undulating ripples.

Again we behold plants or their corollas displaying themselves and opening according to the seasons and hours of the day. So exact are they in their movements, that a sagacious observer, attentively following up these phenomena, soon sees that by means of them he can arrange calendars and clocks, all the divisions of which the charming goddess of flowers indicates accurately with her finger.

It is known that Pliny, having noted with care the times at which plants flower, conceived the idea that we might make use of them to mark the different seasons of the year. Cuvier even asserts that the Roman naturalist proposed to arrange a complete floral calendar; but the project was first thoroughly carried out by Linnæus, and it is one of the most elegant conceptions of his genius.

This floral calendar is accurate enough, and we can see that each month of the year is exactly indicated by the blooming of certain flowers. The first month, despite its snow and ice, sees the black hellebore flower. During the second the alder shakes its catkins and the mezereon seems to smile on the spring, scattering its flowerets over its boughs. In March the wall-flower decorates the old walls with its golden corollas, and in our gardens the crown-imperial opens its treacherous bells. The following month the periwinkle expands its leafy net-work in the shadow of our forests. In May, flowers abound; the iris, the lily of the valley, and the lilac perfume the air on every side. During the months of June and July Flora parades all the pomp of her empire; the foxglove, the sage, the wild poppy, the mint, and the pink bloom in our fields and woods. In August, the asters, dahlias, and helianthus seem to brave the heat of the sun. Finally, in September, the colchicum scatters its purplish flowers all over our meadows, and announces the return of winter. It is the plant which, according to Linnæus, gives the signal of repose to the botanist.

The hour at which each flower opens is itself so uniform, that by watching them floral clocks of sufficient accuracy can be arranged.

Father Kircher had dreamed of it, but vaguely and without pointing out anything; it is to Linnæus that we must ascribe the ingenious idea of indicating all the hours by the time at which plants open or shut their corollas. The Swedish botanist had created a flower-clock for the climate which he inhabited, but as, in our latitudes, a more brilliant and radiant dawn makes the flowers earlier, Lamarck was obliged to construct for France another clock, which is a little in advance of that at Upsala.

This regularity in the opening of flowers strikes every person; some savage races make use of it to divide their days and their toils. These begin at the hour when the marigold opens, and the Natchez, Chateaubriand says, make their love appointments for the time when the last rays of day are about to close the flowers of the Hibiscus.[1]

Other flowers, less regular in their habits, only open under the influence of certain atmospheric conditions, from which they have acquired

[1] There is something very inexplicable in these facts. The Sidas of India expand their flowers in the morning only, while the Abutilons, *which scarcely differ from them in any point of structure*, only unfold their blossoms in the evening.—Tr.

the surname of meteoric. Some of them have gained considerable celebrity. Among these is the rain-marigold, which, so soon as the dark clouds begin to gather, closes its corolla with the greatest care, to preserve it from the storm. The Siberian sow-thistle, of totally different habits, accustomed to hoar-frost, seems to dread our sun; it only expands when the sky is cloudy, and closes its flowerets tightly up so soon as the atmosphere gets warm.

The connection between man and the vegetable kingdom is not limited to these curious investigations; plants, living emblems of the rapid passage of hours and time itself, eternal lessons of wisdom, are associated with all our wants, our pleasures, and our pains.

The hardiest trees serve to build our dwellings with; other plants form our most natural food.

Sometimes the existence of certain tribes depends on a single vegetable species. A palm which grows in the forests at the mouth of the Orinoco, suffices for all the wants of some savage races, who, in company with the monkeys, live almost constantly perched as it were in the midst of its foliage. It yields them food, wine, and even cordage to swing the hammocks on, in which they suspend themselves during the inundations.[1]

In all ages men have prized the beauty and perfume of flowers, and they have become an indispensable ornament of even the least important festival. The ancients had their "coronary plants;" these were consecrated to Venus and at feasts each guest wore a chaplet. But we must also do them the justice to remark, that they employed an ample series of "funereal plants" for the mournful ceremonies of death; each one had its mission or special signification.[2]

[1] The palm spoken of here belongs to the genus Mauritia. It grows by the banks of the Orinoco, along almost the whole course of its stream, and forms remarkable forests near its mouths. "At the time of the inundations," says Humboldt, "the tufts of the fan-leaved murichi (*Mauritia flexuosa*) present the appearance of a forest issuing from the bosom of the waters. The navigator, traversing at night the branches of the Orinoco delta, sees with surprise the crowns of these palms lighted up by large fires. These are the habitations of the Guaranis suspended from the trunks of the trees. These people stretch mats in the air, fill them with earth, and on this bed of wet clay light what fires they require for household purposes. For ages they have owed their liberty and political independence to the treacherous and miry nature of their soil, which they traverse in seasons of drought, and over which they alone know how to pass in safety; to their isolation in the delta of the Orinoco, and to their living in the trees."—Von Humboldt, *Voyage aux Régions Equinoxiales*, t. viii. p. 363.

[2] The history of the funereal plants of the ancients has been worked out in a very interesting way by G. A. Langguth, in his *Antiquitates Plantarum Feralium apud Græcos et Romanos*, Lipsiæ, 1738. He follows up the employment of them from the commencement of the malady to the close of the funeral ceremonies. The author presents us with a true and interesting picture of Greek and Roman manners. When the malady began to

BOOK I.

THE ANATOMY OF PLANTS.

Three men of genius, Grew, Malpighi, and Leuwenhoeck, founded vegetable anatomy almost at the same time in England, Italy, and Holland. This subject was unknown in antiquity, for as it has only been with the aid of that grand revealer, the microscope, that men have been able to penetrate the secrets of vegetable life, the discovery of this instrument necessarily preceded that of the structure of plants.

The microscope very soon taught us that the whole vegetable edifice is built up from the cell, and that this is the creative element of the different organs of the plant, notwithstanding their diversity.

The cells consist of little microscopic vesicles, at first globular, but which by increase and mutual compression become many-sided. And these elements, which conceal themselves from our eyes, animated by an inconceivable plastic force, and multiplying at a prodigious rate, cause new worlds to arise. "Give me a lever and a fulcrum," said Archimedes,

alarm a family seriously, they suspended at the patient's door boughs of the favourite tree of Apollo, the inventor of medicine, in order to secure a favourable turn to the complaint. To the branches of laurel were added tufts of the Rhamnus, consecrated to Janus, and which was supposed to preserve the dwelling from all harm. But if, despite this invocation for aid, death overtook the sick person, they substituted for these plants black boughs of cypress, the emblem of Pluto and Proserpine; or branches of larch, the funeral tree, as Pliny calls it. At a later period, when the body of the defunct had been washed, it was anointed with perfumes—myrrh, frankincense, canella, and cardamom. It was then deposited in a coffin of cypress wood, which the Athenians, as Thucydides tells us, considered to be incorruptible, and on the head was placed a wreath, the composition of which was emblematic of the condition of the deceased. It was formed of olive, laurel, white poplar, of lilies or smallage. Burning branches of pine and stems of papyrus lighted the procession, which advanced to the sound of funereal flutes, in the construction of which only boxwood and lotus were employed. They always made use of a pyre of resinous wood to consume the dead body. Its action was more rapid and its odorous emanations absorbed the smell of the burned flesh. The relatives piously collected the ashes and placed them in urns, mixed with perfumes of myrtle and rose, frankincense and violet. After this they were deposited in the tomb.

"and I will lift the globe." M. Raspail, almost paraphrasing the geometer of Syracuse, was able to say, "Give me a living cellule, and I will reproduce all creation."

And indeed it is these cells, these living atoms, about one three-thousandth of an inch in diameter, but endowed with a mysterious and disproportionate power of production, which each spring cover our soil with verdure, and call to life the awe-inspiring savannah or immense virgin forest.

These creative vesicles, by lengthening, become fibres or vessels, and these anatomical elements, when grouped together, form roots, twigs, leaves, and flowers. Their multiplication takes place with such prodigious rapidity, that a body of them not a hundredth part of the size of a pin's head sometimes produces in a single night a plant which

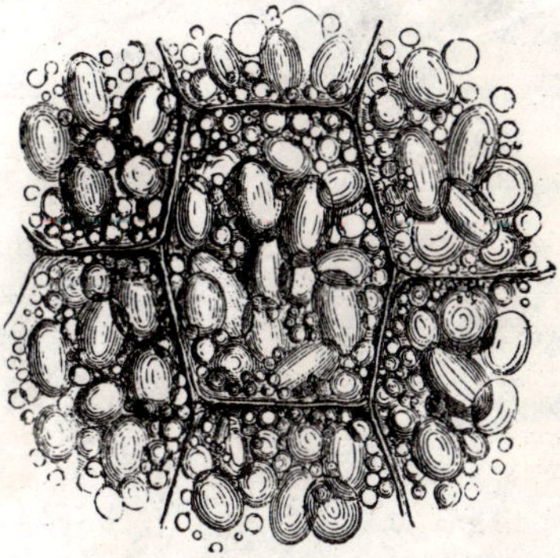

157. Cellular Tissue filled with Fecula, seen with the microscope.

reaches the size of a great gourd! This is what takes place in some Fungi.

In spite of the extreme minuteness of the interior of the cells, they still contain bodies of very various kinds, some of which one is surprised to find there.

In the leaves the cells are all filled with little green granules, which give to vegetation the colour it displays everywhere. Sometimes fine crystals are observed in them. Vaucher and Morren have even found animalcules quite alive in certain aquatic plants. Lastly, M. Trécul has recently demonstrated at the Academy of Sciences,[1] that the cellular tissue of the Caladium is sometimes invaded by numerous rudimentary

[1] Dr. Charles Musset, who has acquired a certain amount of celebrity in the great discussions on spontaneous generation, has had an opportunity of verifying the exactness of the facts put forward by M. Trécul.

plants, the appearance of which, according to this savant, in the midst of this tissue so entirely cut off from connection with the outer world, cannot possibly be explained except by spontaneous generation.

But the substance most frequently met with in the interior of the cellular tissue is our alimentary fecula. Each of the microscopic cells is sometimes quite filled with it. We observe it in all the organs—root, stem, and flower.

We are astonished when sailors tell us that the islanders of Otaheite

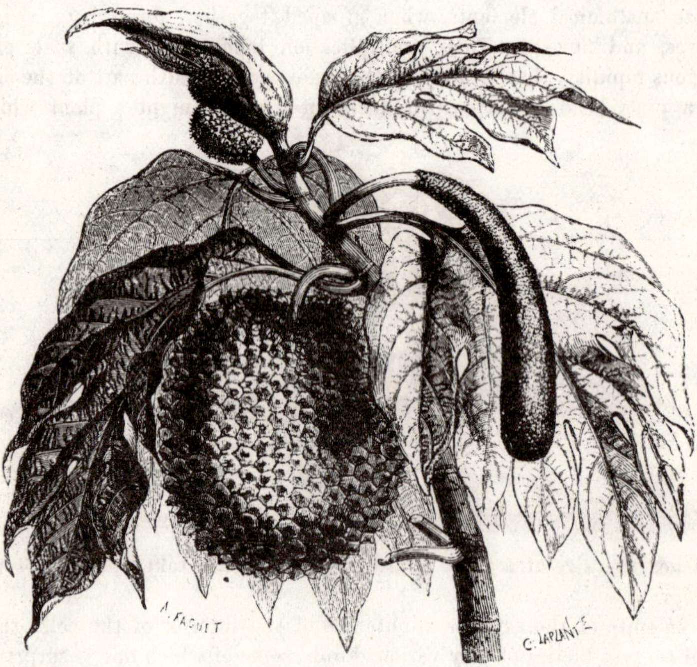

158. Fruit of the Bread-fruit Tree—*Artocarpus incisa.* Very much reduced in size.

actually prepare bread, by simply placing upon a gridiron slices of a large fruit which grows in their island, and that these, when they are taken from the gridiron, have precisely the taste of the bread made by our bakers. This is easily explained. The fruit of the bread-fruit tree, for it is so called, which reaches an enormous size, generally weighing more than two pounds, and sometimes four or five, is crammed with fecula, and owing to this only requires to be sliced and exposed to heat in order to be transformed into genuine warm bread.

Strabo relates, that when the army of Alexander was traversing Gedrosia, the men, being utterly without food, supported themselves for some time on the pith of a certain species of palm. The same thing happened, according to the account given by Xenophon, during the famous retreat of the ten thousand Greeks. All this is also naturally explained by the abundance of alimentary fecula contained in the trunks of certain palms. A similar fact is now repeated every day of our lives. Every one knows that the sago, so frequently used at our tables, is obtained from the central and medullary part of the stem of the sago-palm, which originally belongs to India.

CHAPTER I.

THE ROOT.

Notwithstanding the unseemly look of its tortuous ramifications, and the disorderly appearance of its absorbing fibres, the root of a tree is none the less organically identical with the regular boughs and symmetrical divisions supported by the stem. Anatomy and experience prove this.

We sometimes see in forests large branches creeping along the surface of the earth, their lower half buried, while the other is exposed to the air. The former sends out rootlets which sink into the ground, and the other leaves which expand to the bosom of the atmosphere. The same organ therefore is at once trunk and root.

Experiment proves this fact still better. Duhamel inverted willows, placing their roots in the open air and their boughs in the earth. So identical are these organs, that in a short time the roots were covered with leaves, and the stems, transformed into an underground structure, had put out spongioles. This curious experiment succeeded equally well on a large scale. M. de Raguse, in his memoirs, mentions having seen on the property of a Russian gentleman, an avenue of limes which he had in a whim transplanted upside down. The metamorphosis was complete; all the inverted trees flourished splendidly, and the roots were completely changed into vigorous leafy branches.[1]

[1] In the birch-wood of Culloden there is a larch-fir which was blown down in a storm, and fell across a gully. The branches took root on the other side, and from the parent stem, thus fed, shot up perpendicularly fifteen trees all in a row, which still flourish in all their splendour.—*Science Gossip*, 1865.—Tr.

The identity between the organs is so complete that the physiologist can even transform the middle part of the stem into a root, whilst above and below this it puts out branches covered with leaves, in such a manner that the tree thus represents two trees placed one above the other. Duhamel proved this by a curious experiment. He surrounded the stem of a willow with a cask filled with earth, which was raised from the ground to a higher level than the first branches of the tree. Adventitious roots soon shot out on this part of the trunk, while above and below it was laden with boughs covered with verdure.

159. Adventitious Roots upon a Trunk. Duhamel's experiment.

Anatomy assigns generally three functions to the roots: they fix the tree, feed it, and at the same time fill the office of excreting organs.

In most of the Fuci the root merely represents a sort of cramping-iron, serving just to anchor the plants at the bottom of the sea, without drawing the least particle of nourishment from the rock which it grasps. The myriads of little claws by which the ivy attaches itself to the rugged stone of tombs and walls seem also designed solely to fix it to its favourite site.

On the contrary, the water-lentil, which spreads its carpet of verdure on the surface of our pools, possesses nothing but spongioles. A Pontederia, which floats on the rivers of India, is only furnished with fine rootlets spreading through the water. But these are rare exceptions.

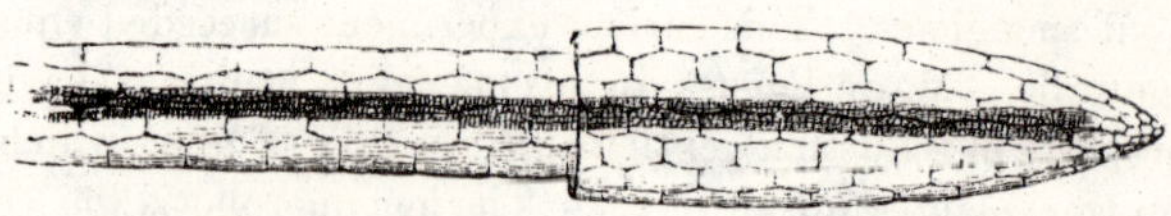

160. Spongiole of the Floating Pontederia (*Pontederia crassipes*), highly magnified.

Buried in the earth, the root there performs its three functions in obscurity. For this purpose each of its capillary filaments is terminated by a little swelling called spongiole, to which the function of absorbing is specially intrusted, and which, like an invisible sponge, sucks up the nutrient juices of the soil which surrounds it.

CHAPTER II.

THE STEM.

Although the diversified forms of stems do not allow us to classify them strictly, we can at least see that they often present themselves under three strictly defined aspects, the types of which are found in our trees, in the palms, and in the grasses.

The stem of our trees—called the trunk, consists of a greatly elongated cone, which becomes very much smaller as it gains in height. In a

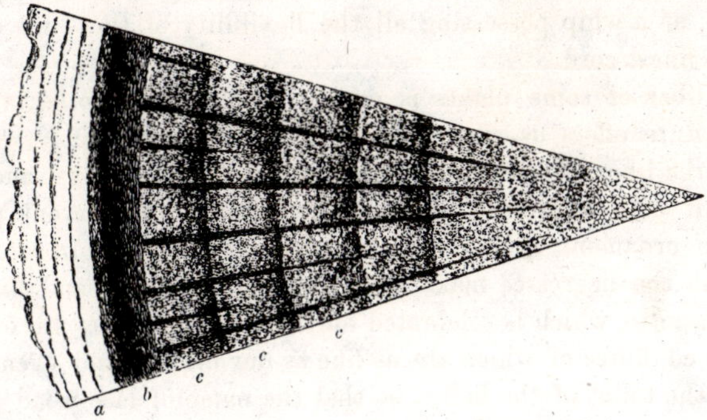

161. Section of Cork-tree. *a*, Layers of cork or suber; *b*, Inner bark and suber; *c*, Concentric rings of wood and medullary rays.

section of it we distinguish three parts clearly defined—the bark, the wood, and the pith.

The bark, which is the outermost, is formed of tolerably numerous layers. The parts most deserving of remark in it are the epidermis or outermost layer, a fine transparent membrane, which generally allows us to see the tissue over which it lies. Under the epidermis is the suberous layer, generally unnoticed on account of its thinness, but which exceptionally attains to a thickness of an inch or so in some trees, particularly in the cork-tree. This layer constitutes the cork of which we make such great use for our domestic wants. In the south of Europe and in Africa it is taken from the trees, and as this tissue grows after being removed, a new crop can be gathered every seven or eight years. The cork then is not the bark, but merely its superficial layer, for when we strip a trunk of its cortical envelope completely it dies; we could not effect several successive removals of it; the trees would be killed if we did.

Beneath the suberous layer is seen the inner bark, characterized at the first glance by its little cells filled with granules, usually green, the colouring of which is seen through the epidermis.

The layers of the liber are found still deeper. They form thin membranes composed of elongated fibres, and often of a beautiful white. These layers are superimposed like the leaves of a book, and can sometimes be separated with facility, whence they have acquired the name of *liber*, and also that of *libretto*, by which they were formerly designated.

The long tenacious fibres of the liber sometimes simply lie side by side, and thus yield valuable textile fabrics. At other times, being closely interwoven, they are worked up by the savages into various objects. By distending the bark of a little switch, the size of a quill, they make a nightcap, or a whip possessing all the flexibility of those we construct with the finest cord.

The liber of some plants is exactly like certain cloths; vestments which nature offers us ready made. The inhabitants of New Zealand convert the liber of some of their trees into strong drapery, and having covered it with impressed patterns, they put it to different purposes, either to ornament their dwellings or to make their dresses of. In Havannah the negresses make their dresses of a softer and finer kind. On the Lagetto, which is celebrated on this account, layers are found, the intertwined fibres of which are as fine as our muslin, and even take its place in the toilet of the ladies, so that the name of lace-wood has been given to the tree which produces them.

The inner layers of the bark are sometimes formed of leaves sufficiently close and compact to constitute a kind of paper. It was from these that the ancient Egyptians made their celebrated papyrus rolls, on which they wrote, and which, spared by the hand of time, reveal to our astonished gaze works which go back to the days of the Pharaohs. The paper-sedge (*Cyperus Papyrus*), which has such a strange aspect, and which grows on the banks of the Nile, has long been understood to furnish this precious object.[1]

[1] The employment of the papyrus for writing upon seems to have preceded historic times. Herodotus asserts that he saw drawn up on this substance a catalogue of 330 kings who had preceded Sesostris. Papyrus was employed even in Gaul up to the beginning of the

162. Egyptian Papyrus—*Cyperus Papyrus* (Linnæus).

The wood is composed of concentric zones lying one within the other, which are the result of the intimate union of a mass of microscopic vessels and fibres.

In the centre of the stem is found the pith, composed almost exclusively of cellular tissue. It is with very thin sheets of this structure, cut by means of a sharp knife, that the Chinese make the beautiful paper on which they paint, and which is incorrectly called rice-paper.[1]

The second type of stem belongs to the palms. This stem, which bears the name of stipes, is usually cylindrical, and is without branches or bark.[2]

Lastly comes the *stalk*, composed of a stem bulging at successive points; it is peculiar to the family of grasses.

seventh century, and to preserve the manuscript books, after every four or five leaves of paper two leaves of vellum were placed, on which the text was continued. In the end the papyrus was replaced by cotton-paper, *charta bombycina*, also called *charta damascena*. The invention of rag-paper, which M. Goury ascribes to about the twelfth century, probably caused the disuse of cotton-paper.

[1] Rice-paper is nothing else than fine layers, cut with great skill, of the pith of the *Æschynomene paludosa*, a plant of the family of the Leguminosæ.

[2] This sort of stem has no distinct concentric layers or medullary rays. The youngest formation takes place towards the centre instead of at the circumference, as in exogens; and the pith *p* (Fig. 163) does not occupy the centre, but is interposed between bundles of

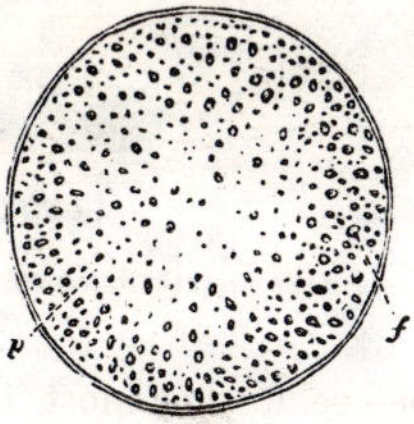

163. Palm—Horizontal Section of Stem.

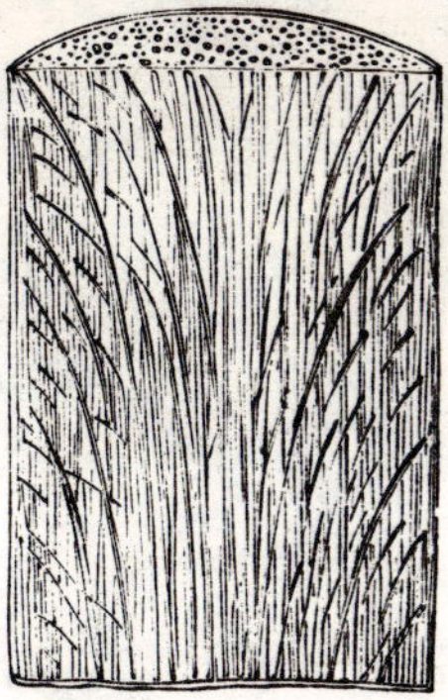

164. Palm—Longitudinal Section of Stem.

woody and vascular tissue *f*, which descend from the leaves, and curving inwards, pass down near the middle of the stem for some distance, as shown in Fig. 164, and then taking an outward course terminate at the circumference. The older formations, being thus continually pressed outwards, become harder and more compact than those in the interior. The stems of palms have no true bark, but are covered with a cortical integument similar to that of exogens.—Tr.

CHAPTER III.

THE LEAF.

To the tunic of leaves by which plants are covered is due all the magnificence of creation. The flowers, indeed, form a charming ornament which attracts and seduces the eye, but they remain unnoticed in the

165. Aërial or Pulmonary, and Aquatic or Branchial Leaves of the Aquatic Ranunculus.

grand scenes of Nature, when she unrolls before us her most splendid landscapes, her sombre forests, or her immense extended plains of verdure.

To the leaf is confided one of the most important functions of vegetable life—respiration. Leaves then are only the lungs of plants. It is seldom that they are unprovided with them, yet such is the case with some Euphorbiæ, the stem of which, inordinately swollen, entirely replaces them, and only bears very insignificant rudiments of such structures.

The leaf is composed of two parts: the petiole or support, and the blade, which is spread out in the form of a membrane. It is only exceptionally that this is perforated so as to look like an elegant net-work, as in the *Hydrogeton fenestratum*, the name of which comes from this singular peculiarity; it is also seen in the submerged leaves of some aquatic plants, which in such an arrangement seem to remind us of the branchiæ, the respiratory organs of fish.

In some plants they are transformed into long capillary filaments, which are seen gently undulating in the current of our rivers, like the tresses of a Naïad floating beneath the limpid water. It is thus that the

166. A River Reach filled with the Floating Leaves of the *Victoria regia*.

leaves of some aquatic ranunculuses are seen forming movable green carpets in the depths of our streams.

If we transport ourselves to the agitated waves of the Amazon, we find there leaves which display themselves on the surface like immense plains of verdure; these are the growth of the *Victoria regia*. These leaves, almost circular, are from six to eight feet in diameter. They spring from a petiole which, issuing from the depths of the river, projects from its stem some twenty feet distance, and ends beneath the blade, forming by its ramifications a solid framework, strengthened by very projecting partitions such as no other plant possesses. The upper surface of the leaves of the Victoria is, on the contrary, very uniform and of a beautiful green; thus seen at a distance they look like so many floating tables covered with velvet. Owing to their framework of nerves, these swimming leaves can support a great weight without sinking. Thus in these burning regions the aquatic birds rest upon them, or pass the night on these cool natural rafts. The daughter of one of the most illustrious botanists in England told me, that when a child, her father had set her upon one of those gigantic leaves, and that she had walked upon it without it sinking.

Indian mythology is therefore not so irrational when it relates, that the god Vishnu, armed with a trident, crossed the abyss of eternal waters on a leaf of the Nymphæa, and that one of these served as a floating seashell for the graceful goddess Lakshmî.

There are some other leaves which, though they certainly do not spread out in elegant sheets of verdure like those of the Victoria, nevertheless in unfolding extend their numerous divisions in a much more extraordinary manner. This is seen in the taliput palm (*Corypha umbraculifera*), a great palm which grows in India, and the specific name of which denotes the broad shadow which its crown of verdure projects upon the ground. Its leaves are supported by a long powerful petiole as high as a man, and under their vast cover forty persons can shelter themselves. We sometimes see leaves of this tree fixed to the ceiling of a collection of natural history, one of them covering it completely.

CHAPTER IV.

THE FLOWER.

When we brush a flower with our fingers, when its colour attracts our attention and its perfume intoxicates us, it seems as if we knew all about it. But this is a mistake. Nothing is more difficult than to conceive an exact idea of what a flower is. Famous botanists like Haller and Adanson have given it up; others have said nothing of value on this head.

"When I am not asked what time is I know it very well; I do not know it when I am asked." These words of St. Augustin, which J. J. Rousseau repeats, are perfectly applicable to the flower, the nature of which every one thinks he knows, and which nevertheless no one ever previously succeeded in describing well. This honour was reserved for the philosopher of Geneva, who admits having found so much happiness in the study of botany.[1]

Difficult as it may be to define the flower with precision, it is not less so to unravel its mysterious genealogy.

While prying deeply into its primordial essence, Goethe, triply illustrious as a naturalist, poet, and philosopher, arrived at a discovery which was quite unexpected. He has scientifically proved, that however sumptuous the beauty of a flower may be, each part of it is nevertheless

167. Petaloid Perianth of the White Lily—*Lilium candidum* (Linnæus).

only a result of the metamorphosis of a humble leaf. We are therefore right in saying that we are stripping the roses of their leaves when tearing off their coloured lobes, for each of these is in fact only a transformed leaf.

When the floral apparatus is complete it is formed of four rosettes, or verticilli, of depressed concentrated leaves.

[1] The only author who has described a flower well is Rousseau, who at one period of his life occupied himself with botany, and even wrote several volumes on this science. "It is," he says, "a local and fleeting part in which, or by which, the fecundation of the plant is effected."—J. J. Rousseau, *Dictionnaire de Botanique*, art. "Fleur."

These leaves are transformed into two kinds of organs. Some become the perianth, the most brilliant part of the flower, a true organ of protection, forming soft swathes for the delicate apparatus which it incloses, and, like a glowing mirror, reflecting heat and light upon them. The others, still further changed, are raised to the dignity of a reproductive apparatus.

Most frequently the perianth is double. Its external envelope, or calyx, is formed by the first whorl of metamorphosed leaves, and as the transformation of these is much less radical than in the other parts, the different parts of this organ, or the sepals, in many cases remind us of the leaves by their structure and colouring. The internal envelope, or corolla, although more brilliant than the other, is nevertheless also

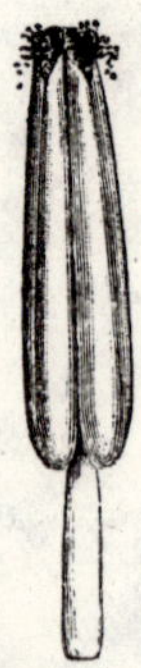

168. Stamen of the Potato.

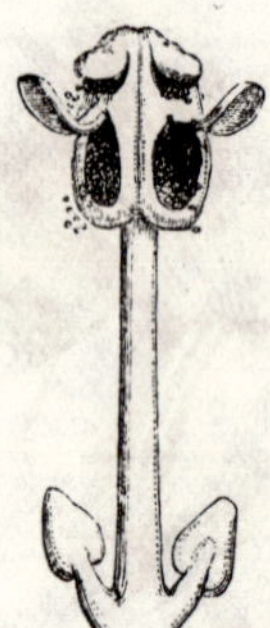

169. Four-celled Anther of the Persian Laurel.

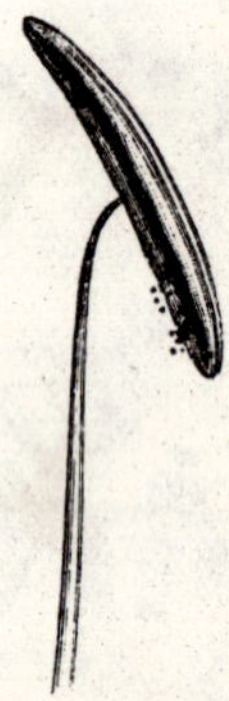

170. Stamen of the Amaryllis.

formed by a whorl of leaves—the second. Each of these leaves is called a petal. The stamens, which represent the male apparatus of plants, result from the metamorphosis of the third whorl of leaves; these depart so far from their normal type that analogy alone shows what their fundamental structure really is. Finally, the pistils, real organs of maternity, are derived from the fourth, or innermost foliaceous ring.

Simple analogy made the naturalists of antiquity suppose that plants, like animals, present two sexes, but they had only very confused ideas about them.

It was only in the seventeenth century that Camerarius, a physician of Tübingen, hit upon the real truth, which he expounded in a letter that has become very celebrated.

This writing lighted up the flames of discord in the camp of the botanists; some warmly espoused the discovery, others combated it to the very utmost. The dispute became violent; the schools took part in it; men quarrelled about it on every side; the pupils on their benches and the professors in their chairs. In the Jardin du Roi, Tournefort and Le Vaillant had a deadly dispute on the subject. Pontedera, a cross-grained obstinate savant, imagining that ascribing sexes to the flowers sullied their virgin purity, treated all those botanists who accepted the new heresy as devoid of decency. And yet there was nothing in it that could alarm even the modesty of a rose.

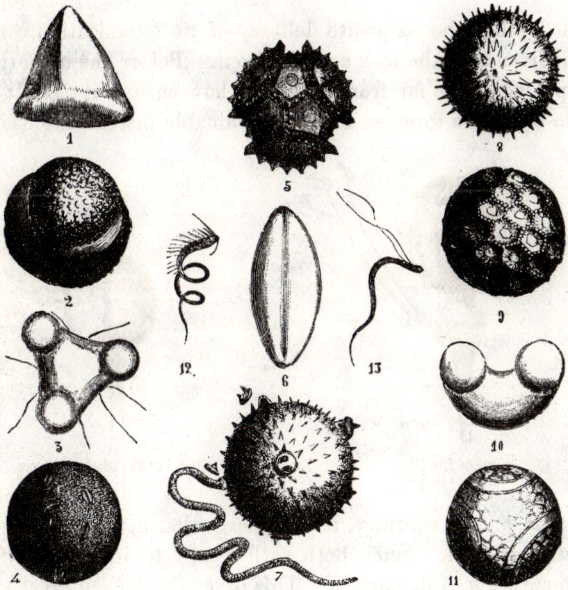

171. Pollen of different Plants, seen with the microscope. 1, Hellebore; 2, Sea Lavender; 3, Wild Oleander; 4, Convolvulus; 5, Scolymus; 6, Lily; 7, Gourd; 8, Hibiscus; 9, Cobæa; 10, Pine-tree; 11, Passiflora; 12, Animalcules of the Pollen of Ferns; 13, Animalcules of the Chara.

But notwithstanding the denials of Tournefort, and the invectives of the old professor of Padua, it became necessary to admit the truth of the discovery, for experiment proved every step in it.

Every person has seen the delicate filaments which rise up in the white flower of the lily. These are the reproductive organs. Six of them, the beautiful yellow dust of which stains the fingers of those who touch it, are the stamens. This dust, which is usually elaborated in two little sacks called anthers, is known as pollen; the German botanists give the anthers the more picturesque name of pollen-ateliers.

They are in fact marvellous laboratories, in which the impalpable agents of vegetable life are imperceptibly prepared. If they are severed the plant dies without posterity.

Most usually anthers throw off their products by splitting up from end to end. Sometimes they become pierced with holes at the top, and the pollen issues forth like a cloud of smoke. Lastly, in some flowers each sack presents one or two little doors in miniature, opening on microscopic hinges, the gaping mouth of which vomits forth the animated dust.

In the pollen the exquisite delicacy of its organization corresponds to the importance of the task confided to it. Before the invention of the microscope men were far from thinking how curious it is. It was considered to be only a formless dust; the valuable instrument has revealed

172. Pistil of the Poppy.

173. Pistil of the Madder Plant.

the fact, that, on the contrary, it possesses a distinctly defined configuration, which varies very much both with regard to its general form and the ornamentation of its surface. This diversity is even great enough to allow some botanists to make it the basis of their classification of plants.[1]

It is generally the globular form that predominates, but there are also grains which are ovoid; some triangular ones are known, and others resemble gourds or pyramids. Their surface is sometimes smooth, sometimes roughened with papillæ, or defended by an armature of spines. But microscopy is not limited to this; it shows us that each of these pollen grains is really a charming little utricle with a double envelope,

[1] Although they possessed very imperfect means of observation, our predecessors were nevertheless struck by the variety of the pollen grains. Adanson, who pushed his mania for classifications so far as to produce sixty-five, and who based them on the first things which struck him, even the smell and taste of plants, did not omit to form a classification based on the configuration of the pollen.—Adanson, *Familles des Plantes.* Paris, 1763. Preface, p. 286.

inclosing a fluid in which sometimes swim myriads of animalcules.[1] This fluid escapes by irregular openings which are caused by the bursting

174. Flowers protected by a Spathe. Florentine Iris—*Iris florentina* (Linnæus).

of the pollen, or by minute valves of microscopic size, but of exquisite

[1] The microscope was very little used by the botanists of last century, and we must come to our own age before we find the pollen perfectly described. Guillemin attentively studied the infinite variety of its forms and surface. The fluid contained in each little pollen-vesicle was particularly studied by Messrs. Mirbel, Brongniart, and Seringe, who all consider the numerous corpuscles which move about in the midst of it as so many microscopic animalcules. The German botanists, such as Schacht and others, designate them under the name of antherozoa, in order to leave no doubt on the subject.

construction, which open at the fitting moment, as represented in the figure of the pollen of the gourd on page 275.

In the lily, which we have chosen as an instance (Fig. 167), the pistil is represented by a little column situated in the centre of the flower. It consists of three parts: the ovary, which forms the swollen base, and which is only the fruit in miniature; the style, which surmounts it, but which is wanting in some other plants; and lastly, the stigma, which expands into a trilobed swelling at its extremity.

Such are the elements of the flower, and these by their close union or their monstrous anomalies produce the infinite variety of forms which we admire throughout the vegetable kingdom.

A ceaseless source of fecundity, the flower is the object of the most delicate protecting care.

When yet scarcely outlined, downy scales lend warmth to it, and form a soft pillow for its first lineaments, and the exterior of the bud is sheathed with thin dry scales, covered with resin to protect the organ against moisture.

As an extreme precaution, some flowers are covered with an envelope, or spathe, which does not fall till the time of opening. In small-sized monocotyledons, such as the iris (Fig. 174) and garlic, this envelope is very thin, membranous, and transparent: whilst in some great species like the palms, this supplementary cradle of the young flowers acquires colossal proportions; it is thick, woody, and resembles a large cup one to two yards long, and this allows the negresses sometimes to make use of it as a bath for their children.

BOOK II.

THE PHYSIOLOGY OF PLANTS.

CHAPTER I.

ABSORPTION.

It is to the root and leaf that nature has intrusted the great source of nourishment—absorption.

The leaves imbibe moisture by the whole of their surface, by every pore, whilst it is only by their fine hair-like fibres that roots take up water from the soil. And still further, in the root absorption is absolutely restricted as to extent; it does not take place through the whole of the capillary filaments, but only by the microscopic spongiole which terminates each of them, and acts the part of a sucker. Hence Linnæus compared the roots to the chyliferous vessels of animals.

The great roots of vegetables, to which the vulgar naturally attribute the principal function of life, have really nothing to do with it. A very simple experiment proves this. If we place the body of the root of a plant in dry sand, whilst the fine ends of the roots are in suitable soil or in water, it continues to grow, displaying the freshest foliage. But if, on the contrary, the main mass of the root be encircled with suitable soil, whilst the fine extremities are scattered in the dry sand, the subject of the experiment fades, languishes, and dies.

An instinctive irresistible power guides the root to its goal. Nothing checks it; to attain this it cleaves the rock, traverses the water, and hangs and twists in a thousand ways.

A New England Acacia, which had become weakly and languishing after having exhausted the sterile soil in which it was planted, at last driven to quench its thirst, threw out one of its roots across a hollow of sixty-six feet, in order to plunge it into a neighbouring well, and spread out its fibres in the midst of the water. From this time, according to Malherbe, to whom we owe the story, the tree reared its sinking boughs and blighted leafage, after which it grew with marvellous rapidity.[1]

The banyan-tree, celebrated in India on account of the veneration with which it is regarded, and of its strange aspect, is still more remarkable. From its powerful horizontal boughs fall here and there fine aërial roots like simple filaments. These appendages sink slowly to the ground, as if attracted thereby, and do not enlarge till they have sunk into it. But everything changes as soon as they touch the soil. These slender shoots then acquire a considerable increase in size, forming all round the mother trunk a splendid vegetable colonnade, the manifold pillars of which uphold an imposing vault of verdure. The Brahmin sometimes places his idols beneath this rustic and mysterious temple, where the Indian bows his forehead towards the sacred Ganges. It is to this custom that the tree owes its common name of the pagoda fig-tree.

The number of aërial roots on this fig-tree is sometimes considerable, and the mother tree produces all round it an impenetrable colonnade, composed of supports of all sizes. There are some on which as many as 350 of these great roots can be counted, to which from 2000 to 3000 little ones are joined; it seems a forest in the midst of a forest. An Indian tradition tells that Alexander passed near one of these gigantic trees which still exists by the Nerbuddah.

The aërial roots of the *Clusia rosea* produce different results. The plant lets them drop from the top of the palm-tree. At first fragile and harmless, they twine themselves innocently round the stems, but very shortly they become welded together, and finding in the soil a superabundance of vital matter, these roots form a thick woody mantle, and their tortuous arms, compressing their protector more and more, finish by fixing it in the middle of an unyielding sheath so as to choke it. Hence the accursed fig-tree, for this is the common name of the parasite, is the living symbol of ingratitude.[2]

[1] Dr. Davy brought forward a case in which a horse-chestnut grew on a flat stone, the roots passing for seven feet up a wall, then turning over the top of the wall, and down again for seven feet to the earth.—Tr.

[2] The *Clusia rosea*, or rose-flowered balsam-tree, is a handsome tree growing to the height of 20 or 30 feet, and inhabiting America. Its seeds are often carried by birds and left upon the limbs or trunks of other trees. Here they take root, the rootlets crawling along the stem till they find some cavity containing decaying vegetable matter. When the nutritious matter of this is exhausted a root is sent down to the ground, perhaps a distance of forty feet, and having fixed itself there it supplies nourishment to the whole plant, which is then no longer a mere parasite.—Tr.

175. Pagoda Fig-tree (*Ficus religiosa*), with its Aërial or Adventitious Roots.

De Candolle admits, without any circumlocution, that absorption is an essentially vital phenomenon, and we share in the most unqualified manner this opinion of the greatest botanist of modern times, which was also that of Sennebier, Saussure, and Desfontaines.

To the suction of the spongiole, which ceases as soon as life is extinguished, are accessorily joined some purely physical forces, such as endosmosis, capillary attraction, and hygroscopic action, which some naturalists have erroneously looked upon as the special agents of it.

The radicles seem to select instinctively from the soil the food of the plant, which is scattered through it, just as out of the midst of the nourishment which fills the intestine in animals, the chyliferous vessels pump up only the fluid which is to regenerate the organism. Like the latter, the spongioles of plants are sometimes deceived, and introduce along with the sap some poison which kills them. But absorption is so little left to the chemico-physical powers that certain plants vegetate in soil charged with deadly substances without suffering in the least from it. In the countries where arsenic abounds there are some which brave its corrosive action. Hence, when everything else is dying round them, certain leguminous plants cover with verdure the rocky soil of Cornwall, which contains fifty per cent. of arsenical sulphuret, while the rest of it consists of silica and sulphuret of iron.[1]

By means of very simple experiments it can be demonstrated that absorption by the roots is a vital act. If, on the one hand, a root be plunged uninjured into a saline solution, and on the other a similar plant be immersed after having its members cut short off, it will be seen at the end of a certain time that the uninjured plant has not absorbed the salt in the same proportion as it is found in the solution, whereas that which has had its roots divided has been abandoned to the dominion of physico-chemical causes, and has pumped up the liquid without making any selection.[2]

Water is the principal food of the plant, but the radicles also take up other substances from the earth. They require carbon and nitrogen. The grasses demand a certain quantity of silica. The stalk of the wheat-plant contains a pretty large amount, but this substance strengthens the powerful stem of the bamboo in a much more decided manner. Accord-

[1] According to Dr. Daubeny, professor at Oxford, the sulphuret of arsenic contained in small quantities in the soil produces no injurious effect upon mustard, beans, and barley. He concludes that, to a certain extent, plants possess the power of selecting from the constituents of the soil in which they live.

[2] The sea, which contains thirty times as much sodium as potassium, furnishes to some of the Algæ, drawing all their mineral matter from it, equal quantities of these two metals, and to many others half as much potassium as sodium.—Tr.

ing to Davy, the latter contains as much as seventy-one parts of silica in a hundred, and like our flints strikes fire with the steel. According to De Candolle, analysis demonstrates that other vegetables absorb iron, and even gold. Copper has also been found in coffee and wheat, and a chemist has computed that in France 3650 kilogrammes (8055 lbs. avoirdupois, omitting grains) of this metal yearly enter into our food through the medium of this cereal.[1]

Seeing the quantity of water that plants absorb every day, Boyle

175. Ice-plant—*Mesembryanthemum crystallinum* (Linnæus).

concluded that this fluid was alone used for their nutrition. The opinion of the celebrated English philosopher was adopted by Van Helmont, and he thought he had proved it to demonstration when he saw a willow continue to flourish which he only watered with rain-water, at that time considered to be wonderfully pure.

[1] It is now considered that the inorganic ingredients in plants are as absolutely necessary to their existence as carbon and oxygen. In addition to such well-known elements of tissue as silicon, chlorine, potassium, &c., modern research has shown the presence of zinc, fluorine, cæsium, rubidium, and manganese. All food, however, presented to the plant must be oxidized, or the plant cannot take it up. It is even probable that all ammonia becomes oxidized before assimilation by the plant.—Tr.

Science has overthrown these views by proving that distilled water is in no way sufficient to support life in the plant.

The aërial organs of vegetable life also play a great part in absorption; watering the leaves of certain plants makes them grow with as much rapidity as if their roots were moistened. Some spongy plants, gorged with aqueous fluid, seem to draw their nourishment exclusively from the atmosphere. It is thus that in the burning days of summer I have found carpets of ice-plants on the most arid rocks in Greece. Although it had not rained for a month, these plants displayed a remarkable freshness, and their leaves were none the less covered with a coating of icicles![1]

The absorption effected by the leaves was known to the ancients. Theophrastus makes mention of it, but we must come to the epoch of Mariotte to reach the demonstration of this phenomenon which the

177. Absorption by the Leaves. Mariotte's experiment.

Greek botanist had only pointed out. The French philosopher attained this result by means of a very simple experiment. He took a bifurcated branch, and placed one part of it in a vessel filled with water, while the other remained exposed to the air. The water absorbed by the former sufficed to keep the latter green and fresh for a long time. Therefore the one absorbed for the other.

We must not omit stating that there are even certain plants in which this function is entirely displaced; the task is confided to the stem only. This is the case with the cactuses—strange existences—which consist solely of a monstrously swollen stem covered with spines. Growing only

[1] The glacial *Mesembryanthemum crystallinum* is a small herbaceous plant well known in science on account of its strange appearance. It has literally the look of a plant covered with drops of frozen water. This appearance is due to excessive development of all the superficial cells of the plant, which are like so many small bags filled with limpid water.

among rocks and sands parched by the sun, where all other plants around them wither into dust, these corpulent plants exhibit a freshness which is inexplicable. By some secret unknown to the myriads of different kinds the desiccated corpses of which surround them, they contrive to imbibe from the atmosphere the abundance of water which swells out their tissues. Among these "heralds of ruined soils," as Ch. Müller calls them, the roots, represented only by a few dried fibres, draw absolutely nothing from the calcined rock which supports them. It is therefore the stem which nourishes itself, the leaves are so rudimentary, so little apparent, that it may be looked upon as entirely deprived of them.

In our hot-houses the same thing may be seen every day. Cactuses, which are never watered, thrive there splendidly by means of the moist and warm atmosphere with which they are surrounded.

CHAPTER II.

THE CIRCULATION IN PLANTS.

The more we study nature the grander does she appear. Science, by penetrating her secrets, often shows us that hidden and imposing forces exist where we only see inertia. The obscure vitality of plants, brought to light by the genius of naturalists, sometimes manifests itself to our eyes in unexpected power.

Plants, like animals, have a circulation. It is to that universal genius Claude Perrault, at one and the same time physician, architect, and naturalist, that we owe the discovery of this phenomenon. The sap, which is in fact the blood of the plant, circulates through its vessels by means of a power possibly greatly exceeding that which drives the blood through the arteries of an elephant. The celebrated Hales made a very curious experiment on this subject. Having fitted a long tube to the stem of a young vine which he had severed, he saw this fluid rise forty-four feet high. These results appearing very extraordinary to the French physiologists, they soon repeated the experiments of the English philosopher, but they were greatly astonished to see that they were within the mark. In fact, De Candolle, who was one of the last to move in the matter, noticed that the force with which the sap rises in the vessels of the plant is equal to the pressure of two atmospheres and a half—a force which enormously exceeds, and indeed almost doubles, the results obtained by the Canon of Windsor, since it is equal to the weight of a column of water eighty feet in height.

Thus in an occult function, which is performed so mysteriously in the vegetable kingdom, experiment reveals a powerful energy — an energy which surpasses the visible and tumultuous circulation in the largest animals. Many physiologists have stated, not without some foundation, that the sap rises in the vessels of the vine with at least five times as much force as the blood circulates in the crural artery of the horse — the most important blood-vessel of the thigh — and with seven times as much force as in the same vessel in the dog.

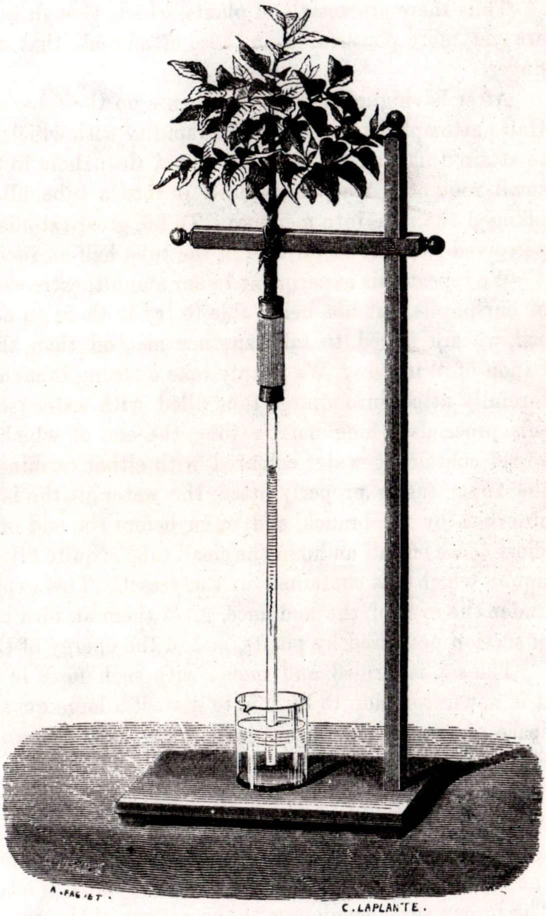

178. Force of Vegetable Circulation and Absorption. Hales' experiment, modified, as shown at the Amphitheatre of Rouen.

It is certain that the blood which the heart projects so violently into the vessels of large animals is not driven with so much power as impels the sap in its ascending movement. Indeed, experiments made on the ox and horse have shown that the impulse given to the arterial blood would only raise a column of blood about $6\frac{1}{2}$ feet; the advantage is therefore not at all on the side where it was supposed to be, since, according to what has been already stated, the vegetable circulation raises a weight fourteen times greater than does that of the largest mammals.

Thus there are vessels of plants, which, though not so thick as a hair, are yet more powerful than those of animals that are thicker than the finger.

After having made his experiments on the force of ascent in the sap, Hales attempted to ascertain the rapidity with which it moved. In order to attain this end, he hollowed out a deep hole in the soil, laid bare a small root of a tree, introduced it into a tube filled with water, and plunged the tube into mercury. To his great astonishment he very soon perceived that the metal rose in the tube half an inch per minute.

We repeat this experiment in our amphitheatre every year in presence of our pupils, but not being able to try it there on a tree planted in the soil, we are forced to take another method than that adopted by the Canon of Windsor. We simply take a strong branch of a tree, which is carefully fitted into a large tube filled with water (see Fig. 178). From this proceeds a long narrow tube, the end of which is plunged into a vessel containing water coloured with either carmine or indigo. When the apparatus is properly fitted, the water in the larger tube is rapidly absorbed by the branch, and often before the end of the lesson, in the short space of half an hour, the small tube is quite filled with the coloured liquid which was contained in the vessel. This experiment, carried on under the eyes of the audience, gives them an idea at once of the force of suction possessed by plants, and of the energy of their circulation.

The sap is formed and moves with such force in certain plants, that it is not uncommon to be able to extract a large quantity of it in a short space of time. The sugar-maple (*Acer saccharinum*), scattered over the mountains of Canada, produces a bucketful in a day. It is from this tree that they get the greatest part of the sugar consumed in the country where it grows.[1]

For this purpose it is only necessary to pierce the tree with a wimble; the sap runs from it, and after being collected is evaporated at the fire. The brown sugar condenses at the bottom of the evaporating pans.

[1] The sap of the sugar-maple begins to rise in the month of February. In order to extract it they simply bore a hole in its trunk a few inches deep, and into this insert a tube which allows the fluid to drop into a pail. When fermented, it furnishes a light and agreeable wine, and when evaporated by a gentle heat, it yields a brown, viscid syrup, as sweet as treacle, which is converted into little sugar-loaves. Each tree produces yearly two to four pounds.

179. Scene in North America—Collecting the Sap of the Sugar-maple—*Acer saccharinum* (Linnæus).

In the tropical countries a tree yields a product not less precious to man—a wine ready made. This is nothing else than the sap of a species

180. The Wine-tree or Wine-bearing Sago-palm—*Sagus vinifera.*

of palm—the wine-bearing sago-palm (*Sagus vinifera*), which grows in Western Africa, and the name of which characteristically indicates the benefits it yields. This vinous sap is mild and sweet when first drawn, but a few hours afterwards it ferments, and then becomes a most intoxicating drink. It is very widely used, and the tree yields it in profusion. The negroes quickly fill their calabashes with it by hanging them to the petioles of the leaves, which for this purpose are cut off soon after their birth.

The vegetable circulation has such energy, and the liquid which it bears away is reproduced at such a rate, that Scott assures us that out of certain birch-trees there flows, in spring, a quantity of fluid equal to their weight.

Looking at results so totally unexpected, we ask what association of mysterious forces produces such phenomena. If the ancients sometimes went astray in exaggerating the faculties of the plant, our epoch has often fallen into the opposite extreme.

Many modern naturalists, retrograding towards the Cartesian philosophy, explain the vital actions of the plant only by the intervention of purely physical or chemical forces. According to some, their circulation is merely a matter of capillary attraction, or endosmosis; according to others, it is a simple fermentation, or a series of electric shocks.

But one solitary objection, one alone, immediately levels with the dust all these hypotheses which the materialist so zealously takes up. These physico-chemical phenomena are so little the initiatory cause of the circulation, that they have never yet proved adequate to reanimate life in a plant which has been killed without changing the tissues; and if the causes of life were absolutely under the empire of material forces, the supporters of these strange opinions which are so much in vogue ought to be able to resuscitate dead organisms.

But we are happy to say that the leading minds in physiology have not fallen into the errors we have touched upon.

Our immortal anatomist Bichat did not hesitate in the least on this point; he set an example to all by attributing the circulation in the plant to the same cause which makes the blood move in the capillary vessels of animals.

The greatest botanists of our time follow the author of *General Anatomy*. De Candolle thinks that the ascent of the sap must be ascribed to the vital contraction of the tissues; its cause he considers is allied to life. Achille Richard, after a general view of the whole power of vegetable circulation, compares it to that of insects.[1]

[1] Achille Richard, so illustrious as a savant, and of so worthy and noble a character, often reverts in his work to the vital power in plants. On this subject he expresses himself, when speaking of the circulation in plants, in the following authoritative manner:—"Here, as in most other functions of animals and plants, we must admit an unknown, powerful,

Schultz of Berlin, who has so deeply studied this function, considers it as essentially due to the vital action of the vessels. By means of the microscope we can, according to him, see these contract in order to propel the fluid which they contain. The learned Prussian even perceives, in reference to this phenomenon, a great analogy between plants and certain inferior animals of the class of worms.

After such authorities it is impossible to hesitate any longer, and it must be admitted that the circulation in plants is essentially due to a vital cause. Then follow, as accessory powers, the various actions of heat, capillary attraction, endosmosis, and electricity. With the aid of the microscope any person can convince himself of the truth of everything here stated. In viewing with this instrument plants in which the sap contains coloured granules, we see these pass rapidly along in the capillary vessels. Professor Schultz even says that in certain cases these vessels may be seen contracting so as to force onward the particular juices which they contain.

CHAPTER III.

THE RESPIRATION OF PLANTS.

The largest animals—the whale, the rhinoceros, the ostrich, and also man—only respire air by one channel, and it is in a certain degree in one retort, the lungs, that all the chemical reactions of their respiration are effected. In this respect plants are better provided for than is generally supposed. Instead of one sole apparatus, the microscopic laboratories in which their pneumatic combinations are mysteriously carried out may be counted by thousands of millions; a single leaf sometimes presents more than a million in its interstices.

Leaves are in fact only the lungs of plants. The microscope discovers on their surface a crowd of elongated openings, with swollen edges, and not unlike the button-holes of our dress. These are the stomata, or open orifices by which the air enters the respiratory chambers. Of extremely restricted size, owing to their being in the thickness of the leaf, these invisible little chambers are hollowed out in the cellular tissue, and their

active force, the result of organization and life, which is their immediate, indispensable agent, and which is designated vital force."—Richard, *Botanique et Physiologie Végétale*. Paris, 1846, p. 238.

roofs are supported by fine colonnades of cells placed end to end, the marvellous labyrinth of which is traversed by the air.

Some aquatic plants, which live in the depths of the rivers, do not present this organization. Having no connection with the atmosphere, these aërial cavities would be of no service; hence they display quite a peculiar arrangement, approaching more that exhibited by fish, which have a special respiratory apparatus, the branchiæ, so disposed as to take up imperceptible portions of air contained in the water in large enough quantity to suffice for their respiration. An analogous disposition is seen in certain plants of the family of the naïads, Naïadeæ,[1] which live in our pools and ditches. Their leaves are unprovided with epidermis, and represent a kind of branchiæ, constructed to act upon the atmospheric particles contained in the medium in which they live. Of this class are the potamogetons or pond-weeds, which, in respect to their respiration, considered in an isolated point of view, are in reality fish-plants.

The respiration of animals is injurious to the composition of the atmospheric air; they vitiate it incessantly, either by absorbing the vital principle oxygen, or by diffusing in it a deadly poison—carbonic acid.

It has been calculated that the human species alone consumes annually 160,000 millions of cubic yards of oxygen, and that animals quadruple this amount.

On the other hand, every man exhales daily about 8 oz. troy of carbonic acid gas, which gives about $2\frac{1}{4}$ oz. troy of combustible carbon. Hence, without reckoning the amount produced by animals, the quantity of carbon poured into the atmosphere by the population of France alone may be computed at about 2,500,000 tons per annum.

This alarming alteration in our atmosphere is enough to startle one; it seems as if it must bring on an entire destruction of animal life. But by the side of the disturbing element Providence has placed the means of reparation; the mantle of verdure on the globe remedies all the disorders called forth by the animal kingdom; each plant represents a regular *machine for purifying the air.*

Plants require a large quantity of carbon for their nourishment and the formation of their solid framework. For this purpose they absorb all the carbonic acid they can find in the air, and then fix its carbon in their tissues by exhaling the oxygen; a twofold action, in the course of which they render the air wholesome, and regenerate it by restoring the vital gas which animals absorb, and removing the poison which they continually diffuse.

[1] Also called Fluviales, a small natural order of endogens.—Tr.

This harmonious contrast will strike every one, and we see that it is destined to counteract the incessant changes which the animal kingdom introduces into the atmosphere, and to protect it from all serious perturbation. According to M. Brongniart, the law of equilibrium is such at this moment, that plants seem to pour into the atmosphere as much oxygen as animals consume.

Nothing is easier than to estimate the quantity of oxygen which plants distil at every pore into the atmosphere. For this it is only

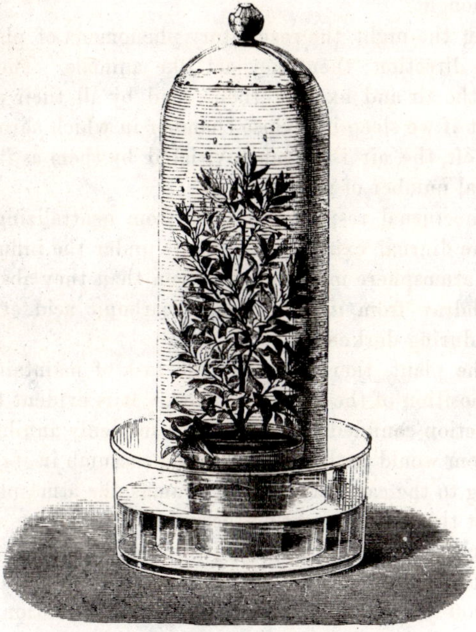

181. Respiration of Plants. Disengagement of Oxygen under Water.

necessary to put one under a bell-glass filled with water; as soon as it is exposed to the light, all its foliage becomes covered with bubbles of gas which are disengaged from it, and rise without ceasing to the top of the vase. If we now analyze the product collected there, we find, from the brilliancy it gives to bodies in a state of ignition, that it is oxygen and in possession of all its attributes.

But it is a remarkable fact that this salutary intervention of plants is only manifested under the influence of light. Were the star from which light emanates to be extinguished, it would cease in a moment, and the globe, plunged in obscurity, would soon be deprived of its green tunic. Lavoisier was therefore right when he said:—

"Organization, feeling, spontaneous movement, and life only exist on the surface of the earth, or in parts exposed to light. One might say that the fable of the torch of Prometheus expressed a philosophic truth which had not escaped the ancients. Without light nature would be without life; she would be dead and inanimate; a beneficent God, by imparting light, has shed over the surface of the earth organization, sensation, and thought."

But during the night the respiratory phenomena of plants take the very opposite direction; then they act like animals. They absorb the vital part of the air and exude carbonic acid by all their pores, to such an extent that if we sleep in a close chamber in which shrubs have been imprudently left, the air is as much vitiated by them as if it had contained an equal number of men.

But this nocturnal respiration is far from neutralizing the benefit effected by the diurnal exhalation. Plants under the influence of light pour into the atmosphere much more oxygen than they absorb by night, and they withdraw from it greatly more carbonic acid every day than they produce during darkness.

It is to the plant, therefore, that the task of maintaining the harmonious composition of the air is intrusted. It is evident that were the important function confided to plants to be suddenly annihilated, all the animal kingdom would within a given time succumb in its turn. However, according to the calculations of M. Dumas, the atmosphere is so rich in oxygen that this event would not occur till after a long series of ages. The learned chemist maintains that it would require at least 800,000 years for all the animals on the globe to absorb the whole of this gas, and that 10,000 years would pass without its diminution being made sensible by our most perfect instruments.[1]

[1] The weight of the air which encircles us is equal to 581,000 cubes of copper, 1093 yards on every side. The oxygen in it weighs as much as 134,000 of these cubes. Supposing the earth to be peopled by 1,000,000,000 souls, and taking the animals on it as equivalent to 3,000,000,000 men, we should find that these together would, in a century, only consume a weight of oxygen equal to 15 or 16 of these cubes of copper, whilst the air contains 134,000.

It would require 10,000 years for all the people on earth to produce an effect on the air appreciable by Volta's eudiometer (an instrument for measuring the purity of the air), even supposing that vegetable life remained annihilated during all that time. Thus the proportion of oxygen the air contains is guaranteed for many ages, even entirely excluding the action of plants. Nevertheless these incessantly return to it as much oxygen as it loses, and perhaps more, for plants also exist as much at the expense of the carbonic acid furnished

By means of ingenious investigations Professor Liebig has even proved that the chemical nature of the atmosphere has not varied sensibly for upwards of 2000 years. He took one of the little glass vases in which on the death of persons who were dear to them the Roman ladies collected their tears, and which, after being partly filled, were hermetically sealed by fusion, and deposited in the sarcophagus with the dead. The lachrymal vase having been broken and its contents analyzed, the great chemist found that the air was of exactly the same composition as the fluid which we respire now-a-days.

M. Lacrèze-Fossat was enabled, by means of delicate experiments, to determine the proportion of respirable gas discharged into the atmosphere by certain plants. This observer noticed that in twelve hours the under surface of the large floating leaves which the yellow water-lily (*Nymphœa lutea*) spreads out on our rivers, produced over ten cubic inches of oxygen. And, according to him, a single specimen of this plant, composed of fifteen leaves, in five months exhaled into the atmosphere 117·7 gallons.

How much then must be produced in a single season by a large tree, the respiratory surface of which is of such a size compared to that of the aquatic plant.

CHAPTER IV.

TRANSPIRATION IN PLANTS.

Vegetable physiology approaches very nearly that of animals. Like them plants exhale moisture abundantly by their whole surface. It is this which, condensed upon the leaves by the cold of night, forms on them limpid little drops of water, which the vulgar incorrectly ascribe to a deposit of atmospheric moisture.

The idea that plants transpire like animals is due to Muschenbroeck, one of the professors who have contributed most to rendering the university of Leyden illustrious. For this purpose he covered with a plate of lead the whole circumference of the root of a white poppy, so as to prevent the vapour of the earth from interfering with his experiment. The plant was then covered with a bell-glass cemented to the lead.

by volcanoes as at that of the acid expired by animals.—Dumas, *Essai de Statique Chimique des Etres Organisés.* Paris, 1842, p. 18.

After that each morning when the naturalist came to visit the imprisoned plant he observed, that even during the driest nights its leaves were covered with an innumerable quantity of those drops of water to which the name of dew is given, and that the sides of the glass themselves were quite obscured with it. It is not then from the air that the dew of the meadow and the leaf comes, but, as the Dutch naturalist learned, from the transpiration of the plant; dew is only their perspiration condensed.

This fact being thoroughly established, it only remained to decide the amount which vegetable transpiration produces. Mariotte tried a very elementary experiment on this head. Having cut off a branch and covered the section with impermeable cement, he observed that the

182. Discovery of the Transpiration of Plants.—Muschenbroeck's experiment.

leaves, while withering, had lost two tea-spoonfuls of water in two hours, at a time when the air was tolerably warm. The naturalist therefore concluded that in twelve hours the branch would lose a dozen tea-spoonfuls.

But such an estimate was far from being exact. Guettard managed better; he conceived the idea of not separating the branch from the plant, but of inclosing it in a globe of glass, terminating outwardly in a neck which was inserted into a flask. When all was hermetically sealed, the moisture transpired, condensing itself on the sides of the globe, fell drop by drop into the bottle situated beneath it, and could be collected without the slightest loss, so that nature was left to herself.

Inclosed in this apparatus, a branch of a cornel-tree weighing only five drachms and a half distilled each day an ounce and three drachms of water; that is to say, it transpired double its weight in twenty-four hours—results which were far from being expected.

When on a burning summer day, exhausted and streaming with perspiration, we see in the by-nook of a parterre the garden sun-flower, we admire its heavy floral crown turned towards the luminary which it ceaselessly accompanies in its course, and its ample and motionless leaves; but this apparent calm vails a most unexpected vital energy.

183. Transpiration in Plants.—Guettard's experiment.

Who indeed would think that the perspiration exhaled by the leaves of the plant is more copious than that which moistens our foreheads? Yet science has proved this; after demonstrating the existence of vegetable transpiration, it has dared to estimate comparatively the extent of it.

An old physician of Padua, Sanctorius, whose originality has become celebrated, had the patience to pass a great part of his life in a pair of scales, weighing and reweighing himself every minute in the day, in order to ascertain how much loss his body underwent by transpiration.[1]

[1] Experiments show that on an average a man loses 2·2 lbs. avoirdupois of watery vapour by means of his skin in twenty-four hours.

Hales, without having the same perseverance, attempted to ascertain what weight of water a sun-flower lost daily by its leaves. For this

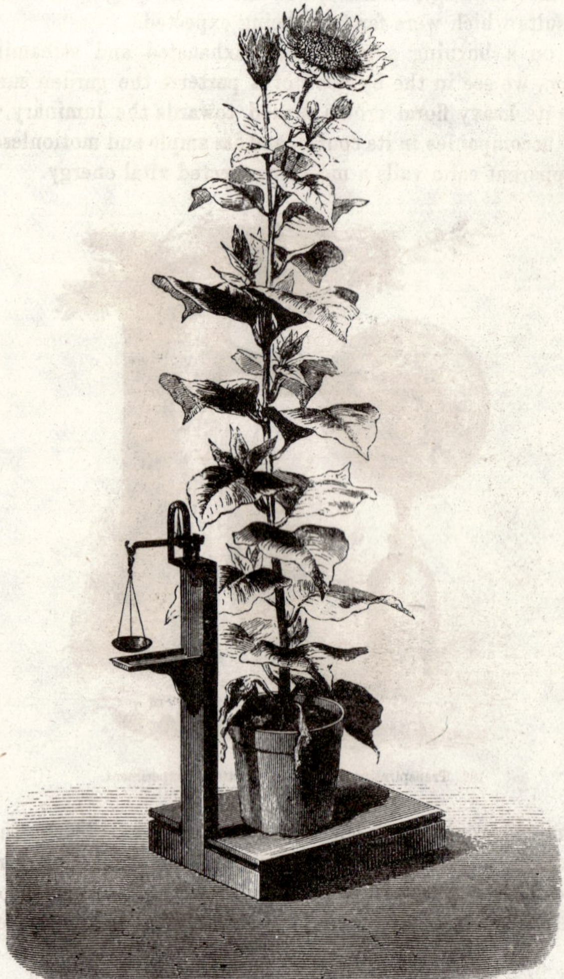

184. Transpiration in the Sun-flower.—Hales' experiment.

purpose he put one of these plants into a pot, the upper surface of which, hermetically closed with a plate of lead, only presented one small neck through which it could be watered. By weighing this sun-flower daily his scales showed him that it lost, by the transpiration of its leaves only, twenty ounces of water in the twenty-four hours.

The experimenter having subsequently calculated the difference in extent between the skin of a man and the leaves of a sun-flower, found

185. Edible Arum—*Colocasia esculenta* (Schott).

that the former is to the latter as 26 to 10, and that consequently, with equal surfaces, the insensible transpiration of the sun-flower is seventeen times as great as our own.

In some plants the phenomenon does not take place so mysteriously; their leaves transpire with surprising abundance; water streams from all their pores.

Ruysch states that an Arum, which he kept in a greenhouse in the botanical garden at Amsterdam, distilled water drop by drop from the extremities of its leaves in proportion, so to speak, as it was watered.

One might think there was some hyperbole in this, but recent and curious observations, which we owe to an experimenter of Toulouse, have proved the thorough exactness of the fact put forward by the great Dutch anatomist. M. Ch. Musset has discovered that a plant of the same family as has been mentioned, the Edible Arum, launches little drops of water in the form of a jet into the air, and that these exhale from the pores which we see on the tips of its magnificent heart-shaped leaves, undulated like the waves of the sea. The ingenious and learned observer of this extraordinary phenomenon noticed, that from each of these orifices from ten to a hundred drops of water were thrown every minute the distance of an inch or more.

But the vegetable marvel in respect to transpiration is the weeping-tree, which was seen some years ago in one of the Canary Islands. The water fell like copious rain from its tufted foliage—a fact which botanists sought to express by calling it *Cœsalpinia pluviosa.* Collected at the foot of the tree, it formed, it is said, a kind of pond, from which the inhabitants of the vicinity furnished themselves with water.[1]

At first I suspected some exaggeration in the accounts given by travellers as to the transpiration of this extraordinary tree, but after seeing an arborescent Fuchsia in one of the greenhouses of the botanical garden of Rouen rain down so much water upon the plants round about it that it was necessary to remove them, I have believed the statements.

The insensible transpiration is demonstrated by the most simple experiment. It is only necessary to place a plant under a dry bell-glass, the base of which is plunged in mercury. In a few seconds all the inner surface of the glass is covered with tiny drops of water, which become condensed and run downwards.

The leaves of other plants, more tenacious of the perspiration they

[1] In the *Historia de la Conquista de las Is'as Canarias*, by Juan de Abreu Galindo, it is stated that there was at Hierro (Ferro) a laurel-tree which, according to M. Roulin, was perhaps the *Laurus fœtens*, that furnished the natives of the island with drinking water. This fluid distilled drop by drop from the foliage, and was preserved in cisterns. This marvellous vegetable fountain was, during part of the day, enveloped in a cloud, from the bosom of which it drew its supply of water. But the tradition of the tree quoted by the old historian of the seventeenth century is no longer found among the conquerors of the island.

186. The Weeping-tree—*Cæsalpinia pluviosa* (*Laurus fœtens*, Ait.?)

distil, collect it in little cups, which are found at their ends, sometimes constantly open, sometimes closing and opening by means of a movable lid.

187. Pitcher-plant—*Nepenthes distillatoria* (Linnæus).

In the first rank we ought to place the famous *Nepenthes distillatoria*, or pitcher-plant, met with in Southern Asia. Its leaves display a strong mid-rib, which extends beyond the blade and ends in an elegant cylindrical cup, provided with a hinged lid, which spontaneously opens and closes according to the state of the atmosphere. During the night this lid sinks down and hermetically closes the little vase, which then fills with limpid water exhaled by its walls. During the day the lid is raised and the fluid evaporates more or less completely. The beneficent nepenthe has often quenched the thirst of the Indian lost in his burning deserts.

In the marshy forests of Southern America Providence has intrusted this task to another distilling plant, the Purple Sarracenia, the structure of which is no less eccentric. Its leaves, uniting at their edges, are transformed into elegant amphoræ, the narrow opening of which is sur-

188. The Purple Sarracenia—*Sarracenia purpurea* (Linnæus).

mounted by an ample green auricle decorated with scarlet red veins, to which the species owes its name. These cups, presents from the empire of Flora, and which rise from spot to spot at the feet of the traveller, are filled with pure and delicious water, for the benefit of which he is all the more grateful that he is encircled by nothing but marshes, the water of which is lukewarm and nauseous.

Generally, transpiration from the leaves only takes place by their under surface. Knight demonstrated this by a very simple experiment. He inclosed a vine leaf between two plates of glass, and observed that only the plate in contact with this side was covered with the secretion. I succeeded still better, and make, I believe, the experiment more scientific, by using a leaf of the Indian chestnut attached to its branch, and sucking up the water into a vase at hand in proportion as it transpires. All the under surface of the leaf is speedily covered with little drops of water visible to the eye, and which obscure the glass it is in contact with, whilst that to which the other surface is applied barely shows traces of vapour.

CHAPTER V.

GROWTH.

The growth of our trees was for long an impenetrable mystery.

Duhamel maintained that it was the bark which produced the wood, and for more than a century this was believed on the faith of the celebrated academician who had made so many experiments on the subject. It did not occur to any one to ask him from whence the bark came.

After many discussions it has at last been shown that the woody structure and its envelope grow at their junction, each in its own way: the bark growing towards the interior, the wood outwards by concentric layers which are piled up one above the other. One is produced each year, so that by counting the circular zones at the base of a trunk, their number gives the exact age of a tree.

Long before this fact had been taught as a dogma by botanists, it was known to the vulgar. Mention is made of it in Michel Montaigne's *Voyage en Italie*, a singular production, wherein, instead of Italy, we find only a list and the effects of different remedies which the illustrious Mayor of Bordeaux employed in every town he passed through. A journeyman turner showed him that he could compute the age of trees very well from sections of them. "He taught me," he says, "that all trees bear as many circles as they have endured years, and pointed it out to me in all those he had in his shop. And that part which looks towards the north is narrower and has closer and denser rings than the other.[1]

At a later date Adanson the botanist was enabled, by means of

[1] M. Ch. Musset states that the trunks of trees are always flattened in a northerly and southerly direction, and expand in an east and west plane: a fact which he considers quite in accordance with astronomical laws.

observation, to prove how exact were the statements of our celebrated writer. An avenue of trees in the Champs-Elysées, planted 200 years previously, being cut down in his time, the same number of woody zones was found in a transverse section of the trunks of each one. This section therefore showed their age.

These views about growth explain certain phenomena which have often been considered miraculous.

When, as an imperishable testimony to their constancy, two lovers carve their entwined initials upon the bark, the chisellings on the tree, alas! do not endure longer than their vows. The incessant separation which the parts of this envelope undergo, owing to annual growth, first distorts and then totally effaces the letters.

But if the engraving penetrate deeper, if the tool pass through the layers of the bark and reach the wood, all goes differently; the workman has carved upon solid matter. As years only cause the deposit of new woody layers upon the surface of the work, this is preserved intact. And when after a long lapse of time the trunk is cleft, the chisellings are revealed to our astonished eyes, in marvellous preservation and in the depths of its layers.

Solid bodies introduced into the wooded layers are speedily covered by and soon disappear beneath them. Professor Desfontaines used to show us regularly at his lectures the horn of a stag which had become almost entirely enveloped by the trunk of a tree, into which the animal had, no doubt, thrust the horn some little way in getting rid of it.

Some few years ago, when a large tree in the environs of Orleans was cleft, a cavity quite closed up was found towards its centre containing a death's-head and cross-bones. The astonishment of the public was extreme, and the prodigy was talked about everywhere. But really the whole turned upon a vital phenomenon of which physiology gives a complete explanation. At a distant epoch some anchorite of the forest, having probably hollowed the tree, prostrated himself and prayed before these human relics, which he placed in the excavation. Then the recluse having disappeared in the course of years, nature took up the work again, and ingeniously preserved the oratory by covering it with thick woody layers.

During the siege of Toulon a ball from the English fleet entered deep into the stem of a pine standing near the town. The wound is now invisible. Should this tradition be lost, how astonished would any one be, on cutting down the tree, to find this enormous mass of iron!

Generally the denser plants are the slower in their growth; on the contrary, the softer their tissues the more rapidly are they developed.

Certain plants astonish us in this respect, and there are even some, the vital energy of which is so active, that we can in some measure pry into the secrets of their evolution; accordingly Cavanilles conceived the idea of seeing the plant grow. For this purpose he directed strong glasses, furnished with a horizontal micrometric thread, upon the end of the stem of certain plants, just as astronomers do when they place the cross-thread of the telescope athwart a star of which they want to ascertain the movement. The Spanish botanist made his observations principally on agaves and bamboos. With the latter the experiments might

189. Gigantic Lycoperdon or Puff-ball—*Lycoperdon giganteum* (Batsch), of one night's growth.—From nature.

yield very clear results, as they grow with such rapidity that we sometimes see them attain the height of a three-storied house in a month.

A bamboo, which grew a few years ago in one of the greenhouses of the Jardin des Plantes at Paris, lengthened out its stem at the rate of about five inches and four-fifths daily, so that it could easily have been seen growing, as its upward movement was as quick as that of the large hand of a time-piece.

But a still more extraordinary fact is noticed with respect to certain Fungi, and it may be said of them, without hyperbole, that they grow visibly. This is the case with the gigantic Lycoperdon (*Lycoperdon giganteum*), which, springing from a seed so small that it absolutely escapes our sight, reaches the size of a gourd in one night, so that it may be said without any exaggeration, that this plant, of a most degraded order, acquires a bulk which our children require ten years to attain. This fungus being only composed of microscopic cells, an immense number are required to make it up, and besides, they must grow with prodigious rapidity. Lindley calculates that a Lycoperdon like this contains more than 47,000,000,000 cells, and that, taking the time of its evolution at twelve hours, it produces about 4,000,000,000 cells every hour, and 96,000,000 every minute.

But what a much more feverish activity must reign in the vital laboratory of those monstrous lycoperdons, nine feet in circumference, of which Bulliard speaks in his *History of Fungi!*

CHAPTER VI.

THE SECRETIONS.

In every part of the vegetable kingdom the most extraordinary contrasts are seen. We find them as well in the details as in the organism viewed as a whole; in the aspect of a plant as in the obscure functions of the cell. The same pores exude at one time a beneficent nourishment, at another a treacherous poison; demulcent juices or corrosive liquids. The same fruit, or the same root, nourishes or instantly kills us.

The tapioca on which the American savage feeds, and which is so often employed at our tables, abounds in the midst of a poison as deadly as the philtres of Locusta. The edible portion is taken out for the purposes of commerce; but the negroes, when they want to commit suicide, eat the root whole. The effect is almost as rapid as that of prussic acid.[1]

[1] Two products which are extensively used as food for man, cassava and tapioca, are elaborated in the midst of the most deadly juices. They are both furnished by the root of the *Manihot utilissima* (the *Janipha Manihot*), found extensively in Africa and the West Indies. The negroes are well acquainted with the virulence of this poison; but as it is very volatile and easily decomposed, being considered analogous to prussic acid, it is easily destroyed and rendered powerless by fermentation, so that the rude tribes of America manage to extract from the starchy root of the manioc the nourishing food so often served up at our tables under the name of tapioca.

On one spot bloom friendly flowers, the folds of which only distil a perfumed nectar that the bee transforms into honey; elsewhere, sombre

190. The Tapioca Plant and its Root—*Manihot utilissima* (Pohl).

It is composed of tolerably pure fecula, which is collected with care, but the farina of manioc, on which so many of the American races feed, is coarser. All they do in order to extract it is to press the roots of the plant; the result of which is a mixture of starch, vegetable fibre, and extractive matter. It is afterwards dried in chimneys, and when desiccation is sufficiently advanced, it is powdered and bread is made of the flour it yields.

corollas like those of the crown-imperial, and some azaleas, exude only venomous juices. Woe to the insect that feeds thereon, for they yield only deadly products. Our readers will recollect the accident which overtook the army of Xenophon near Trebizond, in the famous retreat of the ten thousand Greeks. His soldiers, weakened with hunger and fatigue, having seized eagerly upon some honey which they found near the sea, all fell to the ground a few moments afterwards, dangerously poisoned. Tournefort rightly ascribes this accident to the bees of the country having imbibed the juices contained in the calices of the *Azalea pontica*, which he observed to be poisonous.

The hand of Providence draws freely from the vegetable kingdom to satisfy our pleasures and our wants.

The petals of the rose, the jasmine, and the tuberose are steeped in precious essences which perfume the air all round them, and of which art bereaves them in large quantities for the refinements of luxury.[1]

Other plants of more modest appearance, such as mint, rosemary, balm, and lavender, are better provided in this respect, for their odoriferous oils exhale from all their tissues, and they pour them forth even more freely than the others. The species which contain them sometimes betray themselves by perfuming the air to a great distance. Bartholin tells us that the odour of the rosemary indicates the coast of Spain more than ten leagues out at sea, and the old historian Diodorus Siculus relates something analogous with respect to Arabia.

The sugar-cane (*Saccharum officinarum*), originally from India and Arabia Felix, fills its pith with the alimentary substance which has been for so many ages extracted from it.

Strabo, in his *Geography*, speaking of the productions of these two

[1] The tissues of the plants of India, Mexico, and Peru are impregnated with precious aromatics, but it is from the south of Europe that commerce draws the principal part of the perfumes which we enjoy. The mild temperature of Provence is wonderfully suited to the culture of the sweet-smelling plants of all countries, and hence this province is familiarly styled the garden of Europe. This cultivation is carried on chiefly in the environs of Grasse, Nice, and Cannes.

The consumption of flowers in the establishment of M. Hermann alone, one of the principal perfumers of Cannes, will give an idea of the importance of this branch of commerce. He uses yearly above 153,000 lbs. of orange flowers, 13,000 lbs. of black-currant flowers, more than 153,000 lbs. of rose flowers, 35,000 lbs. of jasmine flowers, 22,000 lbs. of violets, 8800 lbs. of tuberoses, without counting the mint and rosemary which are so common all through Provence. [Great quantities of the flowers grown in the south of France are used by the London perfumers, and the flower season is watched as anxiously there as the grain harvest in other districts. The only blossom for which this climate is better suited than any other, and which is used to any extent by perfumers, is that of lavender, the French being of very inferior quality.—Tr.]

countries, and Dioscorides also, in his great repertory of medical lore, evidently make mention of this grass. The former says it is a reed which yields honey. Dioscorides is still more explicit. According to him the reeds of India and Arabia yield a congealed thick honey as hard as salt, which crumbles between the teeth, and which is called sugar. According to the learned, the Chinese have understood the culture of the sugar-cane and the art of extracting its produce from the remotest antiquity.

Bélon even says that this plant is mentioned in a host of Indian and Arabic works; and Humboldt seems to confirm all this by attesting that it is found drawn upon the oldest China porcelain.

Thus, then, there can be no doubt that the sugar-cane is indigenous in the Old World, and that its culture goes back to a very remote period.

But it was towards the thirteenth century that the merchants who imitated Marco Polo, by bringing the products of India overland to Europe, introduced the plant into Nubia and Egypt, from whence, in the fourteenth century, it was carried to Sicily, Syria, and Madeira. From thence it was finally transported to America soon after its discovery.

Another grass, maize (*Zea Mays*), also contains sugar in its stem, but it was not so much on account of this, as for the sake of its beauty and its use as an article of food, that it became almost sacred among the ancient races in America. The Peruvian virgins, themselves devoted to the worship of the sun, made bread from it which the Incas offered as a sacrifice. And when the sacred plant failed in their gardens, they substituted gold and silver imitations.[1]

Manna, also valuable in many respects, is the ready-prepared sugar furnished by a tree. It runs and hardens on the trunk and branches of the flowering-ash, which is cultivated in Sicily, and from which the white and sugary stalactites are collected by means of a wooden knife.[2]

On the other hand, the trunks and fruits of some curious trees are quite covered with a thick coat of wax, exactly similar to that of the bee, and which is used instead of it for giving light and other purposes.

[1] Maize certainly comes originally from America, though it is erroneously called in some parts Turkish and Indian wheat, under the supposition that it is indigenous to these countries. If this beautiful gramineous plant had belonged to the old continent, the ancient naturalists and authorities on farming would not have failed to mention it, and yet it is not spoken of in the writings of Theophrastus, Pliny, Columella, and Dioscorides. And while no author names it before the discovery of Columbus, we see, on the contrary, the first describers of America constantly speaking of it.

[2] The manna used in medicine is principally procured from the flowering-ash (*Fraxinus ornus*), which is cultivated for this purpose in Sicily and Calabria. Other trees produce analogous substances. The larch-tree (*Larix europœa*, Linn.) furnishes the manna of Briançon. In some countries even herbs are covered with an abundant sugary exudation.

Among these is the wax-palm (*Ceroxylon andicola*) found in the Andes, the stipe of which is incrusted with this substance, which the savages

191. Manna-tree—*Fraxinus ornus* (Linnæus), and Manna-gathering in Sicily.

remove by rubbing it off as they climb the tree. The candleberry-myrtle (*Myrica cerifera*) is another, but in it the precious substance exudes from the fruit, and is extracted by simply boiling it, the wax quickly rising to the top.

Again, some vegetable secretions, formed in obscurity, deep in the stems of certain trees, and gathered by the intelligent hand of man, add to the wealth of nations. Thus the French pine spreads its treasures over the once sterile heaths of Bordeaux. From incisions made in it

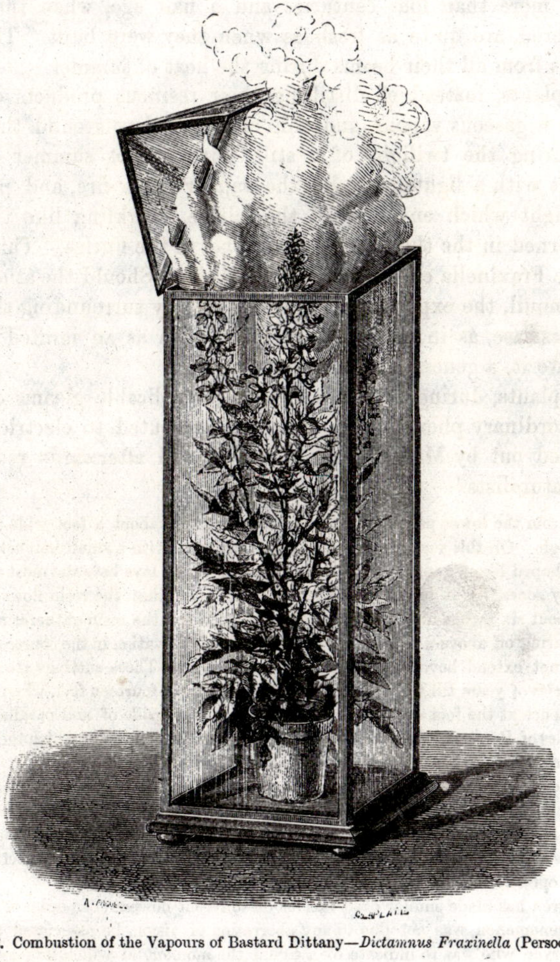

192. Combustion of the Vapours of Bastard Dittany—*Dictamnus Fraxinella* (Persoon).

flows a turpentine which the resin-gatherers, active as monkeys, collect in numberless cups suspended to the trunks of the trees.[1]

It is this secretion that gives to the coniferous woods such power of

[1] The resin is extracted when the maritime pine has reached the age of twenty to thirty years. In order to obtain it, workmen, called resin-gatherers, remove with an axe the

endurance; the more it abounds in their resinous ducts, the greater lapse of ages can they endure. The wood of the Canary Islands pine (*Pinus canariensis*) is quite impregnated with it, and is therefore almost imperishable. The ancient dwellings in Teneriffe, which were entirely built of this wood more than four centuries and a half ago, when the island was conquered, are quite as fresh as when they were built. The resin still exudes from all their beams during the heat of summer.

Some plants, instead of distilling their resinous products drop by drop, form a gaseous vapour, and this clings so close around the plant, that if, during the twilight of a still, burning hot summer day, we approach it with a lighted candle, the vapour takes fire, and produces a bright light which envelops all the foliage, sparkling like the lycopodium burned in the theatres on the torches of the Furies. This can be seen in the Fraxinella cultivated in our gardens. Should the atmosphere be less tranquil, the experiment is easily made by surrounding the plant with a glass case, as in our engraving. So soon as an ignited body is plunged into it, a general combustion ensues.

Other plants, during darkness, project inexplicable gleams of light. This extraordinary phenomenon, which is attributed to electricity, was first pointed out by Mademoiselle Linnæus, and afterwards recognized by some naturalists.[1]

coarse bark from the lower part of the trunk, over a surface about a foot wide and a foot and a half high. On this surface they afterwards excavate with a small hatchet, the head of which is shaped like a gouge, a still deeper cutting, which lays bare the most superficial of the woody zones, for it is between these and the bark that the resin flows; this last incision is about six inches high and four wide. Each week the resin-gatherer renews the surface by paring off above a thin slip, so small that the excavation in the course of a single season does not extend beyond eighteen inches in height. These cuttings are prolonged through a series of years till they reach a height of twelve or fourteen feet, when the workmen recommence at the foot of the tree, and cut others alongside of and parallel to them.—In the landes of Bordeaux the resin is generally received in little cups, which they suspend beneath the cuttings, and into which little spouts conduct the sap.

[1] Mademoiselle Linnæus remarked that during twilight, or towards the beginning of dawn, the flowers of the monkshood produced passing gleams from moment to moment. She communicated these observations to her father, and to several authorities on physics. These species of lightnings were generally attributed to a disengagement of electricity, and this was the opinion of M. Vilcke in particular.

M. Haggren has made similar observations on different flowers. In order to be certain that this phenomenon was not due to any aberration of vision, he associated to himself another observer, who was to indicate by a signal the moment at which he perceived the luminous sparks. The learned Swede became convinced that there could be no illusion, for his companion saw the lights at precisely the same instant that he did. These passing gleams are sometimes seen in quick succession, but they often only appear at intervals of several minutes. They are best seen on flowers of an orange yellow; the pale varieties of the same species do not produce them. They may be observed in the marigold, the monkshood, the tagetes (*Tagetes erecta*, Linn.), and the heliotrope.

When speaking of vegetable secretions, we cannot, in the present day, omit a beautiful tree of the family of Sapotaceæ, formerly considered useless, but which furnishes us with one of the most precious substances —gutta-percha. Spread over the coasts of Sumatra and Java, its produce has only been advantageously worked during the last twenty years. Like the gold of California, this tree has caused great social changes in the countries where it grows.

In Caracas, in South America, grows the cow-tree, which, when its trunk is wounded, furnishes an abundant supply of milk, of which the traveller can confidently drink freely, for it unites all the qualities of the milk of our domestic animal, which it entirely replaces in some countries of America.[1]

One of the trees which yield our internal economy services as important as the preceding is the butter-tree. It furnishes the negroes of the Niger with a secretion which they substitute for the ingredient used in our kitchens, and with which they prepare all their food. It is sold abundantly in their markets, where it is known as shea-butter.

Nature offers us in profusion the greatest contrasts. On one side, with generous and beneficent hand she lavishes food and salutary remedies; on the other, she only distils poison, as though in the laboratory of Medea.

Here we see opium perspiring like a milky dew from the heads of our poppies, and becoming so indispensable to the art of medicine, that Sydenham, the Hippocrates of modern times, said he would renounce his profession were he deprived of this powerful anodyne. There we behold the poisons of belladonna, datura, and henbane, by turns useful and deadly.

But no tree prepares in its invisible laboratories such precious crystals as the cinchona; nature offers us no other medicine which is so potent. The cinchona alone arrests the ravages of deadly fevers in their fatal progress; without it many countries would be uninhabitable, many journeys impossible. Hence, in their enthusiasm about its marvellous power, many physicians, in imitation of Torti, have given it the name of "herculean remedy."[2]

[1] As respects the milk or cow tree, *paolo de vaca*, as it is called in the country, M. Boussingault, who at Humboldt's request analyzed its products, states that its physical properties are exactly similar to those of cow's milk, except that it is a little more viscous. It is remarkable for containing an enormous quantity of wax. This substance constitutes the half of its weight.

[2] The following passages will show how M. Georges Pouchet, following the account of La Condamine, inserted in the *Mémoires de l'Académie des Sciences*, has traced the history of the discovery of the most powerful medicine we possess:—

"In 1638, Count Chinchon being vice-regent of Peru for the crown of Spain, his august

In many trees, instead of the bark being saturated with medicinal juices, it secretes aromatics which are highly prized. This is the case

193. Thyrsus of Flowers of the Yellow Cinchona—*Cinchona cordifolia* (Mutis).

with the cinnamon-trees, which are an element of prosperity for places where, like Ceylon, they are cultivated to a certain extent.

spouse was attacked with a severe fever. The corregidor of Loxa, filled with gallantry for the wife of his immediate superior, sent him word that the Indians of the neighbourhood knew of a bark which cured their fevers, and might possibly have the same effect upon a person of so exalted a condition, and begged of him, should his resources fail, at all events to try this medicine of the savages. The vice-queen getting worse and worse, the corregidor was called to Lima in order himself to regulate the dose and mode of preparation of his

Along with these we must not omit to name a tree which selects the fruit instead of the bark as a store-house for its aroma; it is the nutmeg-

194.—Nutmeg-tree—*Myristica moschata* (Lamarck).

tree. It grows beneath the sun of India, and its nuts, an important article of commerce, are frequently used in the preparation of our food.

medicine. But it may be easily imagined that no one was imprudent enough to administer so extraordinary a powder to the noble patient without some precautions; they therefore decided to try it on some of the common people *in anima vili*, and it was only after they had cured with the corregidor's bark some poor Spanish beggars, shattered with fever, that the vice-queen took it and was cured.

"The inhabitants of the town of Lima, being astonished at this, sent a deputation to the convalescent, begging her to send to Loxa for a stock of the bark, a request which was complied with. The countess herself distributed the remedy to all who required it, and from this time it began to be known by the name of the countess's powder. Some months afterwards she gave up the task, handing over what remained to the Jesuit fathers, who, to their praise be it said, continued to give it gratuitously, and hence it acquired the name of Jesuits' powder, which it long bore both in America and Europe."

Pepper, made known to us by a daring innovator of the name of Le Poivre, governor of the Isle of France, previously spoken of, also has its aroma contained in its fruit.

Whilst the cinchonas and the cinnamon conceal their active juices in the thickness of the bark, other trees, such as the camphor laurel, spread them through all their organs—stems, roots, and leaves. These trees, covered with brilliant glazed leaves of bright green, ornament the regions of India and Java. The camphor which they furnish is extracted in the easiest manner: all the natives have to do is to break up the tree into small pieces, and heat these in water, when the precious essence condenses under the lid of the retort.

In other parts we find, instead of these stimulating aromatics, beautiful mimosas, from the fissures in whose bark flow emollient gums, and mallows swollen with demulcent juices which medicine calls to its aid.[1]

Beneath the burning sun of India, where the naja distils its dreadful venom, the nettles secrete a mortal poison. This analogy to the reptile is doubly exact, so that we are not at all astonished to see a German botanist call the Urticæ "the serpents of the vegetable kingdom." It is in fact by the same kind of organ that the plants introduce the venom into a wound; and if we look at the minute quantity with which one of their hairs inoculates us, not perhaps the hundred and fifty thousandth part of a grain!—at the rapidity and intensity of the symptoms—it is clear that the poison of the nettle is the deadliest known.

Our indigenous species only produce a burning sensation, which is soon dissipated, but those of tropical countries give rise to very serious results. Leschenault says that he has seen the sting of the indented nettle (*Urtica crenulata*, Linn.) bring on the most horrible suffering for a whole week. Another species, which grows at Timor, and which the natives call the Devil's Leaf (*Urtica urentissima*), produces such serious wounds, that, according to Schleiden, amputation is the sole means of saving life.

In the midst of this fearful cohort of deadly plants, the upas-tree of Java stands prominently out as one of those which distil the most terrible juices. Its action is such that a weapon dipped in it at once kills any animal it strikes. Travellers relate having seen several women guilty

[1] The seeds of some leguminous plants are used by the Chinese as soap. Sowerby has suggested that the leaves of the soapwort (*Saponaria officinalis*) might be used for the purpose, as they undoubtedly were in by-gone times, especially it is said by the mendicant friars. The lather formed by boiling or bruising the seeds in water has all the effect of soap, and readily removes grease, so that we here find nature spontaneously developing a great manufacturing product, which under man's hands has taken two thousand years to bring to its present perfection.—Tr.

195. The Camphor-tree, or Camphor-laurel—*Laurus Camphora* (Linnæus).

of adultery die in six minutes after being pricked below the bosom with a lancet dipped in the juice of this tree.

No tree has been the subject of so many ridiculous fables as the upas, and till quite lately they were popularly believed. On the faith of a Dutch surgeon named Foersche, it was related that the upas flowed from a unique and singular tree, which vegetated in the midst of a frightful solitude in Java, "the valley of death." According to this traveller, no living creature could resist the poisonous vapours which it exhaled, and for three or four leagues around only dead bodies and skeletons of men and animals were to be met with. The birds themselves which ventured into the surrounding air fell to the ground as if struck by lightning. Criminals condemned to capital punishment alone essayed the task of wresting its infernal produce from the tree. Many tried the perilous journey, but very few returned from it.

It is disgraceful to be obliged to admit, that we owe the refutation of this fabulous narrative to so recent a writer as Leschenault. This traveller noticed, that the famous poison is furnished by two species of trees which grow amid the forests of Java. So far from exercising a deleterious influence upon all that surrounds them, they are encompassed by a luxurious vegetation, while birds, lizards, and insects lend animation to their boughs and foliage. The learned Frenchman, while examining one of these trees which he had had cut down, had his face and hands covered with exudation flowing from the broken branches, yet he experienced no bad effects from this circumstance.

But it is very different when the juice of the upas is introduced into the organism by means of the smallest puncture. A wound of this kind destroys a dog in five or six minutes, as Magendie noticed in his experiments. Eight drops of the juice injected into the veins of a horse kill it directly.

Other plants, more happily gifted, instead of these deadly poisons, elaborate at the same time medicinal agents and nutritive matters. One of these products furnishes a remedy in sickness, another increases the luxury of our tables. This is the case with the rhubarbs. Their large roots are quite full of purgative and strengthening principles, whilst their leaves, saturated with acidulous juice, display strong stalks which serve for food. In England an enormous quantity is consumed in the spring for pastry and side-dishes, and at this time of the year trains of vehicles heavily laden with rhubarb stalks are seen arriving at the London markets.

For long a kind of sympathy between certain plants has been observed to exist, as if one loved to be under the shade of the other.

Thus on the banks of our rivulets the amaranth-coloured[1] flowers of the purple loosestrife (*Lythrum Salicaria*, Linn.) constantly adorn the vicinity of the willow. Other plants, on the contrary, seem to experience an aversion one for the other, and if man inconsiderately compels them to approach each other, they languish or die. The flax-plant, for instance, seems to have a manifest antipathy for the scabious (*Scabiosa arvensis*, Linn.)

At the present time these peculiarities are explained by assuming that the roots emit products favourable to certain species and hurtful to others; products which Plenck, with all the coarseness of one of Molière's doctors, called the "excrement of plants."

Duhamel, when having some elms cut down, had already noticed that the soil in which they had stood had undergone a certain alteration, having become unctuous.

A Genevese observer, M. Macaire, went even further. He observed that when roots of chicory or Euphorbia were placed in water, they exuded into it a coloured extractive matter, which could only be an excretion.

Lastly, Brugmans, professor at the University of Leyden, pushed the matter still further. Having collected this substance from the roots of violets which he had placed in pure fine sand, he found that it acted like poison upon other plants.

Thus the cause of those curious instinctive mutual advances, already perceived by Mathiolus, who called them the friendships of plants, is demonstrated. Indeed the old botanist, in his work, says that there is so much affection between the reed and the asparagus, that if we plant them together both will prosper marvellously.

In Germany agriculture, guided by science, has learned to profit from these mutual affections, and Schwerz, in his learned works, points out how cereals should be allied in order to augment the produce of our fields.

[1] A colour inclining to purple.

CHAPTER VII.

THE SLEEP OF PLANTS.

The deeper we search into the mysteries of vegetable life the closer relation do we find with animal existence. Exhausted by the functional labour of the day, many plants, when the evening arrives, assume a particular attitude, which they preserve through the night; this is their sleep.

This curious phenomenon, which a fortunate accident revealed to Linnæus, was carried by him to demonstration. He first observed it in a Bird's-foot Lotus growing in one of the greenhouses of the garden at Upsala. Having noticed it flowering in the morning, what was his astonishment, as he passed by the plant in the middle of the night, to find that he could not see its flowers! At first the botanist thought that some unprincipled amateur had robbed him of them; but on looking more attentively at the plant, he found that it was against itself the charge of larceny would have to be preferred. In fact, the naturalist observed that each evening the leaves of this Lotus assumed a particular position, which hid the corollas:[1] it was their way of sleeping.

Thinking that such a phenomenon would not be an isolated one, Linnæus after this passed the nights in wandering about in his garden, with a torch in his hand, to verify the results. In this way he noticed that a great number of plants assume a particular attitude when they give themselves up to sleep: this is due to their need of repose, which, as in most animals, coincides with the want of light.

In certain families of the vegetable kingdom the plants are even so transformed during their sleep that they are not recognizable. The aspect of a forest or a savannah is sometimes absolutely changed by it. Many bring their boughs nearer to the stem, and apply their leaves one to the other, so as to be a mutual protection against the cold. Whoever has seen a sensitive plant during the night, with its boughs drooping, and, as it were, overpowered by fatigue, with its leaflets folded together like eyelids which close, will admit that at such times it rests and sleeps.

[1] The sleep of plants was first observed in India, on the tamarind tree, by Garcias de Horto in 1567; after this in 1581 by Val Cordus on the liquorice; but it was Linnæus who first really demonstrated the nature of it.

The phenomenon we are speaking of is seen in a much more striking form in hotter countries. Humboldt, while traversing the banks of the Magdalena, observed that there plants awake much later than in less

196. Sensitive Plant Asleep and Awake—*Mimosa pudica* (Linnæus).

torrid countries, as if vegetation in these climates shared in the indolence which is observable in all the peoples scattered beneath the equator.

Many flowers close every evening in order to give themselves up peacefully to repose. There are some, such as certain bind-weeds, which are very lazy, falling asleep long before sunset, and only rousing up very late each morning, when the sun darts his rays upon them.

In the evening if we view a meadow in which these impressible flowers abound, its mournful aspect renders it unrecognizable. In full mid-day, when it is enamelled with all these open corollas, it seems a mass of verdure filled with great yellow and blue eyes which gaze at us. But when twilight arrives all these seem to have closed their eyelids in order to slumber: the living aspect of the meadow has vanished; all appears inanimate—its flowers are sleeping.

Men have sought to attribute the phenomenon we are speaking of to the difference between the temperature of the day and the temperature of the night; but when it was seen to take place in greenhouses, where the heat was equal night and day, they were obliged to seek for some other cause.

De Candolle showed by some interesting experiments that within the empire of Flora sleep is to be attributed to the absence of light. By throwing a very bright light upon sensitive plants during the night, and conversely, by placing them in profound darkness during the day, the learned botanist succeeded in completely changing their habits. These plants closed up their leaflets and slept the whole day, deceived by the artificial gloom, and they remained awake the whole night when six lamps projected upon them a brilliance equal to five-sixths of that of daylight.

It is principally among plants which inhabit intertropical countries that the phenomenon in question is seen. It is particularly noticeable in the family of the Leguminosæ, and most of all in the sensitive plants. Many of those in our fields show it plainly.

If at the close of summer we examine a clover field about six o'clock in the evening, we are struck with the aspect which all the plants present at this moment, the first of their sleep. The two side leaflets of each leaf are laid close against one another, and the middle one covers them like a protecting roof: the whole aspect of the crop has changed.

CHAPTER VIII.

VEGETABLE SENSIBILITY.

What mysterious forces preside over the life of plants? These forms so graceful and imposing, adorned with dazzling colours, perfuming the air with the sweetest odours, have they been deprived of all the faculties accorded to the most ignoble animals?

There are two schools which have on this subject put forward equally exaggerated statements: the one has found pleasure in over-estimating the vital essence of plants, the other in degrading it.

The ancients clearly erred on the side of the first of these two excesses. Empedocles did not hesitate to accord high endowments to plants, and some of the followers of the philosopher of Agrigentum have surpassed him in this respect.

The marvellous mandrake was considered by them to be endowed with the most exquisite sensibility. The ancients related that at the slightest wound this plant, with human form, gave vent to mournful groans; and those who were daring enough to gather it were obliged to employ certain precautions in order that they might not be alarmed at these sounds, and might defy its evil influence.

The most illustrious botanist of ancient Greece, Theophrastus, goes so far as to describe the ceremonies which were imperiously demanded for the conquest of this funereal plant. He says that in order to tear it out it was necessary to trace three magic circles round it with the point of a sword, looking all the time towards the east, whilst one of the assistants danced round about, uttering obscene words.[1]

The theories of credulous antiquity have been reproduced, and even exceeded, in our own day. Adanson, a daring spirit, if ever there was one,

[1] The Mandragora, which was one of the most celebrated plants of antiquity and the middle ages, was supposed to grow under gibbets, where it was manured with the remains of those put to death. It was said that it could not be torn out without danger. The credulous supporters of the cabala, in order to avoid all accidents, taught their adepts to extract it from the ground by means of a dog tied to the plant, and which, as the plant exerted all its malevolence over it, was thus devoted to a certain death.

The charlatans of our superstitious ages gave the Mandragora a human form before employing it in their sorceries. The idea that this plant naturally appears under this form had procured for it the name of *anthropomorphos* among the ancients; and it was so was not satisfied, like the Sicilian sophist, with endowing plants with a mere sensitive soul; he contended that each one must have several.[1]

Hedwig a profound botanist, Bonnet more an orator than a really learned man, and most of all Edward Smith, allotted to plants exquisite sensibility, and even sensations of pretty high character.

197.—The Mandrake—*Atropa Mandragora* (Linnæus).

These views have in our day been ardently upheld by two of the most celebrated savants of studious Germany—Von Martius and Théodore

entirely considered as such by our superstitious ancestors, that in certain botanical works of the period of the Renaissance, and particularly in the *Grand Herbier en Français*, we find sketches of the Mandragora plants, faithful enough as regards the foliage and aspect, while their embellished roots present a human figure, some representing a man, and others a woman.

[1] The following curious passage on this subject is found in Adanson's work :—

"Every plant, although without sensation, being animated, possesses a soul, which is not sole nor fixed in any part, but equally spread through all, and divisible, since every one of its integrant parts which participate in a common life possesses in itself an isolated vitality, and because, when separated and detached from them, it grows and fructifies, finally enjoying all the properties and faculties which it possessed before its separation."

Fechner—who consider a plant a sentient being endowed with an individual soul, the latter having carried his temerity so far as to found a sort of vegetable psychology.

Camille Debans, in his charming little work, makes an allusion to the system of these two botanists which is full of poetry and freshness. He draws the picture of a rose so weakened and languishing that the least breath of air, as light as the sigh of a virgin, tears away the suffering and faded petals. And when the murderous breath has at last slain the flower formerly so sweet and perfumed, the gnomes, with tears, bear away its soul to paradise on their diaphanous wings.

Struck with the imposing aspect of the aged denizens of the forests, the ancients revered them, thinking that under their trunks tranquil divinities kept themselves hidden from mortal eyes. Their sombre recesses sent a thrill of religious terror through the breasts of all. The lapse of ages has not yet everywhere rooted out such ideas. In the legends of Japan it is said that cedars which have stood for centuries enjoy such an exuberance of life that drops of blood may sometimes be seen oozing from them as they are cut by the axe; and ancient traditions even add that they have souls exactly like those of men and of the gods. Hence the unspeakable dread of the belated Japanese woodcutter when he passes through these dark forests, in which every gnarled trunk appears like a menacing and terrible shade!

On the other hand, as the genius of Descartes was powerful enough to make the bulk of men believe that animals were only simple automatons, set going in order to accomplish a certain number of acts, so many naturalists, on still more plausible grounds, and in particular Hales, whose beautiful experiments laid the foundation of vegetable physiology, leaned strongly to the view of considering plants as so many structures entirely under the empire of material forces.

But neither of the two views above described finds an asylum at the present day in the severe domain of science. We cannot liken the phenomena of vegetable life either to simple physico-chemical action, or to a supreme intellectual directing power. It is evident that they are governed by a vital force which binds all the springs of existence; when that disappears, nothing preserves the plant from destruction.

All naturalists who have treated the question seriously as physiologists maintain that plants enjoy quite as active a life as many animals, and that they possess traces of sensibility and contractility. Bichat, the most illustrious of modern anatomists, in his admirable *Recherches sur la Vie et la Mort*, admits this without hesitation.

Numerous experiments prove clearly that there are in plants traces of sensibility analogous to animal sensibility. Electricity will kill them; narcotics paralyze or destroy them. By sprinkling opium over certain species they have been thrown into a profound sleep. Messrs. Gœppert and Macaire, in their interesting investigations, have observed that prussic acid poisons plants with as much rapidity as it does animals.

Does not the sensitive plant contract visibly when we irritate it? Do we not know that vegetable tissues shrivel of their own accord so soon as we bring them in contact with any stimulant? Carradori noticed that exciting the tips of the leaves of a lettuce was sufficient to make it eject little drops of its own juice.

If we divorce ourselves from all our old ideas of vegetable life, and simply observe its phenomena, we shall arrive at conclusions which will astonish us. We shall be surprised to find that the energy displayed in the biological actions of plants often surpasses everything seen in the animal kingdom—a fact which has only remained unnoticed because we have wrongly looked upon the turbulent manifestations of animal life as the highest expression of this power.

If towards the close of a burning summer day we enter a greenhouse where the long fluted stems of the *Cactus grandiflorus* twine in a spiny and tangled net-work, we perceive here and there on them lanceolated pointed knobs of moderate size. There is nothing which would lead us to think what a spectacle is about to open to our sight.

But towards half-past eight o'clock, the time when obscurity overspreads the earth, all at once every flower of the Cactus displays its innumerable long yellow and white petals, and its corona of five hundred stamens waves and trembles round the pistil; then its vast calyx exhales an odour of vanilla which perfumes the whole greenhouse. But such an exuberance of life is only very ephemeral. A button two inches round is transformed into a flower a foot in circumference. A few minutes have sufficed to unfold one of the marvels of Flora's empire; a few minutes will equally suffice to destroy it. Towards midnight every part of this nuptial couch, so brilliant and perfumed, fades and totally decays.

What animal displays an organic force at the same time so active and so fleeting? Not one, and yet we have never bestowed a thought on it. This splendid flower lives more in a few hours than does a mollusc in a whole year.

Among divers plants endowed with sensibility, there is not one which vibrates and moves with such animation as the queen of the mimosas, the *Mimosa pudica*. Should the slightest touch stir only one of its leaflets, the whole of them shut up; then in a few seconds the branches droop successively towards the earth, and the plant displays signs of the most profound disturbance, appearing as if struck by lightning.

In vain have certain botanists tried to explain this extraordinary phenomenon through the intervention of chemico-physical forces; it is evident that we have only to deal here with a vital manifestation.

If we preserve a sensitive plant from being shaken, and place upon one of its leaves a drop of acid, the contact of the irritant suffices to make the whole plant shrink up; and if we merely heat one of its little leaflets by placing it in the focus of a burning-glass, the injury seems to be felt through every part of the fragile Mimosa; its boughs and leafage sink down as though it were struck by stupor.

This charming leguminous plant, the subject of so many ingenious comparisons, possesses a delicacy of sensation which we should never think of meeting with in the vegetable kingdom. When Von Martius was traversing the savannahs of tropical America, where it abounds, he observed that the sound of his horse's hoofs at a distance made all the sensitive plants contract as if they had been frightened. A ray of sunlight, or the shadow of a cloud even, is enough to produce a manifest change in the midst of them.

Such very singular phenomena ought to suffice to make us suppose that the vegetable fibre conceals in its hidden folds some traces of the structure which everywhere presides over animal life. Dutrochet even thought he had found in it the regulator of so many mysterious actions —a nervous system. According to him this structure is represented by the granulations interposed between the cells. But with the most powerful microscope the eye cannot perceive anything that can be identified with the nerves of animals.

Although the existence of nerves in plants may still be matter of doubt, it is none the less certain that the irritability shown by the sensitive plant seems to be under the empire of organs analogous to nerves, as it is influenced by the same agents and in the same manner as animals. Narcotics weaken its sensibility as they weaken ours. If opium be sprinkled upon the plant it ceases to feel irritants, and no longer contracts; it is paralyzed. And, as we have said, an electric shock kills it.

But a still more extraordinary phenomenon is, that this plant knows, like ourselves, how to accommodate itself to circumstances. Desfontaines, having placed one in his carriage on a journey, saw it contract all its leaves so soon as it felt the shaking of the wheels. Then, strange to say, while the journey was still continued, the Mimosa, having recovered from its fright, opened all its leaves little by little, and kept them expanded so long as the movement lasted. It had accustomed itself to the motion.

But as soon as the vehicle stopped, the same peculiarity was repeated, and on starting the plant contracted afresh only to open again when farther off.[1]

Many plants perform instinctively almost incredible actions in seeking for the necessaries of their existence. M. Grimard, in his charming work on botany, written with remarkable independence of thought, quotes the history of a Scaly Lathræa (*Lathræa squamaria*, Linn.), which, having germinated at the bottom of a mine, raised itself to the prodigious height of 120 feet in order to reach the light, although it ordinarily attains a length of only five or six inches.

CHAPTER IX.

THE MOVEMENTS OF PLANTS.

Like animals, plants are endowed with the power of movement. The slightest observation shows this, as it does their sensibility; but some of our savants refuse to believe it as obstinately as men opposed the first demonstrations of the rotation of the earth. In vain is it shown that plants move just like the seconds-hand of a watch, that they constantly

[1] In the *Proceedings of the Botanical Congress*, at London, in 1866, there is an exhaustive paper by Professor Caspary, on movements induced in different trees by cold. It seems to be made out that the seat of such movements is the protoplasm, not the outer cell-wall. The contractile power of the protoplasm is strongly marked in the *Selaginella mutabilis*, which, when exposed to a bright light, becomes of a pale whitish milky colour, but resumes its green tint when the intensity of the light is diminished. The rhythmical tremors observed by M. Lecoq in the leaves of *Colocasia esculenta* are so violent, that on one occasion the pot in which the plant was growing was so shaken that it could with difficulty be steadied. The *Oxalis sensitiva*, probably in its own country the most sensitive of plants, is in this country (England) nearly or quite destitute of such a power. One of the most extraordinary of these plants is the *Desmodium gyrans*, or telegraph plant, possibly the same plant described by M. Pouchet as *D. oscillans*, a native of India. The leaves consist of two small lateral leaflets and a terminal one. The latter works up and down according to the intensity of the light, while the side leaflets work day and night like the old semaphore signals. Dr. Masters confirms the statement of Desfontaines as to the effect of travelling on the Mimosa, having noticed it while conveying a specimen by railway. When the ether spray is directed with some force upon the leaves of the *Mimosa pudica* they close up, but if the spray be so directed that it only touches the leaves very gently, they seem paralyzed. Analogous facts are constantly seen in disease. M. Blondeau says that when a direct current from a galvanic battery is passed through the plant it is not affected, but if an indirect current from a small Ruhmkorff coil be substituted, the leaflets roll up immediately.—*Popular Science Review*, vol. vii. p. 22.—Tr.

change their position in order to sleep or protect themselves from injury. Forasmuch as the old doctrine taught that they are insensible and deprived of movement, some timid minds do not wish to emancipate themselves from it.

Yet the movements of plants are susceptible of positive proof, only we cannot discover the acting forces. But do we know more about them in the most degraded of the animal kingdom? Certainly not.

De Candolle and Tiedemann, trampling under foot purely theoretical views, rightly admitted the mobility of plants. The latter physiologist justly observes that it is not necessary for the performance of this act that they should possess fibres analogous to our muscles, and that the

198. Semaphore Plant—*Desmodia oscillans.*

Medusæ and Infusoria move perfectly well without our being able to discern anything of the kind in them.

The movements of plants are spontaneous or accidental. In the one case we see them operate by the instinctive impulse of vegetable life, in the other the plant only withdraws itself from injury when it is irritated.

Under the influence of light and temperature plants exhibit various movements. So great is the action of these upon the organism that it is entirely changed. This is what we see happen in their sleep, which, as we have seen, prevents certain species from being recognized, and totally changes the look of a meadow or forest.

It is particularly in the leaves that we meet this remarkable phenomenon, which approximates plants so much to animal life.

In this respect the Semaphore plant (*Desmodia oscillans*) ought to occupy the first place; the mobility observed in it surpasses enormously that of many inferior animals. It is an Indian plant of the family of Leguminosæ, each leaf of which is composed of a great terminal leaflet and two smaller ones which approximate at its base. When the sun falls upon the Desmodia these two leaflets go through a very remarkable series of continuous oscillations. They advance and retire successively one from the other with a trembling jerking movement, which resembles that of the seconds-hand of a watch or the arms of a semaphore telegraph. There is such a similarity between these movements and those of animals that they cease under the influence of the same agents. If a plant be sprinkled with opium it falls into a state of narcotism and its oscillations are utterly stopped.

The activity of the Semaphore plant is so energetic that it is not arrested in boughs which have been cut from the parent plant. Broussonnet saw the leaflets of a branch which he had plunged into water move for three days after.

In the leaves of the Nepenthes or pitcher plant the phenomenon is not less apparent. Every night, as we have said, the lids of their pitchers close while the water is distilled inside, and in the morning the vase opens spontaneously as if to offer itself to the traveller.

In a host of flowers the stamens and pistils at the time of fecundation are visibly agitated, bending one towards the other in order to accomplish their task. In some, such as the Cacti and the imperial fritillary (*Fritillaria imperialis*, Linn.), it is the stamens that are affected with this unwonted mobility; in others, which is the rarer case, the pistils lean towards the other sex, as is noticed in the flowers of the Nigellæ and the Passifloræ.

There are certain Nympheæ which during the day expand their flowers on the tranquil surface of some river, and at night sleep in its depths.

To these spontaneous acts must be added accidental irritations, from the action of which the organs strive so energetically to escape. We have seen with what extraordinary rapidity the sensitive plant shrinks from the least injury. The shock is so great that the whole plant seems to sink to the earth; the boughs and the leaves fall as if struck by lightning.

The disturbance caused by an insect is enough to agitate the leaves of other plants. This is seen in several little species which have become celebrated on account of their extreme irritability. The most remarkable of these is the Venus' Flytrap (*Dionœa muscipula*), the leaves of which are so many insidious snares for insects, living traps in fact. Their expanded end presents two little palettes, armed with teeth along their edges and united by a longitudinal hinge. Each of these palettes is furnished with three pointed spines, placed towards the middle of it and surrounded by glands which distil a sugary fluid. When some imprudent insect, attracted by the honied juice, lights upon the leaf, this, irritated by the contact, suddenly brings its lobes together, just as we close a book, and pierces it with its darts, compressing it more closely in proportion as it struggles harder. The palettes only open when the animal, quite

199. Venus' Flytrap—*Dionæa muscipula* (Linnæus).

exhausted, ceases to move, but it is then frequently too late; the prisoner is dead. The leaflets contract with such force, that when they are closed they tear sooner than open.[1]

[1] According to an English savant, the Flytrap Dionæa (*Dionæa muscipula*) does not close the panels of its trap merely to punish the insect which irritates it, but to suck out and feed on its juices, so that it would be a carnivorous plant. This observer maintains

One of our marsh plants, the sun-dew, or Round-leaved Drosera (*Drosera rotundifolia*, Linn.), is equally treacherous with respect to little winged insects, but after another method, which we might almost call physico-vital. All the upper surface of its leaves is covered with long slender filaments, each bearing at its end a little drop of glutinous fluid, and every imprudent fly that comes among them for the purposes of plunder finds there a certain death. Its wings and feet being glued with the secretion, all escape is rendered impossible. Whenever on a botanical excursion we find this plant towards the mouth of the Seine, we always observe that its leaves are plentifully garnished with the dead bodies of its victims.

On the other hand, the botanist can succeed in demonstrating vegetable irritability by experiment. For this purpose it suffices to excite certain organs with the point of a needle or a fine scalpel. So soon as we touch the stamens of the barberry, the nettle, or the cactus, we see them shrink quickly from the instrument. In the same way the pistils of the Mimulus bring their blades together when the least prick is made.

Lastly, this mobility is again seen manifesting itself spontaneously with extraordinary intensity in the pollinic animalcules of certain plants, which are furnished for this purpose with special organs or ciliæ, by means of which they swim in every direction in the fluid which contains them! (See Fig. 171.)

Some true animalcule-plants are formed like eels, and move by the aid of two long filaments which they carry on their heads. This is seen in the common Chara of our ponds. Others which flit about in the cells of mosses are exactly like the tadpoles of frogs.

And yet these creatures, the locomotive organs of which we can see so plainly, and which the microscopist beholds capering as nimbly as our

that such food is so indispensable to the plant, that it fades when deprived of it by inclosing it in a framework of wire or perforated zinc; although if from time to time a few morsels of meat be placed upon its leaves, the Dionæa remains healthy even when here.

[The carnivorous habits of certain plants have now been well established by the experiments of Dr. Hooker, Mr. Darwin, and others. Among these vegetable carnivora are the fly-trap and sun-dew mentioned above in the text, the side-saddle plants (*Sarracenia*) of North America, one of which is figured at page 306, and the pitcher-plants (*Nepenthes*) of North America, also figured in the preceding pages. The Venus' Flytrap contracts with such force as to crush and kill a fly between its lobes. A quantity of juice is then secreted by the inner surface of the leaf, and this fluid is of such a nature as to cause the liquefaction of the insect and enable it to be absorbed by the plant. This process of liquefaction and absorption is of the same nature as that by which food is digested in the stomach of the higher animals. The pitcher-plant and others also secrete a digestive fluid which enables them to absorb the nutritive elements of their victims.—Tr.]

mountebanks in their dangerous leaps, are obstinately considered by certain botanists, for the sake of mere theory, as being insensible and incapable of moving. Do some learned men possess eyes only in order not to see with them?

CHAPTER X.

PHYSIOLOGY OF FLOWERS.

In the flower, this glorious and supreme effort of vegetable life, the poetic imagination of Linnæus beheld only the picture of a chaste marriage. The calyx, which grasps the corolla in its rustic arms, was to him only the nuptial couch, of which the delicate and undulating petals formed the mysterious curtains. Lastly, in the centre sat the modest spouses, intoxicating themselves with love, enveloped in a cloud of perfume, and their feet bathed in nectar.

But all plants do not display to us in this way the calm magnificence of their nuptials. The secrets of these are quite hidden in many of them, which the greatest and most ingenious of botanists named for this reason Cryptogamia, signifying secret marriage.

Among plants which are ornamented with visible flowers, these exhibit an endless variety of size, form, colouring, and perfume.

While some, such as the valerians, bear such tiny corollas that we can scarcely make them out, the lilies and irises exhibit grand and sumptuous structures of this class, which rivet every person's attention; and yet some exotic plants leave them far behind in this respect.

The flower of one Aristolochia, which grows on the banks of the Magdalena, presents the appearance of a helmet with great edges. The opening of it is so large that it will admit the head of a man; and Humboldt relates that, when travelling along by this river, he sometimes encountered savages wearing this flower on their heads like a hat.

But it is on the surface of rivers that the pomp of vegetation is displayed. Nature nowhere shows another flower which for size, united to colouring, can be compared to those of the Nymphææ and the Nelumbia, commonly called water-lilies and lotuses. By gentle gradations they pass from the purest white to the most velvety red or the most delicate blue! In every age these magnificent plants have attracted man's attention, and been the object of his admiration. Art has made a splendid

200. Sacred Lotus of the Egyptians—*Nelumbium speciosum.*

use of them, and to them the ancient myths owe some of their most delicate and beautiful conceptions.

They play a great part in mythology and on Egyptian monuments. The colonnades of Thebes and Philæ, which seem to defy the hand of time, are crowned with capitals representing flowers of the Nymphæa in full bloom, with which the sculptors of the Pharaohs have sometimes intermingled bunches of dates.

There is no Egyptian monument on which Isis is not represented surrounded by the lotus, or holding bouquets of it in her hands. This flower was the indispensable ornament of the immortal goddess. In the Hindoo temples it also serves as a seat for Bramah, who is represented sitting and holding in his hands the sacred Vedas.

Yet the brilliant rose and white flower of the *Victoria regia*, which ornaments the waves of the Amazon, attains still more remarkable proportions than the foregoing, being sometimes a yard in circumference.

But the flower of the *Rafflesia Arnoldi*, a perfect monster of vegetation, leaves all these far behind! It is found in the forests of Java and Sumatra. Its outlines and gigantic proportions separate it so widely from everything known, that in spite of the assertions of travellers, botanists refused to believe, and persisted in looking upon the colossus as a fetid Fungus. The discussion did not cease till one of these flowers was sent to London, and examined by R. Brown, who dissipated all doubts. Each flower was found to be composed of a fleshy mass weighing from twelve to fifteen pounds. Its border, the circuit of which was not less than ten feet, showed five lobes, forming a gaping excavation capable of holding a dozen pints of fluid.

This strange and eccentric flower, which botanists still regard as one of the marvels of the vegetable world, looks at first sight like one of the huge Fungi commonly called puff-balls, and it is only when it has displayed its thick and flesh-coloured petals that its true nature is revealed. It exhales a repulsive carrion-like smell.

The naturalist stands stupified at such an exuberant production, but the Javanese prostrates himself before it; he almost makes a divinity of it, and clothes it with supernatural power. Yet its bulk, weight, and fetor will ever prevent us from making use of it for our wants and enjoyments.[1]

[1] Here and there, in desolate spots in South-west Africa, grows one of the most extraordinary plants in the world, the *Welwitschia mirabilis*. It looks perhaps almost as much like an immense red and green Polypus as anything. It has two leaves, nine or ten feet long, and of a pale green colour. Under the influence of heat and drought these split up into ribbons. In the centre is a woody mass, with a rough bark or cork-like surface, rising a foot or so above the ground, and bearing round its edges, just within the insertion of the

Poetry has exhausted all its resources in telling of the perfume and colour of flowers. Nature has surpassed art, and the pencil of Apelles and Rubens could not reproduce them in all their magnificence. And yet one colour, black, is wanting amid this multitude of varied tints. Some corollas, such as those of certain Scabiosæ, are, it is true, of a sombre purple, but a perfect black is never seen in this organ.

One phenomenon occurs in respect to flowers which has been a good deal talked about, namely, the mutability of colour which they exhibit. Pallas, when exploring the banks of the Volga, remarked with astonishment that a species of anemone, the *Anemone patens*, sometimes bore white flowers, sometimes yellow, and sometimes red flowers. This phenomenon, still unexplained, appeared so abnormal that it was mentioned everywhere. It is, however, common enough; and we may observe it any time in France without encountering such a long journey.

The field-pimpernel (*Anagallis arvensis*), so common in our country districts, frequently displays this change. Usually its flower is of a vermilion red, but it is also sometimes of a magnificent sky blue, which made some botanists think there were two different species.

A pretty little plant of the genus Myosotis, which is met with in our arid grounds, varies still more singularly in its colour, for on the same stalk we find at the same time red, yellow, and blue flowers—a peculiarity to which this species owes the name of *Myosotis diversicolor* which has been given to it.

Other plants display a still more remarkable phenomenon, for in them the same flower changes its colour at different hours of the day. This happens with the *Hibiscus mutabilis*, the corollas of which are white in the morning, become rose-coloured towards the middle of the day, and in the evening take on a beautiful red tint.

The successive change in the tints of the corolla is easily conceived; it may depend on vital action or on chemical reactions effected by time; but what is much more difficult to explain is, that flowers having displayed a certain category of changes during the day, go through the same round

leaves, an assemblage of small stems about six inches long, dividing into smaller branches, each of which bears from three to five cones, three inches in length and three quarters of an inch thick, of an elongated oval form and crimson colour, tinted with green in the less developed specimens, and marked with scales like those of a fir-cone. The leaves are so straight-grained that they can be torn from top to bottom without deviating a single line from a straight course. Rain rarely or never falls where this plant exists. The plant seems sometimes to attain a much greater size than mentioned above, the leaves being two and even three fathoms long, and the apex of the trunk, or rather, from the confused account given of it, the flower itself, being six feet wide, and opening like two immense clam-shells, some eighteen inches across.—*Science and Art*, vol. i.—Tr.

of variation the day following. This is observed in the variously coloured corn-flag (*Gladiolus versicolor*, Linn.), the corolla of which, brown in the morning, becomes blue in the evening, and on the day following takes on again exactly the same succession of tints as it showed the day before.

What a variety of perfumes the flower possesses! And yet notwithstanding their thousand and one shades of difference, those whose sense of smell is sharpened by practice can distinguish that of each species.

201. Flowers of Rafflesia Arnoldi.

It is even stated in some works that a young American, who had become quite blind, botanized, guided by the smell only, in the midst of prairies enamelled with luxuriant vegetation, and never committed any mistake in his gleanings.

The odours which exhale from plants are almost always delightful; it is only rarely that they are repulsive.

The poisonous vapours which envelop the poppy and nenuphar reveal their narcotic properties. Infectious exhalations, precisely like those from putrefied meat, escape from the flowers of the Stapelia and Arum, and thus the insect, deceived by them, deposits on their calyces a carnivorous progeny which must infallibly perish. Some plants emit odours exactly like those produced by certain animals; an orchis of our forests (*Satyrium hyrcinum*, Linn.) repels us by its goat-like stench; other plants attract us by their sweetness, thus the musk-mallow (*Malva moschata*, Linn.) distils the same perfume as the musk animal (*Moschus moschiferus*, Linn.)

The perfume of flowers seems to depend upon the volatilization of an essential oil which they secrete in their most hidden recesses. In some plants this is palpably the fact. When the atmosphere is very still the odorous vapours collect round them, and can be burned by means of an ignited substance.

By employing very varied methods, the successors of the skilful perfumers whom Mary of Medici brought to France from Italy, collect the odoriferous essences exhaled from the flowers, and which also saturate many other organs. The otto of roses, one of the treasures of the East, is only this oil in a concrete state.[1] Camphor offers us another under the form of crystals.

The secretion of the perfume is usually continuous, beginning at the time the flower opens and ceasing when it fades. Even when the corolla, being altogether ephemeral, only lives for a few minutes, it is still observed to perfume the air during these brief moments. This is seen in

[1] From what Homer says, it seems that in his time, men already knew how to prepare a kind of oil of roses by infusing these flowers in an oily liquid, and it is certain that in antiquity they were cultivated in order to extract a perfume from them. The Island of Rhodes even owed its name of Island of Roses to the fame of its cultivation of rose-trees, but probably the use of this perfume was discontinued, for rose-water is not mentioned by authors, and it is spoken of for the first time in the works of Avicenna. The Orientals, in the times which preceded ours, employed it with extraordinary profusion. Some historians assert that when Saladin took Jerusalem in 1188, he caused the interior of Omar's mosque to be washed with rose-water, and for this purpose it was employed in such quantities that Father Sanut relates that 500 camels were employed to bring it from Damascus. Mahomet II. also, after the taking of Constantinople, ordered St. Sophia to be washed in the same way. According to Father Catrou's account, the Princess Nourmahal surpassed both, for she collected sufficient rose-water to fill a canal, on which was launched a bark which bore her, accompanied by the Great Mogul. Indeed it was during this remarkable trip that the essence of rose was discovered, having formed at the surface of the artificial lake owing to evaporation caused by the sun.

The essential oil of roses is one of the most exquisite and dearest perfumes, and justly bears the title of attar or sweetest of fragrances. About 100 lbs. of flowers are requisite to obtain nine to twelve drachms (avoirdupois) of this oil, which comes to us from the East and India, and which is often called butter of roses. Hippocrates and Galen were acquainted with this product, and often employed it in medicine; now-a-days it is only employed to perfume linen and rooms.

the magnificent *Cactus grandiflorus.* Quite inodorous a few instants before it blows, it discharges a scented cloud when, towards twilight, its calyx opens; but the enchantment vanishes before midnight, with the death and decomposition of the flower.

Some flowers of nocturnal habits, which do not disdain to lend life to the night, shed their perfumes only during the darkness; these are the bats of the vegetable kingdom. Their sombre mournful hue has often led botanists to saddle them with unpleasing names; *tristis* or *nocturnus* are their designations for nearly all the plants which present this singularity, as for instance the *Pelargonium triste*, the *Gladiolus tristis*, and the *Cestrum nocturnum.*

The emanations from plants produce upon us physiological effects which are well worth studying. If too concentrated they may give rise to serious symptoms, to convulsions and spasms, or they may even induce death.

These different phenomena have been particularly observed in persons keeping nosegays near them during the night. The flowers exhale, as we know, carbonic acid; but in the cases we speak of the accidents ought not to be ascribed to lethal vapours, but to the odorous exhalations from the flowers, which operate, as Orfila says, like certain poisons, for they act fatally upon some individuals and do not affect others in the least.

In 1779 a woman died in London during the night from having kept a large bouquet of irises in her room. Triller saw a young girl perish in the same way from the effects of a bouquet of violets; and it has been stated that workmen, who have imprudently fallen asleep upon bales of saffron, have died in consequence.

The scent of roses, so much sought for everywhere, causes repugnance in some persons and inconveniences others. Catherine of Medici could not endure it, and her aversion to these flowers was so great that it was enough for her to see the painting of one to be seized with some degree of nausea. The Chevalier de Guise was still more easily affected, for he fainted at the sight of a bunch of roses.

Some cases are even told in which the smell of these flowers sufficed to produce instant death, but they are perhaps apocryphal.[1]

[1] The death of one of the daughters of Nicholas I., Count of Salins (in the department of Jura), and that of a Bishop of Poland, are attributed to the emanations from roses. But these facts, related by the historian Cromer, are probably inexact.

CHAPTER XI.

THE NUPTIALS OF PLANTS.

Darwin wrote a delightful poem entitled the *Loves of the Plants.* The chaste pen of the English poet has there sketched, in a most attractive manner, the mysterious history of the fecundation of plants. All is hidden behind a most graceful veil, and there is nothing to alarm the strictest propriety.

As we have seen, the flower is difficult to describe. Linnæus, by the medium of one of the most ingenious metaphors, gives a charming idea of it. It is, he says, the nuptial couch in which the wedding of the plants is celebrated. This yields a delightful perfume of poesy, but so soon as we aspire to more exactitude the difficulty begins.

What is popularly called the flower is but a sumptuous and almost useless ornament; the most essential parts lie unperceived. In the eyes of the botanist the true floral apparatus consists only of the little filaments placed near the centre. These are the spouses; the pistils or brides, and the stamens or bridegrooms.

It is for them that nature displays her most sumptuous adornments. The velvety curtains of their virgin couch, woven by the hands of fairies, steep them in light and fire amidst their folds of purple and sapphire. In one part faithless husbands profusely scatter life and fecundity on everything around them; in another chaste households live retired, and jealous brides conceal their lovers beneath domes of azure and gold.

The delicate envelopes which attract our regards represent only the ephemeral and perfumed palace in which the mysteries of Hymen are about to be accomplished. But so soon as the golden dust of the stamens is spread upon the altar, the odorous sources dry up, the veils of the temple fade and wither, and the marvellous edifice soon lies scattered on the ground, whilst the now fruitful mother silently nourishes her precious offspring.

All flowers do not exhibit such luxury in these organs. Generally they possess two protecting envelopes, and contain at the same time ardent husbands and tender wives. More rarely they present only one sex. In this case the one class, without ornament and without perfume, only contains a few cenobites; whilst others display all the splendour of a harem, the perfumed canopies of which only veil a bevy of sultanas.

Nature's aim is always clearly defined, and she has profuse resources for attaining it. A few grains of pollen, almost invisible, are enough to impregnate a flower, and she pours it out open-handed; ninety-nine hundredths of it may be lost. A single spouse—and this is the case with certain of the Cacti—is sometimes surrounded with five hundred husbands.[1]

It is even observed that nature multiplies her resources further in order to insure the reproduction of plants when the sexes reside each in a separate flower, and sometimes on plants separated by a great distance. The corollas with stamens produce an enormous quantity of pollen dust, which makes up for the difficulty of communication. This strikes every observer who is in the neighbourhood of a pine-forest. The pollen is often borne away from the trees in such abundance that it covers all the surrounding country with its yellow dust. This is the phenomenon known by the name of "sulphur-rain." And indeed, owing to its yellow colour and the way in which it burns with a bright flame, pollen has been thought akin to sulphur by some inexperienced observers. Sometimes when it falls upon the roofs of the neighbouring towns, it tints them all over with a pale yellow.

At the moment when the curtains of the nuptial couch are opened the plants appear to suffer a febrile excitement. Unwonted movements are observed in their floral organs, and the temperature is sometimes raised in a very remarkable manner. It seems, as the physiologist Burdach says, that at such moments the plant issues from its humble sphere and shows us traces of animal life. The stamens are agitated, and quit their places, bending towards the stigmata. More rarely, as if modesty were inherent in the delicacy of flowers, the pistils advance towards their spouses.

[1] When a grain of pollen has fallen upon the stigma, and is retained by the hairs projecting from the surface, a pollen tube is emitted, apparently owing to endosmotic action between the fluid exudation from the stigma and the contents of the pollen cell, which latter bursts and sets free the inner lining of the cell in the form of a cylindrical tube. This tube passes down between the cells of the style, lengthening out till it at last reaches the ovules in the cavity of the ovary. This lengthening was at one time thought to be merely extension, but is now supposed to be due to actual interstitial growth. Having arrived here, the pollen tube enters the foramen at the top of the ovule left by the imperfect closing of its investments, and thus comes in contact with the nucleus and embryo-sac. In this sac there are at the top some minute vesicles called the germinal vesicles, one or sometimes two of which, under contact, lengthen out into a slender cellular thread, and at one end of this thread is the embryo-plant.—*The Life of a Seed*, by Maxwell T. Masters, M.D.—Tr.

By means of thermo-electric needles it has been proved that the elevation of temperature in the flower is a wide-spread phenomenon. In some plants this heat is so great that an instrument of accuracy is not requisite to show it; the simplest thermometer suffices. It is only necessary to touch even the flower in certain arums to observe that it is of a burning heat, and we are astonished that it can support such a temperature without being consumed. De Candolle observed that a thermometer plunged into the spathe of an Italian arum rose to 143° 36′ Fahr.[1]

From the remotest antiquity men seem to have understood the mysterious loves of plants. The question was practically solved, for Herodotus tells us that the Babylonians knew how to distinguish male from female date-trees, and that in his day, in the environs of their immense city, they occupied themselves with the artificial fecundation of the latter.

The first travellers who, in imitation of Prosper Alpinus, taught us true notions as to the manners of the Orientals, state that they were so well acquainted with the fertilizing power of the stamens, that they were accustomed, from the most distant times, to place their female date-trees to the leeward of the males, in order that they might more effectually receive the prolific dust.

At the present day the negroes know perfectly that the loss of the male stems completely checks the production of the fruit. Hence when, in time of wars, they wish to starve their enemies out, they content themselves with destroying the stamen-bearing palms, which are much the less numerous.

In Egypt the harvest of dates has for ages been assured by mounting the palms and shaking the male panicles upon the female flowers. At the time of the French invasion the Arabs were not in a position to take this precaution, being more occupied with war than with agricultural labours; and consequently in this year, according to the statement of the botanist Delille, who was a member of the expedition, the date-trees were barren.

Nevertheless, it must be admitted that if the ancients observed the sexual nature of plants, they often deceived themselves on the subject.

[1] It was Lamarck who discovered that the flower of the arum gives out considerable heat at the time of fecundation. De Candolle verified this fact at Montpellier. It is a very remarkable phenomenon. I observed that at a certain moment the flowers of some Colocasiæ grew so warm, that their heat was felt by the fingers of those who touched them. In other flowers the phenomenon is less evident, still it is general. Brongniart, Dutrochet, Biot, and Schultze have recognized it by means of thermo-electric needles.

Pliny alone, in his thirteenth book, describes the fecundation of the palm-tree with a perfection which it is almost impossible to surpass.

But we must turn to Linnæus in order to see this fact demonstrated experimentally for the first time.

In a charming production entitled the *Marriage of Plants* (Sponsalia Plantarum) the great botanist initiates us into many marvels. In it he relates that having taken two specimens of the annual mercury (*Mercurialis annua*, Linn.), the one male and the other female, growing in separate pots, the fecundity of the latter was more marked in proportion as her spouse was nearer. Even at a considerable distance impregnation still took place; the air becoming the mysterious medium of communication between the plants. But when the stalk charged with stamens, with which the experiment was made, was removed from the greenhouse the abandoned wife remained quite sterile.

A few years subsequently to the time of this learned botanist, Gleditsch likewise proved the fecundation of plants by a transcendent demonstration. He had in his garden at Berlin a female palm-tree, the verdant crown of which yearly overshadowed numerous flowers, and each year these were infallibly stricken with sterility. But having learned that there was a male plant of the same species flourishing at Dresden he conceived the idea of sending for some of the pollen in order to artificially impregnate the one in his possession. The pollen dust was immediately sent to him by the post, and a short time after he had sprinkled it upon the stigmas of his palm-tree he beheld all the flowers fecundated by the contact produce a corresponding number of fruits.[1]

Insects play a great part in vegetable life; some botanists even consider them as the principal agents in fecundity. While working their way among the stamens and pistils they bear off the fertilizing dust from the former and transport it to the others. The farmers on the banks of the Rhine have even remarked, that the orchards in which bees are reared, are more productive than those in which there are none.

In the Levant insects are thought to have a certain amount of influence on the products of the fig-tree. Where cultivation is carried on upon a large scale, they take boughs from the wild species, with numbers of the gall-insects on them which frequent those trees, and lay them upon the cultivated trees. These insects, penetrating into the obscure recep-

[1] On one of my visits to Strasburg, Professor Fée showed me a female palm-tree on which he had repeated Gleditsch's experiment with equal success. It was a dwarf palm-tree, *Chamærops humilis*, the flowers of which were fecundated with pollen sent from a distance. He simply sprinkled it upon them. All the fruit was developing perfectly upon this palm-tree when I saw it in the month of August, 1855.

tacles of their cloistered flowers, spread upon them the germs of generation. This is the operation that is called "caprification."[1]

Thus a single fly which lives upon the fig-tree providentially secures subsistence and commercial wealth to the greatest cities of the East.

A tiny beetle, by means of its dainty taste, imparts a similar benefit

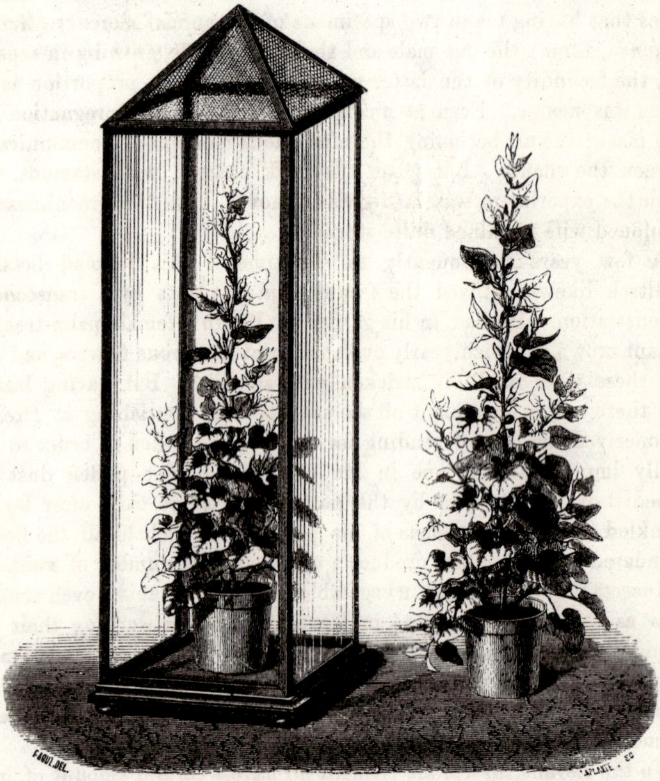

202. Influence of Insects upon the Fecundation of Flowers.—Willdenow's experiment on the Common Birthwort—*Aristolochia Clematitis* (Linnæus).

to Greenland, by aiding in the reproduction of the Kamtchatka lily, the bulbs of which, in the rigorous winters of these polar regions, alone preserve all the population from famine.

[1] Caprification was considered essential for the fructification of the fig-tree. Aristotle, Theophrastes, and Pliny speak of it. Their accounts appeared fabulous, but Tournefort demonstrated their correctness, having had an opportunity of satisfying himself during his

Willdenow, by means of an interesting experiment, showed plainly what a part insects play in respect to fructification. He took an *Aristolochia Clematitis* and placed it under a cage covered with gauze. As this prevented the animals from reaching and penetrating within the flowers, the plant produced no fruit. On the other hand, another Aristolochia of the same species, which stood by the side of it in the open air, so that the insects could visit it as they liked, had all its flowers fecundated.

The idea of the intervention exercised by insects is so predominant with Burdach, that he goes the length of supposing that each nourishes its particular insect, the mission of which is to preside over the mysteries of its espousal. According to the German physiologist, flowers only preserve their original purity because their faithful visitors consecrate the whole course of their ephemeral existence to them, and never wander to another species. The nocturnal plants are also haunted by useful parasites which only awake to animation during the darkness.[1]

Conrad Sprengel even thinks that if so many flowers are stricken with sterility in our hot-houses, even when parading a superfluity of means for becoming mothers, it is because their indispensable insect has not been allowed to bear them company. This is the case with the Vanilla. Since it blossoms in our country, it might fructify if kept duly supplied with heat by means of a hot-air apparatus, and yet it remains quite barren. The same thing happens with the orange-coloured corollas of the Royal Strelitzia.[2]

travels that this practice still existed in the Levant. Linnæus only saw in caprification a step by which insects transport pollinic dust from the male flowers of the wild fig-tree to the female flowers of the cultivated species in order to produce fecundation.

But the part played by the insects is restricted to puncturing the receptacle—a process which stimulates the ripening of the figs, as it does that of our garden flowers, and enables us to obtain a much larger yield of fruit. However, the figs thus punctured are much less finely flavoured than those which ripen spontaneously; but it is asserted that the trees thus operated on bear ten times as many figs as when it is not practised. Tournefort says that a caprified fig-tree yields as much as 280 lbs. of fruit, whilst only 25 lbs. can be got from it when it is not artificially fructified. Ollivier, who also saw this operation practised during his travels in the Levant, and Bosc, the writer on husbandry, look upon it as useless. I quite share their opinions; my travels in the East have enabled me to satisfy myself that in many countries where they do not practise this operation the figs are no less fine and abundant.—Pouchet, *Botanique Appliquée*, t. ii. p. 22.

[1] Dr. Hildebrand of Bonn concludes, from several interesting experiments on the fertilization of *Corydalis cava*, that when the flowers of the plant are protected from insect influence and acted on only by their own pollen they produce no capsules.

[2] The Rev. Conrad Sprengel, who assigned such a marvellous part in the fecundation of plants to insects, in the excess of his enthusiasm called them Nature's gardeners. The proof that the sterility of the Aromatic Vanilla (*Vanilla aromatica*, Linn.) in our greenhouses is owing to the imperfect nature of the fecundation has been given by the experiments of M. Morren, who showed that by placing the pollen itself upon the stigmata of

It is especially in the two great families, the Asclepiadaceæ and Orchidaceæ, the strange flowers of which remind one of the forms and brilliant colouring of insects, that nature seems to call the latter to her aid. In these the anthers, which are like little glutinous clubs, attach themselves to the flies when these come to drink the nectar, and are by them transported from one flower to another and deposited upon the stigmata. But for such visitors these plants would die out without progeny.[1]

With respect to other plants, nature has intrusted the cares of their conjugal union to the wings of the wind. This is the case with the diœcious plants, the sexes in which are separate and dwell on distinct plants, which are often separated a long way from each other. In whirling about the waves of air uplift the pollen, carry it into the clouds, and let it fall upon the flowers like a fertilizing dew.

Science religiously preserves the history of two palm-trees which were born in Italy and displayed a most striking instance of what we have been stating. One of them grew in the vicinity of Otranto; it was a female tree, and annually covered with luxuriant flowers, yet it remained constantly sterile. Every season had for a long time brought forth the same hopes of fertility, to be followed by the same blight. It may be imagined then how general the astonishment was when the palm-tree of Otranto was at last, after so many delusive promises, seen laden with fruit? It was then found that another palm-tree of the same species, but a male, had for the first time blossomed at Brindisi. There could be no doubt about the matter; the wind, carrying away the pollen from the latter, had besprinkled the other with it, and thus the breeze had borne the life-giving dust a distance of fifteen leagues. From this time the palm-tree of Otranto bore a harvest each year.

Flowers only celebrate their chaste union in broad daylight. They require for it waves of air and light, and in order to plunge into these, we frequently see them perform the most unexpected feats.

Aquatic plants are principally remarkable in this respect. The task itself seems to be chiefly intrusted to the peduncle. In some plants growing in the depths of our marshes this support lengthens out, even to an

the flowers fecundation was artificially produced, and that plants were thus soon obtained which for beauty and aroma might rival those produced by America. On the other hand, M. Brongniart artificially fecundated the *Strelitzia regina*, which, left to itself, is with us unproductive.

[1] Sometimes bees, when rifling the flowers of the Asclepiadaceæ or Orchises, come out with their heads and feet covered with the anthers of these flowers like small clubs. In some cases so much adheres that they cannot fly. This is the affection which amateurs call the "club disorder." Ch. Robin, in the beautiful plates of his work on vegetable parasites, gives figures of different insects struggling with this inconvenient burden.

203. Nuptials of the Common Utricularia—*Utricularia vulgaris* (Linnæus).

immense extent if necessary, so as to raise the flower above the surface of the water. This is frequently seen in the magnificent water-lilies (*Nymphœa alba*, Linn.) which ornament our ponds so splendidly with their virgin corollas. When the plant grows at the edge and is quite dry, its peduncles are only an inch or two long; whilst, when it is planted in deep water, these organs stretch out three or four feet, in order that the flowers may expand upon the surface of the wave.

When incapable of executing such manœuvres, these plants make use of some equivalent proceeding instead. This was observed by Ramond in a Water Ranunculus (water crow-foot, or *Ranunculus aquatilis*, Linn.) which he met with in the Pyrenees. Placed in deep water, and not being able to bring its flowers into contact with the atmosphere, the want of this was supplied by an ingenious means. Each corolla had secreted a large bubble of air, which entirely enveloped it in such a manner that, though beneath the water, fecundation was accomplished just as if the floral apparatus had not been submerged at all.

But of all plants the fecundation of the *Vallisneria spiralis* has acquired the most celebrity. This diœcious plant lives in the rivers of the south of France. Its female flowers, attached to peduncles twisted spirally, expand upon the surface of the water, all the movements of which they follow. Like a spring, their spiral lengthens when the water rises, and shortens when it falls. The male flowers, not being provided with this elastic apparatus, find themselves chained to the foot of the plant at the bottom of the water. How are the wedded pair to become united? Nature has foreseen all. When the moment has arrived the peduncles of the male flowers break, these mount to the surface of the water, spread out and form a numerous cortége, floating around the females. Thus is the wedding of the Vallisneria accomplished, and the intent of this curious scene is so clearly marked out, that so soon as the act is over, the fecundated flowers shorten their spirals and sink beneath the water to ripen their fruit.

Our marshes nourish a still more curious plant, the Utricularia, doubly remarkable for its singular look and for its mode of ascent. Yet its fecundation is far from having acquired the celebrity of that of the Vallisneria, poetry not having appropriated it as it has done with the other. This plant at the bottom of the water looks like a confused mass of fibres. When we withdraw it and inspect it, we observe that its capillary ramifications present here and there little vesicular leaves, representing so many utricles in miniature, the gaping mouths of which seem to be guarded by two prominent filaments. So long as the Utricularia is only occupied in providing for its own subsistence, these vesicles remain filled with a mucous fluid, by the weight of which they are overloaded, and the plant, borne down in this way, rests supported on the bottom of the pond, to which, however, it in no way adheres.

But later on, when the period of flowering arrives, the vesicles absorb the mucus which filled them, and replace it with an aëriform fluid. Then the plant having become lighter than the water, escapes from the bottom

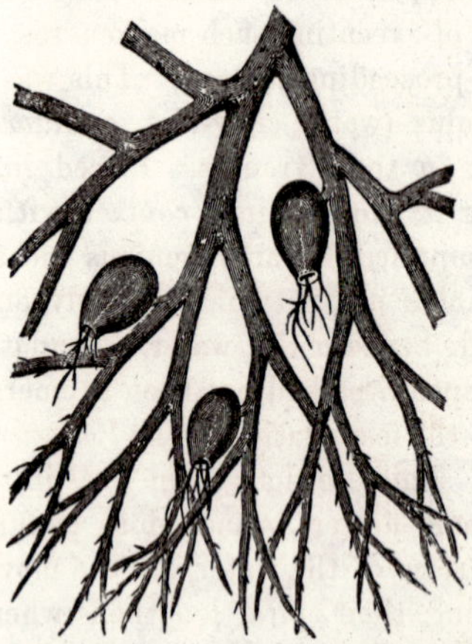

204. Branch of the Utricularia laden with its Hydrostatic Vesicular Leaves.

and rises to the surface, where it floats, and where its pretty golden yellow flowers are expanded and fecundated.

After this, by an unexpected reflex action, and when the torches of Hymen are scarcely extinguished, the vesicles expel the gas which they contain and fill anew with weighty mucus. At this last moment the Utricularia falls again to the depths of the marsh, where the spouses expire in the act of ripening their fruits.

A more robust plant, the Aldrovanda, which grows in the lakes of Italy, attains the same end, but by a method less ingenious, and marked, so to speak, by a certain degree of coarseness. It lives at the bottom of the water, but when the hour of fecundation has struck, its large stem breaks short off close to the root, and all at once it rises to float on the surface of the waves.

Thus by different ways does nature arrive at the same ends.

BOOK III.

THE SEED AND GERMINATION.

The seed is really only a vegetable egg, and Linnæus, when he gave it this name in his botanical philosophy, already perceived all the analogies between the two.

When these analogies are compared we see that the advantage is on the side of the plant, and that its egg is elevated to a higher state of organic development than that of the bird. In the latter it is with difficulty that we perceive the germ of the new being that is to issue from it, whilst when we separate the coverings and membranes of the seed of the plant, we see the embryo already formed. We distinguish in it, even with the naked eye, the little root, the stem, and the delicate leaves; everything is there; it is nothing but a young plant slumbering in its cradle. In many seeds we can even discern the cords by which the little one clings to the mammæ which are to nourish it.

The young stalk of the wheat exists already in the grain which we eat; the little palm-tree, as stiff as the vertical stem which it is about to produce, is also seen in the cocoa-nut; while the embryo of the bean, bent upon itself, reveals the tendency which its stem has to curl itself round everything that finds itself in its way.

The seed, essentially a rudimentary organ, like the egg of the animals shows itself almost constantly in an elementary form: it is generally globular, ovoid, or kidney-shaped; rarely angular.

Some seeds are so small that they are absolutely invisible without the aid of the microscope, as for instance those of the Fungi; whilst others, like the Cocos (*Cocos nucifera*, Linn.) of the Maldive Islands, reach the size of a man's body.

Some only preserve their germinative faculty for a few hours; if they are not sown at the moment when the plant offers them at maturity, as it were, they constantly abort. Others, on the contrary, preserve their latent life through many ages; sheltered in our monuments or buried in an unpropitious soil. After such a long sleep, perchance of many thousands of years, if they are placed in a favourable spot, they germinate, to our great astonishment.

Two parts are to be distinguished in the seed: the integument and the kernel.

The integument or envelope generally presents a coriaceous substance; sometimes, however, as in the case of the pomegranate, it is only formed by a watery layer. Its surface, usually smooth, is sometimes wrinkled, hairy, or finely honey-combed.

In one region of it we see the trace of the spot where the cord adhered which attached the grain to the mother plant, and transmitted its nutritive juices to it. This imprint bears the name of umbilicus.

The kernel is formed of the embryo, a true plant in miniature, surrounded by parts which are to aid in its evolution.

Among these the cotyledons occupy the first place. They are usually fleshy, sometimes foliaceous, organs which prepare for the little plant, issuing from the egg, nourishment appropriate to its delicacy till it can itself take up its food from the soil. There are usually only one or two.

When the cotyledons are little developed their alimentary function is intrusted to another organ, the perisperm. This, which Gärtner compared very rightly to the albumen of the egg, varies a good deal as to its volume and consistence. In the cocoa-palm it is in part milky. Our bread is made from the farinaceous perisperm of the wheat; our coffee is only the same part from the horny seed of the coffee-tree of Arabia.

Plants are known, the perisperm of which is of a firmness much surpassing that of the coffee-tree. Such is the case with the seeds of the Corozo, in which this structure is as white and hard as ivory; owing to this fact different objects are made from it in trade which are put forward as being fabricated from this substance. This peculiarity has procured for the Corozo palm the name of the *elephant-plant* (Phytelephas), and for its fruit, cargoes of which are brought to France, that of *vegetable ivory*.

It was Leuwenhoeck who first of all noticed that the seed contains the young plant in miniature, traced out in the midst of its envelopes, and only waiting for favouring circumstances to expand its leaves and flowers. Thus, looking philosophically at the subject, we may say that certain plants are viviparous. There are even some in which the impatience of the embryo is so great, that in order to reach the air and light more quickly, it precipitately escapes from its egg while this still adheres to the mother.

This peculiarity is seen in the mangroves (*Rhizophora gymnorrhiza*,

205. Forest of Mangroves.

Linn.), strange plants, half-tree, half-fish, living half-plunged in the sea or the lagoons of tropical America and India. Suspended above the water by their bent branches, often quite covered with oysters, these trees let drop through their foliage long roots of embryos which have germinated in the fruit. These, perfectly adapted to the work they have before them, are like little pointed clubs, and have attained a length of from ten to fourteen inches at the time when they are to fall into the water; so that they sink deep into the mud which encircles the mother plant and form a family group around her.

Germination, which is really vegetable suckling, is only the development of the embryo up to the fall of the cotyledons.

This act is almost always accomplished in the ground; it is only aquatic plants which effect it under water. Some parasites, however,

206. Germination of an *Arundo indica.*

germinate on the plants or animals on the surface of which we find them. This occurs in the microscopic Fungi which attack our hair and beard, and bring on most harassing diseases, tetters, tineæ, &c., as the labours of the microscopists of our day have placed beyond a doubt. Similar to these are certain parasitic plants, which are never found except upon certain insects.

At other times germination takes place under very strange conditions. Vandermonde saw children in whose noses peas had germinated from having been imprudently introduced. Another physician, Bréra, mentions having opened the body of a soldier whose stomach was filled with barley which was developing itself there.

There are two classes of actions to be considered in germination: physiological phenomena, and chemical phenomena.

Let us first of all examine the former, we can discuss the others farther on. So soon as ever the seed is confided to the earth it imbibes water and swells. Soon afterwards the integument tears irregularly and the young plant appears outside. Sometimes, however, this act is effected symmetrically. The seed presents a kind of lid or little door, which the young plant opens by pushing it so as to direct itself towards the soil, as we see in the Indian reeds. After that the root sinks downwards and the stem shoots up towards the light.

This double phenomenon has occupied physiologists a great deal. At first the direction of the roots was attributed to the humidity of the ground or to its chemical composition. But Duhamel having noticed that young roots did not sink into wet sponges between which seeds had been made to germinate, and Dutrochet having remarked that seeds suspended in boxes filled with earth left them in order to penetrate more deeply, it became necessary to renounce these two hypotheses.

Knight and Dutrochet, seeing that when seeds are made to grow in the buckets of a wheel set in motion by mechanism, the rootlets always tend outwards and the stems inwards, concluded that the divergence of these organs was owing to the influence of terrestrial gravitation.

It was also thought that the direction of the roots was due to their trying to escape the light, but by means of experiments in which suspended plants were lighted from below, it was ascertained that these organs directed themselves towards the light. Hence this hypothesis really explains the cause of the direction which plants take no better than the others.[1]

In proportion as the embryo is developed, the cotyledons, as Malpighi remarked, become filled with vessels, the office of which is to secrete the first nutritive fluids of the young plant, for this could only find in the ground food too active or too coarse for its yet undeveloped tissues. Then when these vegetable mammæ, as Bonnet called them, have accomplished their function, and when the roots are vigorous enough to nourish themselves, the part of these organs being played out, they fade and fall. Such is the last phase in the evolution of the young plant.

At the same time that these different vital actions are carried on, the germination is the theatre of important chemical phenomena. For its accomplishment it imperiously demands a certain amount of warmth, water, and air. If one of these factors be wanting, this first manifestation of life becomes an impossibility. At the temperature of zero all vegetation ceases.

[1] M. Blondeau, in a memoir read before the French Academy, stated that exposure of some seeds to an induced electric current has the effect of making the stem and leaves grow down into the earth, while the roots come up and take their place.—Tr.

When cold fastens upon seeds it preserves them for an indefinite period of time, just as it preserved the companions of Bilbao, the discoverer of the South Sea, whose corpses were recently found in the snows of the Cordilleras; and as it preserved the remains of the antediluvian elephants and rhinoceroses, the skeletons of which, still enveloped in their flesh, were discovered in the ices of Siberia.

207. Roots Lighted from below and directing themselves towards the Light.

The course taken by the water, which is to soak into the grain and prepare the way for its evolution, is not always the same.

In seeds which have a coriaceous husk, not easily permeable by moisture, the liquid enters by the umbilicus. Poncelet and De Candolle proved that all the outer surface of these seeds might be covered with wax, and yet that would not prevent them from germinating if the precaution were taken of not covering the umbilical cicatrix.

In seeds the skin of which is soft and easily imbibes water, such as those of the haricot bean for instance, it is this structure that principally gives access to the water which is so indispensably necessary to primordial life.

The air also plays a great part in the chemical phenomena of germination. The learned Homberg denied the importance of it, because he saw seeds develop in the receiver of his pneumatic machine. But Boyle, Muschenbroeck, and Boerhaave demonstrated that this agent is absolutely necessary to vegetable evolution, and that if the great chemist stated the contrary, it could only be attributed to the defective construction of his instruments which enabled him to obtain but a very imperfect vacuum.

All the air, however, is not employed in the first phase of vegetable life; of its two principal elements the oxygen is here alone of service. It is to the chemist Scheele that the glory of this great discovery is due.

Some seeds only absorb a small quantity of it; one or two thousandths of their weight is enough; this is the case with wheat. Others, such as the haricot bean, consume according to Saussure and Woodhouse, as much as a hundredth part.

At the time when seeds germinate they exhale carbonic acid and water, and set free a noticeable amount of heat.

Divers causes accessorily hasten the evolution of the plant.

Electricity is one of these. It was the Abbé Nollet who discovered its action. More recently Sir Humphry Davy and A. Becquerel observed that it is only negative electricity that gives energy to this phenomenon; whilst positive electricity, on the contrary, retards it.

Indeed, if we pass an electric current beneath a sown surface, the seeds develop much more quickly than in a part which has not been submitted to electricity.

The difference is well marked when we experiment with seeds which germinate very quickly. One patch will be covered with close green vegetation, while on the other not a single plant has yet issued from the ground.

Following Ingenhouz and Sennebier, men have long taught that light was opposed to germination. This is an error, as Saussure noticed. Nevertheless all the coloured rays of light are not favourable to it; the chemical and the calorific rays have each an opposite action upon this phenomenon. The former, which are the blue and the violet rays, clearly increase its activity; the latter, the red and yellow rays, are hurtful to it.[1]

[1] With regard to the action of light, the balance of evidence seems to be in favour of the opinion expressed by Mr. Hunt, which is very much to the same effect, viz. that the blue rays promote germination, while the yellow light-giving rays impede it.—*Popular Science Review.*—TR.

A knowledge of the fundamental conditions demanded by vegetation explains certain phenomena which have occasionally astonished the vulgar. When these conditions are wanting, seeds are often preserved torpid for a long time in the place which incloses them, and then when they find themselves under the influence of favourable circumstances, they cover a site with a form of vegetation unknown there within the memory of man.

Thus, according to the account of Ray, after the great fire of London, the hedge-mustard (*Sisymbrium Irio*) all at once grew thickly on the ruins of this city where previously it was unknown. When certain forests are burned we see plants spring from their soil which were never previously known there. Analogous facts have been noticed after old marshes have been dried up. Their beds laid bare are sometimes covered with an entirely new form of vegetation, quite unknown in the country, and arising doubtless from seeds having been buried under the water and preserved there till, having been exposed to the air, all the conditions necessary to germination, which were previously wanting, were now brought to bear upon them.[1]

[1] Thompson's weed (*Lepidium Draba*), a plant which gives much annoyance to agriculturists, appears to have been introduced in the straw of the beds brought back from the disastrous expedition to Walcheren. The troops being disembarked at Ramsgate, the beds were ripped up and the straw thrown into an old chalkpit belonging to a Mr. Thompson. It was subsequently used as manure, and wherever this manure was laid down a plentiful crop of the new weed was the result. This weed has now spread over a great part of Kent.—*Popular Science Review*, vol. v. p. 492.—Tr.

BOOK IV.

EXTREMES IN THE VEGETABLE KINGDOM.

CHAPTER I.

THE LICHEN ROCK AND THE VIRGIN FOREST.

The vegetable kingdom is the emblem of diversity in harmony. While its extreme limits offer the most manifest contrasts, everything still is chained and bound together by imperceptible links, and bears evidence of the divine wisdom which presided over its distribution. In certain families force and majesty predominate; others attract attention by the delicacy of their forms or the charm of their beauty. On one side are seen robust forms sculptured by the hand of giants, on the other delicate outlines traced by the fingers of fairies.

What an astonishing contrast between this palm-tree, the crown of which daringly rends the clouds as it waves above the tropical forest, and this gray lichen, a thin layer of coloured matter staining our statues and walls! What infinite variety, what a series of gradations, from the splendid flower of the *Victoria regia* to the imperceptible corolla of the nettle; from those indestructible plants which grew on the warm mud of our new-born globe to the ephemeral organisms which die as they issue from the earth; from the wood which is substituted for iron to the gelatinous plant which the slightest touch crushes! And yet in the midst of this inextricable chaos, science reveals to us order and eternal wisdom.

The sceptre of vegetation belongs to the oak. When in the depth of night we wander amid the sombre and stately precincts of Mount Etna, the imposing majesty of these denizens, centuries old, and the huge shadows of their agitated and groaning summits, fill us with awe and terror, and announce that we are in the presence of the king of our forests. One dreads to hear the plaintive groans which froze Dante with terror as they issued from the black boughs of the Wood of Suicides.

208. Forest of Palm-trees on the Banks of the Nile—*Phœnix dactylifera* (Linnæus).

The palms, decorated with their waving crowns, are, in the eyes of all, the emblem of tropical vegetation. Poets have often sung of their magnificence; and Linnæus, impressed by their brilliant appearance, decorated them with the name of "princes of the vegetable kingdom."

But those who travel in the East, which the great Swedish botanist never did, find that masses of palms are far from having the grand and imposing look of our European forests. They form only a vista of naked and monotonous columns, the leafy dome of which allows the rays of the sun to pass through; hence a popular saying of the ancients tells us that "no person can travel with impunity beneath the palm-trees." Explorers of the valley of the Nile who were really in earnest about their work, have justly observed that the poets would not have written their idylls on these trees if they had found themselves beneath the date-palms of Egypt in the hottest hours of the day.

There is one solitary exception, the doum-palm of the Thebaïs (*Cucifera thebaica*, Martius). Its wide-spread branches, terminated by numerous tufts of large leaves, to which hang monstrous bunches of fruit, give to its forests a diversity, a picturesqueness, which its congeners do not partake of.

The palm-tree really displays all its splendour and its strength only when it shows itself in little groups, boldly planted in the midst of rocks, the crowns of which, waving in the tempest, seem only to bend in order to defy the fury of the waves breaking tumultuously at their feet.

The beauty of the Liliaceæ, the great flowers of which are enamelled with the brightest colours, also charmed Linnæus. He looked upon them as "the nobles of Flora's empire," spreading forth their blazonry on the segments of their resplendent corollas.

Lastly, according to the legislator of botany, among the numerous families of plants which enliven the globe, the great but humble family of Graminaceæ represents the people. "They are," he said, "the plebeians, the poor, the peasants of the vegetable kingdom. They form the simplest, the most numerous, and the most sprightly part of it; hence it is in them that power and force reside, and the more we trample upon and maltreat them, the more do they multiply."

Fleshy plants give the strangest of aspects to equatorial landscapes, as for instance in Mexico, the privileged land of the cactuses. It is there that we find growing in almost a miraculous manner the gigantic torch-cactus (*Cereus giganteus*, Engelm). One is quite astonished at finding it upon the most sterile rocks, where the eye with difficulty detects a few particles of earth. How can a plant so bulky, fleshy, and watery, grow without taking up anything from the soil, and draw the elements of nutrition from the burning air around it? When this cactus is fully developed, it presents the appearance of an immense chandelier, attaining a height of as much as sixty feet, and it is surprising to see that the tempest spares it.

When we pass from animals to the vegetable kingdom, we find, that notwithstanding the calm and silence which here preside over all the acts of life, there is yet an energy, a tenacity, which one would never have suspected. To the extremes of size are opposed incalculable differences in duration. No animal grows with the prodigious rapidity which we see in certain plants, nor does any attain the fabulous longevity which is the attribute of many trees.

One plant passes away like the last hour of the Ephemera which flutters in the twilight over the banks of our streams; a ray of sunlight sees its birth and fall. Another defies the power of ages: the offspring of creation, it seems as if it ought only to sink with the wreck of the globe.

Some of our more common moulds pass in one day through all the phases of life; this lapse of time is sufficient for them to appear in, fructify, and die. But by a singular contradiction, some plants of the same class only grow with inexplicable slowness. One of those lichens which show like plates of golden yellow on the roofs of our houses, was watched for forty years by Vaucher, without his seeing that it increased to a perceptible extent. Accordingly De Candolle said that the lichens which cover our rocks possibly go back to the times of the cataclysms which laid them bare!

But it is particularly in the dicotyledonous plants that longevity is so extraordinary. Some of these grow so slowly that ages seem scarcely to alter their dimensions.

If we look at vegetable life scattering its great families over the globe, we everywhere find the same contrasts—misery by the side of grandeur. The bare rock which raises its shattered masses on the mountain slope is only coloured with a crust of lichens and mosses, which dot its surface like so many pencil marks. Below these regions, where the severity of the air destroys everything, we find pines and oaks twisted and dwarfed, while lower down rise magnificent and sombre forests of Coniferæ encircling the mountains with their girdle of black.

The palms compose numerous groups in all the equatorial regions. But vegetable life reveals itself peculiarly with all its variety and splendour in the immense virgin forests of the tropics, where the axe has never yet shorn it of its exuberance. Some present such a profusion of aged trees entwined with ferns and creepers, that they are absolutely impenetrable, unless some stream of water happen in its winding course to furnish the daring traveller with a natural path.

The special character of the vegetation in some of these forests gives

209. Arborescent Ferns of the Forests of New Zealand.

them quite a characteristic aspect. When the parasitic orchises predominate, they form on every side elegant chandeliers, as it were, of verdure and flowers; or they hang here and there in long slender pendants, looking at a distance like so many gigantic spiders displaying their mighty claws and balancing themselves now and then at the end of their threads.

Again, as in New Zealand, arborescent ferns, with the aspect of palms, give these distant landscapes an appearance which is seen in no other part.

The impenetrable virgin forest alarms us by its sombre and terrible aspect. On one side vigorous parasites assail the aged trees, forming with them an inextricable net-work which the axe can scarcely cleave, whilst all progress through it is impeded by bushes and tall herbs, where so many redoubtable enemies lie concealed. During the day all is silent: the frightful heat paralyzes the tenants of this realm of vegetation, and sleep reigns everywhere. But when night arrives all becomes full of life; birds, mammals, and reptiles declare war on one another, and every part rings with groans and hoarse cries of pain and death.

CHAPTER II.

GIANTS OF THE VEGETABLE KINGDOM.

Like animals, plants may be infinitely little or infinitely huge; the latter astonish us by their colossal proportions, while the former escape our ken, and are only revealed by the microscope.

The study of the development of plants in respect to their mere size presents us with some curious contrasts.

Some rudimentary plants, such as the Ascophori, Mould Fungi which so frequently invade our bread, and the Aspergilli which we often see forming in the fluids we drink glairy repulsive-looking films, possess an almost invisible stalk. Woody plants, on the contrary, often astonish us by the enormous dimensions of this part.

The old authors who describe Germany tell us that there were trees there, from the trunk of one of which boats were made which carried as many as thirty men.

From the times of antiquity the luxuriant growth of the plane-trees on the banks of the Bosphorus and the Black Sea has been the subject of remark, and the botanists of our day have proved that what our forefathers said was in no way exaggerated.

Men were almost inclined to disbelieve the account of Pliny, who states that in his time there was in Lycia a stout thriving plane-tree in the trunk of which was seen a vast grotto eighty-one feet in circumference, the whole extent of which had been tapestried by nature with a green and velvety hanging of moss. Licinius Mutianus, governor of the province, charmed with the delicious coolness of this rural hall, gave a supper in it to eighteen guests from his suite. After the orgy they transformed the scene of their festivity into a dormitory, and comfortably passed the night there.

This fact has been fully confirmed by modern travellers. De Candolle relates that according to one of them, there still exists in the neighbourhood of Constantinople an enormous lime-tree, the trunk of which is quite as ample as that of which we have been speaking. It is 150 feet in circumference, and also presents a cavity 80 feet in circuit.

Ray, the celebrated English botanist and geologist, speaks of an oak existing in his time in Germany which was of such dimensions that it had been transformed into a citadel. To confine ourselves more strictly to the truth, let us just say that its interior served as a guard-house. We may here mention another tree of the same kind, still growing in Normandy, and which, in contrast to the other, has been consecrated to piety. This is the chapel oak of Allouville, in which there is an altar dedicated to the Virgin, where on certain days mass is said. The ample hollow of this tree not only furnishes an oratory, but above this a sleeping-room has been scooped out; there is a bed in this room, to which access is gained by steps outside: it is the abode of an anchorite. This tree, which perhaps sheltered in its shade the companions of the Seigneur de Bethencourt, when on their way to embark for the conquest of the Canaries, is held in great veneration in the country.

One of our most illustrious and philosophic botanists, Marquis, renowned alike for his eminent position and knowledge, measured the trunk of this tree, and found that it was thirty feet in circumference near the ground.

I have also seen on the banks of the Bosphorus plane-trees the trunks of which were pierced with enormous cavities. In the neighbourhood of Smyrna there is one of these trees celebrated for its size and antiquity. The stem, which is hollowed right through, is spread widely out at the base, and represents three columns, which converge towards each other, forming a sort of porch beneath which a man on horseback can pass easily.[1]

Yet the baobab on the banks of the Niger, in its splendid luxuriance

[1] In their learned works on forests Evelyn and Loudon have represented several other trees, which, like the Platanus of Smyrna, present openings through which a knight completely equipped could pass freely. — Evelyn, *Sylva*, 1664. Loudon, *Arboretum Britannicum.* London, 1838.

210. Chapel Oak of Allouville, Normandy.—From a sketch by Marquis in 1824.

of growth, surpasses even all the giants of the Bosphorus. It is especially remarkable for its thickness, contrasted with its want of height. It is a colossus of ungraceful look. Almost always without leaves, bearing them only in the rainy season, its whitish conical trunk, scarcely fifteen to twenty feet in height, is more than a hundred feet in circumference at the level of the ground. This short and robust support is necessary to sustain its incredibly large dome of leaves, the bulk of which is sometimes so great that, seen from a distance, the baobab looks rather like a small forest than a single tree. Its large branches are fifty to sixty feet long. When time has hollowed out the stem of one of these noble trees, the negroes make use of the cavity. Sometimes they turn it into a place of amusement, a rustic retreat where they can smoke their chibouques and take refreshment; at other times they convert it into a prison. One of these is known of which the Senegambians have converted the interior into a council-hall; the entrance is covered with sculptures which point out the high destination reserved for it.

But the marvel of the vegetable kingdom in respect to its colossal dimensions, is assuredly the famous chestnut-tree growing on the lower slopes of Etna. Count Borch, who measured the trunk very exactly, accords it a circumference of 190 feet. A house which shelters a shepherd and his flock has been built in the immense hollow of its trunk. During the winter the wood of the tree serves the inhabitant of this solitary retreat for fuel, and its abundance of fruit supplies him with food during the summer.

This colossus of our forests, which is called the "Chestnut of a Hundred Horses," owes its name to the vast extent of its foliage. The inhabitants of the country told the painter J. Houel "that Jeanne of Aragon, when travelling from Spain to Naples, stopped at Sicily, and, accompanied by all the nobility of Catania, paid a visit to Mount Etna. She was on horseback, as were also her suite, and a storm having come on, she took shelter under this tree, the vast foliage of which sufficed to protect the queen and all her cavaliers from the rain. It is from this memorable adventure, they add, that the old tree took the name of Chestnut-tree of the Hundred Horses."[1]

Yet whatever astonishment we may feel at the extraordinary dimen-

[1] The celebrated journey of Jeanne of Aragon to the *Castagno di Cento Cavalli*, as the chestnut-tree of Etna is called in Sicily, is only a fable. Count Borch maintains that it owes its name merely to the fact that fifty horses could be placed within its trunk and fifty round about it. Some botanists, however, think that this colossal tree is only a fusion of several individuals of the same species. But this is scarcely probable; the vicinity presents several specimens which are almost as vast, and which, for that reason, are known

sions attained by the trunks of certain trees, the height to which others reach strikes us still more than their growth in diameter. The king of our forests, the oak, which poetic fiction looks upon as the emblem of passive force, rears its crown of leaves one hundred feet above the soil.

In the East the imposing remains of the ancient forest employed in building the temple of Jerusalem, the cedars of Lebanon, the object of so much veneration, and which the pilgrim only approaches with the sounds of a hymn on his lips, spread forth their dark sheets of verdure to a height of 150 feet above the mountain.

Supported only by its flexible column, which yields and bends beneath the force of the tempest, the wax-palm on the Andes balances its waving crown in the bosom of the clouds 200 feet above the heights whereon it grows.

But no tree rears its head towards the sky so boldly as the gigantic cedar of California, the *Wellingtonia gigantea*. One colossus of this species, now hurled down and stretched upon the rock, presented when it stood erect and threatening a height of more than 490 feet, that is to say, about eight times the elevation of a house of five stories. It was above 130 feet in circumference.

The bark of the trunk of one of these giants of the American forests was transported in part to the Crystal Palace at Sydenham, where it formed one of the most splendid curiosities, until accidentally destroyed by fire in 1866. It was a monstrous column, above 130 feet in height, and which at the level of the ground had a diameter of nearly thirty-four feet. I stood inside this tree along with fifteen people. At San Francisco a piano was placed and a ball given to more than twenty persons on the stump of a Wellingtonia which had been brought thither. The age of this colossus corresponds to its dimensions. By counting the number of annual rings in a transverse section, it was ascertained that these monstrous trees must be 3000 or 4000 years old, so that they seem to have been almost contemporary with the biblical creation, and have stood erect and unshaken amidst all the commotions of the globe.

Alongside of these giants stretched prostrate on the ground, man only looks like a pigmy and feels his littleness. He calls them the *mammoths of the forest*, to show that, like those frightful animals which surpassed

by distinct names in the country. Count Borch, who has carefully examined the Hundred-horse Chestnut, says that at the first look one might think it arose from the junction of several trunks, but that when it is attentively studied we find that it is only one tree. This fact has been placed beyond doubt by the Canon Recupero, who had it dug round, and saw that the five trunks end in one single colossal root.—Borch, *Lettres sur la Sicile*. Turin, 1782, t. i. p. 121.

211. The Great Chestnut-tree of Mount Etna, called of a Hundred Horses.—After a drawing by Houel in 1784, *Travels in Sicily.*

212. Gigantic Cedar of California—*Wellingtonia gigantea.*

all others in their size, they tower above all the vegetable kingdom. One of these cedars, hollowed out into a deep cavern, owes its name of "the Riding School" to the fact, that a man on horseback can penetrate sixty-five feet into the dark excavation.

However, these prodigies of vegetation do not seem to be the supreme manifestation of creative power. In penetrating into regions of Australia previously quite unknown, some gold-seekers have just discovered Eucalypti that surpass in size even the *Wellingtonia gigantea.* Ferdinand Müller, the botanist, says that trees of the species *Eucalyptus amygdalina*, 480 feet in length, were met with lying on the ground; and this seems perfectly confirmed by the statement of Mr. George Robins, who saw in the mountains of Berwick one of these trees standing which had, near the ground, a circumference of 81 feet, and the height of which he estimated at 500 feet. This Eucalyptus, therefore, could overshadow the great pyramid of Egypt and the spire of the cathedral of Strasburg, for the former is only 480 feet in height and the latter 466. Thus these vegetable giants dethrone all others that have hitherto been regarded as the forest monarchs of our globe, and must be added to the marvels that Australia may yet have in store for us.

When from these noble trees, proudly cleaving the clouds with their tops, we pass to those whose humble stem creeps upon the ground, we find that even the latter at times acquire a length which has something of the prodigious in it.

Struck with the aspect of the vines in Italy, the manifold garlands of which entwine from branch to branch and disappear amid the foliage of the trees without our being able to see either the beginning or the end, Pliny maintained that they grow for ever: *Vites sine fine crescunt*, said the Roman naturalist.

But we have more precise data as to the size of sundry other plants. Thus in the virgin forests of India, the *Calamus Rotang*, which climbs upon the trunks of aged trees, and stretches from one to another, sinking to the ground to rise again, attains, according to the traveller Loureiro, a length of 400 or 500 feet.

The Gigantic Fucus (*Fucus giganteus*, Linn.) reaches much more extraordinary proportions; the waves of the ocean, according to Humboldt, yield strips which are sometimes 1500 to 1600 feet long.

In an interesting article in the *Revue Germanique*, M. A. Boscowitz says, that in the botanical garden of Caracas there was a Convolvulus which in six months attained the incredible length of 6000 feet.

It must therefore have grown at the rate of more than a foot per hour, and its growth must have been visible to the naked eye!

CHAPTER III.

VEGETABLE LONGEVITY.

But if anything ought to astonish us in the life of trees it is their longevity; we might even go farther, and speak of the principle of eternity which is clearly latent in some species, the death of which seems rather to depend upon fortuitous circumstances than on the fact of age.

The life of animals is quite ephemeral compared to that of our trees. Minute investigations have thrown considerable light upon the chronology of many of them.

The pine and great chestnut can assuredly extend their existence to a term of 400 or 500 years. In the island of Teneriffe are found many venerable pines and enormous chestnut-trees, which in all probability were planted there by the Conquistadores at the commencement of the fifteenth century, the epoch of the invasion of this island. The former, the *Pinus canariensis*, are distinguishable from the others, owing to the conquerors having in their piety decorated them nearly all with little madonnas, which are still seen suspended to their boughs.

The lime-tree of Morat, planted at Fribourg on the day of the celebrated battle, is one of the oldest trees in Europe. This glorious event in the history of Switzerland having occurred in the year 1476, the venerated tree, which is encircled by a colonnade, and of which the aged branches are upheld by a framework of wood, must be now 400 years old.

The fir attains a still greater age. In some of the most ancient forests of Germany, situated on the summit of the Wurzelberg in Thuringia, as many as 700 annual layers have been counted on some of the trees cut down there.

The olive-tree, so revered in ancient Greece, and which inspired such beautiful verses in the tragedy of *Ædipus at Colonus* by Sophocles, reached a much greater age, according to the ancient myth. Pliny even asserts that in his time the celebrated olive-tree which Minerva caused to spring from the ground at the epoch of the foundation of the city of Cecrops was still to be seen in the citadel of Athens.

The ancient races, struck with the noble aspect of our oaks, have in all ages enveloped them in the clouds of their legends, and carried them

213. The Lime-tree of the Battle of Morat.—From a sketch by M. Pouchet, 1858.

back to the remotest antiquity. Of this class was the mighty holm-oak, which in the days of Pliny still existed near Rome, on the trunk of which there was an Etruscan inscription in letters of brass, stating that before the existence of the Eternal City it was already the object of popular veneration. The Roman naturalist also asserts that in the environs of Heraclea, in the kingdom of Pontus, there was a tradition that two oaks which overshadowed the altar of Jupiter Stragius had been planted by Hercules.[1]

The origin of certain trees is lost in even more remote antiquity.

The imposing terror of the Hercynian Forest has deeply impressed all those who have described Germany, and Pliny and Tacitus especially. The aged oaks of its sombre vales, where wandered the elk and the aurochs, especially aroused the admiration of the Roman historian; he cannot refrain from speaking of them in the most lofty terms: "The majestic grandeur of the oak in this forest," he says, "surpasses all imaginable belief: this tree has never been touched with the axe; it is contemporary with the creation of the world, and appears to be the symbol of immortality!"

Pliny does not restrict himself to this splendid image; he adds further details: "I wish," he says, "to preserve silence as to things so extraordinary as to be considered fabulous; but one thing is certain, viz. that where the roots are found they raise the earth into little hillocks, and if the soil will not yield, the roots press against each other and form lofty mounds which rise to the branches: they interlace with each other so as to form complete arcades, below which whole squadrons can ride on horseback."

This idea of immortality in trees is often met with in the works of the ancients. The historian Josephus, in his *Jewish War*, relates that in his day there was near the city of Ebron a turpentine tree which was as old as the days of Adam (book v. chap. xxxi.)

It was reserved for modern naturalists to show that these assertions however extraordinary they may appear, are still rigorously correct, and that many of our trees, in some sort indestructible, may have witnessed the final scenes of creation, and after braving the action of so many ages, are still upright and living to this day.

[1] In the Crimea some trees are met with which possess a certain amount of celebrity. The chief one is a nut-tree in a plain near Balaklava, at the spot where stood the temple of Iphigenia in Tauris. It is considered to have been in existence at the time when the Greek colonies exported their nuts to Rome, and that its age dates back several thousand years. At present its fertility is so great that it bears every year as many as 100,000 nuts, which are shared without any jarring among five Tartar families, to whom it belongs.

It is now a hundred years since Adanson, by ingenious calculations, showed the learned that such ideas, though extraordinary, are yet facts of the most scrupulous exactitude. This naturalist, by a happy chance found in the interior of the trunk of a baobab in one of the Cape Verd Islands an inscription which had been traced on it by the English 300 years previously. Starting from this point and comparing the diameters of the stems of many of these bulky trees, the French savant succeeded in proving that the most vigorous of these primitive inhabitants of the African forests might be at least 5000 years old.

A bareheaded cypress, a venerable patriarch of the vegetable kingdom, has possibly traversed a still longer vista of ages! It is seen at the present day on the road from Vera Cruz to Mexico, and is celebrated for having sheltered the whole army of Fernando Cortez beneath its mighty shade. Its birth, according to some botanists, seems to date from an epoch so remote as to be almost beyond our ken. As its trunk, which is 117 feet in circumference, surpasses that of the baobabs, and as its growth is slower than theirs, De Candolle supposes this tree may be not less than 6000 years old, which carries back its origin to the times anterior to the period usually assigned to the Mosaic creation.[1]

Meanwhile we ought not to be astonished at seeing some botanists look upon trees as so many beings, the life of which is unlimited, and many of which, born amid the débris of former cataclysms, still vegetate full of sap and vigour.

De Candolle, who puts forward this opinion, admitting the hypothesis of Gaudichaud, considers the giants of our forests as so many aggregates of individuals, or buds, annually succeeding on the stem, which thus represents a living soil. This stems grows on century after century, and only succumbs by accident, as when struck by lightning, or when its suckers cannot find nutritive juices.

Thus then, we repeat, actual science demonstrates what antiquity had only dimly seen.

1 History has preserved for us the number of soldiers that composed the little army of Cortez, and this knowledge enables us to estimate how far the shade of the cypress in question must have extended. The army consisted of six hundred Spanish foot soldiers, forty horse, and nine small pieces of artillery.—*Hist. Gen. des Voy.* t. xii. p. 389. According to M. Schacht the calculations of Adanson are liable to the charge of inexactness on account of the rapidity with which this tree grows. In forty years a baobab at Santa Cruz gained a circumference of about ten feet four inches.

Strabo mentions trees still more extraordinary, but without appearing to believe in them. He says that beyond the Hyarotis there was one the shade of which was so ample that it extended five plethra (505 feet), and could shelter ten thousand persons.—Strabo, *Geography*, book xv.

214. Gigantic Baobab of the Virgin Forests of Africa—*Adansonia digitata* (Linnæus).

To us a tree is no longer a simple individual; it is an agglomeration, a republic of isolated beings which fashion its branches, as the polype of the coral constructs its boughs; in fact it is a vegetable polypidom.

The slow development of the trunks of certain trees at once calls up

215. Dragon's-blood Tree of the Island of Teneriffe—*Dracæna Draco* (Linnæus).

images of immobility and eternity. The dragon's-blood tree of the Canaries awakens such thoughts.

Thrice famous for its strange look, its vast size, and its antiquity, this dragon's-blood tree is equally so for the stationary condition of its growth. In the legends of Teneriffe we are told that this singular tree was worshipped by the Guanches, its original inhabitants; and it is related that in the fifteenth century mass was celebrated in the interior of its trunk, a fact even lately attested by the vestiges which were seen of a little altar. This tree grows so slowly that after a tolerably long interval of time it was not possible to verify any change in its circumference. It was accurately measured in 1402 by the companions of Bethencourt at the time when they discovered the island, that is to say, more than 460 years ago, and since then it has in no way increased in diameter. Time has passed over without touching it.[1] Humboldt, when he ascended the peak of Teneriffe in 1799, measured this tree a little above the level of the ground, and found it forty-five feet in circumference.

CHAPTER IV.

DENSITY OF PLANTS.

As the duration of life in trees presents such vastly opposite limits, we expect to meet equally enormous differences in their density; and this is the case.

Those singular plants the Tremellæ, which after a wet night, or even merely a storm, suddenly bestrew the earth in the shape of so many tremulous masses of jelly, covering the ground where a few hours before there was not a vestige, and which, on account of the unexpected manner in which they appear, were looked upon by the alchemists as a supernatural production, an emanation from the stars, are so soft that the least pressure crushes and reduces them to water.

In the same class to which these gelatinous plants belong, we find others of a surprising degree of firmness. This is the case with certain Algæ scattered over the shores of Asia, and in particular with the *Fucus tendo,* the toughness of which has been compared to that of the tendons which convey movement to the limbs of animals. In appearance this marine plant is exactly like a cord, and as it possesses the strength of cordage, the Chinese, who are so ingenious in everything, make use of it in order to tie up bales of goods. In Japan this fucus serves for making fishermen's nets.

In some trees of considerable size the trunk is scarcely harder than in these plants: for instance, that of the *Bombax Ceiba,* or cheese-plant, is as soft as the article of food after which it is named.

[1] [This tree is said to have been destroyed by a storm in 1867.—Tr.]

On the contrary, iron-wood (*Siderodendrum triflorum*), which can be polished like metal, is so dense that savages often employ it to make their war-clubs and other formidable weapons of.

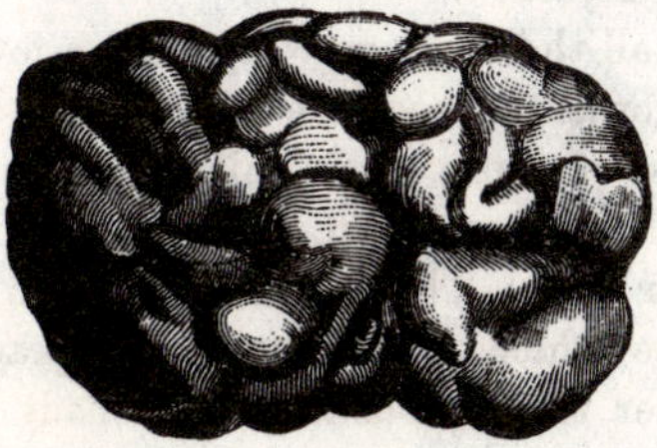

216. The Green Tremella—*Tremella atro-virens* (Bulliard).

The finger-nail will pierce the fleshy stalk of some euphorbias and cause abundance of milky juice to flow. But, on the other hand, the stalks of some bamboos in India almost turn the file, and, as we have said, are so indurated with silica, that sparks can be drawn with the steel from them.

BOOK V.

MIGRATIONS OF PLANTS.

Nothing reveals to us the resources of nature in a more imposing way than the facility with which she covers all the surface of the globe with vegetation and life. At times she seems to trust solely to the immense fecundity allotted to the species; at others she employs the most ingenious and varied proceedings in order to transport her fruits and seeds from one pole to another.

The large number of seeds which certain plants produce insures their incessant reproduction, and in this respect calculation often gives very unexpected results. Ray counted 32,000 seeds on one poppy stalk, and

Linnæus says that a single stem of tobacco sometimes yields 40,000. Dodard carries these figures still higher in respect to the number of fruits that can be collected from an elm. According to him, this tree annually produces more than 529,000.

It is clear that if all the seeds grew up, only a few generations would pass away ere these forms of vegetable life covered the entire surface of the globe. But a host of causes arrest this menacing invasion. Animals, the rigour of some climates, and man, whose civilization encroaches upon nature, place a barrier to it. The first invaders of a virgin soil are pitilessly stifled by those which follow them; the prairie gives way to a thicket, and soon after this dies beneath the shady vaults of a vigorous forest.

The fecundity of some fungi is quite extraordinary. Fries counted more than 10,000,000 reproductive bodies in one individual of the *Reticularia maxima.* Other plants of the same family rear a still larger progeny, the abundance of which is prodigious, and which indeed cannot be numbered by all the resources of the human intellect.

The immeasurable fecundity of the gigantic Lycoperdon is such that its microscopic grains must be counted by thousands of millions. Now, although they are invisible to the eye, each of these may yet give birth to a voluminous fungus which often in one night acquires the size of a gourd. And it may be said, without hyperbole, that if the little seeds of this plant were miraculously dispersed over the whole globe, and were to be simultaneously developed, the earth would be absolutely paved with them the next day.

The air certainly plays the most important part in the dissemination of vegetable life. A host of light seeds seem to have been decorated with little plumes and membranous wings only in order to be borne away by the winds.

For this purpose the seeds of many Syngenesiæ are surmounted by plumes of outspread fibrillæ, forming complete parachutes which the slightest breath of the zephyr bears away. Torn from the mother plant, the seed, by means of its aërial skiff, accomplishes the longest journeys. The slightest breeze carries it up from the depth of the valley to the mountain peaks. If the tempest rise, the little parachute, borne away on the powerful wind, mingles with the stormy clouds, traverses oceans, and then effects a descent upon some distant shore. We are told that after certain hurricanes it is not unusual to see the soil of Spain covered with different aërial seeds brought from America. It is to the action of the winds that Linnæus ascribes the importation into Europe of the *Conyza cœrulea* of Canada, which now infests the north of France.

The air does still more; in its commotions it carries away entire plants and bears them to a long distance, to let them fall there like an abundant living shower.

Certain lichens from the mountains of Asia, travelling thus amid the clouds, suck up watery vapours from them and grow during their accidental peregrination. Torn away from the soil when they are scarcely so large as the head of a pin, they have reached the size of a small nut by the time when, their aërial journey over, they fall far from their native rocks upon the ground below them. This happens with many edible species, which after a storm are soon scattered over the sand of the deserts.

These plants, which seem thus to fall from the sky, sometimes form thick layers on the soil and yield the exhausted traveller an agreeable

217. Edible Air-borne Lichen—*Lecanora esculenta.*

food. The providential manna, on which the Hebrews fed while wandering in the desert, doubtless arose from showers of edible lichens, for it is these plants which seem always to produce such showers.

Some years ago, Thénard, the chemist, presented to the Academy of Sciences one of these wandering plants, which had been carried away from the summit of Mount Ararat, and been borne by the wind to a great distance from the celebrated mountain. In the countries where it had been strewed upon the soil, people maintained that *it had come from heaven.* This rain of plants sometimes forms in those places a layer five or six inches thick. Men feed upon it, and what they cannot consume is given to the cattle.

Some seeds, too weighty to be carried by the winds, accomplish long voyages by sea, and, borne by the currents and waves, traverse oceans. The cocoa-nuts of the Seychelles, protected by their woody coverings, are carried away by regular currents, and arrive at the coast of Malabar, after performing a journey of more than 400 leagues by water. The Hindoos, astonished at this unexpected fecundity, which is renewed every year, can only explain it by supposing that the depths of ocean nourish the trees which produce those enormous fruits.

The hard fruit of the cocoa-palm, the immense husks of the climbing

Mimosa, which are often more than three feet in length, and many other fruits from Equatorial America, torn away by the waves and cradled by the storms, are frequently stranded on the shores of Scandinavia, where the want of heat and light is the sole obstacle to their development.

The regular currents of the sea also bear to a distance certain cosmopolitan plants, for the most part the offspring of seeds, the impermeable envelope of which for a long time resists the action of water. Thus, according to Karl Müller, the great current which springs from the eastern coast of South America has been known to bear a flotilla of thirteen species of plants from Brazil and Guiana to the shores of Congo in Africa. Another grand oceanic current, traversing an immense space of the torrid zone, constantly transports fruits from the shores of India, which its waves tumultuously scatter on the rocks of Brazil.

The most important migrations in the vegetable kingdom are due to the movements of fresh waters, rivers, and streams. Pascal says that rivers are moving roads, but the plants seem to have found this out before he did. Carried by the fugitive waves, seeds sometimes travel great distances to seek a new country. It is thus that the rivers which spring from the glaciers of the Upper Alps deposit in the plains of Munich some of the species which grow on their lofty peaks; others descend from the spurs of the Andes, to seek a humble shelter in the isles by the mouth of the Orinoco. Plants are known which fall from the lofty heights of the Himalayas, and pass safely through the turmoil of their foaming cascades, to expand their corollas on the enchanting borders of the delta of the Ganges.[1]

Dreading the agitation of torrents and waves, some nautical fruits trust to tranquil waters only; thus upon the waves of the Nile sail peacefully the floating cradles of the lotus. For this purpose its fruits form little circular boats, the interior of which contains the precious progeny. At maturity the waves carry off these reproductive germs *en masse* and transport them to a distance. Then when the rude shocks of the voyage have finally torn the little skiff, the seeds of the sacred plant, which have remained intact amid the waifs and strays, sink into the mud and water, and thus fertilize the burning banks of the king of rivers.

Even masses of ice, especially at some prehistoric epochs of the globe, have played a certain part in the dispersion of plants. Karl Müller

[1] An alpine moss (*Bryum alpinum*), certainly torn away in the Thuringian forest, is borne by the water to the porphyry rocks near Halle. Darwin thinks that the forests of peach and orange trees which cover the mouth of the Parana owe their origin merely to seeds carried by the river.

thinks that the wandering blocks, which the glaciers drive before them in their efforts, carry certain seeds from place to place. This grand phenomenon, which poured immense seas of ice over countries where now a mild temperature reigns, might certainly have precipitated some plants from the mountain tops into the depths of the valleys.

Thus at the present day we see growing in the north of Germany lichens, mosses, and some woody plants, in particular the Swedish cornel-tree, which have evidently descended from the mountains of Scandinavia, and have been borne away by the icebergs which, along with them, transported to the plains of ancient Germany the granite boulders with which they are strewn.

At other times the aid of another process is requisite to enable icebergs to transport plants from one hemisphere to another. Their floating islands becoming detached from the shore, carry away with them fragments of rock still covered with animals and plants. After having been long worn by the waves and currents, these islands at last light upon some propitious shore, and, sinking there, deposit their living population. Thus along with the polar bears which so frequently travel on the ice-blocks, some seeds torn from the boreal regions often reach happier climates.

Animals also contribute freely to the dissemination of vegetable products. Marmots, dormice, hamsters, heap up fruits in their underground abodes. Frequently a part of the booty accumulated by their active foresight is left forgotten in the ground, germinates there, and develops with the return of spring. At other times the weapon of the sportsman slaughters the owner of the store, and his hoard turns to the profit of vegetation. Squirrels break down the cones of the pine in order to devour the seeds, of which they are very fond. But during this occupation some of the seeds escape them, fall, and take root in the ground.

Some mammals assist the process of dissemination by a still more simple means; the seeds cling to their wool and are transported hither and thither by them during their peregrinations. The seeds of the burdock, which end in a hook, are very well adapted for this purpose. Those of the goose-grass (*Galium aparine*), roughened with fine points like so many fish-hooks, cling to the skin of any animal or the dress of any man who may happen to pass near them, a peculiarity which acquired for this plant the surname of *philanthropos* among the witty Greeks.

Although animals consume a large quantity of seeds for their food, nature by a happy compensation finds in this consumption an inexhaustible source of regeneration.

In this way great troops of reindeer which are scattered over the plains of Siberia, emigrating in masses on all sides, sow, as they pass along, a host of plants, the seeds of which, swallowed with their food, have resisted their digestive powers.

It is to the thrushes, which eat with avidity the fruit of the mistletoe, that we owe the propagation of this sacred plant, so celebrated in ancient Gaul, and which the Druids gathered with a golden sickle.

As Theophrastus remarked, these birds swallow the berries of the mistletoe. But as the pulp alone is absorbed, and as the seeds defy their digestive powers, these, like the worm of Hamlet, which only effects its migration by traversing the body of a beggar, fall with the excrement upon the branches, and there take root. Here the mistletoe soon forms those parasitical tufts which invade the crowns of the giants of our forests; beautiful globular tufts, decorated with perpetual verdure when winter has already stripped of leaves their powerful supporter.[1]

Other birds also propagate a great number of plants by similar means. Travellers relate that the Dutch having destroyed the nutmeg-trees in several of the Indian Islands, in order to confine the cultivation of these trees to Ceylon, the nutmeg-eating pigeons, which are very fond of this fruit, sowed the tree afresh in almost every spot where Dutch vandalism had extirpated it. The pulp of these fruits being all that is absorbed by the process of digestion, the seed is voided by these birds intact and still capable of germination.

The part played by birds in the general harmony of the globe does not end here. According to some botanists it is the birds that carry off the coral-red service-berries, and thus plant the tree on the crumbling porticoes of our castles and our old ruined churches. The grape of America (*Phytolacca decandra*), recently introduced near Bordeaux, has been disseminated by the winged songsters of our forests all through southern France, and even as far as the desert gorges of the Pyrénées. It is to the magpie of Ceylon that the propagation of the cinnamon-trees in that island is often intrusted, and this fact is so generally known that the inhabitants afford it ample protection.

Certain islands, which everything proves were formed after the great continents near them, owe the principal elements of their colonization solely to birds and to the marine currents. This is particularly the case with Iceland, which has been observed to be furnished with plants

[1] Once adherent to the branch the seed of the mistletoe germinates there, plunges its root into the bark, and lives at the expense of the tree. The stalks of this plant possess the peculiarity of extending with equal facility in every direction. The fruit is white, and of the size of a currant.

brought to it from Greenland and Northern Europe, carried thither by the innumerable birds which annually migrate in these latitudes.

It is also to birds that the varied flora seen in the interior of the Coliseum at Rome is owing. In fact the entire vegetation which covers these celebrated ruins, from the fig-trees, the powerful roots of which split its arches, to the humble grass that blooms upon its fallen stones, has been introduced into the vast structure solely by means of animals.[1]

In like manner some mammals even of the most carnivorous kind eat sundry fruits of which their digestive organs, though possessed of great energy, only act on the pulp, and as they wander about they deposit the seeds intact along with their excrements. In this way a species of civet in Java and Manilla takes an active part in disseminating the coffee-tree. It greedily eats the fruit, and the pulp being like that of the cherry is easily acted upon by the intestines, which afterwards expel the seeds still in a fit state for germination.[2]

Man himself ought to be considered as one of the most active agents in the dissemination of plants. His vessels and caravans, traversing the ocean and the desert, transport unknown to him seeds and plants which invade new countries.

In this way, through the importation of American sheep into France, certain seeds attached to them have become localized in France. In one locality in the neighbourhood of Montpellier, where a large quantity of wool is received from Buenos-Ayres and Mexico, several species of plants derived from the flora of these two countries are now seen growing on every side. The botanists of the celebrated school of Montpellier—the Decandolles, the Delilles, and the Dunalds—were perfectly aware of the fact, and from time to time made their way to this spot in order to botanize amid the products of the tropics without fatigue and without peril.

At other times, in order to satisfy the requirements of commerce or his own pleasure, man extirpates certain species from their native country

[1] According to Sebastiani, an Italian author, the number of species of plants growing in the Coliseum of Rome which have been transported thither by the birds is not less than 261.

[2] In Java it is the civet called *Viverra Musanga* which effects the dissemination of the coffee by scattering it here and there with its excrement. Karl Müller, following the authority of Junghuhn, relates that this coffee which has passed through the digestive organs of this mammal is even considered by the Javanese as of superior quality, and that they do not disdain to collect it for their use from the excrement of the animal. The American grape (*Phytolacca decandra*, L.) was introduced into the neighbourhood of Bordeaux in order that it might be used for colouring wine, and it is from thence the birds have spread it so widely. The so-called sparrow which in Ceylon sows the camellias in every direction is the *Turdus Zeilanicus*, a kind of thrush.—K. Müller, b. i. s. 91, 92.

in order to enrich distant lands with them. In short, it is sometimes to the armies of conquerors that we owe certain exotic plants.

Yet there are countries which are sometimes invaded by a vegetation neither the arrival nor the vigour of which can be explained. It grows in its new country with such energy, that it stifles everything that previously grew in the spots where it fixes itself. Thus a large everlasting, the *Helichrysum fetidum*, transplanted from America to France, has become a despotic ruler in many of the southern districts of that country.

In opposition to this, the common artichoke has exiled itself from France in order to establish itself victoriously in certain districts of Patagonia, and dispossess the rightful owners. In bringing our most useful cereal from Asia we have brought with it the cockle, the wild poppy, and the corn-flower, which enamel our harvests with such lively colours.

Our wants have caused us to import the greatest part of our alimentary plants from Asia. Wheat evidently comes from Persia; Michaux and Olivier observed it there in the wild state. The vine, the olive, and the walnut tree were brought to us from the mountains of Asia. The citron-tree comes originally from Media, and the orange-tree from China.[1]

It is owing to this variety in the means of transport that vegetation has established itself with such great rapidity on all parts of the globe which have been laid bare. Its most elementary representative forms first appear on the naked rock; the air seems almost to suffice for their nourishment: these are the lichens and the microscopic fungi. Then appear mosses, which, leaving mould behind them as they decompose, form for the future a soil thick enough to nourish the grasses. Lastly

[1] The wild radish (*Raphanus raphanistrum*, Linn.), often called the white charlock or twisted charlock, which is originally from Asia, was clandestinely introduced into our fields when the cereals were brought hither. Spinach comes from Media. The lentil (*Ervum lens*, Linn.) and the common haricot (*Phaseolus vulgaris*) are probably derived from Arabia; melons and cucumbers from the banks of the Euphrates and Tigris; the lilac (*Syringa vulgaris*) first came from Asia to Vienna, and then spread through Europe. The lily (*Lilium candidum*) is from the mountains of Syria. The weeping willow (*Salix Babylonica*, Linn.) was transplanted from the plains of Babylon, and spread through Europe by means of the poet Pope, who received a specimen from Smyrna. Tradition relates that the father of all our orange-trees in Europe is still to be seen in the convent of St. Sabina, on the Aventine Hill in Rome, and it is maintained that it was planted by St. Dominic, A.D. 1200. The Hortensia, dedicated by Comerson to Hortensia Lepaute, who distinguished herself in astronomy, comes originally from Japan, whence it only arrived in 1788. It is from this island also that the camellia comes, having been brought from thence by R. P. Caméli. Mexico also furnishes an abundance of cacti. The dahlia was imported from Mexico, and thus named in honour of a Swedish botanist, Andrew Dahl.

come shrubs and bushes, and then a verdant forest is soon seen rising in a district formerly stricken with sterility.[1]

The vital resistance of seeds, which varies between the widest extremes, comes also to the aid of dissemination. In fact, while there are some grains the organic development of which seems as if it could not be checked, and which are so impelled towards life that they germinate even on the plant which produces them, as we have seen is the case with the Rhizophoræ; there are others which on the contrary yield embryos in the bosom of which life may slumber through a succession of ages.

The seed of the coffee-tree, notwithstanding the thick coriaceous covering of its embryo, in a very short time loses the power of germinating. Should the planter defer sowing only for a few days, the seed will be incapable of reproduction.

But on the other hand some seeds, apparently less hardy, preserve their germinating power for a long time. Haricot beans have been obtained from seeds taken out of the herbarium of Tournefort, which could not have been less than one hundred years old.

More delicate seeds resist destructive causes even much longer than this. A few years ago a successful attempt was made to grow seeds from the heliotrope, lucerne, and clover, which had been found in a Gallo-Roman tomb more than fifteen hundred years old.

An analogous fact, which it seems impossible to doubt on account of the high reputation of the botanist who relates it, is that which is mentioned by Lindley. This savant assures us that seeds of the raspberry which had been taken from a Celtic burying-ground dating about seventeen hundred years back, having been sown in the garden of the Horticultural Society of London, produced bushes of their species which are still to be seen.

But life seems to make a still longer stay in the embryo of some other plants. Many learned men maintain that grains of wheat of such anti-

[1] In my youth I travelled through the celebrated valley of Goldau in Switzerland, where, twenty years previously, a whole mountain had given way in the most frightful manner, crushing several villages, and covering an immense space with fragments of broken rocks. All these rocks, lately quite bare, were already covered with a luxuriant vegetation, and the tortuous and uneven road which had been cleared through this vast sheet of ruin was everywhere smiling and fresh, and covered with pines and shrubs of the most charming aspect. M. Boussingault mentions a similar instance which he observed in America. In ten years a mass of porphyry rocks, which had fallen down, was covered with massive acacias. —Boussingault, *Economie Rurale*. [Lees, on weighing together and separately a tuft of *Bryum capillare* and the soil attached to it, found that it had collected and retained on the tiled roof where it grew five times its own weight of humus. —Tr.]

quity as to go back to the epoch of the Pharaohs, have germinated and yielded a harvest after having been intrusted to the earth! They had been found in Egyptian burying-places by the side of mummies, and thus in all probability had been reaped on the borders of the Nile three or four thousand years ago.[1]

According to some English botanists the bulb of the maritime squill presents a longevity not less extraordinary.

Being the object of a special worship in ancient Egypt, where temples were even reared to it, this sacred plant was sometimes swathed in small bandages and solemnly deposited in the sarcophagus. The daring genius of naturalists sought to pry into these vegetable mummies, in order to see if they did not yet retain some spark of life after so many ages of sleep. And we are told that these corpses of roots, withdrawn from their double prison and placed in a favouring soil, quickly vegetated again, becoming decked with flowers and fruits.

[1] This assertion is based on the experiments of Sternberg, who says he saw grains of wheat obtained from Egyptian tombs give birth to new wheat. Schacht, professor at the university of Bonn, seems to admit this fact as proven. It is, however, necessary to state that Messrs. Vilmorin and Payen think this assertion doubtful. The celebrated chemist even maintains that the germinative faculty of wheat does not last more than sixty years.

An English experimentalist sent me twenty years ago stalks of wheat which he assured me had grown from grains collected in an Egyptian sarcophagus. These blades were twice as high as those of our cereal, and the ears were of a peculiar character. But as M. Louis Figuier judiciously observes in his work on botany, we ought to be on our guard about such prodigies; the malignity of the vulgar has in such matters only too often deceived the good faith of some observers.—*Histoire des Plantes.* Pari 1865, p. 198.

GEOLOGY.

"While Caesar's chambers and the Augustan halls
Grovel on earth in indistinct decay."

Manfred, act iii

Nous retrouvons encore des vestiges des fleurs antédiluviennes qui animèrent les premiers gazons du globe!

We still find vestiges of the antediluvian flowers which gave life to the first meadows on earth.

BOOK I.

FORMATION OF THE GLOBE.

CHAPTER I.

APPEARANCE OF ANIMALS AND PLANTS.

When learned men began to occupy themselves with the theory of the earth, they became divided into two very clearly defined opposite parties:

The Plutonists, who attributed the formation of the crust of the globe exclusively to fire; and

The Neptunists, who, on the contrary, derived everything from the action of water.

The truth is that fire and water have had their share by turns. One part of the terrestrial crust is the result of heat, the other that of the deposit from water.

It is evident that the globe was originally a purely incandescent mass. Descartes had divined this great fact, and had stated that the earth was only a sun crusted over and partially extinguished, the chilled skin of which hid the central furnace from view.

Leibnitz developed this hypothesis in his *Protogæa*. It was afterwards successively confirmed, partly by the observations of Buffon and Cuvier, partly by the calculations of Cordier, La Place, and Fourier.

The globe on fire, and launched into space, necessarily obeyed the laws of the radiation of heat, and when after a long succession of ages it had sufficiently cooled down its surface became solidified, and constituted the primitive crust.

When this cooling down had made sufficient progress, the vapours from the earth, an immense atmosphere of which enveloped the globe, became condensed and poured over the surface in torrents of rain. Gleams of lightning and incessant peals of thunder accompanied these imposing scenes of the birth of our globe, of which our imagination will never yield us more than an imperfect image. Such was the origin of the first seas.

At the same time that in the course of ages the crust of the earth augmented in thickness, the cooling down, by contracting the globe, forced its envelope to yield and break. These efforts produced the mountains which now roughen its surface.

Whilst the crust of the earth was yet thin, a slight effort of the central heat sufficed to rupture it, but this only produced insignificant elevations. When this crust had acquired sufficient firmness and thickness, its rupture, inasmuch as it demanded much greater force, was only effected by means of the most violent plutonic movements; it was then that the Cordilleras rose into the clouds.

The upheaval of each mountain chain was necessarily accompanied by enormous perturbations in the level of the sea; from thence came these grand scenes of deluges mentioned in the cosmogonies of all nations. These upheavals, of which at least fifteen or sixteen have been made out, terminated by the rising of the chain of the Andes, the result of an immense rent extending almost from one pole to the other. This, by lifting up the two Americas above the ocean, raised the prodigious mass of water which submerged the ancient continent, and produced the Mosaic deluge. Thus fire and water successively remodelled the surface of the globe.

It is to be remarked that the crust of the earth in breaking follows a fixed determinate direction. Von Buch, Humboldt, and M. Elie de Beaumont have, in speaking of this subject, called our attention to the fact, that all the great mountain chains have been developed from the north to the south as the Andes and Ural, or from west to east as in the Atlas chain.

It is evident that each telluric phase had its peculiar organic forms, and that the species of animals of one geological epoch neither lived before nor after this epoch. Humboldt himself, the most illustrious philosopher of modern times, embraces this opinion without any qualification. "Each upheaval," he says, "of these mountain chains of which we can determine the relative antiquity, has been signalized by the destruction of ancient species and the appearance of new organisms."

It is impossible to be more explicit. The Rev. Dr. Buckland professes the same opinion, and says that numerous groups of animals and plants have already had their beginning and their end, and that creative intervention must have manifested itself at the appearance of each of them.

Telluric phenomena have not been abandoned to the fluctuations of chance. Governed by harmonious laws, each of them links itself with the past and loses itself in the future. And thus every generation that appears is only the corollary of that which is expiring, and the prelude of that which is about to spring into life. The stages of creation, except some rare oscillations, follow a rising scale. Nature seems to proceed by a succession of essays before fashioning her more splendid *chefs-d'œuvre;* sundry minute crustaceans, a few molluscs precede the reptiles, and these prelude the creation of birds and mammals!

The earth is only an immense cemetery where each generation acquires life at the expense of the débris of that which has just expired; the particles of our corpses form new materials for the beings which will follow us. But we have now reached an epoch of transition; the exhausted creative powers are experiencing almost a period of arrest; they are waiting till new telluric perturbations awaken them from their torpor!

The first compact crust which enveloped the globe was only formed by the cooling down and solidification of its superficial, once incandescent layers. Hence the beds which compose it are called primitive or plutonic, in order to indicate their antiquity or igneous origin.

The strata which overlie the primitive rocks owe, on the contrary, their formation to deposit from the waters; and for this reason are called alluvial or neptunian strata. These are divided into four leading groups: the transition rocks, secondary rocks, tertiary rocks, and diluvium.

CHAPTER II.

PRIMARY EPOCH.

When the globe had sufficiently cooled down, the frightful ocean of fire which enveloped its entire surface stilled its burning waves, leaving to float hither and thither a few black and smoking islets—the first traces of the terrestrial crust. These soon increased in thickness, and at last invaded all the space that had formerly been in combustion. Thus were formed the primary rocks; they are all of igneous origin, and all bear marks of fire.

These first steps towards the solidification of the globe produced the granites, which seem to be only the result of the incandescent mass on the surface of the globe being chilled; hence these rocks are found everywhere. They form the skeleton, the supporting arch, so to speak, of the other layers which in the lapse of ages have accumulated upon them.

But in the beginning these chilled waves only produced thin beds, which were often broken up again by the fiery ocean below; in consequence of this the granites exhibit great differences, indeed, as M. Elie de Beaumont happily remarks, "Perhaps not a single page of these first archives of our globe remains intact." The gneiss, for instance, seems to be only granite which has been fused again in the central fire.

The rocks of the primary epoch being all the product of a mass in a state of ignition, it is needless to say that we do not find among them any trace of organized beings, but by way of compensation they contain the principal riches which Nature elaborates in the splendid laboratories of her alchemy.

Metalliferous layers often lie in veins, huge cracks in the globe filled with divers materials. Philosophers guided only by the power of intuition—Descartes and Leibnitz—had taken up perfectly correct ideas as to the theory of their formation. They considered that the ores and other substances met with in the rocks had filled up the clefts by solidifying there, having escaped in a state of vapour from the burning beds below. Werner demonstrated this in a very plausible way, and modern geologists have accepted his views, at the same time modifying them a little.

In his beautiful work *La Vie Souterraine*, M. Simonin maintains that these metallic emanations may reach the fissures in two ways. "They are deposited in the fissures which constitute the veins either in the state of vapour by a *dry method*, as in the craters of volcanoes or the chimneys of smelting furnaces; or in a state of chemical precipitation by a *wet method*, as in the solutions of our laboratories."

This hypothesis, as the author tells us, meets all objections, explaining at the same time the deposit and the formation of the matrix which envelopes it.

Granite and porphyry must be classed among the richest metalliferous rocks, but beds of ore are also met with in the old transition rocks. It is in these that gold and silver are found. The *placers* of California are often formed merely by the detritus of granite rocks and schists filled with particles of gold, deposited on the beds of ancient rivers which had borne them away.

The rich family of precious stones, the diamond, ruby, sapphire, and emerald, seem to owe their formation to the same cause as the masses of metal. Volatilized in clefts of the igneous rocks, these stones there turned into brilliant crystallizations—tears of nature, as M. Simonin calls them.

CHAPTER III.

TRANSITION PERIOD.

It was at the transition period that the dawn of life began to show itself. No animal could have lived upon the burning surface of the globe during the plutonic period. But so soon as it was sufficiently cooled down to admit of living creatures appearing on it, we see them at once enter upon the scene. This is characteristic of this epoch.

The earth, imperfectly cooled down, still maintained a very high temperature, and this temperature was the same from one pole to another; the sun only brought with it useless supplementary heat. There were neither seasons nor climates; the torrid zone and the polar regions were peopled with the same plants and animals; their fossilized remains are identical whether found beneath the ice of Spitzbergen or in the rocks of burning tropical countries.

SILURIAN PERIOD.—This name is derived from that of a part of England inhabited by the ancient *Silures*, and is given to the strata of this epoch because they have been chiefly studied there.

The globe at that time supported nothing but a very small number of sea-animals, belonging to classes of the lowest order of organization, as if nature, still feeble and undecided, were in their production making the first trial of her strength.

The seas, still warm, occupied at this time nearly all the surface of the globe, and only very small portions of land had emerged from the waters—islets lost in the midst of a boundless ocean. Crustaceans, a few scattered molluscs, polypoids, and a small number of fish, were the sole tenants of the deep.

But among the silurian animals, those which especially predominated were the trilobites, the name of which is derived from the arrangement of their articulated bodies formed to a certain extent by three long lobes ranged side by side to each other. No living representative of these crustaceans, which were the most ancient inhabitants of the globe, is now found in our seas; they are absolutely struck out of the catalogue of created beings.[1]

CARBONIFEROUS PERIOD.—Later on, the first layers that cooled down became covered with a luxuriant vegetation, the fossilized remains of which now constitute our coal-beds—antediluvian forests, which the genius of man extracts from the depths of the earth, to serve the wants of industry and his own dwellings.

During this period the whole surface of the globe was covered with strange and dense forests, where proudly reigned a host of plants, the representatives of which at the present day play but a very humble part. Here were palms and bamboos, there gigantic Lycopodia, which, now humble creeping herbaceous plants, at that time bore straight stems towering to a height of eighty to a hundred feet. Then came the Lepidodendra, the stem of which reminds one of a reptile's scaly cuirass. Lastly came trees of the family of our Coniferæ, their boughs laden with fruit.

These vast primeval forests, which the course of ages was to annihilate, sprang up on a heated and marshy soil, which surrounded the lofty trees with thick compact masses of herbaceous aquatic plants, intended to play a great part in the formation of coal.

[1] Although thousands, perhaps millions, of years separate us from the period at which the trilobites existed, yet, by a fortunate accident, geologists have sometimes met with specimens so perfect that the delicate structure of the eyes could be made out in them; and it has been shown that these organs were constructed upon exactly the same plan as those of the crustaceans which now inhabit our seas.

These revelations suffice to establish a parallel between the extreme points of creation; and hence Buckland, after an examination of this apparatus, daringly painted the condition of the globe at the time when these strange crustaceans lent life to it. "The results," he says, "arising from these facts are not confined to animal physiology; they give information also regarding the condition of the ancient sea and ancient atmosphere, and the relations of both these media to light, at that remote period when the earliest marine animals were furnished with instruments of vision, in which the minute optical adaptations were the same that impart the perception of light to crustaceans now living at the bottom of the sea.

"With respect to the waters wherein the trilobites maintained their existence throughout the entire period of the transition formation we conclude that they could not have been that imaginary turbid and compound chaotic fluid from the precipitate of which some geologists have supposed the materials of the surface of the earth to be derived, because the structure of the eyes of these animals is such that any kind of fluid in which they could have been efficient at the bottom must have been pure and transparent enough to allow the passage of light to organs of vision, the nature of which is so fully disclosed by the state of perfection in which they are preserved.

"Regarding light itself also we learn from the resemblance of these most ancient organizations to existing eyes that the mutual relations of light to the eye and of the eye to light were the same at the time when crustaceans endowed with the faculty of vision were first placed at the bottom of the primeval seas as at the present moment."

218. Imaginary View of a Forest of the Coal Period.

The luxuriant vegetation of the coal period was certainly favoured by the enormous heat which the terrestrial crust still preserved, as also by the dampness of the atmosphere, and very probably by the great abundance of carbonic acid which it then contained.[1]

Although a thick and magnificent mantle of foliage covered the globe, everything wore a strange, gloomy aspect. Everywhere rose gigantic horse-tails (*Equiseta*) and ferns, drawing up an exuberance of life from the fertile and virgin soil. The latter in their aspect resembled palms, and at the least breath of wind waved their crowns of finely-cut leaves like flexible plumes of feathers. A sky, ever sombre and veiled, oppressed with heavy clouds the domes of these forests; a wan and dubious light scarcely made visible the dark and naked trunks; on all sides reigned a shadowy and indescribable hue of horror. This rich covering of vegetation, which extended from pole to pole, was sad and silent, as well as strangely monotonous.. Not a single flower enlivened the foliage, not one edible fruit loaded its branches. The echoes remained absolutely mute, and the branches without a sign of life, for no air-breathing animal had as yet appeared amid these savage scenes of the ancient world!

One might say, in fact, that there was then no animal life to be seen, for amid so many remains of the coal flora, which geologists have so admirably reconstructed, they have only met with a few rare vestiges of one small reptile, the Archegosaurus. This great contrast between the richness of the vegetable and penury of the animal kingdom is explained by the great quantity of carbonic acid at that time mixed with the atmosphere, which, though particularly favourable to the life of plants, must have been fatal to all animals endowed with active respiration. But though the atmosphere was poisonous, the seas, on the contrary, uniting together all conditions most favourable to life, were peopled with shelled molluscs and fish.

After having lent life to the primitive ages of the globe, these strange forests completely disappeared in the lapse of ages, and they have now become almost impossible to recognize, owing to the transformations they have undergone in nature's immense subterranean store-houses.

[1] At the present time the atmosphere only contains a thousandth part of carbonic acid, whereas, according to Mons. A. Brongniart, there were at the carboniferous period seven to eight parts in a hundred. This acid being an indispensable part of the food of plants, to which it gives up all its carbon, its presence easily explains the great development of the antediluvian forests of this period, and as such a quantity of acid in the air would clearly have been fatal to animals of a higher degree of development, such as mammals and birds, so none are met with at that time. Reptiles and mammals only appeared when the plants and trees, by their absorption of the carbonic acid as food, had necessarily purified the atmosphere sufficiently to allow of animal life going on freely.

There can, however, be no doubt about the matter. It is clearly the débris of these antique forests of our gradually cooled-down planet that constitutes the coal of the present time. Science, carrying its torch even into the dark regions from whence this débris proceeded, has discovered all its constituent parts. Amid the black and gleaming masses of the coal strata abundant impressions have been found of the plants which produced the antediluvian combustible, and from these primitive medals of creation we have seen science weave the history of the dawn of terrestrial vegetation.

But by what mysterious phenomena was this extraordinary transformation effected? At first it was thought that the forests of the coal era had been overthrown or borne away by the violence of currents, and that their trunks, locked together after having floated about like immense rafts, had collected in creeks, and there become changed into layers of coal.

But this theory, though seductive from its simplicity, is inadmissible, because the trunks, in spite of their bulk, would yield only a very thin layer of coal. M. Elie de Beaumont, on the other hand, thinks that it was the compact, herbaceous vegetation enveloping the great plants of the coal-forests which played the principal part in the production of coal, and that by its ceaseless renewal and change the coal was produced by a transformation analogous to that which our aquatic plants undergo when transformed into turf. This theory offers a better explanation of the abundance and thickness of the coal-seams. We do not exactly make out the nature of the chemical phenomena which must have taken place during such a fundamental metamorphosis; but what is clear is, that this was principally effected under the influence of the immense pressure and great heat which the plants experienced during the time they were submerged under water, owing to the subsidence of the soil on which they had lived and died.

CHAPTER IV.

SECONDARY EPOCH.

In this epoch everything strongly contrasted with that which preceded it. In the latter the vegetable kingdom predominated during its whole course to an extraordinary extent; in this the animal kingdom seems to have absorbed all the vital forces of the globe.

219. Imaginary Landscape during the Secondary Epoch, with Pterodactyls. Lias Period.

The secondary strata were peopled by a fauna altogether new, and more and more exuberant. The reptiles astonish us by their number, their gigantic size, and their unwonted forms; antique and incomprehensible inhabitants of the globe, reproduced in all their parts to our wondering eyes by the genius of a Cuvier and an Owen! It is to this epoch that the name of the Reptilian Age may be most appropriately given, so completely did these creatures then predominate on the globe; it was the age of the Ichthyosauri, the Plesiosauri, and the Mosasauri—a throng of frightful lizards, compared to which our own are mere pigmies, and which spread terror through the antediluvian seas.

At this period we see innumerable molluscs, the shells of which have been carefully preserved by the rocks. Some belong to genera which are no longer met with in our present seas; all to species which are absolutely unknown at the present day.

Already at the time we speak of, the previous extreme heat of the earth had declined. The sky had grown clearer and the atmosphere become less heavy; still there was a decidedly high temperature, which, combined with great humidity, favoured the luxuriant vegetation which developed itself vigorously under the influence of the luminous brightness of the sun.

The more ancient of the secondary rocks have interested geologists on account of the innumerable remains of shells which they contain, and owing to which they have been named conchylian.[1]

At the time when these strata were being deposited lived one of the most extraordinary reptiles that we know of. It was a kind of monster toad, so enormous as to equal an ox in size, and the teeth of which, resembling the windings of a maze, have procured it the name of Labyrinthodon. The strata of this ancient epoch have contributed to teach us some even of the anatomical details of this animal, having preserved the impressions of its footsteps. On the same beds have been observed the prints of three-toed feet, considered by some geologists as traces of the first birds that animated our globe.

To this period belong the Jurassic strata, which play so important a part in the formation of the Jura Mountains, from whence they derive their name. This formation is rich in animal fossils, which give it quite a special character. It may be divided into two sections—the *Lias* and the *Oolite*.

The liassic seas fed numbers of animals, and their deposits are distinctly characterized by the gryphæas, ammonites, belemnites, plagio-

[1] This era most probably means here the coarse, shelly limestone of the forest marble, and the great oolite; possibly also including the muschelkalk of German geologists.—Tr.

stomata, and encrinites, which are peculiar to it. But what impresses a special stamp upon it is the presence of strange marine reptiles, the remains of which are found in it remarkably well preserved.

At this time lived the Ichthyosauri, veritable fish-lizards, as is indicated by their name. These reptiles, which must have spread terror through the ancient seas, attained a length of about thirty-three feet. Their whole organization is a series of paradoxes. With the vertebræ of the fish they have the fins of a dolphin; and while armed with the teeth of a crocodile they display an optic globe which is without any parallel. This eye, the bulk of which was sometimes as large as a man's head, was protected in front by a framework of bony plates, and was beyond all doubt the most powerful and perfect visual apparatus ever seen in creation. Hence Buckland maintains that the Ichthyosauri could discover their prey at the greatest as well as the shortest distances; in the profound darkness of night, and in the depths of the ocean; the delicate

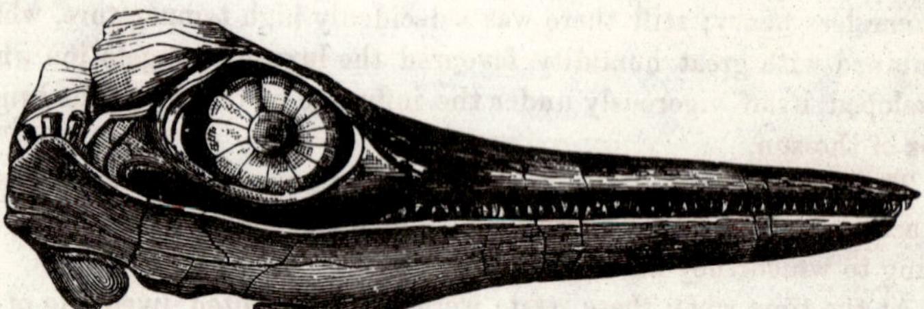

220. Head of Ichthyosaurus—*Ichthyosaurus communis.*

structure of the organ of vision being protected from the pressure of the water and the shock of the waves by the osseous buckler which surrounds the transparent cornea.

Naturalists have investigated the remains of these animals with such skill, that in spite of the destruction of the softer organs thousands of years ago, they have been enabled to make out the structure of the intestinal tube! It has been shown that this was formed exactly like an Archimedian screw, and was strictly analogous to that of our sharks and rays. At the same time the nature of the food of these voracious reptiles has been discovered. These two facts were revealed by an examination of the fæces or coprolites of Ichthyosauri, which are found in large quantities in some localities. Their form, moulded on that of the intestine, showed the structure quite clearly, while the petrified remains of food which were discovered proved that these animals devoured an enormous quantity of fish, and even occasionally their own species,

221. Gnomes of the German Legends laying bare the Skeleton of an Ichthyosaurus.

for small Ichthyosauri have been met with in the bellies of the large ones.

With these terrible dominators of the Jurassic seas lived the Plesiosauri, reptiles equally strange, and which Cuvier considered as the most abnormal races of the ancient world. They were remarkable for their turtle-like fins, and especially for the thinness and extreme length of their serpent-like necks. The arrangement of the skeleton in the Plesiosaurus led Mr. Conybeare to think that it swam ordinarily on the surface of the waves, curving back its long flexible neck like a swan, and darting forward with it from time to time in order to seize the fish which approached it. Their paws, analogous to those of the sea-turtles, induced this learned Englishman to think also that the Plesiosauri, like these reptiles, sometimes issued from the sea and sought refuge amid the plants, in order to evade their dangerous enemies, which were beyond all doubt the Ichthyosauri.

If any of the animals which the remote periods of the globe present to our notice are to be looked upon as monsters, we submit that in this respect the first place is due to the Pterodactyli, which remind one of the ancient dragons of legendary tradition. Their structure is so paradoxical that one does not really know where to place them; they were alternately looked upon as birds, mammals, and reptiles. De Blainville, embarrassed, as, indeed, all the learned world were, formed a separate class for them in the animal kingdom.[1]

The aspect of the pterodactyl was necessarily very strange. When naturalists tried to restore their frames, the figures they produced were more like the offspring of some diseased imagination than realities. They were really reptiles furnished with large wings, and resembled enormous bats, having a very pointed head supported on a slender neck. The smaller species certainly lived on insects, for the remains of these have been found among fossilized skeletons.[2]

Certain naturalists, among them Bory de Saint-Vincent, have been almost inclined to think that these fantastic animals may have suggested the first idea of those images of dragons so frequently represented on the monuments produced in the infancy of art, or whose existence is affirmed by inspired writers. This savant supposes that some pterodactyls,

[1] There were air-cavities in the bones of the pterodactyls, and the coracoid process, the scapula, and the broad sternum with its median crest, allied them in anatomical points to birds.—*Popular Science Review*, vol. vii. p. 242.—Tr.

[2] To these amphibious reptiles must now be added several others. Three new genera have been recently discovered in the Castlecomar coal-measures in Kilkenny. Remains of another new genus, the Pliosaurus, presented to the British Museum, show that the skull of this creature was nearly five feet long.—Tr.

having survived the era of general extinction, may have been contemporary with the first men; that these, struck with their strange appearance, possibly preserved a few likenesses of them among their imperfect hieroglyphic designs, and that mythological tradition afterwards more or less distorted the type.

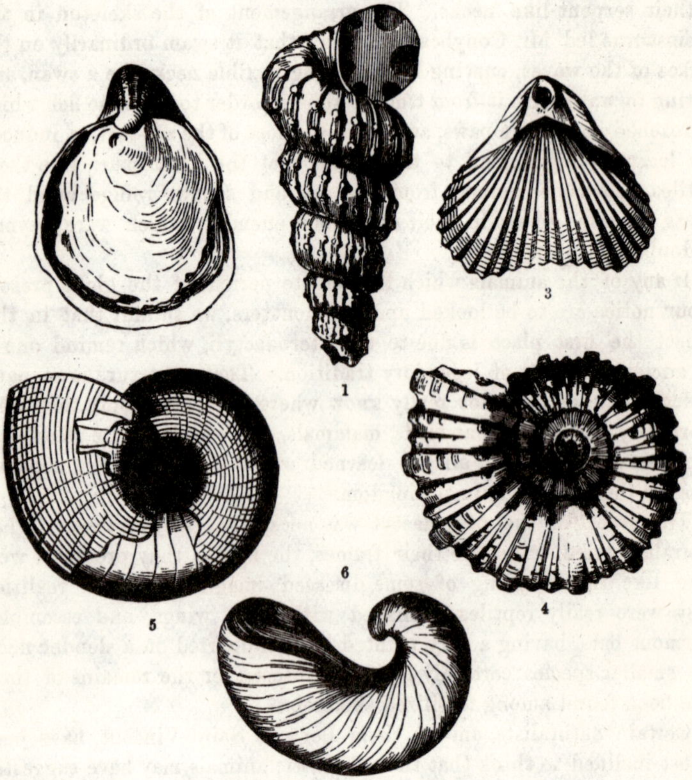

222. Fossil Shells of the Secondary Period.

1, *Turrilites catenata, Protogœa.* 2. Oyster—*Ostrœa columba* (Lamarck).
3, Terebratula. 4, Mammillary Ammonite.
5, Striated Nautilus—*Nautilus striatus.* 6, Curved Gryphæa—*Gryphœa incurva.*

The second section of the Jurassic period often displays in its strata small yellowish sub-globular concretions, resembling in their appearance fish-eggs, which has procured for it the name of Oolite.

The great feature of this period is the first appearance of mammals. The only vestiges found of them are two little jaws, belonging to species very like the opossum, so well known from the habit of the female of carrying her young family in an abdominal sack, or bearing them on her back.[1]

The oolite abounds in molluscs, polypoids, and fossil plants. Insects and crustaceans are also found in it.

The last group of the secondary strata, the cretaceous or chalk formation, plays an important part in geology, partly owing to its depth, partly to the great extent over which it is found. It is scarcely necessary to say that it owes its name to the chalk (carbonate of lime), of which it almost entirely consists. The cretaceous strata form many of our mountain chains.

During this period both land and sea appear to have been still under the domination of reptiles of colossal size. The Mosasaurus, long called the "great Maestricht animal," an immense marine lizard, attained a length of more than sixty-five feet, whilst contemporary species are not more than a yard long. It must have spread terror on all sides.

With the cretaceous seas were extinguished all those races of strange reptiles, to whose voracity the exuberant brood of ocean fell an easy prey. But at the same time their mission was now intrusted to voracious sharks of enormous size, which for the first time appeared in the waters of the globe.

In the same seas those families of microscopic Foraminifera, the débris of which, as we have seen, constitute large mountains, swarmed alongside of the gigantic Nautili and Ammonites.

To use the happy expression of M. L. Figuier, "the state of the vegetation in the cretaceous period might be looked upon as the vestibule of the vegetation of our days." The dicotyledons augment in number, whilst the ferns and inferior plants lose their supremacy little by little, and are replaced by trees analogous to those that now afford us their shade.

But if the forests of this epoch already approached ours in the character of their vegetation, they differed very widely as to the nature of their inhabitants. Where now we only meet inoffensive lizards a few inches long playing on the sward, there were then creatures of

[1] The oolite which produced the famous lithographic slate of Solenhofen, yielded the first bird, the skeleton of which has been so far preserved that its nature could be clearly decided upon. This is the Archæopteryx, now in the British Museum. It exhibits a closer approximation to reptilian structure than any modern bird. The tail is very long, and in this respect more like that of a reptile than that of a bird. Two digits of the manus have curved claws, much stronger than those of any existing bird.—*Pop. Science Review*, vol. vii. p. 241.—Tr.

this class which dragged through these solitudes their vast frames forty-five to fifty feet in length. Such were the Megalosauri and the Iguanodons.[1]

CHAPTER V.

TERTIARY EPOCH.

We have just seen unrolled before our eyes a phase of creation in which all animal life was under the dominion of a legion of frightful reptiles: in the tertiary epoch these had disappeared into the abysses of the globe, and peaceful and luxuriant nature was animated for the first time with varied races of inoffensive mammals, which spread over the whole earth from pole to pole. Among the remains of these animals, dug out of the soil and reconstructed by the skill of the anatomist, some astonish us by their singular forms, others by their colossal size. The creation of the present time seems to have quite degenerated when compared to these giants of the animal kingdom! Hence, looking at its predominant feature, this epoch might be called the epoch of the mammals. They predominate throughout.

In the course of ages the crust of the earth, augmenting in thickness as it steadily cooled down, had become compact enough to intercept the central heat, and hence the solar influence, gaining the predominance, now began to mark out the separate climates.

The tertiary fauna displayed extreme richness, and among the animals it offers in profusion, the list of those belonging to contemporary genera is visibly increased. We find monkeys, bats, genets, marmots; and now for the first time cetaceans appeared in the seas.

But the most remarkable of all the animals of that day were the Palæotheria and Anoplotheria, curious pachyderms which belong solely to this epoch and vanish utterly with it.

The Palæotheria, with their heavy forms and small trunk, resembled our tapirs. According to Cuvier, they lived like them on the banks of rivers and lakes, as is shown by the remains of lacustrine and fluviatile

[1] Neither the Iguanodon nor the Megalosaurus has as yet been found in England of such proportions as these. Owen computed the length of the Iguanodon at thirty-five feet, but a thigh-bone was found just west of Sandown Fort which clearly belonged to a larger animal, one possibly forty-five feet in length.—Tr.

223. Imaginary Landscape during the Tertiary Period, with groups of Palæotheria and Anoplotheria.

animals scattered amid their calcareous winding-sheets. These mammals, remarkable for having three toes on each foot, were sometimes as big as a horse, as was the case with the great Palæotherium; others scarcely reached that of a hare.

The Anoplotheria were of more slender make, and had long powerful tails. According to Cuvier, the *Anoplotherium commune* had some analogy with the otter, but was of larger size. This naturalist thought that it dived with ease, in order to seek for the roots and succulent stems which composed its food.

The remains of the Palæotheria and Anoplotheria abound in the gypsum of the quarries near Paris, and there are some in which they lie so thick that every blow of the pickaxe exhumes some of their remains from these antediluvian charnel-houses. This fact evidently proves that these mammals lived in dense herds near the banks of the ancient fresh waters of the Paris basin.

It is in this tertiary epoch that we also discover the bulkiest terrestrial mammals, the Dinotheria, in shape analogous to the elephant, but much larger.

An animal which has been an object of interest to every one, the great Mastodon, belongs to the same period. It was at first called the elephant of Ohio, on account of its shape and the place where it was discovered; but afterwards, as its teeth were found to be provided with strong projecting elevations, a separate genus was formed for it.

Although of such vast size, the remains of this species are extremely common in Canada and Louisiana. Along the river of the Great Osages are found skeletons almost complete. Sometimes mastodons have been exhumed entire and standing upright, in places where they seem to have been caught alive; some appear to have been so suddenly overtaken by the alluvial floods that we still find in their stomachs the food which they had just swallowed. The nature of this food has been made out: it consisted of herbs and small branches of trees; and thus science has again shown on what one of the most ancient creatures of the globe used to feed!

Towards the same time we find the Glyptodons, huge armadilloes which were more than double the size of those living in our days; and then the Megatheria, a kind of monstrous sloths which were as large as elephants, while those of our epoch are scarcely the size of a dog.

Lastly came the frightful Sivatherium, found in India, and to which this name, derived from that of the God Siva, worshipped there, has been given in consequence. This animal, as Owen tells us, is certainly one of the most gigantic and extraordinary of the extinct races known to us. It was a stag as large as an elephant, its head being surmounted with four horns.

In the tertiary epoch we meet with few reptiles, but one of them enjoys a great celebrity. It was a gigantic salamander, which the dictum

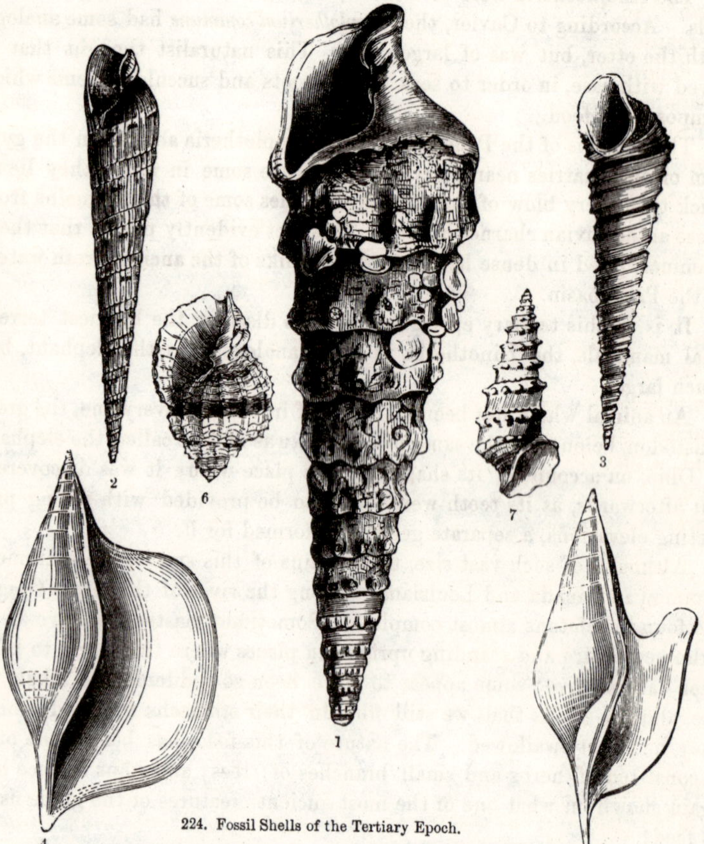

224. Fossil Shells of the Tertiary Epoch.

1, Gigantic Cerithium. 2, Bichambered Helix.
3, *Turritella imbricata* (Lam.) 4, *Rostellaria macroptera* (Lam.)
5, *Rostellaria columbata* (Lam.) 6, *Cancellaria cancellata* (Bonn.)
7, *Cerithium thiara* (Lam.)

of a theological naturalist caused to be long considered as an incontestable relic from the hecatomb of the biblical deluge.

During this phase of creation of which we have sketched the history, new races of molluscs arose on all sides, while the ancient ones perished to return no more. The ammonites, formerly so numerous, disappeared altogether, whilst tiny nummulites, the size of lentils, were forming imposing chains of mountains in different parts of the globe. The miliolites, infinitely smaller, multiplied at such a prodigious rate that they deposited vast strata, which, as we have seen, are now-a-days quarried to build our dwellings with.[1] It was also during this period of organic evolution that the seas of the Paris basin abounded in such rich deposits of shells, in those places where the great city was one day to parade its splendour. It is amongst these that we discover the gigantic Cerithium (*Cerithium giganteum*, Lam.), which attains a length of nearly twenty inches, and a host of other shells, in the most marvellous state of preservation, some of which are represented in the above engraving.

The vegetation of the tertiary epoch is remarkable for the approach it makes towards ours. M. A. Brongniart expresses himself as follows: "Looked at as seen in Europe," says this learned botanist, "this vegetation displays, in particular, a great analogy with the present flora of the temperate regions of the northern hemisphere."

We are in fact astonished to find in the ancient strata of this epoch unimpeachable remains of our present flora. Nymphææ allowed their beautiful flowers to float on the surface of the tranquil waters of the new world, whilst the Potamogetons or pond-weeds displayed their leaves in the depths. Lastly, we find here also Coniferæ, oaks, elms, and other different contemporary genera.

CHAPTER VI.

QUATERNARY OR POST-TERTIARY PERIOD.

The first phases of this epoch are connected with the tertiary period, and it is during one of those which follow that we finally see man appear —man whose supreme essence shows like a grand crowning of the work of creation.

The post-tertiary is then the epoch to which we belong, and nearly all the creatures which serve to enliven it are those we see at present contributing their share to beautify animated nature. But this period, which perhaps contains many myriads of years, was far from being so tranquil as many geologists would have it. Though we no longer see the immense seas which rolled their untamed waves from pole to pole,

[1] See page 24.

we find great deluges, the upheaval of mountain chains, and horrible invasions of ice, which waste or engulf everything living.

This last epoch abounds less in new animal forms than those which preceded it; but the creatures which were brought forth at this time are often remarkable for their vast size, their number, and the extent to which they were disseminated. In every part of the globe their vestiges, disinterred by patience and learning, prove the truth of these assertions.

We have seen invisible antediluvian Infusoria, heaped up into mountains by the waters of the globe, exist through a cycle of ages, and present themselves to our astonished gaze with all the details of their organization. In the diluvium, on the contrary, we find a population of colossi belonging to the ancient world. Elephants, mastodons, rhinoceroses, and hippopotami are spread over regions far from where they now live. France itself supported numerous cohorts of them, and they existed in the midst of the ices of Siberia.

In antediluvian times this latter country was even peopled with such herds of elephants and rhinoceroses, that travellers say the soil of some islands in the Icy Sea is at present literally stuffed with their bones.

Art, which from the remotest epoch has employed so much ivory for ornament and statuary, finds without any search a rich mine of this precious substance in the teeth of the fossil elephants which abound in these ancient charnel-houses. At present the north of Asia furnishes an enormous quantity for commercial purposes. The ivory mines of New Siberia and of the island of Lachoo are so rich in these débris that their soil is absolutely a mass of sand, ice, and elephant tusks. Every time there is a storm the waves throw up a great number of these, some of which weigh as much as 100 kilogrammes (233 lbs. avoirdupois).

The richness of these cemeteries in the arctic regions, and the colossal size of the remains which they inclose, surpass everything that can be imagined. The Siberians and Tartars are themselves struck with them. One of their myths assigns them to subterranean animals which abhorred the light. In relation to this subject it is curious to observe, that in several very ancient Chinese books mention is also made of these fossil elephants, for it must be these animals that are referred to. In the *Ly-Ki*, a treatise on ceremony written 500 years before the Christian era, it is said that there exists an animal called Tin-Schu, or the mouse, which hides itself, which lives in obscure caves, and is of the size of a buffalo; the least ray of sun or moonlight kills it instantly.

Klaproth relates that a similar fable is met with in Mantchoo manuscripts. It is said there that this colossal mouse attains the size of an elephant!

Amongst the most remarkable discoveries of recent times must be ranked that of one of these elephants of the extreme north, which was found by some fishermen in the ice near the mouth of the Lena in 1799. Its flesh, enveloped in a block of ice, had been preserved through many thousands and perhaps millions of years! The bears and dogs flocked thither to make an antediluvian repast off it. Almost the whole skeleton of this animal was saved, and it may now be seen in the museum of St. Petersburg.

The human mind, face to face with all these gigantic races, engulfed by the latest telluric convulsions, turns back to search amid their remains, striving to penetrate into the cause of these grand disasters.

At one of the epochs nearest to us, when the whole surface of the soil which we inhabit, lighted by a radiant sun, was covered only with splendid forests and magnificent prairies, in the midst of which wandered troops of elephants, mastodons, and rhinoceroses, all at once the whole of this exuberance of life disappeared in one common shipwreck. A horrible mantle of snow and ice covered all northern Europe, and extended its folds even to the plains of Germany. Overpowered by the cold, all those great races succumbed and were buried beneath this grim winding-sheet; a luminary dim and pale alone lighted up these lifeless solitudes, and the silence of death reigned everywhere.

What was the first cause of these unexpected phenomena of this period, justly called the glacial, which swept over the globe formerly so heated? It will perhaps long remain unknown, but its ravages have left everywhere indelible traces. The waves of this immense sea of ice, rolling down the mountains, tore off the projecting portions, bore them away in their movement, and scattered them everywhere on their passage. In this way numerous fragments from the loftiest peaks of Scandinavia were transported to the plains of Germany and Novogorod others, violently torn away from the summits of the Alps, were strewed over the slopes of Jura.

Up to the present time geologists had supposed that these fragments of rocks, these *erratic blocks*, as they are called, which are met with far from the mountains of which, as their structure shows, they once formed part, were transported by the violent action of the waters, and that they had been carried away by the waves of deluges. Agassiz, in his work on *Glaciers*, has shown that this hypothesis is inadmissible, and that to the great movements of the seas of ice must be attributed the transport of rocks which we often find far from the spot where they were formed.

It is to this severe cold which raged over a large part of Europe that we must refer the great hecatomb of those myriads of elephants, mastodons, and rhinoceroses, which formerly lent life to every part of France, Germany, and Italy, and of which their soil displays such numerous vestiges on every side.

The cause was clearly sudden, for if all these animals had not been frozen as soon as they were killed, different agents would have dispersed their remains, whilst on the contrary we often find entire skeletons on the spot where they had expired. As we have just said, elephants have even been discovered contained in the ice and still covered with skin and the long and extraordinary hair of which they possessed a thick covering!

In the post-tertiary epoch other events again greatly disturbed the globe; these were the mighty deluges which poured in tumultuous torrents over its surface, and deposited abundance of débris on it. Hence these strata are known by the name of *diluvium.*

But although an attentive study of the earth points out to us with great accuracy the succession of its epochs, all the power of modern science is inadequate to say what space of time these great phases endured; and how many years back we must place all these deluges, these cataclysms, and lastly the creation of man.

Notwithstanding the apparent youth of the new continent, some geologists assign a very remote period to the great shock which gave it birth by rending the globe almost from pole to pole. One of the most learned men whom England loves to honour, Sir Charles Lyell, resting his arguments upon authorities of great weight, maintains that the Mississippi has run in its present bed more than 100,000 years; and Dr. B. Dowler, who shares this view, asserts, from observations on vegetable physiology and the examination of some pottery and certain Indian burying-places, that the delta of this great river has been inhabited by man for more than 50,000 years!

On the other hand, G. Cuvier makes creation much more recent, and does not date the appearance of man further back than tradition. According to this illustrious zoologist, the history of the human race attests that man has not ruled over the surface of the globe for more than a very limited number of years.

The Hebrew nation is the only one which possesses annals written before the reign of Cyrus. Homer, the first of poets, and Hesiod his contemporary, lived about 2800 years ago. Herodotus, who was the first profane historian, wrote about 2300 years before our time.

From national pride the Indians and Egyptians boasted that their origin was lost in the darkness of ages; and in order to gain credit for their recitals, they often interwove fables invented by the Magi or Brahmins, whom many reasons led to falsify history!

Among the Indians, the Vedas, or sacred books, which they assert were revealed by Brahma in the very beginning of the world, scarcely go back farther than 3200 years. The works on astronomy of this nation, and the tables of the state of the heavens which were thought to be of such vast antiquity, have on the contrary been shown to be quite modern. It has been discovered that they were antedated. The Brahmins boldly announced that the most ancient of these astronomical tables had been compiled more than 20,000,000 years ago. For a brief space of time men were deceived by their assurance and the authority of Bailly. But Laplace proved that their calculations had been made after the events, and, moreover, that they were false. Bentley even asserted that they were composed only 700 years ago.

The Egyptians, though less pretentious, nevertheless carried back the origin of their nation to a period much more remote than is consistent with fact. When Herodotus visited their country, the priests told him that they possessed a history which dated back 11,340 years; and in order to give a semblance of veracity to their recitals, they added that during this space of time the sun had twice risen near the horizon where it sets.

The cyclopean monuments, the vastness of which astonishes us, seem to be the result of labours which belong to the infancy of society. The almost shapeless stones of which they are composed, and the enormous proportions of their architecture, which in no way approaches that of the Greeks, have led authors to ascribe the execution of these monuments to the first men who inhabited the earth, and some of the learned, exaggerating their antiquity, have regarded them as anterior to the deluge. But these vast constructions, more extraordinary for their mass than for the taste displayed in their construction, seem to have been reared by a seafaring people to resist the encroachments of the sea. Although there is some difference of opinion among the learned as to the epoch to which they belong, everything seems to prove that they were erected by the Phœnicians.

Astronomical monuments support the antiquity of the human race still less. The famous zodiac of Dendérah, to which Dupuis accords an antiquity of 15,000 years, is considered by the astronomer Delambre as later than the epoch of Alexander, and, according to Biot, represents a state of the heavens which appeared 700 years before Christ. Besides, the Egyptian temple in which this singular zodiac was discovered was built during the Roman rule, as is proved by an inspection of the hieroglyphics, and even by an inscription consecrating this sanctuary to the welfare of the emperor Tiberius.

Notwithstanding all these reasons, which, besides, are only derived from a civilized state, the opinion of G. Cuvier has been assailed by the recent conquests of science.

In past times some theological naturalists used every effort to find some vestiges of fossil men contemporaries of the deluge. One of them thought he had succeeded, and gave the pompous name of *homo diluvii testis* to the fragments of a skeleton discovered in Switzerland by Scheuchzer in the quarries of Œningen. But Cuvier scattered all this to the winds by showing that this precious "man, a witness of the deluge," valued at its weight in gold, and venerated as a holy relic, was nothing more than the skeleton of a gigantic salamander. Doubt was no longer possible. The head of the reptile had been taken for the hip-bone; the teeth could be seen, and the French naturalist had only to scrape the stone a little in order to lay bare the claws.

At present this biblical ardour seems replaced by quite an opposite tendency of argument. Scientific facts, the value of which cannot be contested, clearly establish the antiquity of the human race, notwithstanding which, for some inexplicable reason, certain geologists make every effort to nullify this great discovery.

From time to time vestiges of our species had been found among the débris of animals which had become extinct in the latest revolutions of our globe.

On the other hand, a learned archæologist, M. Boucher de Perthes, supported by the most laudable perseverance, succeeded in collecting a tolerably large number of flint instruments, which had clearly belonged to pre-historic races of men destroyed in the great diluvian catastrophe.

There was no longer any doubt in the mind of the illustrious Lyell. These implements shaped out of flint—axes, arrow-heads, and knives—which are found in the drift, were the work of a race which preceded ours—a race which was contemporary with the cave bears and hyenas, and even with the rhinoceroses and elephants, which formerly inhabited our soil, and of which we find only the fossilized remains.[1]

[1] M. Boucher de Perthes has just made a discovery as fortunate as it was unexpected, which confirms his former views. He has at last found in the drift gravel, in the neighbourhood of Abbeville, human remains mixed with flint implements. These precious remains consisted of a human tooth and jaw, and were found at a depth of nearly 15 feet. The concurrence of opinion among the English and French naturalists who examined these relics leaves no room for doubt: they belong to a race of men anterior to the deluge.

[It seems difficult to understand how any unprejudiced person who has really examined the evidence can refuse to believe that man lived on this globe many thousands of years before history began. It is as certain as anything can be that flint implements wrought by human hands have been found, not in one or two, but in many places, *especially undisturbed caves*, beneath or embedded in stalagmite containing remains of the great cave-bear, the cave-hyena, the mammoth, cave-lion, and rhinoceros, and that man's era certainly goes

The discoveries, then, of geologists and archæologists reveal to us that vestiges of antediluvian races exist in the ground. Lyell, Lartet, and M. Boucher de Perthes are unanimous on this point.

Is it not then strange to hear, that at the very time when modern science was making every effort to deny that man and the great races of mammals were contemporary, the affirmative was in some measure already interwoven in the rhapsodical traditions of the North American sr .ages? Jefferson says the Virginians are convinced that the mastodons, the bones of which are so often found in their country, lived there at the same time as their forefathers, but that as they (the mastodons) destroyed all the animals which were useful to men, the Great Spirit destroyed them all with his thunderbolts, except the strongest of their males, the mail-clad brow of which shook off the bolts as they struck him.

The lake dwellings, of which so many remains have been recently discovered in the lakes of Switzerland, Scotland, and Denmark, also attest the antiquity of man on the globe. It is no longer possible now-a-days to deny that these singular constructions, raised on piles, served in pre-historic times to shelter the first human races. We can no longer doubt respecting this point, now that among these primitive vestiges of art have been found different implements which their inhabitants made use of—mill-stones, stone knives and weapons, besides collars and bracelets in bronze or Baltic amber, and even human skeletons.[1]

back to at any rate the decline of the great glacial period, even if he did not exist before it. They have been met with also in river-drifts interbedded with the bones of the mammoth and rhinoceros, and in fresh-water formations, together with the bones of the elephant.—*The Stream of Life on our Globe*, chap. ii.—TR.]

[1] Our learned naturalist Victor Meunier gives the following curious details about the lacustrine dwellings:—

"In New Guinea the Papuans also build on piles, but these are sunk in the sea at a certain distance from the shore, and parallel with it. They support, at a height of eight or ten feet above the water, a flooring formed of round pieces of wood, which in its turn supports circular or square cabins, formed of stakes placed near each other, and of interlaced rushes, and covered by conical or two-fronted roofs. One or two narrow bridges lead to the shore.

"Except in the difference between a lacustrine and maritime site, the habitations of these Pœonians on Lake Prasias whom Megabyzus could not subdue were exactly similar.—*Herodotus*, book v. cap. 16.

"The settlements of those Africans whose aquatic city, built in a creek of the river Tsadda, caused so much astonishment some ten years ago to Dr. Baikie, the English naturalist, then a member of the expedition in the *Pleiad* on the Niger, are also constructed quite on the same plan.

"On the approach of strangers the inhabitants issued from their abodes, the water being up to their knees. One child was up to the waist. 'We saw some of these huts,' says the doctor, 'which the inhabitants, if they be inhabited, could only enter or leave by diving like beavers. We could not have imagined,' he adds, 'reasonable creatures forming,

Such are the grand scenes of the temporary creations which successively lent life to the earth, and during each of which the sublime essence of life seems to be constantly progressing over matter till it reaches our species, the genius of which appears the highest reflection of the divinity.

But it is in this intellectual supremacy that man inevitably finds the source of the doubts which overwhelm him. His life is exhausted in vainly attempting to efface the past and fathom the future. His thoughts, uncertain and inquisitive, sweep him along like an impetuous river which loses itself in a boundless ocean: like the favourite heroes of Goethe and Byron, all his efforts are directed towards unravelling the impenetrable shadows of his destiny. Hence philosophers and learned men of the highest class, looking at the incessant change in created beings, have asked themselves the question whether the human species was really the master-piece and the last effort of creative power, or whether it will in its turn disappear in some new shipwreck, to be succeeded by creatures of still purer essence.

Looking at the progress which each creation shows, some of the German savants admit, with Bremser, the latter hypothesis, and among them are some daring enough to attempt to prove the point by figures.[1]

In his remarkable work on Geology, M. Louis Figuier has written on this subject a beautiful passage, which we are happy to lay before the reader. "It is not impossible," he says, "that man may be a step in the ascending and progressive scale of animated beings. The divine power which strewed on earth life, sensation, and thought; which gave to the plant organization; to the animal movement, sensation, and intelligence; to man, besides these manifold gifts, the faculty of reason, doubled by the

as it were from taste, a colony of beavers, having the manners of the hippopotami and crocodiles which infest the neighbouring marshes.'"—Victor Meunier, *La Science et les Savants en 1864*. Paris, 1865, p. 86.

[1] Bremser thus explains himself in reference to this subject:—

"It may still be presumed, supposing there should be a new radical change, that beings more perfect than those which resulted from preceding ones will be created. In man mind bears the same proportion to matter as 50 to 50, with slight differences more or less, for sometimes mind and sometimes matter predominates. In a subsequent creation, supposing that in which man was formed not to be the last, there would probably be organizations in which the mind would act more freely, and where it would be in the proportion of 75 to 25. It results from these considerations, that man was formed at the most passive epoch of existence on our earth. Man is a sad middle state between the animal and the angel: he aspires to elevated knowledge and cannot reach it, albeit our modern philosophers fancy such is not the case. Man wishes to fathom the first cause of all that exists, and cannot attain to it; with fewer intellectual faculties he would not have the presumption to want to know these causes, which on the other hand would be quite clear to him if he were endowed with a more extended mind."

power of aiming at the ideal, perhaps proposes to itself to create one day, along with man or after him, a still superior being. This new creature, which modern religion and poetry appear to have foreseen in the ethereal and radiant type of the Christian angel, would be provided with moral faculties, the nature and essence of which elude our understanding.

"We ought to satisfy ourselves with laying down this redoubtable problem without attempting to resolve it. This great mystery, to use the beautiful expression of Pliny, is concealed in the majesty of nature, *latet in majestate naturæ*, or better, in the thoughts and omnipotence of the Creator of worlds."

BOOK II.

FOSSILS.

If, in ending this sketch of geology, we now inquire from what sources the learned have been able to decipher the dark phases through which earth has passed, we see that they have managed to extract most valuable data from the numerous vestiges of creatures which successively peopled it, and which are found scattered on its surface or in its deep layers.

In fact, the fossiliferous rocks only represent the catacombs of the former creations, miraculously preserved through ages, and the ineffaceable impressions which they have left in every terrestrial stratum seem like so many medals destined to mark the various revolutions of the globe.

The different layers of our sphere have faithfully bequeathed to us vestiges of all that once animated their surface; nothing has been lost in this great medal-cabinet of nature. The Dragon-fly, with its wings of gauze, is quite as well preserved as the ponderous skeleton of the mastodon. The carapace of a microscopic infusorial animal lies by the side of the bony case of a gigantic tortoise. Some of the flowers which perfumed the first meadows on the globe have been found, if not in all their freshness, at least retaining all the delicacy of their forms. Certain vegetable secretions themselves have escaped the ravages of cataclysms. Thus we discover the resin of some antediluvian Coniferæ, and in the

225. Fossil Libellula or Dragon-fly of the Secondary Epoch.

midst of its transparent lumps lie yet the winged insects which it imprisoned as it flowed; this is the source of our yellow amber.[1]

For those who know how to fathom the most mysterious revelations

[1] The history of yellow amber has been unfolded by M. Göppert, who has remarked that this precious substance, the origin of which was so long a mystery, is only the resin produced by a species of antediluvian Conifer, the *Pinites succinifer*. This amber-tree, which seems decidedly analogous to our red fir (*Abies rubra*, Mich.), distilled its resin more abundantly than the trees of the same family do in our forests now. Hence, as it flowed in large quantities over the surface of the bark, its voluminous concretions imprisoned insects and flowers, which its transparence allows us to see.

According to K. Müller we sometimes find in the midst of morsels of amber little fir-cones and remains of woody tissue, which may be recognized as having proceeded from the trunk of some species closely resembling the red-pine. In antediluvian times the succiniferous pines formed, beyond doubt, dense forests on the borders of the Baltic, and the amber buried beneath its waves is now thrown up by violent tempests. It is found mingled with floating wood and marine plants, which are withdrawn from the waves by means of nets. When the mass is rescued from the sea the women and children seek for the precious substance. In the interior of Europe the amber is dug out like fossil products. Beds of it are found in Switzerland, in Poland, and in Italy. It is also met with in Greenland.

This valuable material flowed so abundantly from the pine-trees that it often accumulated on the ground in masses of considerable size. Here the resin, combining with the oxygen of the air, became transformed into succinic acid. The largest piece of amber known of nature she unveils other and quite unexpected facts; traces of certain acts or certain phenomena which have lasted only an instant!

The antiquary no longer finds on the sand any trace left by the bloody feet of those proud conquerors who marched their savage hordes from one end of the earth to the other, whilst humble tortoises, or a few isolated lizards, separated from us by twenty cataclysms, still display to the astonished naturalist the passing impress of their steps, upon a soil scarcely consolidated in the most ancient times of our globe. And, moreover, who would think we should even find indications of the storms

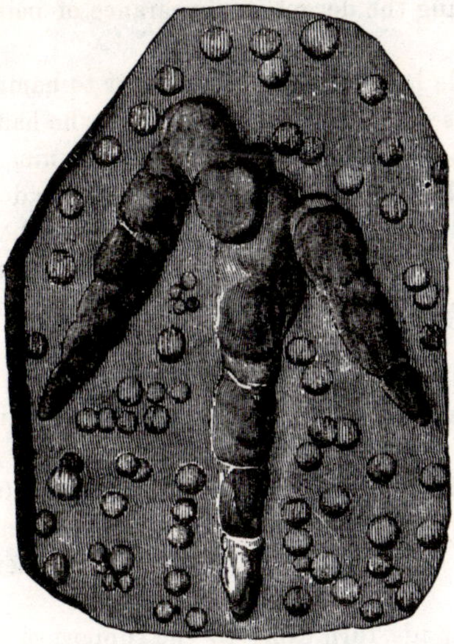

226. Impressions of Rain-drops and Animal's Footsteps on Antediluvian Rocks.

of the primitive epochs of the earth? Rain-drops, falling upon the sand, formed impressions upon it which it has preserved by becoming transformed into a solid freestone![1]

is in the Museum of Natural History at Berlin; it weighs more than thirteen pounds. Its value is estimated at £1500, although only the tenth part of this price was paid for it, for, like diamonds in Brazil, amber is considered in Prussia the property of the crown. The shores of the Baltic, which produce the most amber, yield annually about 150 tons.—*Cosmos*, b. i. s. 329. K. Müller, *Merveilles du Monde Végétal*, t. i. p. 168.

[1] These impressions of rain-drops have been photographed by J. Deane from rocks in Connecticut. They are evidently due to showers falling on sand still moist and soft, which later on became dry, and was transformed into freestone. In other rocks of America, figures of which can be seen in Buckland's work, we find the marks of tortoises' feet and of the footsteps of lizards.—Buckland, *Geology and Mineralogy in their Relations to Natural Theology.*

Yet in spite of this marvellous preservation of ancient beings, men long persisted in regarding fossils as only freaks of nature, *lusus naturæ*, as they were called.

In vain did the earth yield up its most delicate skeletons with all their fine, thin bones; in vain did it present shells with their most charming tracery, sometimes even with their ancient colouring; in vain did we find in the midst of rocks birds yet enveloped in their feathers, and insects with their transparent wings; up to the sixteenth century all these things only passed for accidental products begotten by chance, and merely possessing the deceptive appearance of beings which life had animated.

No slight trouble had to be taken in order to hammer the truth into the refractory brains of some savants. The first who had the courage to do this was a potter, poor in fortune but great in genius. It was Bernard Palissy who in his lowly state taught a lesson to the doctors of Paris, and showed them that the shells which are found in the soil were carried thither by the sea, which of old occupied the place where we find them. It was this humble and fervent man who thus became the founder of positive geology.

But whilst the different fossiliferous rocks were being deposited, whilst the earth was renewing its living races, plutonic forces, in ceaseless agitation, from time to time shook the crust of the globe, or fractured it in various places. Its fragments formed our mountains, and these, issuing from the depths of the seas, bore aloft to the regions of the clouds the charnel-houses of the animals which had formerly peopled their abysses.

When Buffon in his turn came to the support of the view that the shells scattered over the summits of the Alps and Apennines only proved that the globe had undergone convulsions, he found himself contradicted where no person could have expected it. This was by Voltaire, who in his *Physique* attacked with biting sarcasm those who adopted this opinion. He maintained that all the shells found on our mountains had been scattered there by pilgrims on their return from Rome.[1] Only a few words were needed to have silenced the immortal writer, but these few words Buffon never uttered. He could have told him that we find these fossil vestiges everywhere, even in the two Americas, whither

[1] The idea of ascribing to the pilgrims from Rome the fossil shells found in the mountains was not long upheld by the philosopher of Ferney. He shrank from the idea of seriously embroiling himself with the illustrious overseer of the Jardin des Plantes. "I do not," he said, "wish to quarrel with M. Buffon about shells."—Voltaire, *Physique*, chap. xv., "Des Singularités de la Nature."

certainly these pious travellers never carried them; whilst, on the other hand, there are even imposing chains of mountains which are absolutely formed of shells.

Notwithstanding the perfect preservation of many fossils, the love of the marvellous which predominated over our ancestors made them misunderstand nature, and these relics were almost constantly assigned to some extraordinary creature or other. The bones of bears, which were obtained from the caves of Franconia, passed in Germany for a sovereign antidote, and were sold in all the apothecaries' shops as the remains of the fabulous unicorn.

For the elephants and mastodons there was generally another story. As many of the bones of these animals present in their forms striking resemblances to those of man, at an epoch when the imagination of our forefathers, roused to enthusiasm by the legends of olden times, elevated the stature of heroes to the height of their heroic poems, the bones of the great mammals found in the earth were constantly referred to some celebrated personage.

Thus, according to the statement of Pausanias, the knee-cap of an elephant, as large as a circus discus, found near Salamis, was considered as having belonged to Ajax. The Spartans prostrated themselves before the skeleton of one of these animals, in which they thought they recognized the skeleton of Orestes. Some remains of a mammoth found in Sicily were considered as having belonged to Polyphemus! . . .

The learned were not more exempt than the vulgar from these kinds of errors. Father Kircher, in his remarkable work on the subterranean world (*Mundus Subterraneus*), gives figures of these giants alongside of men of ordinary size.

The skeleton of an elephant discovered in Switzerland, at the foot of a tree torn up by the wind, was considered by F. Plater, the anatomist, as the skeleton of a giant nineteen feet high. He even restored it by means of a sketch which became celebrated, and which was to be seen some time ago at Lucerne in an ancient college of the Jesuits.

In the reign of Louis XIII. there was found on the banks of the Rhone a skeleton which attained great celebrity. It was shown as that of Teutobocchus, defeated by Marius in a most sanguinary struggle. It was said to have been exhumed from a tomb bearing this inscription, "Teutobocchus rex:" in which were also found some medals with the same title. But despite all this evidence, the remains of this too famous king of the Cimbri, which gave rise to so many bitter disputes among the faculty and physicians of Paris, were recognized by De Blainville as being nothing more than those of a narrow-toothed mastodon (*M. angustidens*).

The name of the Field of Giants is even often given to places in which the bones of elephants and mastodons abound.[1]

BOOK III.

THE MOUNTAINS—CATACLYSMS AND UPHEAVALS OF THE GLOBE.

It is in the midst of lofty mountains that Nature develops her most magnificent scenes. Their winding-sheets of eternal snow, their diadems of ice, and their burning volcanoes, by turns strike and astonish the traveller. "It seems," says Rousseau, "as if, when we rise above the dwellings of men, we leave behind all low and earth-born sentiments, and that in proportion as we approach the ethereal regions, the soul contracts something of their unchangeable purity!"

Here we are penetrated by a sense of the divine majesty and human weakness. Before their colossal masses, their frightful and sombre clefts, we can say with the old German miner, "Man is only an atom on the mountain, though he is a giant in the mine."

The aspect of the sea is monotonous compared to that of the frowning crests of the globe; if it have its gales and tempests, they have their hurricanes and avalanches. Mountains are also of importance in the harmony of the globe. These grand chains, the summits of which pierce the lofty regions of the atmosphere, seem, says De Saussure, to be the laboratory of nature, and the reservoir from whence she draws all the blessings and ills which she pours upon earth; the rivers which water and

[1] Near Bogota, at a height of 2660 metres (about 8750 feet), there is a field filled with bones of mastodons, called there the *Campo de Gigantes* (field of the giants), in which Humboldt had some excavations made with great care.—*Cosmos*, b. i. p. 321.

the torrents which ravage it, the rains which fertilize and the storms which desolate it.

The mountains are only the result of upheavals of the crust of the earth caused by throes of the incandescent mass which it envelops. The globe, in cooling, is necessarily forced to contract. When the elasticity of the crust has reached its farthest limits, it splits, and its fragments produce eminences, the elevation of which is in direct proportion to the thickness of the covering and the intensity of the volcanic effort.

In the earliest times the surface of the earth presented no mountains, and those which first appeared were very low. The solidified crust being then very thin required but little effort to raise it. But in proportion as it became thicker the mountains acquired a proportionate elevation, and in order to cleave it an effort of the most prodigious kind was necessary.

Great shocks, as we have already said, have at times rent the globe almost from one pole to the other. As a particular instance we may mention the upheaval which formed the New World, during which the Cordilleras appeared, stretching away from the Icy Sea to Tierra del Fuego, producing the great wall which traverses the two Americas.

When we think of the ravages which are occasioned in our own time by simple earthquakes, we at once conclude that these cataclysms must have been accompanied by an uproar and an amount of confusion, of which our minds could never form but a very imperfect image.

The birth of lofty chains of mountains has occasioned great disturbances among the ancient oceans. Some, as we have seen, gave rise to those disastrous inundations mentioned in the cosmogony of every race possessed of written annals. According to Messrs. d'Omalius d'Halloy, Beudant, and Elie de Beaumont, the most imposing catastrophe of historic times, our Mosaic deluge, was probably only the effect of the mightiest upheaval of the globe, that of the Andes; and the uplifting of America above the ocean, which was the result of this, gave rise to the immeasurable flood which broke tumultuously against the old continent.

In his work on cataclysms M. Frederick Klee has laid down some very remarkable views on this subject. According to him the axis of the globe has suffered displacements, and it was the last of these that occasioned that terrible event the deluge.

Nothing checks M. Klee in his daring conceptions. He even thinks that some of the contemporaries of this great telluric revolution may have passed safely through it, and that to those who thus survived we owe the legends which erudition has discovered in some ancient writings. According to this geologist, it is to the witnesses of this irresistible convulsion that we must ascribe the mythical traditions in which it is said that during the catastrophe of the deluge the sun, moon, and stars changed their places in the heavens.

If, indeed, the axis of the globe had been displaced, man, regarding the earth then as being immovable and in the centre of the universe, would naturally think it was the stars which had deviated from their path across the celestial fields.[1]

In the Scandinavian mythology we discover some pictures of the great events which then took place in the earth and in the heavens. The *Edda* paints the ravages of the volcanic eruptions and of the waves of a wild and untamed ocean. This collection even contains some rhapsodical descriptions of our cataclysms. This is the character of the prophecies of the *Vala*, where it borrows its principal images from the sombre catastrophe of the deluge. The inspired sibyl relates that at this time the sun rose in the south, and that the east was invaded by polar ices. M. Klee considers that these assertions support the theory of a change in the axis of the globe.[2]

Naturalists are almost agreed as to the cause of the great deluge; but their opinions vary greatly as to the epoch to which we should refer the appearance of America and the antiquity of the human species. Here modern science relapses into speculation.

As our cataclysms indicate the different stages of a ceaseless force, it is evident that others still menace us. Everything indeed seems to foretell that ages to come will see other plutonic phenomena display themselves, and new systems of mountains arise. Hence as the upheavals follow a progressively ascending scale, we are quite led to expect new outbursts and more terrible convulsions.

[1] Bernardin de Saint-Pierre, long before M. Klee, had enunciated a system exactly corresponding to that of this geologist. He believed that it was the successive increase in the tropical vegetation and of the polar ices that made the globe move alternately one way and another. According to our celebrated writer this system also explained the ancient traditions of the Egyptian priests, in which it is said that formerly the sun rose where now it sets.—*Harmonies de la Nature*, Paris, 1806, t. ii. p. 96.

[2] The following are fragments of the prophecies of the *Vala* drawn from the Scandinavian *Edda*, in which allusion is made to the convulsions of the globe:—

"I remember," says the sibyl, "nine worlds and nine heavens. Before the sons of Bor (the gods) raised the globes, they who created the gleaming Midgaard, the sun shone in the south. In the east was seated the old woman in the forest of iron (the polar ices). The sun is covered with clouds, the earth sinks in the sea, the shining stars disappear from the heavens, clouds of smoke envelop the all-nourishing tree, lofty flames mount even to heaven; the sea rears itself violently towards the skies and passes over the lands. Neither earth nor sun exist any longer, the air is overcome by glittering streams. . . . she (the sibyl) for the second time sees the earth, covered with verdure, rise from the sea."—Fr. Klee, *Le Déluge*, p. 223.

Man has been enabled to verify these assertions, and himself to behold mountains issue from the bosom of the earth. In 1538 one formed in the environs of Naples. In 1759, at two or three days' journey from Mexico, Jorullo, since so celebrated, reared its volcanic plateau. Above a plain formerly dedicated to agriculture, a surface of ten square leagues was raised into the air and transformed into numerous and ever-active craters.

This may be a fitting place to say, that many contemporary geologists maintain that these telluric changes were not the effect of sudden transition, but of slow insensible progress. To the school of Cuvier, which

227. Modern Upheaval—Jorullo in Mexico.

proclaimed the infallibility of this great man, has succeeded another, more sceptical, which maintains that, instead of violent cataclysms returning at successive periods to convulse the globe, it has been governed by harmonious laws, which, without shocks, without violence, transformed its surface and perfected there slowly and progressively the work of creation. This daring school, which has seated itself upon the wreck of that of the celebrated naturalist, demands that the name of cataclysm should be struck out of science. At its head stand Messrs. Lyell, Lartet, and Darwin.

Modern geologists refer, in support of this new theory, to certain regions of the globe which in our days are incessantly rising. The ancient *Sagas* tell us that many parts of the beach of the Baltic, formerly almost on a level with this sea, and upon which ample troops of seals climbed to play and bask in the sun, were the scenes of great hunts by the Finns, who slew them with their arrows. Now Von Buch and Lyell have shown that these very places are at the present time raised to a great height above the waves, and are quite inaccessible to these animals. "In 800 years," says Humboldt, "the eastern shore of the Scandinavian peninsula has risen perhaps more than 330 feet, and if this movement continue at a uniform rate, in 1200 years parts of the bottom of the sea now covered with fifty fathoms of water, will begin to emerge and become dry land."

Darwin and many other authors have affirmed that some very extensive regions of South America were formerly the theatre of slow and progressive upheavals, which gave birth to the plains of Patagonia, all over which are scattered recent marine shells, bearing eloquent testimony to the youth of these realms.

It is to the ancient continent that the loftiest eminences of the globe belong. It was thought that Chimborazo in America rose above every other, but since a more accurate study has been made of the Himalaya range, which lords it over the chain of Thibet and towers to a height of above 29,000 feet,[1] men have been forced to greet it as the king of the mountain chains.

Yet notwithstanding its positive height, this imposing mass forms a scarcely perceptible elevation on the surface of the globe. An attempt has been made in works on geology to give an idea of this fact by repeating, that the loftiest mountains on the earth produce on it asperities comparable to those of an orange. But the comparison is far too forced, for the highest mountain chains on the globe only form on its surface projections equal to those of a grain of sand (say $\frac{1}{50}$th of an inch) on a sphere six feet in diameter.

When we revert to the vast commotions which took place at the upheaval of mountains, and to their geological constitution, we feel at once that their lofty summits must present very varied aspects. This is the case. Some mountain chains, like those of Calabria, have crests toothed like saws; others resemble pointed crystals, as is seen in Savoy, where on this account they are called *aiguilles*. Often the tops are rounded and form a succession of paps; finally at other times, as for instance is seen in the peaks of Tierra del Fuego, these asperities of the globe are perfectly conical, slender and pointed, exactly like gigantic sugar-loaves.

[1] The Kaurisankar, or Mount Everest, is 29,002 feet high.

228. View in Tierra del Fuego. Conical Peaks of Admiralty Strait.

The exploration of lofty mountains is not always free from danger. But the deplorable accidents of which they become the theatre are often due to the imprudence of travellers who attend little to the advice of their guides. A good guide holds in his hands the lives of those who accompany him; it is therefore necessary to make a careful choice and to treat him kindly. I have always done so, and have met with devoted men, who years after have preserved the memory of my ascents.

When we have arrived at a moderate height, the ascent of any mountain becomes a heavy toil. Movement and respiration become extremely difficult in proportion as we rise. There even comes a time when, as De Saussure remarks, one is obliged to stop every fifty yards overwhelmed by an inexplicable fatigue. Then the rarefaction of the air renders the oppression greater and greater, and the heart beats as if it would burst from the chest, and the traveller feels every instant as if he would faint. Twice Baron Müller, abandoned by his guides and companions, fainted quite away on the borders of the crater of Orizaba, whilst torrents of blood gushed from his chest.

After long journeys in the snow the traveller, subdued by cold and lassitude, experiences an insurmountable desire to sleep, and yet dare not, for all the world contains, yield himself up to it, for this sleep conducts him to inevitable death—a fact known to all travellers.

On the frozen shores of Tierra del Fuego, Solander, lost in the mountains, said imperiously to his companions in misfortune, "Whoever sits down will sleep, and he who sleeps will never wake again." Yet so overpowering, so unconquerable is this tendency to sleep, that several of the men yielded to it, and Solander himself, a few moments afterwards, sank down upon the snow, where his friend, the illustrious Sir Joseph Banks, had all the difficulty in the world to arouse him.

But when we have arrived at the summit of a mountain, the splendour of the sight makes one quite forget the fatigue of the ascent. This I experienced lately on climbing Mount Etna when I had reached the borders of the crater.

There, upon this throne, round which the lightning plays, we overlook heaven and ocean. Behind us the growlings of the thunder reverberate at the bottom of the immense gulf, according to ancient theogony the entrance to the empire of Pluto, but which the rustic mountaineer only knows as the Casa di Diavolo. Standing on cinders which burned my feet, and the sulphureous vapours of which almost suffocated me, the most splendid spectacle in creation expanded itself before my eyes. The dawn began to appear, and its pale light gradually extinguished the wavering glimmer of the stars. Then soon after, the sun appearing in all the pomp of the east, issued from his opal bed, his forehead bound with purple and gold.[1]

From this prodigious elevation the eye embraces all the circumference of Trinacria, stretching like a warm and luminous cincture along the blue waves which bathe its shores, its advanced promontories reminding one of the three legs which symbolized Sicily on ancient medals. In the distance the waves of the Ionian Sea blend with the azure of heaven; and on the other hand the mountains of Calabria, with their jagged outlines, bound the panorama with inexpressible magnificence; while Malta appears like a dim point upon the confines of a horizon 300 leagues in circumference.

Near Sicily rise from the middle of the sea the Cyclopean Rocks, like so many black projections contrasting with the brilliant shore. Vestiges of the most terrible commotion of the elements, their basaltic masses, produced amid the convulsions of the volcano, go back beyond historic epochs.

It was on the loftiest of these rocks that the frightful Polyphemus, having combed himself with a rake, delighted to play upon the flute in order to charm Galatea, the fairest of the Nereïds. It was with the highest rock that the furious Cyclops crushed Acis, his favoured rival. The others he launched at the vessels of the companions of Ulysses when they escaped him. Farther on we see the little port where Homer makes the fleet of the King of Ithaca touch. All here is imprinted with poesy.

When we look down on the flanks of the giant we behold his frightful progeny, a perfect pleiades of thirty-five to forty little volcanoes. From this point their craters show like so many circular lips, broad and depressed or pointed and projecting, and crowning sugar-loaf cones. Seen thus in a bird's-eye view, all these volcanoes exactly resemble those of the moon, and it seems as if we had before our eyes a magnified section of our satellite. I don't know whether this comparison has ever been made; it is, however, strictly correct. The ascent of Etna might be useful in this respect to many astronomers.

To this splendid picture of vales and mountains unrolling themselves before the eye, and melting away in the mists of the horizon, are sometimes joined remarkable phenomena. There are some elevated peaks

[1] [In addition to this the colouring *of the crater itself* is in most of these views a magnificent sight. The hues include every variety of yellow, passing into the purest white on one side and deep orange or brown on the other. Occasionally we find vermilion and other reds. "The brilliancy of these colours," says Professor Ansted, "is such that no pencil could imitate it, and the appearance can only be compared to the hues of the clouds during an autumn sunset in a warm climate. These bright tints are almost entirely due to deliquescent salts of ammonia, soda, and iron."—Tr.]

229. Spectres of the Brocken in the Harz

where, if a person places himself on a projecting eminence at sunrise, his outline is traced on the distant clouds in singular and gigantic proportions. This can often be seen on the summit of the Brocken, one of the loftiest mountains of the Harz, and it is this curious phenomenon that is known by the name of the Spectres of the Brocken.

But during journeys among mountains, the enchanting prospects from their summits are not the only ones that excite moving impressions, and the vales which show in the distance like insignificant irregular lines, if they do not present such vast horizons, display at any rate unexpected and marvellous appearances. Here and there we find profound and narrow gorges, immense abysses, the sombre hollows of which the eye cannot fathom, and in the depths of which often rolls a furious torrent, its thunders multiplied a hundredfold by the echoes. Everything threatens the daring traveller who ventures to plunge into their abysses. On one hand the avalanche hangs suspended over his head, and on the other every now and then fragments of rock fall down and threaten to crush him.

Almost all these imposing gorges are the effect of convulsions of the globe, and the first glance shows that they have resulted from a violent fracture of the mountains and separation of the fragments. We can identify these great fissures by the similarity which their walls present in respect to the layers of which they are formed, and by the irregularity of their chasms, in the depths of which reign shade and terror. Our superstitious ancestors, overcome by the awe which these darksome clefts inspired, often gave them names expressive of the dread they gave rise to, as for instance calling them hell valleys, hell holes, or devil's gorges.

In all high mountains, such as the Alps and Pyrenees, we see some which are thus designated. But certainly one of the most remarkable of these gorges is the Hell Valley in the Black Forest. I passed through it during a severe winter, and nothing could equal the dark horror it inspired. Masses of snow hung suspended on its buttresses, and their whiteness contrasted strongly with the gloomy mouth of the infernal abyss. This portico to the domains of Pluto, though ample of entrance, was yet shrouded in impenetrable darkness towards the bottom. The ancient Hercynian Forest, which we had just traversed, was buried under half a yard of rime; the cold was 25° below freezing-point (Fahr.); and our vehicle, in spite of the skids, which made large showers of ice fly on all sides, dragged us with frightful rapidity towards the precipice. It was altogether superb, and vividly recalled the icy forests of the north.

Sometimes, on the contrary, the mountain tops in splintering off have left upright here and there long narrow segments of rock, which, seen from afar in the dim mists of night, seem like so many fantastic shades hovering in the clouds. These are the witch-dances of the superstitious inhabitants of the Harz forests.

When the rending asunder of mountains takes place on a grand scale, and their flanks are deeply cut into, advantage is taken of the natural openings thus formed in order to trace out roads or passes, distinguished by the name of *gates*, because they offer easy means of communication between nations. The Iron Gates of Algeria have acquired a certain degree of celebrity.

It should also be remarked, that certain gorges are due to the erosion of the waters alone, which, rolling over their walls, incessantly wear them away, and in time form large valleys. These gorges of erosion are less rugged than those caused by rents; the waters, by the friction of the fragments carried down by them and by their own movement, having smoothed their sides. Often also rivers roar at the bottom of these ravines, leaping over the pebbles, or precipitating themselves from fall to fall amid the rocks.

Many of the cascades which we meet with among mountains issue from gorges of erosion. There are some which, like the cascade of Taurus, spread out in large sheets at the place where they fall; others precipitate themselves in the form of simple runlets of water from lofty heights, and fall in vast basins at their foot, as in the Circus of Gavarnie; some spread themselves like a net-work of streams on a gentle slope, and resemble a skein of white silk, whose silvery gleams undulate softly on the verdure of the hillocks. Seen from a distance one might say it was a tress of hair agitated by a gentle wind; these are what the mountaineers in their picturesque language call the "Locks of the Magdalen."

Instead of these mountain cascades, the variety of which pleases the eye, and the distant murmur of which charms the ear, when great streams meet with obstructions in their way, cataracts and falls are formed of the most formidable aspect. In some cases large sheets of water, as at Niagara, precipitate themselves to the bottom of an immense gulf with a roar which seems to shake the surrounding rocks; in other cases, as in the falls of the Zambesi, the river divides into several masses and gives origin to a series of vaporous columns, which rise in eddying swirls towards the clouds and fall in fine rain.

230. Valley of Erosion—Cascade in the Gorges of Mount Taurus, near Annasha-Kalessi, N W. from Adana.

BOOK IV.

VOLCANOES AND EARTHQUAKES.

After the mantle of snow which envelops the summits of the mountains, that which strikes us most is their volcanoes. Seen from afar they only give a very imperfect idea of what they are. To appreciate their phenomena and their ravages, our eyes must survey their depths. All is then changed, and the grandeur of the spectacle strikes the imagination, graving terrible images on it. We are astonished at the immensity of their fire-spouting mouths, and at the vastness of the lava streams which flow from them at certain times.[1]

The mythology of Greece gave to these mountains an origin altogether independent of the forces that act at the surface of the earth. "According to the Hellenes," says M. Elisée Reclus, in his remarkable work on the *Earth*, "water and fire were two distinct elements. Each had its separate domain, its genii, and its gods. Neptune reigned over the sea; it was he that unchained the tempest and raised the waves; the tritons followed in his train, the nymphs, the sirens, and the monsters of the deep obeyed his orders; and in the valleys of the mountains the solitary naiads poured in his honour the murmuring water from their urns. In the depths of unknown gulfs sat enthroned the sombre Pluto, Vulcan forging by his side, with the anvil ringing under the blows of the Cyclopes around him, while from their furnaces belched forth flames and melted

[1] Some men of science have expressed their wonder that the interior of the earth can furnish matter sufficient for these eruptions, but a little reflection will show that no great contraction of the crust of the globe is required to feed them. Violent eruptions do not usually emit more than 1300 cubic yards of lava, and seldom so much. This quantity, supposing it spread equally over the surface of the globe, would not form a layer so much as $\frac{1}{500}$th of a millimetre (or about $\frac{1}{12000}$th of an inch) in thickness. Thus we see that a contraction of the earth sufficient to shorten its radius by one millimetre would furnish matter for five hundred violent eruptions; and on consulting the history of recent volcanic phenomena we arrive at the conclusion that a contraction of $1\frac{1}{8}$ inch is sufficient to have supplied the lava thrown up in all the eruptions that have occurred on our planet during the last 3000 years.

matter, terrible for mortals to behold. Between the god of the sea and he of fire there was nothing in common, unless that both were sons of Chronos, that is, of Time that changes all things, that overturns and renews, and by its incessant labour of destruction prepares the place for the innumerable germs hurrying to enter upon life."

But we shall afterwards see that though this opinion seems to be the expression of the truth, certain geologists of the present day endeavour to dispute it.

The loftier volcanoes are, the less frequent are their eruptions. The

231. Goenong Api, Banda Islands, in the Moluccas.[1]

lava which they vomit forth, issuing from furnaces the depth of which is probably the same in every case, it is clear, that for the waves to mount in the chimneys of those which are very high, a much greater force is required than in the others. Thus one of the smallest of all, Stromboli, is always throwing out flames; since the days of Homer it has served as a beacon to navigators approaching the Eolian Islands. On the contrary, the volcanoes which animate the crests of the Cordilleras, and which are six or eight times as high, seem condemned to long intervals of repose, and in many cases only break out from century to century.

[1] The island of Goenong Api is one of the most active volcanoes in the Indian Archipelago. It forms an immense cone 7880 feet high, and is covered with luxuriant vegetation except where this has been destroyed by recent eruptions of lava. By the proximity of this volcano the Banda Islands are subject to frequent and destructive eruptions and earthquakes. The strongest recorded were those of 1598, 1615, 1632, 1691, 1711, 1798, and 1820; but the most fatal in their consequences were those of 1629, 1683, 1686, 1743, and 1816. So terrible were the ravages of the eruption and earthquake of 1691, that all the more wealthy inhabitants fled the islands, and the establishment was almost totally broken up.—Tr.

The volcanoes which lord it over the frozen summits of the Andes often produce phenomena equally striking and unexpected. When they melt the snows which crown their craters, their eruptions produce impetuous torrents, which, precipitating themselves, bear with them smoking scoriæ, fragments of rock, and blocks of ice.

At a great distance most volcanoes look just like pointed cones vomiting flames or vapours by a very narrow fissure. But when patience and courage have carried us to the rugged crests of their burning mouths, or when we have penetrated their sides, we are astonished at the scenes of grandeur which present themselves to our eyes in the midst of these frightful and dangerous abysses, where the heat and deleterious gases threaten to suffocate the traveller. I had felt astonished at the dimensions of the ancient craters of France and Italy, the one filled up with lakes, the other transformed into forests. I experienced the same feeling in exploring Vesuvius and Etna; but nothing in their fiery mouths can be compared with what is found in America. The immense crater of Orizaba, according to Baron Müller, is not less than 20,000 feet in circumference. Persons standing on the opposite sides of it are almost invisible to each other.

On another mountain in Mexico we find again a crater of very remarkable dimensions, that of Popocatepetl. Placed on the summit of a crest in the Cordilleras, from whence can be seen at the same time the two seas which bathe America, and in the distance Mexico encircled by its fairy lake, this crater, which is nearly circular, is, according to M. Boscovitz, 5000 feet in its longest diameter. The gullet of this giant has never been disturbed since the discovery of the New World; but in former times it must have thrown out flames abundantly, as thick beds of its ashes are found for more than twenty leagues round about. Where it has been possible for them to accumulate, their mass sometimes displays a depth of more than fifty metres (about 164 feet). The top of this volcano is covered with eternal snow, and by a strange contrast its once blazing summit, now almost extinct, has become an emblem of the alliance between the rigours of winter and the empire of fire. The crater of Popocatepetl is about 1000 feet deep. The descent, which is effected by the assistance of a cord wound on a windlass, is made for the purpose of seeking sulphur. Arrived at the bottom we find a mass of snow, and long stalactites of ice which hang from its walls or occupy the soil in every place where the sun does not reach, and which are not heated by the jets of hot vapour seen springing up here and there. Some writers think that Cortez obtained sulphur from this mountain to make powder when he ran short of it. What is more certain is, that some of his daring companions tried to reach the crater, and that they failed the first time.

The crater of Masaya, which struck the first conquerors of the New World with terror, seems to be even larger. Oviedo, who visited it, was appalled. He relates that in its depths there is a space so vast that a hundred horsemen could easily manœuvre in the presence of a thousand persons. Moreover, at that time there could be seen a furnace where a burning wave rose and fell at intervals, which the pious explorer of America estimated at about six times as long as it would take to repeat the *Credo.* As he moved away from the precipice quite stupified, he exclaimed, "I cannot believe that a Christian could contemplate such a spectacle without thinking about hell and repenting of his sins."

The fire-belching mouths have always alarmed the inhabitants of volcanic countries, and everywhere they have been compared to the gulfs of Tartarus. The crater of the mountain we have just spoken of was called by the ancient American caciques the Hell of Masaya.

"The island of Java," says Elisée Reclus, "owed to the beauty and the violence of its volcanoes the honour of being entirely consecrated to Siva, the god of destruction; and it was in the very craters of the mountains that the worshippers of terror and death constructed their temples." At the present day some pious worshippers of the terrible divinity take up their abode in the neighbourhood of these craters, and at certain times make them offerings of seeds such as are used for food, which they cast into their fiery and bellowing mouths. But these dreadful volcanic gods are not always appeased by such offerings, and with the voice of thunder call for human sacrifices. "Innumerable sacrifices have been offered to the volcanoes in order to appease their wrath," continues the author of the *Earth.* "By a mixture of fear and ferocity the priests of many religions have with great pomp thrown victims into the yawning gulfs of these enormous furnaces. Scarcely three centuries ago, when the Christians were exterminated throughout the whole extent of Japan, converts to the new faith were precipitated by hundreds into the crater of Unsen, one of the most beautiful volcanoes of the archipelago; but this offering to the offended gods did not calm their wrath, for about the end of the eighteenth century this same mountain of Unsen and the neighbouring summits caused by their eruption one of the most terrible disasters of which the history of volcanoes makes mention. Through a sentiment of fear analogous to that of the Japanese priests, the Christian missionaries of America saw in the burning mountains of the New World not the hand of God but the hand of Satan, and went in procession to the edges of their craters in order to exorcise them. The legend says that the

232. View of the Interior of the Crater of Popocatepetl, seen from a breach in its side.

monks of Nicaragua climbed the terrible volcano of Momotombo in order to quiet it by their spells, but never returned—the fire having consumed them."

Many countries of our globe, now buried in the most perfect repose and covered with a vigorous vegetation, were, at an epoch that cannot at present be definitely fixed, everywhere convulsed by volcanic fires; rich harvests now abound where formerly rolled burning streams of lava. Ancient craters now display only grass and moss in the depths of their mouths, which formerly vomited torrents of fire. This spectacle is even met with in the centre of France, in all the mountains of Auvergne.

Active volcanoes are common at the present time on the surface of the globe. But by this it is not meant that they are agitated by perpetual convulsions. Nearly all awake to their terrible activity only at long intervals, and during the space of time between the eruptions their internal turmoil is only revealed outwardly by slight and deceptive phenomena.

Humboldt states the number of active volcanoes at 223; Keith Johnston raises it to 270, of which more than the half (190) are comprised in the great volcanic belt which forms almost a circle of fire around the Pacific Ocean.

When a formidable eruption breaks out it is often accompanied by dull roars which seem to shake the mountain. In a short time the fiery mouth launches into the air sheets of flame and smoke, as well as masses of cinders and burning rock. In 1553, in one of its most terrible eruptions, Cotopaxi projected to a distance of three leagues blocks of trachyte more than a hundred cubic yards in size. During this time the lava escapes with violence from the entrails of the mountain, and pours over its sides like so many streams or cascades of fire, consuming everything in their path.

In very lofty volcanoes the lava, in order to rise to the crater in which they culminate, must require an almost incalculable force; hence it often happens that it makes its way out before reaching it, and having burst the flanks of the mountain near its base forms a small additional volcano, in which, for the future, all the efforts of the eruption are concentrated, and from which pour streams of lava of a magnitude we should not expect from so low an elevation.

In high volcanic mountains we often find at the base of the great cone a series of small accessory volcanoes: as we have seen, Etna possesses quite a family scattered over its flanks. In fact, it is these that have in particular ravaged the surrounding countries.

The most frightful eruption of Etna in modern times was produced by one of these young volcanoes, the Monte Rosa. From it issued in

1771 the long river of lava which rolled its burning waves over a distance of nine leagues, fired great part of Catania, and only stayed its passage

233. Eruption of Cotopaxi in 1741.

when it plunged into the sea amidst a most tumultuous struggle between the waves and fire.

Notwithstanding its smaller proportions, Vesuvius has experienced fearful eruptions. One is especially celebrated for the destruction of two rich and important cities which rose on its sides, Herculaneum and Pompeii. The former was in part invaded by a lava stream, the second absolutely buried under a prodigious mass of ashes. This eruption took place in the year 79, and possibly attracted more notice from having been the cause of the death of the naturalist Pliny than for the ravages it produced.

In our time Vesuvius, in its throes, has produced lava floods which

234. Etna—Cascade of Red-hot Lava during the Eruption of 1771.

have annihilated some small towns. In 1794 its burning waves submerged all the habitations in Torre del Greco, rising above their roofs. Recently again (in 1861) the same volcano destroyed a part of this country town, which had been rebuilt after the disaster.[1]

[1] [In 1872 another eruption took place, which, though not the greatest on record, was the greatest within the memory of man. It began on the afternoon of April 23 without warning of any kind. By 8 o'clock on the evening of the 24th orifices had opened in the mountain here and there on all sides, sending down rivers of lava, and thrusting out long and broad tongues of fire, which now appeared, now disappeared. These subsidiary cones

The great lava floods sometimes present a tolerably smooth surface, like that of a river which has descended peaceably from the mountain heights to the bottom of the valley. The lava then forms a ready-made road, and I have traversed several which the fire of the volcano seemed to have thus prepared for the wants of man. But more frequently these immense lava fields, as is seen in the approaches to Etna, Hecla, and so many other volcanoes, are contorted and broken like a furious sea which the wand of a fairy had suddenly transformed into fractured and blackened rocks, only that they are still more horrible than any sea. A man who lost himself for many hours in these frightful solitudes would infallibly perish.

Some volcanoes in their eruptions throw out mud, and these occasionally constitute a very remarkable phenomenon. A very learned Japanese writer, Tit-singh, relates that in 1793 a volcano of the island of Kiou-siou, one of the largest of the empire, suddenly ejected such torrents of liquid matter, that more than 50,000 of the inhabitants perished, swept away by the waves. Similar circumstances have taken place in America. A large village near the equator was destroyed in 1797 by a river of volcanic mud.[1]

This strange phenomenon is due to a communication being formed between a crater and a subterranean lake concealed in the side of the mountain. This fact also accounts for the enormous quantity of fish mixed with the water and mud which Cotopaxi and other volcanoes of

were fourteen in number, and the lava issuing from so many different points threatened to carry devastation far and wide. By the night of the 27th the horrors had partly ceased, and the mountain gradually returned to its ordinary condition. This eruption was attended with a melancholy loss of life, over twenty persons being killed on the spot or mortally injured by the lava and mephitic fumes from two cracks which suddenly opened in the ground where they were standing for the purpose of witnessing the magnificent spectacle. The villages of San Sebastiano and Massa di Somma were to a great extent destroyed by the lava.—See *Volcanoes and Earthquakes*, published by Blackie & Son.]

[1] [Instances of submarine volcanic eruptions are not uncommon, and the Bay of Santorin, the ancient Thera, in the Grecian Archipelago, contains several small islands which owe their origin to this cause. The last eruption occurred in 1866. It began about the end of January with a noise like a heavy cannonade. In a short time flames issued from the sea, rising sometimes to the height of fifteen feet. This continued till the 14th February, when the eruptions became more violent and the sea more troubled. Gas forced its way upwards from the bottom with terrific noise, flames arose in several places, and a dense column of white smoke mounted steadily to an immense height. A new island appeared next morning, which by the 28th had reached a height of thirty feet, with a circumference of 300 yards at the sea-level. It was composed of a heap of loose clinker and lava. During this time a new volcano had arisen on the island of Neo Kaimeni (itself produced by volcanic action in 1707), and part of that island had sunk below the sea. The new island lay a little to the south-west of Neo Kaimeni, but by its gradual increase it became united with that island, and now forms its south-western extremity.—Tr.]

America sometimes eject. And this explanation is so much the more plausible, because the species which is ejected at such times is the only fish which lives in the most elevated water-courses of the Cordilleras, at a height of 9000 feet. This fish belongs to the family Siluridæ, and naturalists have recently given it the name of *Pimelodus cyclopum* (Pimelode of the Cyclopes) in recognition of the singular changes to which it is liable in the course of existence.

These eruptions containing fish are not rare. Humboldt relates that

235. *Pimelodus cyclopum*, ejected from volcanoes.

in one of them Cotopaxi ejected such a quantity of Pimelodes on the estate of the Marquis of Selvalègre, that they poisoned the air all round. Towards the close of the last century the town of Iburra was ravaged by a malignant fever, which was attributed to the miasmata arising from an enormous mass of these fishes vomited by a neighbouring volcano.

Astonished at the grandeur and variety of volcanic phenomena, the learned of all ages have sought to explain the mystery of their origin. Numerous hypotheses have been put forward for this purpose, and have successively fallen into oblivion. We shall mention only some of the most celebrated.

During the era of the encyclopedists, in the eighteenth century, when all kinds of audacious theories were put forward, volcanoes were explained very variously. One of the ideas then most in vogue was that they only resulted from the ignition of a mass of coal and pyrites which happened to be in the strata of the mountain in question.

Lémery the chemist proposed another hypothesis. In his experiments in the laboratory he had produced a sort of small artificial volcano by mixing together finely powdered sulphur, iron-filings, and a little water. In a short space of time such an amount of chemical action was set up in this mixture that it took fire. According to the professor of the Jardin du Roi, similar phenomena take place in burning mountains. All those who saw this experiment went forth convinced. Buffon himself adopted this hypothesis. "Behold," said this great man, "what a volcano is in the eyes of a master of physics!"

Another philosopher, the illustrious Sir Humphry Davy, also proposed a very ingenious chemical theory, too ingenious perhaps, for which reason it came less into favour than that of Lémery. Having discovered certain metals, potassium and sodium, which have the singular property of taking fire so soon as they are brought into contact with water, the English chemist supposed that the flames which issue from volcanoes are only the product of the combustion of these metals taking place in the depths of the globe when the water reaches them.

Notwithstanding the great celebrity of its author, this hypothesis had only a very brief existence: phenomena so powerful and general could not have their source in local chemical reactions. The geologists of our epoch are almost unanimous in admitting that all volcanic phenomena are to be attributed solely to the central fire of the globe making greater or less efforts to project outwards the superfluity of its incandescent materials. It is certain that this theory explains easily and better than any other what happens during eruptions, and all those who have visited volcanoes admit it without hesitation.

However, the fact that volcanoes are almost always situated in the neighbourhood of the sea leads us to suppose that it must play a certain part in their phenomena; and such indeed is the opinion of several philosophers of the first rank. According to M. Sainte Claire Deville, the so-called smoke that issues from volcanoes is composed even to the extent of 999-thousandths of the vapour of water, and it is to the condensation of this in the upper regions of the atmosphere that the deluges of rain that sometimes accompany great eruptions are due. Thus the ancient legend would appear to be realized that represents Mount Etna vomiting in vapour the waves that are sucked down into the whirlpool of Charybdis.

Earthquakes are essentially united to volcanic phenomena, and often accompany them. They apparently result from the effort which the igneous materials of the globe make to launch themselves from their furnace. In countries where there are volcanoes they are looked upon as being in some measure safety-valves; so long as they are in full activity, and the centre, when overfilled, empties itself by the fire-spouting mouth, the country is tranquil.

No phenomenon offers such a dreadful spectacle as the earthquake. The naturalist who explores a dangerous volcano arrives at it armed with patience and courage. He knows the monster he proposes to face, its fury is announced by warning signs; whilst the earthquake, in the twinkling of an eye, entirely annihilates a large town.

The celebrated earthquake of Lisbon took place the 1st of November, 1755. Nothing had occurred to make men suspect such an occurrence, when, at five-and-twenty minutes to ten in the morning, at a time when all the people were quietly preparing themselves for business, a frightful subterranean noise struck all the inhabitants with stupefaction, and six minutes afterwards this great city was only a heap of ruins, under which lay an immense number of victims.

In the catastrophe of Messina, in 1783, the movement was still more rapid; in two minutes the town was utterly overturned, and, to add to the horror, fire devoured the ruins which the earthquake had heaped up.

But if these shocks thus concentrate their principal action upon one point—if a city collapse entirely without the neighbouring districts suffering any notable damage—volcanic action, on the other hand, is sometimes so powerful that it shakes the crust of the earth from one pole to another. Thus all Europe and part of Africa were shaken when the commotion of Lisbon took place. The Alps and the Pyrenees trembled to the base, the sea rose and fell on the coast of Sweden, Norway, the British Isles, and also upon those of America. At the time when Lisbon collapsed all the richest cities of Morocco were almost totally destroyed. Near the capital of this state an oasis with 8000 or 10,000 inhabitants disappeared.

Earthquakes are sometimes accompanied by very unwonted phenomena. Some curious ones were noticed during that which ravaged all Calabria in 1785. According to Hamilton, mountains were seen to rise at one moment and sink again some time after. Dwellings, with the persons they contained, were transported from one place to another without the least damage; some were moved to higher places than they had previously occupied; others descended quietly into the valleys. The earth cracked from place to place, and engulfed men and beasts in its great fissures. At the time of such a disaster it has been sometimes remarked that objects were carried by a rotatory movement which is

236. Grand Geyser of the Firehole Basin in the Yellowstone Region.

quite inexplicable. The upper layers of the stone pyramids in front of the gate of the monastery of St. Stephen del Bosco were twisted round upon their axis by a circular impulsion, whilst their bases remained fixed. M. A. Boscovitz, in his remarkable work on volcanoes, also relates that during the convulsion of the island of Majorca, in 1851, the shocks impressed a horizontal rotatory movement on a tower, and that in the interval they lasted it was displaced about 60° on its axis.

We cannot terminate this rapid sketch of volcanic phenomena without mentioning the singular geysers of Iceland, which are essentially connected with them. They are hot springs which at certain times issue from clefts in the ground, and rise into the air in the form of a great jet of boiling water. In the Great Geyser the watery eruption is preceded by dull sounds like artillery, at the end of which a jet of vapour and boiling water is launched into the air to a height of a hundred feet.[1]

It is also to volcanic efforts that we must refer those gigantic crystals of basalt which seem to have been pushed out of the earth by a prodigious force, in order to form at the surface, in one place, those remarkable

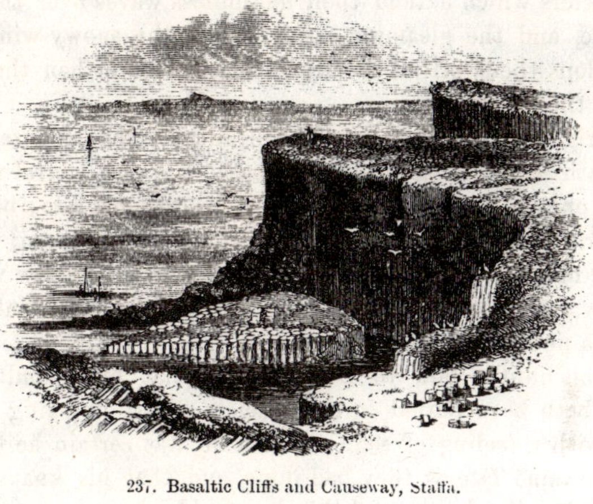

237. Basaltic Cliffs and Causeway, Staffa.

"giants' causeways," which are a favourite haunt with the inquiring; in another, those islands and grottoes which, rising from the bosom of the waves, astonish us by their mass or the arrangement of their prismatic columns; such as the rocks of the Cyclops near the coast of Sicily, and especially Fingal's Cave in the island of Staffa.

[1] [The geysers of Iceland are small when compared with those of the Yellowstone Region in the Rocky Mountains. From its remarkable natural features a portion of this region, 65 miles long by 55 broad, situated in the territories of Wyoming and Montana, has been set apart as a national park. Over this tract are scattered numerous hot springs and geysers, the most remarkable of the latter being found in the valley of the Firehole River. Here there are upwards of 1500 hot springs and geysers, showing a great variety in their times of action, force, mineral deposits, and colour of water. The Grand Geyser, of which we give an illustration, is the largest and most magnificent. It begins an eruption by filling

BOOK V.

GLACIERS AND ETERNAL SNOWS.

The glaciers which extend their motionless waves over the summits of the globe, and the gleaming splendour of the snowy winding-sheet which envelops them, strike the traveller still more than the aspect of the sea and the desert.

All is frightful amid the frozen solitudes of the mountains, and a horrible death seems at each step to threaten the rash mortal who enters them. On one side the avalanche threatens to bury him; beneath his feet open frightful chasms in which he would be shattered, while cold and hunger may destroy him. Every day the names of new victims are inscribed in the records of deaths, and yet each day some intrepid traveller tries a new enterprise.

A chamois-hunter said to De Saussure that his grandfather and father had both been buried in the glaciers whilst pursuing game, and he added, with a feeling of sadness, that he was certain he should experience the same fate as they had done, and that his knapsack would be his shroud! Yet in spite of this he would never renounce his fatal passion. Some years after this conversation the Genevese savant, return-

its basin with boiling water, forming a well 20 by 25 feet across, and having a visible depth when quiet of 100 feet. The explosion is preceded by clouds of steam rushing up to a height of 500 feet; the great unbroken body of water then succeeds, ascending in one gigantic column to a height of 90 feet; while from the apex of the column there rise five great jets slightly radiating, which shoot up to the unparalleled height of 250 feet from the ground. "The earth trembles under the descending deluge from this vast fountain; a thousand hissing sounds are heard in the air; rainbows encircle the summits of the jets with a halo of celestial glory." After playing for about twenty minutes the water gradually subsides till it sinks into the crater out of sight. Another remarkable geyser here is the Fan Geyser, which sends out five radiating jets to a height of 60 feet, the falling drops and spray giving the appearances of a feather fan. For a description of these and other natural wonders the reader is referred to *The Wonders of the Yellowstone Region* (Blackie and Son, 1874). There are also geysers in the North Island of New Zealand, one of which is said to more than equal the Great Geyser of Iceland.]

238. A Bay in Spitzbergen, from the Voyage of the Corvette *La Recherche.*

ing to this part, learned that the hunter's sad foreboding had been realized.

In Europe, the mantle of eternal snow, which buries in death all the upper regions of our mountains, generally begins at a height of 8900 to 9200 feet. In equatorial America the limit of these incessant frosts is almost half as high again, while at Spitzbergen it sinks to the level of the sea (see Fig. 238).

This imposing shroud of snow, by its calm majesty, sometimes gives an air of fantastic lightness to the loftiest peaks. When these are softly undulated they are often taken at a great distance for a transparent curtain of motionless clouds scattered upon the horizon. The chain of the Alps often appears like this. The eye is frequently deceived, especially towards evening, and the conviction that they are really mountains

239. Mount Erebus, Antarctic Regions.

is only acquired by observing that the false clouds do not undergo the least change of form, whilst if they were true ones, a few minutes would suffice to change their outline.

Sometimes also the diadem of snow which crowns a mountain becomes the theatre of the most unusual phenomena: fire and ice are at war, and it is a struggle as to which shall overwhelm the other. This happens in the inaccessible Erebus, a volcano of the polar regions, discovered by Sir James Ross. Enveloped in snow and ice from the base to the summit, and resembling an immense block of rock-crystal, its crater is yet in perpetual activity.

It is in these lofty mountain regions that we hear the thunder of the avalanche growl—their most terrible and most imposing phenomenon. Here the traveller may every instant enjoy this grand spectacle, for it is almost incessant wherever the snow and ice extend their covering over slightly inclined smooth surfaces.

Avalanches are generally formed by enormous masses of snow which from the height of the mountains precipitate themselves into the valleys. It is particularly in spring and during summer that they occur, at the time when the heat of the day makes itself most felt. At such times the least agitation in the air produces the fall. There has been only too often occasion to regret their ravages; they frequently engulf travellers, and sometimes carry with them forests and villages.

In the mountain passes where there is most reason to dread them, the muleteers always travel before day, the time when they are least to be feared; and in order not to agitate the air, they observe absolute silence, and even stuff the little bells on the harness with linen. But notwithstanding these precautions, the avalanches engulf every year a certain number of victims. At different times hundreds of men have perished at once, crushed under their mass. The most deplorable accident due to this cause upon record is that which befell 400 Austrian soldiers who, in the fifteenth century, were buried under one of these falls of snow.

Glaciers are met with most frequently in the valleys of high mountains. From thence they are sometimes seen to descend to a considerable depth, far below the line of eternal snow, and display themselves in the midst of a luxuriant vegetation, among the forests of conifers and the flowers of the valleys which surround them. In the Arctic seas, as at Spitzbergen, they even launch their gigantic crystalline masses into the waves of ocean (Fig. 240).

These icy plains, sometimes formed of obtuse and nodulated blocks, sometimes bristling with immense crystals, the azure of which contrasts with the dead white of the snow when they are heaped up in the mountain gorges, appear to our eyes like oceans, the waves of which have been solidified by magic, in the midst of their most frightful commotions, and destined to eternal immobility. They are really seas of ice, six to eight leagues long, which climb the valleys and clear the elevated passes of mountains in order to cross from one side of a mountain chain to the other. Frequently vast blue and diaphanous grottoes open at their bases, from which spring fountains, which soon become impetuous streams or rivers.

During fine nights, when the silvery gleams of the moon light up the glaciers which wind along the gorges of the Alps, these resemble long and imposing opal shrouds spread silently over the mountain sides, while their numerous crystals here and there sparkle pale and luminous.

240. Glaciers in the Bay of the Magdalen, Spitzbergen.

Notwithstanding their apparent immobility, these *seas of ice*, as they are called, possess a very decided movement of their own, the force of which no power can stop. They constantly tend towards the base of the valleys, where the milder temperature transforms their mass into the water which forms our river-sources.

The first geologists who announced that glaciers move like rivers, though much more slowly, found their views very ill received by their colleagues.

However, this phenomenon had been suspected ever since it had been noticed that a small stone hut, situated on the side of the Lower Aar Glacier, in the Upper Alps, had descended towards the valley.

Desirous of clearing up this mystery, Agassiz had the courage to go thither, and for two years to confine himself to a residence on this glacier in a hut sheltered by a fragment of rock—a rude abode which, since the sojourn there of the illustrious naturalist, has enjoyed a certain celebrity, and which is now known only as the Hôtel of the Neufchatelese. What a hôtel! A room excavated in the ice, and a bed of stone covered with a mattress of hay!

Soon after he had been installed in this frightful desert Agassiz discovered the hut we have spoken of; it had descended about 4930 feet in thirteen years, showing that the annual movement of the glacier was about 380 feet.

But notwithstanding their aspect of grandeur and terror, notwithstanding the too frequent sacrifice of life they occasion, what are the glaciers of the Alps in appearance and extent when compared to the congealed deserts of the polar regions, as for instance the glaciers of Spitzbergen, and especially the Humboldt Glacier, which presents to the traveller an impenetrable barrier twenty-five leagues in length?

In one or two days' travel we cross the most redoubtable glaciers of the Alps; we pass the Col du Géant, or we climb Mont Blanc. But in fact, despite the majestic splendour of their cold realms and charming passes, the picture of their perils and their extent is diminished in effect when they are contrasted with the horrible solitudes of the boreal regions, where navigators have wintered several seasons inclosed by bergs or mountains of ice, and where they have sometimes traversed three or four hundred leagues of frozen sea.

For long a sombre and seemingly impenetrable mystery veiled from us everything that happened in these latitudes, and all that men knew of them was derived from the mournful and obscure legends of superstitious whalers, until a painful accident directed to these regions the attention of the civilized world.

Towards the commencement of this century it was supposed that the north of America, long considered as a land that prolonged itself over the pole, was perhaps occupied by a sea which might permit a passage from Europe to Asia by a shorter route.

Two intrepid navigators, Parry and Ross, had in the course of their celebrated voyages in vain braved tempests and wintered in the midst of ices in order to seek out this passage.

But after their attempts, a final expedition, commanded by Sir John Franklin, already known for his arctic explorations, not having returned, all the European nations were seized with a strong desire to find some traces of the noble-minded navigator, and it was during the expeditions fitted out everywhere for this purpose that the passage round the north of America was discovered by Captain M'Clure. Being a man of great resolution he exclaimed at starting, "I will discover Franklin or the passage;" and he kept one of his two promises.

Men had dreamed of the existence of a polar sea, but it was thought to be completely blocked with eternal ice. Captain Parry, when he started from Spitzbergen with sledges, promised himself that he would reach the pole and plant the flag of Great Britain upon the axis of the globe. But in proportion as the expedition advanced towards the north over the frozen sea, he found to his great astonishment more and more openings in the ice which were not frozen over, and it became necessary to return, as they were equipped for travelling on the ice, not for navigating an ocean.

In course of the researches made in the north of America with the view of discovering the remains of Franklin's companions, it was found out that this region is formed solely of a congeries of large and small islands, separated by tortuous channels. The voyages undertaken for this purpose have revealed a host of surprising facts, and among others the existence of an immense and furious sea, the waves of which extend over all the pole, till then believed to be only an icy desert.

All navigators have drawn striking pictures of the polar latitudes. Though sometimes on all sides only a luminous sea was to be seen, over which rose fairy and splendid colonnades of ice, letting their rigid stalactites droop on all sides, more frequently islands of ice, driven by the violence of tempests, seem, every instant, on the point of engulfing the vessels, or of inclosing them within their prodigious masses.[1] Then we

[1] *Breaking up of an iceberg.*—"We have just witnessed what was for the moment a perfect cataract of ice, with all its motion, and many times its noise. Quick as lightning and loud as thunder, when bolt and thunder come at the same instant, there was one terrific crack, a sharp and silvery ringing blow upon the atmosphere, which I shall never

241. A Chain of Icebergs in the Polar Regions.

have, besides, the monotonous descriptions of those long and trying winters passed amid darkness and snow, under latitudes where man has to struggle on all sides against a cold which freezes mercury. Here the sole event which sometimes breaks in upon the uniformity of life is the visit of some Esquimaux tribe, men of iron who alone resist this frightful climate, and who, incredible as it may seem, prefer it to happier countries. Their appalling nights, six months long, their huts of snow, their dresses of skins, which give them the look of beasts, have more charms for them than all the sweets of civilization, and all the benefits of a sun which daily ripens rich harvests.

It was one of the boldest explorers of these boreal regions that discovered the waves of the new ocean beyond the barrier of ice which bars the path to the pole against our vessels.

Instead of finding, as he advanced towards the pole, a more and more rigorous climate, Captain Morton beheld the bloom of a new spring, and life, instead of becoming extinct, appeared to revive. The boreal flora became richer, and at the same time immense flocks of ducks, sea-gulls and other birds plunged into the waves or sported upon the shores. But very soon after, the indefatigable traveller, vanquished by obstacles and exhausted by so many fatigues, yet transported with the view of the sombre polar sea which he had just discovered, with a failing hand planted his flag upon a cape which had never been reached by the foot of man; and then, pale and wearied, saluted that ocean which no vessel had yet ploughed, and after a few hours of repose commenced the arduous task of returning.

forget nor ever be able to describe. The spectacle was nearly as startling as the explosion. At once the upper face of the berg burst out upon the air as if it had been blasted, and swept down across the great cliff a huge cataract of green and snowy fragments, with a wild crashing roar, followed by the heavy sullen thunder of the plunge into the ocean, and the rolling away of the high-crested seas, and the rocking of the mighty mass back and forth, in the effort to regain its equilibrium."—*After Icebergs with a Painter.* By the Rev. L. L. Noble.—Tr.

BOOK VI.

CAVERNS AND GROTTOES.

The upheaval of large mountain chains frequently produces deep and winding caverns in their sides. In some places there are really so many of these that the interior seems to be only a succession of vast galleries, so rugged and profound that the boldest man dare not attempt to traverse them. This state of things is seen in the cavernous Alps of Carniola, which present a considerable number of water-courses in their recesses; indeed these seem to be more numerous in the bowels of the mountains than on the surface of the ground.

Some of these subterranean rivers are known to run several leagues. They even nourish peculiar animals which never see the light, as for instance the Proteus, a singular animal provided with both lungs and branchiæ, which thus appears to combine all the attributes of an amphibious being.

Among the numerous grottoes which have been explored there is one, that of Antiparos [not far from Trieste], which has become celebrated, not from its extent, but on account of the excursion which Tournefort made to it during his eastern travels. The entrance to it is narrow, and the descent is effected by means of a rope-ladder. "When we arrive at the bottom," says the celebrated botanist, "we have to creep some time among the rocks, sometimes on one's back, sometimes on one's face, and after all this fatigue we at last reach this celebrated grotto." It only presents an extent of 900 feet in length and a width of 150; but on every side the marble forms clustered pillars, is twisted into columns like the trunks of trees, or hangs in numerous stalactites which awaken every one's admiration. These varied forms astonished Tournefort, and the view of them recalled his favourite hypothesis, the dissemination of life. "It seems," he said, "as if these marble trunks vegetate." And further on, perceiving the altar with its beautiful flutings of dazzling whiteness, he exclaimed, "This pyramid is perhaps the most beautiful marble plant in the world!" It was the error of a great genius.

Although this celebrated grotto is very small, the Marquis of Nointel, one of our ambassadors to the Sublime Porte, took the fancy of celebrating midnight mass there on Christmas eve. He descended into the grotto accompanied by a great number of persons of his suite, of merchants and pirates, and then had 100 torches of yellow wax and 400 lamps lighted up, which illuminated all the interior. At the moment of the holy sacrifice of the mass, fireworks and cannon, arranged at the entrance to the grotto, aroused the echoes with their detonations, whilst the

242. Proteus of the Subterranean Rivers of Carniola—*Proteus anguinus* (Laurenti).

trumpets sounded. This being over, the Marquis of Nointel did not end there; he wished to sleep in the famous grotto to which he had taken such a fancy, and there he slept.

Another cavern, the Mammoth Cave of Kentucky in the United States, owes its renown not to the celebrity of those who have visited it, but to its extent, which is perhaps greater than that of any other existing cave.

Although imperfectly known up to the present time, it has been found possible to penetrate about ten leagues into it. The entrance is narrow and low, but after progressing for a few minutes by torch-light through a subterranean passage, the scene changes, and views of the most grand and varied kind unfold themselves. On one side is seen the magical splendour of stalactite halls decorated with pillars twisted in a thousand shapes, and fantastic statues draped in their crystal mantles; on another are seen regular churches formed of precious stones, gleaming with different coloured lights, the splendour of which dazzles the traveller.

In this obscure labyrinth every spot has its historical name. One is

243. Cyprinodons of the Mammoth Cave.

called the Chamber of the Spirits, or haunted chamber, thus called because it was found strewed with mummies of Indians, most probably from the people who of old inhabited this part of America. In another place a still more striking scene presents itself, for we arrive beneath the Dome of the Giant, the immensity of which strikes one with stupor. Enveloped in profound darkness, notwithstanding the great fires lighted by the guides, the eye of the explorer cannot make out the cupola suspended at a height of about 430 feet above his head.

At some depth below, the Styx slowly rolls its sad waters beneath

244. The Styx, a Subterranean River in the Mammoth Cave of Kentucky.

dark vaults, the windings of which are indented by a thousand rocks. In this subterranean river, the course of which we follow in a boat, dwells a very peculiar fish, the Cyprinodon, which is said to be blind, and which, in fact, ought to be so, for what purpose could eyes serve in the midst of waves where the most perfect darkness reigns!

Further on, in this immense Mammoth Grotto filled with rivers, cataracts, and subterranean lakes, the traveller is astonished to find himself beside a large sheet of water on which glide slowly a few boats, the dull

245. Dead Sea in the Mammoth Cave of Kentucky.

glare of their torches being lost in the obscurity of the distance without lighting up the banks and projecting rocks.[1] This dark and calm mass of water is called the Dead Sea.

[1] The Mammoth Cave is always an object of great curiosity with the Americans. They go there in crowds, and there is not always accommodation to be found in the great hôtel intended to receive the tourists, although it is arranged for 300 guests. The exploration requires five or six days, and an army of guides is always kept ready for the service of travellers.

Each site in this celebrated cave bears a picturesque name. There is the Starry Cavern, dazzling with stalactites; the Chamber of the Spirits, formerly encumbered with Indian mummies, which by an act of profanation has become a species of refreshment-room, where

As happens in many of the cavernous openings in the globe there are in the Mammoth Cave certain abysses which seem bottomless. The guides throw down ignited substances, which are seen to descend for an extraordinarily long time, whirling round and round, and at last, to the great surprise of travellers, become extinguished on their obscure journey before they reach the bottom.

Other cavities of only very small extent attract the attention of naturalists much more than those of which we have spoken. These are the bone-caves, in which we find heaps of bones of carnivora, principally bears and hyenas, which lived at an epoch very near our own, and the numbers of which in such places we cannot very well explain. It is, however, probable that they were brought thither by currents of water. Sometimes, too, we find mixed with them traces of the handicraft of the most ancient human races, and sometimes human crania.

But the difficulties presented by the exploration of grottoes and mines, the desert nature of the country where their mouths open, and the ignorance of the rude inhabitants of the mountains have always kept us from seeing a great part of the treasures scattered in the ground. On the other hand, those inflammable gases which by their frightful ravages carry desolation into mines; those poisonous vapours, those *spiritus lethales*, as Pliny calls them, which instantly destroy life and extinguish a torch, were they not calculated to freeze with horror those who should dare to penetrate into the abysses of the mountains?

Superstitious alarms also long hindered men from gathering the mineral riches which the bosom of the earth incloses. As they are principally found in countries which have been the theatre of the most violent convulsions, it was with unmixed terror that men approached the wild and gloomy spots where they lay stored up; and sometimes gross credulity spread the belief that they were guarded by dragons, jealous of the suprem-

the wives of the guides supply liquors and newspapers to those travellers who are already fatigued with the subterranean journey and glad to make a short halt. There is also a kind of hospital here, where some medical men keep patients afflicted with chest affections, thinking the sulphureous atmosphere of these caverns would be favourable to them. In the centre of this hall an almost entire skeleton of a mastodon has been set up. It is also at this part of the Mammoth Cave that the wives of the guides show and sell to those who care for such things, the extraordinary little blind fish, the Cyprinodons, which are caught in the water-courses of these immense caverns.

Further on is seen the Devil's Arm-chair, which, like a gigantic crystallization, rears itself all gleaming on the brink of a dark bottomless abyss. Besides the Styx and the Dead Sea, these caverns, in which underground windings 20 to 25 miles in length are known, possess other bodies of water. Up to the present time 226 avenues have been made out, besides 57 domes, 11 lakes, 7 rivers, 8 cataracts, and 32 abysses, some of which are of an immense depth.

acy of their dark domains. To these all the accidents which happened to miners were attributed: at the moment when the fire-damp exploded, it was said that they were seen in the shape of horses, with fiery manes, passing through the ruins and the fire.

Pacific spirits, however, everywhere effaced the work of these evil genii; this was a rooted belief in all the mining districts, brutalized by isolation and the most degrading superstition. The venerable father of mineralogy, Agricola, influenced himself by the legends of the workmen, in his celebrated work describes these spirits as minutely as if he had held them in his hand; not a detail of form or dress is wanting.

The belief was a last ray of the antique philosophy which held that every particle of created matter was animated by invisible intelligence, and possessed sensibility and a spirit of harmony.

According to the believers in the Cabala, there existed innumerable legions of gnomes, which were scattered through the bowels of the earth. The humble German miner believed there were elves (Kobolds) hidden in every nook and corner of the caverns, working silently and spreading everywhere activity and life; pigmies of the mountains dressed like miners, whose instinctive foresight enabled them to forge metals, to heap up precious stones in veins, and also to collect mysteriously in the darkness those singular petrifactions which were one day to reveal to us unknown worlds. Although they loved him greatly, these Kobolds fled before the approach of man. They had been rarely seen, but every happy event in the ancient mines was attributed to them.[1]

[1] Schleiden took a far bolder flight than Agricola had done. The old mineralogist of Suabia had only described the genii of earth, Schleiden represented them at work. In his work on *The Plant* (*La Plante*) there is a beautiful engraving representing little gnomes laboriously occupied in laying bare all the riches of earth. Some hew the rock in order to withdraw large trunks of fossilized trees; others collect or solder together the torn fragments. Each gnome or Kobold appears under the form of a little laborious and decrepit miner. The back-ground of the picture is occupied by a cascade which bounds and foams among the rocks.—Schleiden, *La Plante*, pl. 13.

BOOK VII.

STEPPES AND DESERTS.

"Let him," says Humboldt, "who wishes to escape from the storms of life, follow me into the depths of the forests, across the deserts, or over the lofty summits of the Andes."

The illustrious philosopher was right, for face to face with these great scenes of nature, man feels his passions and sorrows die out, and contemplation absorbs all his being. St. Bernard felt this deeply when he said to his disciples, "Believe my experience of it; you will find in our forests something more choice than in books; the trees and rocks will yield lessons preferable to those of the ablest masters."

The vast solitudes of nature themselves present their harmonies and contrasts. Sometimes the deserts only represent a sea of sand, calm and boundless like that of Libya, which fills the mind with a sense of infinitude. Sometimes, as in the steppes of America and Asia, they are covered with a carpet of verdure. Lastly, other deserts, as we see in the Arabian chain, are wholly composed of a stony and rugged soil like the arid surface of a planet waiting for the creation of organic life.

A desert of sand possesses a tranquil beauty; a desert of stone is horrible. In the former the horizon develops itself before our eyes, it is accessible and on the confines of it are liberty and repose. In the other the horizon seems impassable, death separates us from it, it is a disordered mass of rocks, burned by the sun, irregular and rugged; there is no practicable road, and it is easy to imagine that a few hours' stay in such a frightful place would prove fatal to the most robust traveller. The frightful aspect of such a desert cannot be better compared than to that which the old engravers gave of the sea in a tempest. It was thus that the desert of Assouan on the borders of Nubia looked to us.[1]

[1] About 100 miles south of Assouan occurs the remarkable desert of Korosko. For the space of two days' journey southwards from the town of Korosko (lat. 22° 35′ N.) the desert is covered with remarkable conical hills, among which winds the path of the traveller. On

And yet in arid deserts an oasis here and there, rich in shade and coolness, rejoices the heart of the Arab, for it is here that he quenches his thirst and rests his caravan. Poetry, usurping the place of truth, has generally promulgated the belief that these spots only consist of a group of palm-trees, protecting with their foliage some limpid desert spring, where the camels slake their thirst on their halt. But these healthful stations, scattered over the sand, to use the expression of Ptolemy, like the black spots on the yellow hide of the panther, are sometimes large spaces, abundantly supplied with springs and sheltered by a vigorous vegetation. In the Sahara there are even some which

246. The Great Desert of Korosko.—Tremaux, Soudan Oriental.

form small but populous kingdoms, and which the caravans take several days to cross.

When reviewing the steppes, those living deserts, other pictures unfold themselves to our gaze. In them we see diversity of vegetation sharply defined, so that we might fancy each zone had at first its own

the slopes of these hills lie moving sands, liable to be displaced by every storm; the winds disperse them generally on the slopes opposed to their course. These hills are formed of a quartzose sandstone. They are not due to upheavals or convulsions of the earth's crust, but are formed by horizontal irregular strata of different density, some only slightly knit, but others united by argillaceous-ferruginous cement, and more capable of resisting the destructive effects of the atmosphere. The upper layers are those that seem less hard, but none of them are very homogeneous. From this geological formation there result the most picturesque effects: the sands are driven along the bottom of the valleys, which they fill up horizontally to a certain height, leaving exposed only the tops of the hills.—*Imperial Gazetteer.*—Tr.

special sheet of verdure. As Humboldt says, "The history of the vegetable envelope of our planet, and of its gradual propagation over the naked surface of the earth, has its epochs, like the most ancient history of the human race."

In some places we find steppes which display only an attempt at vegetable life; extending over immense spaces and losing themselves in a boundless horizon, they open out before the eye like the ocean, but without offering the charm of the perpetual movement of its waves. All is sadness.

In other regions these great spaces, the surface of which is only slightly irregular, are covered with a perfectly uniform vegetation; one species rules there despotically and stifles all the others. Such is the spectacle presented by the Landes of Bordeaux, exclusively pervaded by heath, which at the time of flowering waves gently like a sea of purple, whose waves agitated by the breeze melt away in the azure of the distant horizon.

Struck by the monotony of their steppes, thickly overgrown by the humblest plants, the Mongols named them the *land of grass.* But it is particularly in America, where they bear the name of *pampas*, that they dismay the traveller by their immense extent and often by their impenetrable nature. There, according to Humboldt, exist some which occupy a space of 16,000 square leagues.

Grasses and leguminous plants cover the surface as far as the eye can see. In other places the steppe bristles with tall thistles, which form impenetrable spiny barriers.

The steppes of Southern America, being covered with a light clothing of plants, and being periodically inundated by torrents of rain, often present a luxuriant growth of grasses. These solitudes are at such times traversed by legions of animals, which there find water and an ample supply of nourishment.

But the scene changes so soon as the drought sets in. Then death and aridity appear everywhere. The tropical heat allows only a very ephemeral duration for this luxuriant vegetation. When the heat of the sun is no longer tempered by the rains, and when he darts his vertical rays upon the steppe, the marshes are soon dried up, all the plants wither and turn to dust, and a sea of ashes succeeds to an ocean of verdure. The extreme heat stupifies the crocodile and the boa-constrictor; like the hybernating animals of the polar regions, they sink into the mud and remain there motionless till the return of the rains. All the animals express their sufferings by deep groans, a few only understand how to quench their thirst with the succulent stems of certain Cacti, the spiny armour of which tears their mouths and makes them bleed.[1]

When this consuming drought has wasted or burned up the steppe, the torrid heat kills numbers of wild animals which can find no place to slake their thirst, and their corpses strew the ground in thousands. Night brings no relief to such sufferings. Frightful bats attack the exhausted animals, and like the vampires of the old German legends

247. Travellers attacked by Vampires.

suck their blood, only that they assail living flesh and blood instead of betaking themselves to the corpses in the graveyards. Man himself

[1] "The mules," says Humboldt, "more circumspect and wily, endeavour to satisfy their thirst in another manner. A plant of spherical form and bearing numerous flutings, the Melocactus, contains a very watery pulp under a spiny envelope; the mule, by means of its fore-feet, separates the spines, puts down its mouth carefully, and ventures to drink the refreshing juice. But it cannot always drink at this living vegetable spring without danger. Animals are often seen which have been lamed in the hoof by the spines of the cactus.

"To the burning heat of day succeeds the freshness of the night, which equals the day in duration; but the cattle and horses cannot even then enjoy repose. During their sleep is not safe from their voracity. When some traveller overtaken by night falls asleep in the open air, he wakes in the morning greatly exhausted, scarcely able to stand upright, and finds one of his feet in a pool of blood. This is the work of the vampires, as they are called, which have assailed

248. The American Vampire—*Vampirus spectrum* (Linnæus).

him during the night with so much skill and precaution that he has not been even awakened by their punctures.[1]

monstrous bats fasten like vampires on their backs, suck their blood, and occasion purulent sores, in which horse-flies, mosquitoes, and a host of other stinging insects establish themselves. Such is the painful life of these animals so soon as ever the heat of the sun has made the water disappear from the face of the earth."—Humboldt, *Tableaux de la Nature*, b. i. s. 39.

[1] It is really from their habit of sucking the blood of animals that naturalists have given them the name of vampire. La Condamine asserts that they exhausted and destroyed the earliest troops of cattle and sheep which were imported into some regions of America. Man himself is not safe from the attacks of these bats. The traveller Azara was several times bitten when sleeping without shelter. The wound is like that of a leech, and is not perceived till waking, when the feebleness which results is felt and the blood is seen all round.

After the sufferings occasioned by the heat, the dangers of inundation ensue. Some steppes in America are then totally submerged by the overflowing of the rivers, and only look like a vast sea which threatens the animals with imminent death. Some seek a refuge and gather in groups on the heights. Many are drowned; others are attacked and devoured by the crocodiles, which have now regained all their vigour. A redoubtable eel, the *Gymnotus electricus*, adds to the dangers run by the mammals, the shocks it gives being powerful enough to kill even horses.[1]

The aspect of the desert is more monotonous. With the exception of the oases which it displays here and there it is, in Africa, completely arid. In one of the deserts of Upper Egypt, situated between the Nile and the Red Sea, the eye only perceives an unbroken sheet of burning sand. And yet upon its borders I found, to my great surprise, braving the heat of the sun and never refreshed by a single drop of water, numerous tufts of an asclepiad (*Asclepias procera*, Willd.), the large, moist and velvety leaves of which glistened with freshness. It was an inexplicable problem!

But this last effort of life soon disappears, and we see before us only an ocean of sand and a horizon of death. Not a cry, not a murmur is heard, and scarce even a loitering vulture devours the last fragments of some camel which has fallen on the sand, and the bleached skeleton of which will soon be added to so many others now marking out the desert routes. Not a cloud tarnishes the azure of the sky, not a breath refreshes the air; a sun, the ardour of which nothing moderates, pours down its sparkling light and fiery rays, burning even through one's clothes. The motionless and heated atmosphere tortures the face with its fiery breath, and even the sand attains an extreme heat; my thermometers being broken I tried to ascertain the temperature by plunging my hands into the superficial layers, but at the end of a few seconds a stinging pain compelled me to withdraw them. The soil also, by reflecting the solar rays from the spark-

[1] Humboldt says that it is not only the crocodiles and jaguars that lay snares for the horse. This animal has also a formidable enemy among the fish. The marshy waters of Bera and Rastro are filled with electric eels, the slimy bodies of which, covered with yellow spots, spontaneously emit violent shocks in every direction. These Gymnoti (the name they are known by in science) are five to six feet long; they are strong enough to kill the most robust animals when they put in action all their organs, armed as they are with an apparatus of numerous nerves, at the same time and in a suitable direction. At Uritucu it had become necessary to change the road across the steppe owing to the eels having so increased in a little river, that every year many horses, struck with paralysis, were drowned in passing the ford. All the fish fly before the approach of these formidable eels. They even assail unawares men fishing with a rod, the moistened line often forming a medium for communicating the fatal shock. In this case the electric fluid is discharged even from the bottom of the water.—Humboldt, *Tableaux de la Nature*, t. i. p. 45.

ling fragments of mica and quartz, sometimes becomes insupportably dazzling to the eye.

Instead of the rolling waves and cool breezes of the sea, this funereal region only gives out burning gusts, scorching blasts which seem to issue from the gates of hell; these are the *simoom* or poison-wind, as the word signifies in Arab. The camel driver knows this formidable enemy, and so soon as he sees it looming in the horizon, he raises his hands to heaven and implores Allah; the camels themselves seem terrified at its approach. A veil of reddish black invades the gleaming sky, and very soon a terrible and burning wind rises, bearing clouds of fine impalpable sand, which severely irritates the eyes and makes its way into the respiratory organs.

The camels squat down and refuse to move, and the travellers have no chance of safety except by making a rampart of the bodies of their beasts, and covering their heads so as to protect themselves against this scourge. Entire caravans have sometimes perished in these sand-storms; it was one of them that buried the army of Cambyses when it was traversing the desert.

Maxime du Camp, in his charming work on the Nile, describes in the following terms one of these desert tempests, to the least violent of which the name *khamsin* is given in Egypt: "It comes towards one," he says, "growing, spreading, and advancing as if on wheels. Its overhanging summit is of a brick colour, its base deep red and almost black. In proportion as it approaches it drives before it burning effluvia, like the breath of a lime-kiln. Before it reaches us we are covered with its shadow. The sound it makes is like that of a wind passing through a pine-forest. So soon as we are in the midst of this hurricane the camels halt, turn their backs, throw themselves down, and lay their heads upon the sand. After the cloud of dust comes a rain of imperceptible stones, violently hurled about by the wind, and which, if it lasted long, would quickly flay the skin from those parts of the body unprotected by the clothes. This lasted five or six minutes, and was frightful. Then the sky became clear again, and gave the same feeling of sudden change to the eye as a light suddenly brought into a dark place."

It is in the sand deserts that the phenomenon of the mirage takes place most frequently. I was enabled to see it once in all its splendour.

The captain or reis of our escort had asked leave to stay at a part of the Nile where stood one of his harems, in order to pass the day there with his wives and family. I say one, for he had several, ingeniously established along the river, the scene of the continual voyages which he made. He stopped by successive stages at each of his establishments, in such a way as not to excite the jealousy of any of the sultanas whom he maintained.

I had profited by this halt to make an excursion into the desert, and

249. The Mirage in the Desert.

had started when the reis, seeing me in the distance, came with some Arabs of his tribe to beg I would accept the hospitality of his roof. In the East, to refuse such an offer would be almost an offence, so I turned towards the oasis which he inhabited. It was a delicious hamlet, crowned with date-trees, and the entrance to it was picturesquely decorated with some tombs of a most charming appearance.

After the frugal repast of dates and milk which was offered me, I plunged into the desert, and I was already at a distance when the idea came into my head to salute this hospitable abode for the last time. But everything was transformed. The picturesque village seemed enveloped in a magnificent sheet of the most transparent waters, in which the dwellings, palm-trees, and tombs were reflected in a marvellous manner. The phenomenon was produced with such exactness, and the sheet of water was so beautiful and limpid, that if I had not a few minutes previously traversed the spot which it occupied on the burning sand, I should have thought it real. Such is the mirage, which so often and so painfully deceived our worn-out soldiers when they traversed these very regions. Exhausted with fatigue and dying of thirst, they thought they saw in the distance the water they longed for so much, while it was only a bitter delusion!

Yet other phenomena engage the view of those who traverse the deserts of Africa. Among these is the rising of the sun, the splendour of which, as Byron says, is without equal!

After traversing the great cataract of the Nile, we resolved to rest for a few days in the island of Philæ, situated at the entrance into Nubia. So soon as we had anchored our boats on the east shore of the sacred island, crowded as it is with religious monuments, we set to work to erect our tent on the platform of one of the great gate-towers or pylones of the temple of Isis. It so happened that there was at this place a complete gathering of scientific men: M. Grimaux, my friend and travelling companion, whom Rouen numbers among her chosen men of eminence; Captain Tuifort, who commanded the advanced guard in the expedition to the sources of the Nile which we had just rejoined, and my sons Georges and James Pouchet, the one naturalist to the expedition, the other an engineer on the Suez Canal. There, each evening, plunged in melancholy meditation, and tranquilly reclining on the ancient balustrade of the building, I watched the setting of the sun as it sank behind rocks as black as ebony; and there also, having slept under the open sky, I rose so soon as the first gleams of day began to disperse the night, in order to seat myself upon the lofty parapet of the great gate-tower, in order to enjoy the indescribable spectacle of the dawn.

The setting of the sun is each day the same uniform spectacle. Rolling through a sky of which its rays have absorbed all the vapours, it plunges into the sea of sand like an immense globe of fire hung in a burning horizon. After its disappearance, the blazing luminary only

250. Island of Philæ, or the Sacred Island, Nubia.

leaves a fiery hue, which extends over an immense portion of the distant plain. If at this time a caravan happen to pass the desert on the west of us, the men and camels are clearly defined against the reddish tint of the sky like so many animated silhouettes of an intense blackness; they might be taken for some of the well-known Chinese shadows. Then all at once the night comes on, for the twilight in these burning zones is only of short duration.

The dawn on the contrary is infinitely varied, and presents by turns the most majestic spectacle one can imagine. The freshness of night has condensed all the vapours on the surface of the desert, and the lamp of day which lights us has first of all to disperse the thick veil of mist ere it can appear in all its splendour.

In our foggy country night fades away in tranquil majesty. When dawn begins to appear behind the forest or the icy diadem of the mountain, the first gleams of day scarcely illume the pale azure of the sky. And if we were permitted to see our pale Aurora athwart the last folds of the tunic of Morpheus, she would appear with that fresh and pleasing countenance which ancient poesy gave her.

But in the East, that palace of light, this phenomenon shows itself in forms as varied as they are marvellous; the richness of our most fairy-like decorations is left behind by reality. When the paling splendour of the constellations announces the advent of day, the region where the sun is soon to launch himself into the heavens is covered with an immense and thick black curtain. In a short time this sombre veil of clouds is irregularly rent, as if, in their aërial dances, the joyous sylphs had torn it here and there in order to discover to us the dazzling fire on the horizon. Then the Nubian Aurora appears, looking as if she had issued from the furnaces of Etna. She is no longer the fresh and timid goddess whose tears distil in transparent pearls on our morning flowers, but an intoxicated bacchante, with burning eye and purple visage, whose black tresses float loosely over the azure vault, and who with fingers of fire opens the blazing gates of the East. Then sparkling corruscations are shot from every fragment of night's mantle, which breaks up in all directions; whilst the festoons on high allow us to catch a glimpse between them of celestial vistas of sapphire and opal.

BOOK VIII

THE AIR AND ITS CORPUSCULES.

The aërial ocean which envelops the earth is from fifteen to sixteen leagues high. It is the medium for diffusing animation and life, and its disappearance would be immediately followed by a general destruction of animals and plants, and the silence of death.

The vital principle of the air, or oxygen, enters into its composition to the extent of $\frac{21}{100}$. It has been generally thought that this element is found in the same proportion over the whole surface of the globe. According to M. Martins, the air of the Faulhorn, one of the highest mountains in Switzerland, yields the same percentage of oxygen as that of Paris.

Paradoxes have always had a certain success. Some chemists have maintained that the air in hospitals, drains, and even the foulest places, maintains all its purity.[1] Notwithstanding these different assertions, as a great deal of oxygen is consumed in populous cities, whilst plants are continually pouring it out into the atmosphere, it seemed *a priori* as if we ought to find more respirable gas in the air of the country than in that of towns. Experience began by invalidating this view; then it was found that the respirable gas is nevertheless a little more rare in the latter than in the midst of the fields. M. Houzeau, one of our most able chemists, in some experiments carried on upon a large scale, found that oxygen is really a little more abundant in the depths of forests, which distil it incessantly from every pore of their leaves, than in our towns, where a hundred thousand mouths absorb and consume it.

This is what we know for certain relative to the chemical composition of the air; let us now speak of its microscopy, so easy to study, and which has yet given rise to so many puerile fables.

The ancient theogonies, full of mystery and poesy, peopled space

[1] In a prize memoir of a provincial academy Julia Fontenelle has maintained that the air of hospitals, and even of sewers, is as pure as that of our fields.

with an infinity of invisible and charming divinities, who animated every part of creation. The gnomes were scattered in the depths of the earth, the fire had its salamanders, the naïads sported beneath the crystal waters, and the sylphs, light and diaphanous as the plains of air, everywhere lent life to the atmosphere in the long and graceful gyrations of their dances.

Modern philosophers, without being more precise than antiquity, have been less happy. Instead of sylphs, they have filled, nay, surcharged the air with an incalculable quantity of germs, always ready to shed everywhere fecundity and life. Fiction for fiction, we like that of our predecessors better; it is much more attractive, and, moreover, much less crude.

By means of these germs disseminated in every part, and entering by myriads wherever the vehicle in which they live finds access, the learned of the eighteenth century explained the appearance of those innumerable swarms of microscopic animals or plants which inevitably attack all created things given up to putrid disorganization.

Nothing could evade their terrible inroads. The wonderful minuteness of these destructive agents allowed them to clear all obstacles, and to insinuate themselves into the most sheltered cavities! Human intelligence was quite at fault in attempting to penetrate into the secret of their transmission through the most compact tissues of animals and plants.

In order the better to prop up their systems, at an epoch when the talent of the orator was often substituted for real learning, some of the philosophers attributed most paradoxical properties to these germs. It was as much as glass could do to stay their invasion, or the hottest furnace to consume them. Nothing arrested Bonnet on the subject of these germs: he believed that they resisted the most destructive chemical agents; and even maintained that by means of a circulation which was more than marvellous, they penetrated the entire economy of animated beings.[1]

[1] "Every organized body," says Bonnet, "presents itself to me under the image of a little earth, where I perceive in miniature all the species of plants and animals which are found on a large scale on our globe. An oak appears to me composed of plants, insects, shells, reptiles, fish, birds, quadrupeds, and even men. I see innumerable germs rise into the roots with the juices designed for their nutrition. I see them circulate in the different vessels and lodge in the thickness of their membranes in order to augment their growth in every direction."

Who would believe then that such a science found supporters in the nineteenth century? Yet this has taken place. M. Le Vicomte Gaston d'Auvray, in order to save from shipwreck the old doctrine of panspermism, and the theories of M. Pasteur, has assumed that there exist in the air myriads of eggs and spores, the vitality of which resists boiling for eight hours and even a white heat.

The supporters of the unlimited dissemination hypothesis did not stop here: one absurdity brings others in its wake. Some of them, falling back into the conceptions of the hermetic philosophy, constituted these germs imperishable metaphysical entities, descended according to them from the Mosaic creation, capable of traversing ages and cataclysms, and arriving at our epoch full of fecundity and life.

All this was the result of one false idea; for if the air were filled with all the generative elements which would be necessary to its part of universal dissemination, it would be so thick that we could not move about in it, and we should be plunged in the most profound darkness. In fact, if some globules of the vapour of water are sufficient to produce thick and choking fogs, which as at London often force us to have recourse to links in mid-day, what would the atmosphere be if it were loaded with eggs and seeds?

The name of *panspermism* has been given to this pretended universal dissemination of the reproductive bodies of animals and plants. But this perfectly gratuitous hypothesis falls so soon as it is submitted to the criterion of observation.

There are plants which only appear under circumstances so exceptional and so extraordinary, that the mind revolts at the idea of their tiny seed loading the atmosphere for century after century in order at long intervals to fertilize some imperceptible part of the globe. This would be inutility in immensity.

A fungus is known which never grows except on the bodies of dead spiders; another only appears on the surface of horses' hoofs in a state of putrefaction. One little parasite of the same family, the Isaria of the sphinx, has hitherto only been observed on certain nocturnal moths. The chrysalides and larvæ of these are never attacked by it; other species infest them. Unless one possessed the imagination of a Bonnet, is it possible to suppose that nature would uselessly have burdened the air of the whole globe for the mere purpose of scattering seed on the bodies of a few spiders and moths; and that there was always a stock ready for the perfect insect, its chrysalis, and its larva?

Still more curious facts are known; for instance that of a fungus never found but on the neck of a caterpillar of tropical countries. It is always solitary on this, and of enormous size in proportion, being often four to five inches high. In this fortuitous case is the air necessarily choked with seeds in order that from time to time one may be planted on a particular spot not more than a square millimetre (·00155 sq. inch) in extent?

As a particular vegetation is present in every form of fermentation,

251. The New Zealand Swift-moth (*Hepialus virescens*) and its Larva; the latter with a Fungus (*Cordiceps Robertsii*) growing on it and rooted by it in the Soil.

its germs, according to the panspermists, must have floated loose in the atmosphere from creation up to the time when any new fermented liquor was discovered. Did they rest so many ages unoccupied, awaiting the moment when Osiris invented beer? And even now does the atmosphere, loaded with these little seeds, drift them from pole to pole till the Greenlander or Patagonian sets to work to brew a few quarts of this drink, or till it can fecundate the new ferments which each chemist may invent in the silence of his laboratory?

If it really were so, we might groan over the fate of the atmosphere!

Again, botanists are acquainted with a peculiar plant, the *Racodium cellare*, which has never been found except on the casks in our cellars. Where did the germs dwell before these were invented, during the long ages when our forefathers only employed amphoræ?

Bérard, a physiologist of the faculty of medicine, even speaks of a plant which only lives on the drops of tallow which the miners in working let fall upon the soil. Were the seeds of this singular species produced

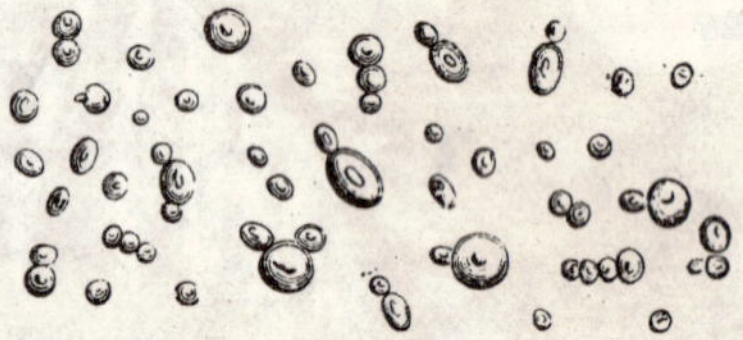

252. Spontaneously formed Microscopic Grains which are found in Fermentations—*Cryptococcus cerevisiæ* (Auct.)

then at creation, in anticipation that mines would be worked by the aid of our common means of lighting!

Lastly, do not all botanists know that every sick or dying plant is certain to be attacked by its special parasite? There is no explaining the introduction of the seedlets of this fatal guest, and we may say that there are as many varieties as there are species of plants. Who then could dare to maintain that the air suffices to furnish so many destructive germs?

Reason revolts before so daring a supposition. In fact, if panspermism were anything but a fiction, the atmosphere ought to be so obstructed with eggs and seeds, that all movement and respiration would become impossible, and we should perish by suffocation.

Microscopy has by one single word for ever overturned this strange hypothesis. It says, "These eggs and these seeds are tangible things; one can generally feel and see them; whoever speaks of them is bound to show them. Then show them!" But this is what no one has yet done.

I have vainly sought for these atmospheric germs, invented to support certain hypotheses, and have never been able to find them. Two observers, equally illustrious for their learning and the splendour of their diction, P. Mantegazza of the university of Pavia, and N. Joly of the faculty of Toulouse, have not been more fortunate than myself.

But although the atmosphere is not surcharged or saturated with these indiscoverable eggs, it must yet be admitted that notwithstanding its transparence and penetrability, there are an immense number of invisible corpuscules floating in it. Is there any one who has not recognized this in entering a dark place traversed by a ray of light. The beholder is quite surprised to see the infinite variety of all the objects whirling about in it, rising and falling, so as to form iridescent and sparkling waves.

These light corpuscules represent the remains, the detritus of all bodies on the surface of the earth, which have been borne away by the agitation of the atmosphere.

In the open sea and in calm weather, scarcely any motes are seen in a ray of light; a few specks of dust detached from the ship alone float in it.

On the summit of a lofty mountain we notice the same paucity of corpuscules. Near the crater of Etna the breeze only brought to us particles of ashes and sulphur thrown out by the volcano.

But so soon as we abandon the solitudes of the sea or the mountains, the nearer we approach populous cities, the more does the air become loaded with invisible particles. The catalogue of these is in reality only the summary of all that man makes use of for his wants or pleasures. We find atoms of food, of our clothes, of our furniture, and of our dwellings, everything in short is represented there.

The flour of wheat, which constitutes the basis of our food, and is used everywhere, is disseminated everywhere by the air. By means of this fluid it penetrates into the most secret recesses of our dwellings and monuments. I have discovered it in the most inaccessible nooks of our old Gothic churches, mixed with dust blackened by the antiquity of six or eight centuries; I also found some in the palaces and crypts in the Thebaïs, where it perhaps dated from the epoch of the Pharaohs!

In our cities it is one of the most abundant corpuscules in the air, the falling snow and the wheeling insect take up an enormous amount as they traverse it. I have counted as many as forty or fifty grains on the wings of certain flies. It also attaches itself to the surface of the body of man and large animals.

We also discover in the air the skeletons of different infusoria, and what is still more extraordinary, we even find there animalcules perfectly alive. We also frequently meet with the débris of insects, filaments of wool, silk, or cotton, tinged with the most various colours; likewise abundant refuse of the soil, and even particles of smoke expelled from our manufactories and household fires. Everything is found here, and with a little practice can be readily recognized; and the only thing we do not encounter, or what is at any rate prodigiously rare, is the eggs and seeds with which the panspermists burden it.

All atmospheric corpuscules penetrate with the air into our respiratory organs. Hence our lungs always contain a certain amount of fecula. I have even discovered microscopic crustaceans living in those of a dead man.

It is known that the bones of birds, instead of being filled with marrow, are perfectly hollow, and that by means of a curious mechanism they communicate with the lungs and assist respiration; hence these pneumatic bones are well suited for retaining the aërial corpuscules which reach their cavities. A peacock bred in a chateau, presented in its bones abundant filaments of wool and silk tinted with the most magnificent colours; these were clearly remains of the rich dresses of the noble ladies of the place, or of work executed by their delicate hands. On the contrary, in fowls from the humble abode of a baker the pneumatic cavities were almost solely stuffed with meal and the remains of coarse clothes: in those of a charcoal-burner they displayed numerous particles of charcoal.

In woodpeckers, which inhabit none but the most solitary parts of our forests, the respiratory passages contain only the remains of leaves and bark. In contradistinction to this, the bones of the crows, which pass part of their lives on our roofs and part in the fields, are filled with everything that circulates in the different places which they frequent. We find in them variously coloured filaments of wool and cotton, flour and smoke, which they acquire on the roofs of our dwellings, and lastly fine vegetable particles which they inhale in the midst of the woods.

It is curious to see the habits of animals told thus by an examination of their respiratory canals.

But everywhere, whether we examine the air or the innermost organs of animals, we only find a very insignificant quantity of those eggs or seeds with which the panspermists, we repeat, nevertheless maintain that the air is loaded.

THE

SIDEREAL UNIVERSE.

. . . "On a sondé ces régions voilées,
Les bornes du possible ont été reculées.
Un mortel a pu voir, armé d'un œil géant,
Osciller des lueurs aux confins du néant!" . . .

J. J. Ampère.

Man has plumbed these veiled realms, the boundaries of the possible have been extended. A mortal, armed with the eye of a giant, has been enabled to see gleams of light oscillating on the confines of empty space!

BOOK I.

THE STARS AND IMMENSITY.

CHAPTER I.

THE STARS.

Kepler, whose genius surmounted all obstacles, was the first to trace the great physical laws of the spheres. All the stars are, according to him, only suns like ours, each of which has its planetary system. And our luminary, with his whole host of satellites, is itself thrown, like a wandering star, into the ocean of worlds, where it forms the central point in the stellar cloud which we call the Milky Way.

All round the sun, disseminated in immensity, the stars majestically lend life to the vault of heaven. Their splendour, the dazzling spectacle which they display to our eyes, fill the soul with a sense of humility and nothingness. It is in the valleys of the glowing Thebaïs, never wetted by a drop of water, that we ought to yield ourselves up to such contemplations. One enjoys there nights which are eternally serene; and under their magnificent dome the stars, these immortal flowers of heaven, as St. Basil calls them, raise the spirit of man from the visible to the invisible. The heavens relate the glory of God: *Cœli enarrant gloriam Dei.*

The number of known stars, the orbits of which have been calculated, is considerable. Astronomers compute the number that can be seen by the naked eye on the horizon at the same moment at 3000. The sharpest sight, favoured by an extremely clear night, can only number nearly 6000.[1]

[1] Argelander, director of the observatory of Bonn, says, in his *Nouvelle Uranométric*, that on the horizon of Berlin 3256 stars are seen with the naked eye in the course of a year. A Munster astronomer, M. Heis, asserts that his sight is so penetrating that he can see 4000 more than his brother worker. According to Humboldt 4146 are counted at Paris. But the difference becomes very great so soon as we examine the sky with even feeble instruments. Thus in a corner of a constellation of the Twins, where the most practised eye can only make out six stars, a good glass shows a mass of more than 3000.

This starry wealth became embarrassing, and at a very early period, for more convenient study, the necessity was felt for making distinct groups, to which the name of constellations was given. Nearly all these assemblages are named after living beings, sketched out on the celestial sphere.

But this grouping into constellations, the origin of which goes far back into antiquity, has only been carried out by successive attempts. According to Clement of Alexandria, it was Chiron, the preceptor of Jason, who, 1420 years before our era, first divided the starry sky into distinct constellations, tracing them out on a sphere which he presented to the Argonauts. Such is also Newton's opinion.[1]

However, the first authentic proof of the division of the heavens only belongs to the times of Hesiod, much nearer to our epoch. In his book, the *Works and Days*, written about eight hundred years before Christ, this poet speaks of the Pleiades, Arcturus, Orion, and Sirius.

The Odyssey and Iliad are barren in respect to astronomical allusions. Homer, however, relates that Ulysses steered his ship guiding his course by the Pleiades and Boötes; and the prince of poets, when he describes the shield of Achilles, mentions several constellations, and among them the Great Bear, "which alone never sinks in the waves of the ocean."

The invention of almost all the constellations is generally attributed to the Greeks. As to those which lie near the equator, and which are called zodiacal, the learned consider that they emblematically recall the Egyptian divinities. The Virgin represents Isis, and the Goat Mendès. The Ram is consecrated to Jupiter Ammon, the Bull is only the emblem of the god Apis, and the Lion that of Osiris.[2]

[1] Several of the constellations, however, are already mentioned in the Bible at an epoch anterior by some years to that in which the celebrated Centaur is said to have lived. In the book of Job allusion is made to the constellations of Orion, the Pleiades, and the Hyades. The grouping of stars thus goes back nearly three thousand three hundred years.—Arago, *Astronomie Populaire*, t. i. p. 346.

We also find on the monuments of ancient Egypt indications of the grouping of constellations. But we now know that many of these monuments are much more recent than was thought at first.

[2] Among the Greeks the Bull recalled to mind the carrying away of Europa by Jupiter. The sun, when he arrived at the sign of the Crab, indicated, by his moving backwards to the equator, the way in which this crustacean progresses.

According to M. J. Coulier, the Egyptians, by the sign of the Lion, intended to indicate the great heats which occur towards the summer solstice—a time when the lions are very abundant and very dangerous in Ethiopia. The Virgin is said to have represented the Egyptian goddess Isis. The Balance anciently indicated the place where the sun is found at the autumnal equinox, the time when the days and nights are of equal length. The sign of the Archer doubtless recalls the season for hunting.—J. Coulier, *Dictionnaire d'Astronomie*. Paris, 1824.

This division of the celestial sphere, though very ancient, has been successively adopted by the learned of all epochs, notwithstanding the attempts which have been made to reform it. Towards the eighth century some theological astronomers, scandalized at seeing all the divinities of Olympus scattered over the vault of heaven, attempted to depose them and to substitute for mythological designations, names borrowed from the sacred writings. But this attempt, of which Bede was the promoter, failed completely. However, those curious in such matters quote calendars wherein St. Peter replaces the Ram, St. Andrew the Bull, while David, Solomon, and the three kings of the Magi, have also their places. Sir John Herschel, more exact, looking at the difficulties presented by attempts to settle the boundaries of the constellations with accuracy, proposed to trace simple quadrilaterals on the celestial sphere, and to class the stars in each of them. But this system met with no success.

Guided by calculations and instruments of admirable precision, the astronomer in our days boldly penetrates to the spheres scattered towards the confines of immensity. He weighs them and calculates their volume and density, as if they were placed on the scale of his balance.

Modern science draws ample supplies from its splendid storehouses, whilst in its cradle all was wanting but genius! Hipparchus and Ptolemy had no instrument to scrutinize the heavens with. The astronomers of the Renaissance, such as Regiomontanus, Copernicus, Tycho-Brahé, and Kepler, were scarcely more favoured, and yet how many immortal discoveries do we owe to them! They seem with their lynx-eyes to have seen or divined everything.[1]

The first telescope made, Galileo's feeble instrument, only magnified objects seven times, and yet with it he discovered the satellites of Jupiter.

At present our astronomers explore the stars with instruments which multiply 6500 times. Lord Rosse fathomed the depths of the heavens with a telescope having a six-feet opening, and fifty-five feet in length. Thus by the potency of this immense optic tube, in which a man could walk with ease, we see several nebulæ, which had defied all our instruments, resolved into dense swarms of stars.[2]

We see that at the present time our means of investigation have given

[1] The first telescope which was constructed of large dimensions was that of Sir William Herschel. He discovered the sixth satellite of Saturn with it. The tube of this instrument being extremely heavy, movement could only be communicated by a very complicated mechanism—a mass of ladders and masts, forming a gigantic pyramid. Its length was nearly 40 feet; its diameter nearly 5.

[2] Euler maintained that in order to see the largest animals in the moon it would be requisite to have a telescope several hundred feet in length. Hooke thought a glass 10,000 feet long (nearly two miles) would be necessary, and projected the construction

gigantic proportions to the field of science. When the sidereal world was only explored with the naked eye, the catalogues of stars compiled from antiquity up to the Renaissance, from Hipparchus to Tycho-Brahé, only made mention of about a thousand stars. In our days the vault of heaven, seen through a telescope twenty feet long, is found, according to M. Struve, to contain more than 20,000,000 stars.

253. The great Reflecting Telescope constructed by Lord Rosse.

But Sir W. Herschel pried yet more deeply into the mysteries of the heavens. By means of his telescope, 40 feet long, the Milky Way, this long white train which the Arabs called the Heavenly River, has been

of one. The telescope of Lord Rosse has shown that we can obtain this advantage much more easily.

"It is," says Sir David Brewster, "one of our most marvellous combinations of art and science." "This magnificent instrument is fixed in the midst of walls which resemble segments of fortifications." The telescopic tube is 55 feet in length, and weighs 14,575 lbs. avoirdupois. With it one can gauge the immeasurable depths of the heavens. It is thought that by means of this instrument we could easily perceive a monument the size of the pyramids of Egypt if any existed on the moon. The surface of this planet is there as accurately depicted as a terrestrial landscape.

The telescope of Lord Rosse, says M. Babinet, would certainly not show us a lunar elephant, but a troop of animals like a herd of American buffaloes would be quite visible. Troops marching in order of battle would be clearly perceptible. The observatory at Paris, Notre Dame, and the Louvre would be very easily seen. We must therefore conclude that if we see nothing of this kind on our satellite it is because its surface, formerly all flame and volcano, and now all ice, did not or does not contain anything of the kind.

resolved into a stellar cloud, in which the English astronomer counted 18,000,000 telescopic stars.

And yet can we say that with these overwhelming numbers,—these numbers which confound the imagination,—we have reached the extreme bounds of science, and that it has traced out the farthest limits of the sidereal universe? Probably not. Other revelations, not less marvellous, may yet astonish our descendants!

The aspect of this star-formed cloud, dispersed through the firmament, only gives us an imperfect idea of the grandeur of the heavenly regions. Number and distance weaken the impression. It seems as if the stars, so abundant and apparently so heaped together, could only be luminous points! It is science that gives objects their real importance by calling calculation to our aid. In order to give the dimensions of one of these bodies with precision, we will quote the exact words of M. A. Guillemin: "Wollaston," he says, "affirms that the apparent diameter of the most brilliant star in the sky, Sirius, is not equal to the fiftieth part of the second of an arc. But we may at once say that this calculation would still leave a large margin for the real dimensions of this star, seeing that at the distance at which it is from us, an apparent diameter so small would yet represent a real diameter of 4,500,000 leagues, which is twelve times that of our sun."

Does not this simple quotation prove that the phenomena of nature possess proportions not less extraordinary than unexpected? Thus when man begins the study of the sciences, it is with profound astonishment that he recognizes that the marvels which they reveal to him far surpass the most audacious fictions of antiquity.

Let us prove it by a few instances.

The ancient philosophers thought they gave a grand and majestic idea of the sun by comparing its dimensions to the superficies of the Peloponnesus. But what a mean comparison! This torch of the world, this *lucerna mundi*, as Copernicus called it, is of such proportions that if we supposed the earth placed in its centre, the mass of the sun would extend beyond the orbit of the moon, and our satellite would only accomplish its revolutions while still buried under the thick incandescent layers of the star which gives us light.[1]

[1] The volume of the sun is more than 600 times as large as that of all the planets put together. It turns round its axis in twenty-five days and a half. We may form an idea of the immense bulk of this star relative to that of the earth by means of a comparison mentioned by Arago in his *Astronomie Populaire*. "A professor of Angers," he says, "hit upon the idea of counting the number of grains of average size contained in the measure of capacity called a litre; he found there were 10,000. Consequently a décalitre ought to contain 100,000, a hectolitre 1,000,000, and 14 décalitres 1,400,000. Having collected

In his *Theogony*, Hesiod, wishing to give an idea of the height of the firmament, tells us that an anvil of brass, falling from the summit of heaven, would sink nine days and nine nights through space before reaching the earth.

How vastly the imagination of the poet of Bœotia is below the truth; a truth which quite confuses one! Indeed, on one hand, physics prove that a solid body, falling by gravitation during this space of time, would only traverse 143,000 leagues; whilst, on the other hand, the astronomy of the nineteenth century teaches us that a ray of light issuing from Alcyone, the most brilliant of the Pleiades, takes five years to traverse the intervening space before reaching our eyes. And yet light is so rapid that in the tenth part of a second one of its vibrations will pass round the globe. But the depth of the heavens does not stop short at the group of the Pleiades: on the contrary, they belong to its nearer regions.[1]

Space being infinite, and our minds finite, they can only take in some small portions of it, and yet, though these are very limited compared to the field of immensity, they are enough to confound the human comprehension. It would be puerile to try and define them by numbers: all the resources of our intellect would not suffice for such an attempt. The space which light traverses in a year far outstrips the measure of our perceptive faculties; we are not surprised when we remember that it clears the distance separating us from the sun, that is to say, 91,328,600 miles, in 8 minutes 18 seconds; and yet it is this light which in its dazzling progress serves to measure the vast distances between the globes, and to give us a grand idea of some fragments of the infinite!

As light passes through 77,000 leagues in a second, the speed of any-

the 14 décalitres of wheat, he showed his audience a single grain, and then said to them, 'This is the size of the earth, while the heap represents the sun.' This comparison occasioned infinitely more surprise among the students than the statement about the relative size of 1 to 1,400,000 in abstract numbers had done."

If we wish to compare the weight of the sun with that of the earth astronomy weighs them with as much precision as though each were placed in one of the scales of a balance. The weight of the sun is 2,096,000,000,000,000,000,000,000,000 tons. That of the earth is only 5,875,000,000,000,000,000,000.

The physical constitution of the sun has only been made out by the astronomers of our epoch. The body of this star is almost entirely dark, but it is surrounded by three envelopes —one, formed of vapours, which touch it; another, which is luminous, placed at a great distance, and which is called the photosphere; and, lastly, a third, which covers the latter, and in which float the clouds. The spots on the sun are occasioned by perforations in the photosphere, which allow us to see the earthy nucleus of the star.—*See* Guillemin, *Le Ciel*. Paris, 1865.

[1] The Alpha of the Centaur, one of the nearest stars to us, which is only about 8,000,000,000 geographical leagues from the earth, sends us its light in three years, and the pole-star, which is more than 70,000,000,000 leagues, in a quarter of a century.

thing we can place beside it is low indeed. Compared with it sound is propagated with ridiculous slowness.

Supposing the immense abyss interposed between the earth and the sun were capable of transmitting sonorous undulations, it has been calculated that sound produced on the surface of the glowing torch of the world would take fourteen years and two months to reach our ears.

If we attempt, by an interesting calculation, to compute how long it would require by means of our most rapid locomotion to accomplish a journey from the star which lends us light, we are altogether astonished at the result. According to the calculations of M. Guillemin, an express railway train, starting from the earth on the 1st of January, 1865, and travelling at the rate of thirty-one miles an hour, would only reach the sun in the year 2212; that is to say, in 347 years: a journey performed by light in a few minutes!

We have said what a great lapse of time a luminous ray starting from the Pleiades would require to reach the earth. But the conquests effected by the genius of man over the infinite are not limited to these constellations; sidereal astronomy, aided by the accurate instruments of our epoch, has shown, as we have stated, that the Milky Way is only a congeries of telescopic stars. Now, Sir John Herschel thinks that, according to his photometric calculations, these stars are at such a prodigious distance from the earth, that a ray of light starting from one of them would take 2000 years to reach us.

Yet human investigation penetrates much farther than this. When the observer carries his investigations more deeply into immensity, when he reaches those nebulæ which lie on the confines of space, the distances are so great that they confound the imagination, and figures no longer suffice to represent them. According to calculations, says Humboldt, which are not devoid of probability, light, notwithstanding its tremendous speed, requires more than two millions of years to traverse the enormous distance which separates us from these stars. Hence, while the telescope still displays to our eyes the luminous gleam of one of these nebulæ, it may be that more than two million years ago this mysterious body was extinguished in space. Thus the history of the heavens traversing the night of time passes through ages, and then appears to us like contemporaneous events! This is, as has been said, the most authentic proof of the immense antiquity of matter.

CHAPTER II.

THE NEBULÆ.[1]

The investigation of the universe is not limited to the stars. By means of large telescopes we discover at the farthest distances in the heavens white patches of different shapes, which were long regarded as simple cosmical, phosphorescent vapours, or as germs of the universe ready to be condensed into new worlds. It is to these white gleams that the name of *nebulæ* was given, in order to designate their diffused appearance and the uncertainty of their nature. But by means of newly-invented powerful instruments it has been made out that these luminous clouds, in which it was thought man had discovered globes in the process of formation, are only groups of small telescopic stars, often aggregated in considerable numbers, and assuming the most varied and unexpected figures.

Some nebulæ are nearly globular, others, like those in the constellations of the Virgin and the Greyhounds, are like a spiral whirlwind, and there are some which resemble a ring. The nebula of the Bull shows like a luminous body lengthened out, from which project claw-like appendages formed by long trains of stars. Struck with its appearance, Lord Rosse,

[1] "Nebulæ" is a name applied to certain celestial objects from their cloud-like appearance, which gives them a resemblance to faint comets or specks of luminous fog. Many nebulæ, though cloud-like to the naked eye, and even to many telescopes, are resolved into clusters of stars when seen through a telescope of sufficient power; but there is likewise a class of nebulæ which cannot be resolved into star-clusters, being shown by the spectroscope to consist of masses of glowing or incandescent gas. To these latter bodies the term nebulæ would be more strictly applicable, but at present both classes are called by the same name, though so different in constitution. The number of nebulæ at present known amounts to somewhere about 5700. Sir W. Herschel discovered 2500 nebulæ, his son, Sir John, revising his father's work, discovered 500 more, and, proceeding to the Cape of Good Hope, added 1700 southern nebulæ to the list. Mr. Huggins first successfully applied the spectroscope to nebulæ. In August, 1864, he first turned his stellar spectroscope on a planetary nebula in the constellation Draco. To his astonishment he found it to consist of an incandescent mixture of the gases hydrogen and nitrogen. He has since examined the spectra of a great number of these objects. Of the twenty which he had examined in 1870 about one-third are evidently gaseous. It is found that the close association of points of light in a nebula must not be accepted as an indication of resolvability into stars, for these luminous points in many cases only indicate the existence of places of greater gaseous density than common. See art. *Nebula* in the *Popular Encyclopedia* (Blackie and Son).

when he saw it for the first time through his immense télescope, gave it the name of the Crab nebula, an animal of which its singular form puts one in mind.

The nebulæ mark the limits of sidereal investigation. In proportion as with our new means we extend our researches further into the starry

254. Spiral Nebula of the Constellation of the Greyhounds (*Canes Venatici*).

sphere, we find new luminous bodies of this class. But in the extreme depth of the heavens there are still a certain number which cannot be resolved.

Already 4500 nebulæ are known. They are scattered through both hemispheres, and the least of them consists of a perfect swarm of suns, for each of their imperceptible stars represents a sun.

The stars which form the nebulæ are so massed together that they cannot be counted with exactness. Astronomers have only been able to calculate approximately the number in several of those which present a globular form. Arago asserts that there are as many as 20,000 in some of those celestial lights which are in appearance not more than one-tenth of the magnitude of the moon's disk.

These bodies are scattered irregularly enough over the celestial vault. Large spaces seem entirely without them, whilst in other regions they

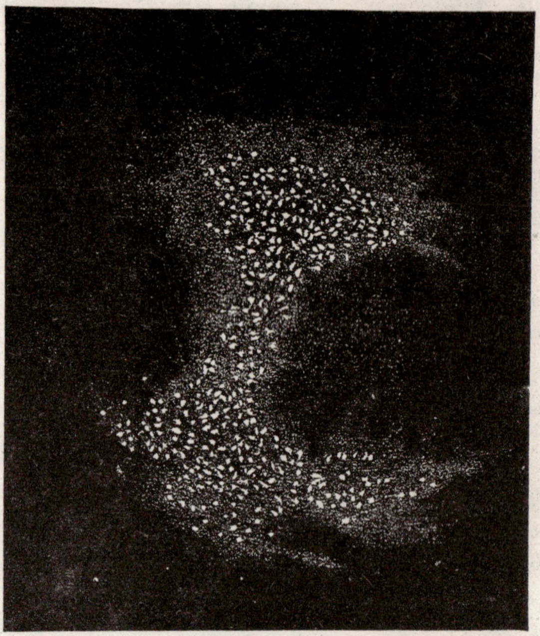

255. The Dumb-bell Nebula—Constellation of the Fox (*Vulpecula*).

are dispersed like numerous archipelagoes, and the observer can, for instance, particularly near the Virgin, see more than 300 traverse the field of the telescope within an hour.

Although the dispersion of the nebulæ apparently does not follow any plan, yet some exact law seems to have presided at their formation, for there are generally very few stars in their vicinity, as if they had drawn towards their centre all the cosmical particles of the regions in which they are placed. Thus Herschel, in his nocturnal explorations, when he saw few stars pass before his instrument, calculated upon a nebula appearing in their place, and was so certain of this that he used to tell his secretaries to be ready to take a note of them. "Be ready to write," he would say, "the nebulæ are coming."

The Clouds of Magellan, those luminous patches which cover so large a space in the southern region, and look like rags torn from the Milky Way, present a complex composition, being analogous to a certain extent with the nebulæ. Sir John Herschel says they are formed of isolated stars, of swarms of stars, and lastly, of nebulæ, more compact than those which we find near the Virgin and in the Tresses of Berenice.

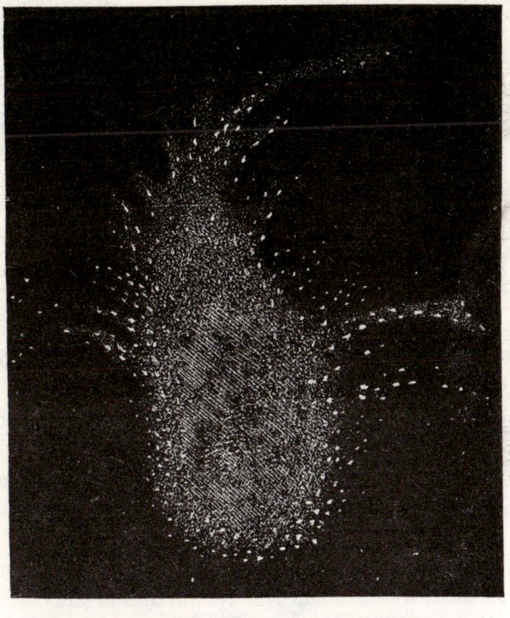

256. The Crab Nebula—Constellation of the Bull (*Taurus*).

The first mariners who ventured into the southern seas were also struck by certain phenomena of a totally opposite character; these were black patches irregularly outlined on the vault of the heavens, to which in their imaginative language they gave the name of *coal-sacks*. According to astronomers, these patches, the most celebrated of which are near the Southern Cross, are due to the sky being at these parts to a great extent without stars. They seem to be really holes, according to the expression of Humboldt, by means of which our vision pierces into the remotest spaces of the universe.

BOOK II.

THE SOLAR WORLD.

CHAPTER I.

THE SUN.

This flaming star, to use the beautiful metaphor of Theon of Smyrna, is the heart of the universe, vivifying everything with its pulsations. Of all those lights that gravitate in the immensity of the heavens, the dazzling splendour of the sun first captivates the attention. Yet great as may be its apparent size, and vivid as may be its light, it is still only one in those myriads of stars which form the Milky Way. But for us it is the centre of a system, or of a family of globes, of which it was the cradle, and which, after being separated from it, revolve eternally round their common parent. Like a sovereign seated on his shining throne, it sits in the centre of its satellites; its invisible power upholds them in space, directs their regulated course, and disseminates everywhere movement and life.

For if its light were extinguished, eternal night would envelop the globe, and with that would come the destruction of all created things, which its rays alone protect from the horrible mantle of ice perpetually threatening to invade them.

Compared to our globe and to the other orbs which it enchains in their orbit round itself, the sun is of enormous dimensions. It is about a million and a half times the bulk of the earth, and has been calculated to contain seven hundred times the mass of all the planets together which circulate in its system.

Astronomers have not rested content with knowing the volume of the sun; they have attempted to estimate its weight, and have succeeded. By comparing its weight with that of the earth, they have made out that it would require a large number of the latter to counterbalance it. If we supposed the existence of a prodigious balance, which allowed us to place the sun in one scale, we should have to put 350,000 terrestrial globes into the other in order to weigh it properly.

The orbit of the earth is rigidly limited to 91,000,000 miles from the sun. Some planets roll at a much greater distance from this luminary; others much nearer. He scorches the one and condemns the other to the empire of eternal frost. Mercury, his nearest neighbour, almost in a state of combustion, is only 37,000,000 miles off. Neptune, which is

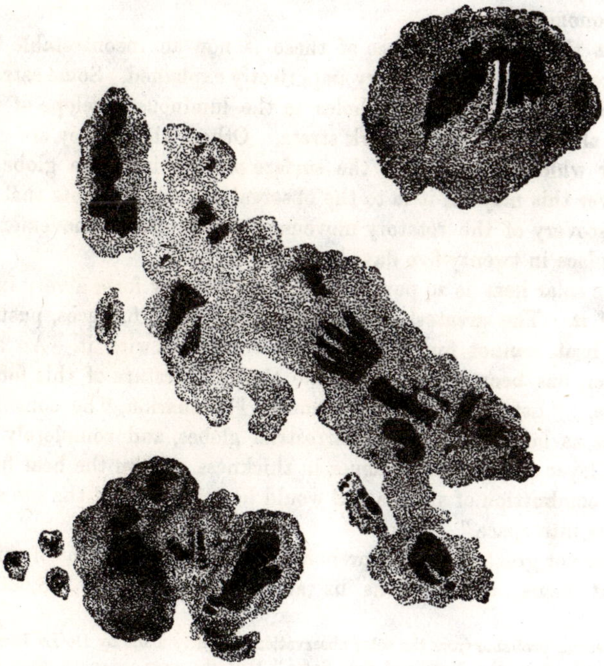

257. Spots on the Sun.

doubtless all covered with ice, rolls in the furthest orbit of the system at 2,854,000,000 miles from the blazing star, and thus it only accomplishes its revolution in 164 years, which constitute its year!

However dazzling may be the splendour of the sun, it was discovered 250 years ago to display here and there some black patches, very small, it is true, in comparison with the extent of its surface, but in reality of vast extent relatively to the dimensions of our globe. Although the eye cannot generally perceive these spots, some of them are nevertheless as much as 75,000 miles in diameter, and if we suppose that they represent gaps in the solar envelope, the earth might be engulfed in them with the greatest facility.

Although the existence of these spots is as easily proved as anything can be, yet when they were first pointed out, and even after the great Galileo had attested their reality, some theologians, founding their convictions upon false philosophic ideas, resolutely denied the fact. They maintained that the pure and radiant star was perfectly immaculate, and that its pretended blemishes only existed on the glasses of the telescopes of astronomers.

But though the existence of these is now an incontestable fact, yet their real nature is as yet very imperfectly explained. Some astronomers maintain that they are only holes in the luminous envelope of the sun, which allow us to see its dark strata. Others think they are clouds of vapour which wander over the surface of this immense globe of fire. However this may be, it is to the observation of these spots that we owe the discovery of the rotatory movement of the sun—a movement which takes place in twenty-five days.[1]

The solar heat is so powerful that we can only form a very imperfect idea of it. The greatest combustion in our blast-furnaces, pushed to a white heat, cannot for a moment be compared with it. An attempt, however, has been made to estimate the temperature of this formidable furnace. "Let the sun," says Camille Flammarion, "be considered as a globe as large as 1,400,000 terrestrial globes, and completely covered with a layer of coal seven leagues in thickness. Then the heat furnished by the combustion of all this coal would be equal to what the sun annually projects into space."

And yet great and incomprehensible as may be the heat of this incandescent focus, which burns us at a distance of 91,328,600 miles,

[1] It seems probable from the solar observations recently made by De La Rue, Stewart, and Loewig, "On the Nature of Sun Spots," that the spots are colder than either the photosphere or the sun; that this greater cold is not due to the general body of the sun at the bottom of a spot being of a lower temperature than the photosphere, and is not produced by any chemical or molecular process, but by matter coming from a colder region, and that when a spot is formed there is a down-rush and melting of photospheric matter. In a paper by M. Faye in the *Comptes Rendus*, the author deduces from Mr. Carrington's researches the conclusions that sun spots are depressions beneath the surface of the sun's photosphere from 20,000 to 40,000 miles in depth; that many of the apparent irregularities of their motion, attributed to cyclones, are probably explicable by the continued variation in the motion proper to each successive parallel of the photosphere; and that the great regularity of their motions seems incompatible with any hypothesis of mere superficial or local movements in the photosphere, and rather points to some more general action arising from the internal mass of the sun.—Tr.

astronomers are so daring that they have ventured to calculate the quantity of water necessary if not to extinguish it entirely, to put out at any rate the surface conflagration.

CHAPTER II.

THE EARTH.

We have previously spoken at length of the earth in reference to geology; here we only have to speak of its position as a planetary body forming part of the solar system.

The earth represents a sphere a little flattened towards the poles. It is subject to two movements, one which takes place round the sun in an orbit of which it traverses the circuit in a year, the other is performed in about twenty-four hours round the axis which passes through its poles. It is the latter movement which occasioned the belief that the sun and the heavens turned round the earth in a direction from east to west, whilst on the contrary it is the terrestrial globe that turns from west to east. Copernicus was the first to demonstrate this great astronomical fact, and Galileo, with all the influence of his genius, confirmed it.

The terrestrial surface is estimated at 196,000,000 square miles, and the learned have calculated that to cover it completely would require a thousand kingdoms the size of France.

Our planet is entirely enveloped by a thick layer of air, which forms round it the softest cushion imaginable, and of which the depth, according to the calculations of Laplace, is about twenty-six miles. Notwithstanding its apparent lightness, this atmosphere weighs heavily upon all bodies on the earth, and exerts greater pressure in proportion as they offer a larger surface. Physiologists consider that each of us has a weight of about 32,000 lbs. to support, but this great weight is not usually felt, because it is counterbalanced by a counter-action equal in all directions, so that the one destroys the other.

The earth is not rich in respect to satellites, possessing as it does only one, which however is of dimensions ample enough as compared to it; this is the moon, the faithful companion of its course. Other planets, it is true, like Jupiter and Saturn, are more richly endowed, and have from four to eight satellites; but again there are others which do not possess any, as is the case with Venus and Mercury.

From one pole to the other our globe is full of animation, and on it life manifests itself with all its strength. In the torrid zone, as well as in the frozen regions, the air, the earth, and the depths of the sea, have their animal inhabitants, and their plants, which have succeeded each other from age to age. When one generation becomes extinct another takes its place, displaying forms before unknown. A series of new creations will doubtless yet follow, up to the time when the whole will be annihilated in one common wreck. The earth, in fact, after its period of incandescence and of life, will in cooling pass successively through the different stages that the moon has already passed through, and like it will one day be but a dead and frozen star. Everything on its surface indicates that it is slowly undergoing the same transformations as its

258. Comparative Dimensions of the Earth and Moon.

satellite has undergone. It has been calculated that $\frac{1}{50}$th of the primitive ocean has been already absorbed. The rest is doubtless destined to rejoin this other portion, and this disappearance will take place with the greater facility in proportion as the terrestrial crust gets thicker by the effect of cooling, for it has been calculated that the earth could easily absorb fifty oceans such as its own.

The surface of the earth will then crack and split like that of the moon at the present day, and its atmosphere will rush into all the hollows, while long before that life will be everywhere extinct; so that the earth will be nothing but a corpse. This strange catastrophe, however, which the study of the moon indicates as inevitable, will take place only at a period far distant in the future, for, according to the experiments of Bischof, 9,000,000 of years would be required to lower the temperature of the earth only fifteen degrees.

CHAPTER III.

THE MOON.

This sole and faithful satellite of the earth, formed by a fragment detached from it, now cold and wan, rolled round us when it began a red and blazing sphere, vomiting torrents of fire from its whole surface. Whilst gravitation was regulating its form and path, the moon, in the course of thousands of years, gradually exhausted its fires to show us at last its pale and silvery face, the sad luminary of our nights, the splendid nocturnal mirror which reflects to us, pale and cold, the divergent rays of the sun.

Compared to the immeasurable distances of the nebulæ and stars, the space which separates us from our satellite is quite insignificant; she is our next-door neighbour, and the eye can so clearly discern her form and peculiarities, that she seems almost to touch us. But this insignificant distance, abstractly considered, is yet vast enough. The distance from the earth to the moon is about 237,000 miles. If it were possible to get there by means of steam, it would require 1 year and about 322 days for a locomotive starting from our globe and travelling at a high rate of speed to reach the moon and land its passengers. A heavy body, projected from the lunar orbit, would, it is true, reach us much quicker. In his charming work on celestial marvels, M. Camille Flammarion says, it would arrive at the surface of the earth in 3 days, 1 hour, 45 minutes, and 13 seconds.

The moon is in every part roughened with eminences of different shapes, but they only very rarely group themselves into mountain chains comparable to those of our globe. The Alps, Caucasus, and the Apennines represent the principal ones. Certain isolated summits have received the names of celebrated men, but those of past times have been chosen in order not to excite any jealousy; we travel from the mountain of Aristotle to that of Hipparchus, from that of Ptolemy to that of Copernicus. The astronomers have very properly not forgotten their claims.

The highest lunar mountains attain an altitude which surpasses most terrestrial elevations, a fact which may well astonish us. Generally they do not rise beyond 22,750 feet. But in proportion to the size of the planet, we may say that the mountains in the moon are much loftier than those of the earth. The summits of Mount Dœrfel are 24,700 feet above the valleys which environ it, whilst the crest of Mont Blanc only rises 15,632 feet above the level of the sea.

Most of the mountains of our pale companion are of volcanic origin, and its surface has been so shattered by subterranean fires that in many places the craters are heaped up close beside each other. Probably no star was ever so horribly torn by the fury of volcanoes. These even attain proportions far beyond what is seen on our globe. Some of those lunar craters are four or five leagues in diameter, and the gaping mouth of the volcano of Aristillus, still more prodigious, is ten leagues from one

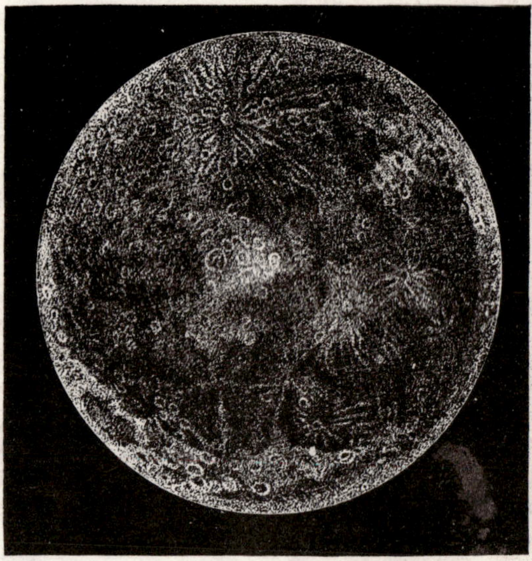

259. Appearance of the Moon when Full.

edge to the other! Our glasses enable us to see these extinct craters in such proportions, that none of their details escape us; whilst, were we on the moon, our telescopes, according to Humboldt, would scarcely enable us to make out terrestrial volcanoes. Seen from the earth many lunar volcanoes appear very much depressed, and the edges of their craters resemble so many flattened rings, projecting very little above the plains. Some regions are so riddled with them that their mouths touch. Others surmount lofty summits, and their crenellated ramparts surround enormous excavations, which pierce deep into the mountains below the level of the plains.

At the present day the volcanoes with which the moon is riddled are quite extinct, and our satellite is really and truly a *dead star*. This opinion, which is held by Beer and Arago, has been developed in an ingenious manner by M. Stanislaus Meunier in his remarkable lecture on the geology of the moon. Evidence of this fact seems to be furnished by the large clefts or furrows which are observed in the surface of this

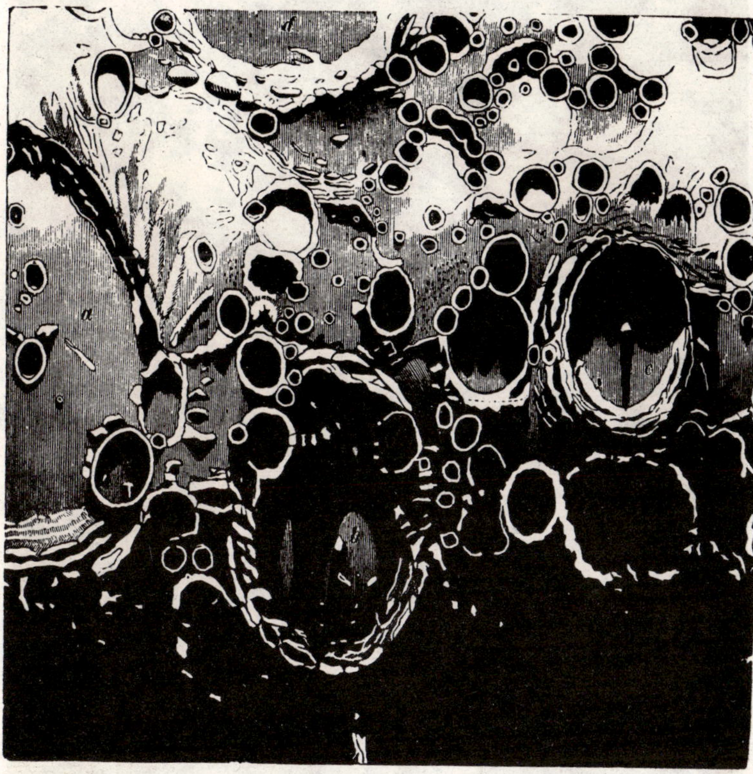

260. Craters on the Moon's Surface, at Sunset.—After Julius Schmidt.
a Clavius, *b* Maginus, *c* Tycho, *d* Longomontanus.

body, and which have sometimes a breadth of more than three-quarters of a mile, and a length of 150 miles. These clefts, according to M. Lecoq de Clermont, are the result of the absolute cooling of the mass of the planet.

Formerly the dark patches which cover part of the moon's surface were considered as representing lunar seas, but at present men are

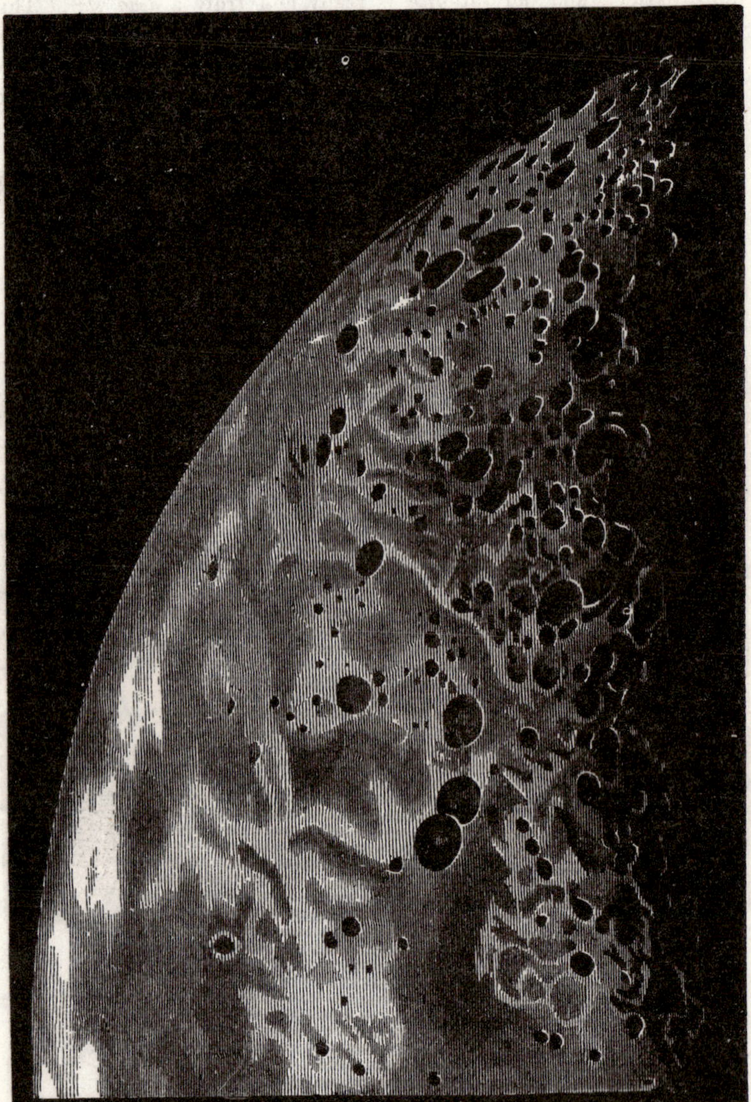

261. Part of the Moon's Crescent during the First Quarter.

disposed to look upon them as only immense plains. The first astronomers gave them names full of poetry. There was the Sea of Tranquillity, the Sea of Clouds, the Sea of Nectar, the Ocean of Tempests, and the Sea of Serenity.

The rocky and shattered soil of our satellite is perfectly bare; not a blade of grass grows there, not a flower opens. Totally deprived of water and air, life is an impossibility. A threefold death would overtake the least animal that happened to alight there; a squirrel would perish of hunger, thirst, and asphyxia! In these cold and horrid realms of the moon everything is plunged in torpor and silence; the echoes are mute, nothing alters the dull monotony of the heavens, and the breath of a zephyr never plays round the summits of the rugged mountains.

By means of our instruments, which have now been brought to so great perfection, we can pry into the minutest details of our satellite, and examine them with as much accuracy as if it were some distant view on earth; hence we can to a certain extent make out its geological disposition. The precision of our glasses has been carried to such a pitch, that we could with them easily perceive large buildings, if any existed on the lunar surface; we could even make out troops of animals moving about. It would, it is true, be impossible to perceive one of its inhabitants traversing the valleys of its silver crescent; but if the much-spoken-of Selenites existed, we should certainly perceive their movements when they were collected into dense masses. According to Humboldt, however, there is only a noiseless, silent desert there.

CHAPTER IV.

COMETS.

Among the myriads of stars scattered through the vault of heaven, there are none which have so much taxed the imagination of the learned as comets. They have often given rise to the most opposite and most ridiculous hypotheses. Descartes thought they were only old stars which had become crusted over and sick, and which being too feeble to maintain their places, were borne away by the vortices of neighbouring stars.

The regular movements of comets seem to have been suspected by Seneca, but it was Newton who taught the method of calculating them. These vagabond stars, however, frequently move in such a way as to deceive all the sagacity of astronomers. The reader may recollect, in reference to this point, that Jacopo Bernouilli had announced the return of the comet of 1680 for the 17th of May, 1719; it ought, at this time, to have made a majestic entry into the sign of the Balance. Voltaire says, that in order to see this beautiful spectacle, not a single astronomer went to bed that night; but the comet did not appear. These wandering meteors are sometimes guilty now-a-days of the same want of politeness.[1]

The learned themselves have contributed largely to all the errors circulated by the vulgar about these strange stars, and even astronomers, though least of all, have supplied their contingent. At one time the appearance of comets inspired such dread that people shut themselves up

262. Donati's Comet on 5th October, 1858, near Arcturus, as seen with the naked eye.

in their dwellings in order not to see their horrible aspect; now-a-days, on the contrary, we rush out of doors the better to gaze upon their luminous tresses. Naturally enough ignorant crowds were alarmed when the most enlightened men, such as J. Bernouilli, maintained that the tail at

[1] Seneca suspected not only the regular movements of comets, but even the possibility of tracing their path by means of calculation. "I look upon them," he says, "not as wandering fires, but as works that are eternal in their nature. Every comet has its defined limits."—See *Just. Astron. de Lemonnier.* To Newton belongs the honour of having first demonstrated their course by calculation.—Newton's *Principia.* Euler has equally contributed to throw light upon the movements of these stars.—*Theoria Planetarum et Cometarum*, 1744.

least, if not the body, of comets might be looked upon as a sign of celestial wrath.

The imagination of Maupertuis gave way to all sorts of phantasies in respect to these nebulous stars. He never forsook the idea that they were probably peopled by a certain race of men; and in their phosphorescent tails the astronomer saw only a dazzling train of jewels. In speaking of such a contingency as a comet falling upon our globe, he expresses himself thus:—"Earth would enjoy the rare treasures which a body coming from so far would bring to it. We should perhaps be much surprised to find that the remains of these bodies which we despise are formed of gold or diamonds; but which would be the more surprised of the two, ourselves or the inhabitants whom the comet would land upon earth? What a strange appearance we should wear in each other's eyes!"

Although the vulgar cannot fathom all the mysteries of the heavens, their imagination receives some compensation in the strange fancies which comets engender, as they have always enjoyed the privilege of creating ecstasy or horror.

The history of these wandering stars, from the beginning to the end, is really only a determined abnegation of the evidence of our senses and the testimony of the masses. In respect to them fiction has been pushed to the wildest extravagance. In every age comets have been considered as sinister omens. In ages of credulity their gleaming tails appeared to the vulgar like formless heaps of flaming swords or bleeding heads and daggers, precursors of the most murderous wars. At other times the fascinated imagination of our forefathers saw in them hairy stars which threatened the world with a general conflagration.

Such erroneous ideas were so deeply rooted in men's minds that some learned men of the Renaissance, even the most advanced, represent comets in their works under the most grotesque shapes; a fault of which even Ambrose Paré is guilty.[1]

[1] In Ambrose Paré we may see to what an extent even the shrewdest men allowed themselves to be misled respecting comets. The illustrious surgeon, who was certainly not superstitious, gives in his valuable work most fantastic figures of some of these stars.

In the chapter entitled "Des Monstres Célestes," Ambrose Paré speaks of bearded and hairy comets, of comets like a shield, a lance, a dragon, or a battle in the clouds. And he there describes and represents in all its details a bleeding comet which appeared in 1528. "This comet," he says, "was so horrible and frightful, and engendered such terror among the vulgar, that some died of fear, and others fell sick. It appeared to be of excessive length, and was of the colour of blood; at its summit was seen the figure of a bent arm holding a large sword in its hand, as if about to strike. At the end of the point were three stars. At both sides of the rays of this comet were seen a great number of axes, knives, and swords of the colour of blood, among which were a great number of hideous human faces, with rugged beards and locks."—*Ambrose Paré*, chap. xxxii.

Kepler himself, though an eminent astronomer, was so subjugated by the superstition of his epoch that he saw in comets a kind of monsters, similar to those produced by the sea, and wandering vaguely in the heavenly regions.

Although in its progress science has eradicated these absurdities, still on the other hand it has given rise to some fears. It was dreaded every instant that the shock of one of these wandering stars would shatter the earth into fragments. The theory of Buffon and the assertions of Kepler in no way reassured men. The former, it may be remembered, had put forth the view that our globe was only a fragment struck off from the sun by the shock of a comet; and the danger seemed only the more imminent when Kepler, in his picturesque language, said that "there are more comets in the sky than fish in the ocean." The worst was to be feared.[1]

But modern science has swept away a part of the danger. At the same time that it has shown the immense size of these stars, it has also demonstrated their inoffensive nature. The tail of a comet, which the Chinese fancifully call its broom, because it seems to sweep the azure of the sky, and which to our eye appears only like a luminous fan, sometimes exceeds 2,000,000 leagues in length. This luminous cone may even attain much more prodigious dimensions, and has been known to equal the distance which separates the earth from the sun.

But notwithstanding these frightful proportions, comets ought to produce scarcely any fear for the earth, as they are of all stars those of which the material particles show the greatest looseness. Their mass sometimes does not reach $\frac{1}{5000}$th of that of the earth, which induced Theon of Alexandria to give them the picturesque name of *wandering clouds.* Some observers have looked upon them as even much lighter than this—so light, indeed, as to surpass everything one can imagine. Comets, says M. Flammarion, have been seen several million leagues long, the weight of which was yet so trifling that one could have carried them on one's shoulders without fatigue.[2]

We have, therefore, no reason to dread their contact, and may sleep securely. In 1770 astronomers saw a comet bar the path of Jupiter's

[1] Arago adopts the hypothesis of an equal distribution of comets in all parts of the solar system, and founding his calculations on the number of comets observed between the sun and Mercury, computes the number of these stars which circulate within the known limits of the solar system, that is to say the orbit of Neptune, at 17,500,000.—Guillemin, *Le Ciel.* Paris, 1865, p. 348.

[2] Mr. Huggins, who has examined the subject very carefully, has come to the conclusion that the nucleus of comet 1, 1866, was self-luminous, that it consisted of matter in the shape of ignited gas, and that this matter is similar in constitution to the gaseous material of some of the nebulæ. The coma was found to shine by reflected light, and as from its

system, and envelop the planet on every side, without the slightest perturbation to the course either of the great star or that of its satellites. On the contrary, it was the nebulous star that suffered from the contact. Besides, it seems that during the passage of certain comets in our vicinity their tails may have penetrated into our atmosphere.[1]

However, according to Maupertuis, though there are some comets so small that their collision with the earth would only destroy a few kingdoms, without shattering its mass, there are others the contact of which might be fatal to every living thing on the globe.

In his *Lettres Cosmologiques*, Lambert leads us to dread the most serious accidents. According to him, the shock of a comet might pulverize our globe, and prove the destruction of everything living on it by means of a deluge of water or a general conflagration; or comets might even carry off our moon by sweeping it away in their orbit, or hurl us beyond the regions of Saturn, where hideous winter reigns for ages together.

But even supposing that comets are not so marvellously light as to allow of a man carrying them off upon his shoulders without being as strong as Atlas, and if too their shock is far from being so formidable as Buffon supposed; yet certainly these bodies are too imperfectly known for us to lay down general rules about them. M. Guillemin, in his remarkable work on the heavens, speaks as follows: "If there be comets the nebulosity of which is quite gaseous, and so transparent that small stars can be seen through their substance, there are others the nucleus of which is without doubt very dense, as their light was bright enough to be perceptible in full day, even in the vicinity of the sun."

The mass of Donati's comet has been estimated at about the seven-hundredth of that of the earth. "That is to say," says M. Faye, "the same weight as a sea of 16,000 square leagues surface, and 330 feet in depth. It must therefore be admitted that such a mass, impelled with great speed, might produce sensible effects by coming in contact with the earth."

Is it not possible, in cases where the tail of a comet is formed of atoms widely scattered, that the brilliancy of their nucleus may just be the result of incandescence? and then, even supposing there was nothing to

extreme diffusion it cannot be supposed to contain solid or liquid matter at the high temperature necessary for incandescence, it seems almost certain that it reflects the light of the sun. The nucleus of meteors is probably a fragment of mineral matter, of which sodium is one of the chemical ingredients. Their spectra are often highly coloured and continuous like those from solid matter at a white-heat.—Tr.

[1] According to Humboldt, the tails of the comets in 1819 and 1823 must have reached our atmosphere. The same thing is supposed to have happened with the last great comet observed in our latitudes.

fear from the shock, would not the approach of such a furnace be enough to make us dread being burned up?

The phenomenon of shooting-stars strikes the untutored mind less than the appearance of comets, and yet notwithstanding its frequency the explanation of it is not free from obscurity on some points.

The distance of the stars does not allow us to ascribe to them the long trains of light which we see so frequently traverse the heavens;

263. Swarm of Shooting-stars at Sea.

hence this phenomenon is at present attributed to bodies entering our atmosphere.

Twice in the year the sky is constantly traversed by a prodigious quantity of these luminous trains; in a single hour we may at such times occasionally count 200 or 300. One of these periods occurs from the 10th to the 12th of August, and it is to this phenomenon, which has long astonished the vulgar, that the name of *St. Laurence's rain* has been given, on account of his festival falling on the 10th of August. These brilliant lights are looked upon by Irish Catholics as the burning tears of the venerated saint.

During the night of the 12th and of the 13th of November, the same

264. The Aurora Borealis in the Arctic Seas.—After M. L. Figuier.

abundance of shooting-stars has been observed. Humboldt and Bonpland, who were witnesses of it in Cumana, relate that the number of luminous trains traversing the sky was so great that the spectator might have thought it was some magnificent display of fireworks, at a prodigious height. At sea the phenomenon is no less extraordinary; it looks like so many rockets which fall towards the horizon.

An attempt has been made to explain this abundance of shooting-stars at the two periods we mention, by supposing that the sun is encircled by a ring composed of myriads of little bodies, which ring the earth passes through annually at these times.

The number of these meteoric bodies which penetrate into our atmosphere in this way, and appear under a luminous form, is computed at millions. There are some which, according to Humboldt, seem almost to graze the summits of Chimborazo.

Meteoric stones, which have all the appearance of shooting-stars, but which are much bulkier, and leave behind them a long stream of fire, which for a moment lights up the earth like the moon, must be briefly noticed.

They sometimes burst with a sound like that of a cannon, and let fall on the earth a number, sometimes considerable and at others not, of meteoric stones, which drop smoking and burning.

While speaking of the mysterious phenomena which attract our wondering eyes to the celestial regions, we must not in such a work as this omit to mention the great lights which often illuminate the heaven of the polar regions during the long nights of winter, a phenomenon known as the Aurora Borealis or Australis.

Whilst this lasts the heavens sometimes present the most splendid spectacle. On the black and starry back-ground of the sky we see traced out a vast luminous cupola, or kind of panelled vault, formed of colonnades of stalactites heaped together and pendant, and which suspended in the clouds reflect the brightest hues of the rainbow. Sometimes they resemble fireworks which dart their sheets of flame in every direction, and seem to set on fire the horizon, forming one of the most imposing spectacles it is possible to enjoy amid the ice of the north.

POPULAR ERRORS.

MONSTERS AND SUPERSTITIONS.

I purpose to terminate this sketch of the glories of nature, by giving as a contrast a short account of the ridiculous fictions which our forefathers were too often pleased to substitute for them. We shall then have completed the picture of the march of science.

The people of antiquity had their superstitions and their fabulous legends, but those were never so widely diffused as they became in the middle ages, a period of simple ignorance and ardent faith. "At that time," as M. Figuier says in his excellent work on this epoch, "all classes of the people, and even a great part of the nobility, the magistracy, and the clergy, believed in magic."

The Renaissance itself did not throw off this weakness of the human mind; on the contrary, learned men vied with each other in collecting all the fables of their forefathers and recording them in their works. They found monsters in every kingdom of nature, and equally in the depths of the sea, as in the heavens. Ambrose Paré even devoted a chapter to "Celestial Monsters," in which he describes the fabulous comets we have spoken of.

All that a fantastic imagination could beget, all that diseased minds could discover wild in tradition or terrible in legend, was for many ages looked upon as expressing occult truths. Fools gave themselves up to punishment and death accusing themselves of unheard-of acts, while the judges never noticed their delirium!

In the middle ages magic was confounded with science; it was not attacked; but in the sterner times of the Renaissance the fagots were lighted. The victims that suffered for imaginary crimes cannot be numbered.

But if so many and such serious errors spread through the vulgar, we must with sorrow admit that they were in great part the work of the learned men of these later times. The most eminent men of the middle ages and the Renaissance, who could discuss all branches of human knowledge of that day with perfect clearness, seemed to become struck with blindness so soon as ever the question turned upon monsters: instead of dissipating error, they lent all the weight of their authority to sanction it. And this deplorable mass of superstition issued neither from the smoky laboratory of the alchemist nor from the mysterious cave of the cabala; the fountain-head is to be found in the works of scholars the most esteemed and religious of their epoch.

In fact all these fabulous traditions, which credulity still collects with such avidity, were put forth as so many realities by the naturalists of past ages. This is what we see in the writings of Albertus Magnus, Olaus Magnus, Aldrovandus, Gesner, and Scheuchzer. Not content with simple recitals, they ornament their works with figures representing all these fantastic creatures, as if they had been drawn from nature. Who could doubt after that?

When we analyze the works of all these writers we are astonished to find side by side so much science and credulity, so much exactness and error! Thus Scheuchzer, a naturalist deeply imbued with religion, in his *Itinerary of Switzerland* describes with minute precision all the localities in the Alps, all the animals to be found there, and every flower that blooms in their valleys. Every object is drawn with extraordinary skill; there is so much delicacy in his engravings that the humblest moss may be recognized. But along with these faithful representations of nature, we find frightful aërial monsters; winged dragons which swarm in the obscure windings of roads, and stop the alarmed traveller. The perusal of the work of this author might well have sufficed to prevent our credulous ancestors from venturing into the gorges of the Alps or searching into their dark caverns!

Kircher the Jesuit, who was one of the most progressive men of his epoch, fell into the most deplorable errors. He represents frightful dragons which guard the riches of the earth, and which must be vanquished before obtaining possession of them. And as we sometimes find in caverns the bones of bears, hyenas, and other mammals, this was enough in times of such credulity to make men assign (as was particularly the case in Franconia) the fossilized remains of these ancient animals to fabulous reptiles.

It is particularly at the height of the Renaissance that we see this love of monstrosity reach its climax; every author then thought himself obliged to devote a few chapters of his work to it. Aldrovandus, a naturalist of Bologna, a profoundly learned man, even wrote a big work on monsters, in which are delineated some of the most fantastic kind.

Ambrose Paré, surgeon to Henry III. of France, though he had long travelled with the army, was no less credulous than the others. In his celebrated work he represents sirens, monks, and men-at-arms of the sea all covered with scales, and as fresh as if they had been just withdrawn

265. Dragon of the Caverns of Mount Pilatus.—Facsimile taken from the *Mundus Subterraneus* of the Reverend Father Kircher.

from the gulfs of Neptune. One asks with astonishment how the old Huguenot could believe such rubbish. I will not speak of the treatise on monsters by Licetus, as that is an important work, in which the anatomist has only exaggerated some details in order to give interest to his subject.

But if anything can surprise us more it is the fact that the history of monsters is found with all its exaggerations at two periods widely distant from each other. We find it in the height of its extravagances in the *Bestiaires* of the middle ages and in the books of the Renaissance, and then at the beginning of the present century it returns in order to astonish us by the audacity of its flights.

In the middle ages it was the sombre countries of northern Europe that harboured this belief, and it is in the works of Olaus Magnus, the Albertus Magnus of the North, that we find the most incredible display of it. From this work our moderns have taken their horrible sea-serpent. The author does not rest satisfied with giving a description of this creature; he delineates it, and in his engravings we see the reptile issuing

266. Sea-serpent.—Facsimile taken from Olaus Magnus: *De Gentibus Septentrionalibus*, 1555.

from the waves, and launching itself upon the ships in order to devour the crews.[1]

Elsewhere the Bishop of Upsala represents Cetacea which crush ships in their formidable jaws!

[1] "The old Scandinavian writers attribute to the sea-serpent a length of 600 feet, with a head closely resembling that of a horse, black eyes, and a kind of white mane. According to them, it is only met with in the ocean, where it suddenly rears itself up like a mast of a ship-of-the-line, and gives vent to hissing noises which appal the hearer, like the tempest roar. The Norwegian poets compare its progress to the flight of a swift arrow. When the fishermen descry it, they row in the direction of the sun, the monster being unable to see them when its head is turned towards that planet. They say that it revolves sometimes in a circle around the doomed vessel, whose crew thus find themselves assailed on every side."—*The Mysteries of the Ocean*, by Mangin.—Tr.

And yet though it seems incredible, our epoch, in respect to the history of marine monsters, leaves the old legends of the middle ages and of the Renaissance far behind. In fact it is impossible to dream of anything more fabulous than what Denis de Montfort in comparatively recent times gave out as a feast for the credulous. His mind must really have been diseased.

The lucubrations of this naturalist have found a place in the great edition of Buffon's works. He there states, without the least hesitation, that in the northern seas there are cuttle-fish of such a size that a whale

267. Cetacean attacking a Ship.—Facsimile from the Work of Olaus Magnus: *De Gentibus Septentrionalibus*, 1555.

is a pigmy in comparison with them. According to him these molluscs are even of such prodigious dimensions, that when they rest motionless and half out of the water their bodies, which ages have covered with tufts of marine plants, have sometimes been taken for islands floating on the surface of the waves. It is even related in some old Scandinavian chronicles that sailors, deceived by this treacherous sign, have been known to anchor their ships on the flanks of these sea monsters, and land on their backs.

In those times of credulity, when the life of the sailor was so full of anxiety and terror, such facts were held to be quite authentic. Thus we see Olaus Magnus represent in one of his works a company of fishermen warming themselves and cooking their food at a glowing fire lighted on the body of one of these fantastic creatures; but the author has sketched a cetacean, not a cuttle-fish. Gesner, a zoologist of the Renaissance, seems to believe such fables, for he reproduces the figure given by the learned Swede.

In the wide field of absurdities, Denis de Montfort displays credulity almost surpassing belief. He asserts, with a strong sense of conviction, that amid these great seas there are gigantic cuttle-fish, which, by means of their immense arms thickly covered with suckers, encircle ships and wreck them by plunging them into the abyss.

The naturalist even attributes the inexplicable disappearance of some of our ships to these formidable tenants of the ocean. He is so convinced of the truth of this fact, that he devotes one of the plates of Buffon's work to the exhibition of it. We there see a monstrous cuttle-fish with flaming eyes, the horrible arms of which are twined round the masts of a ship of war, which they are tightly straining, while the animal looks as if it would devour it.

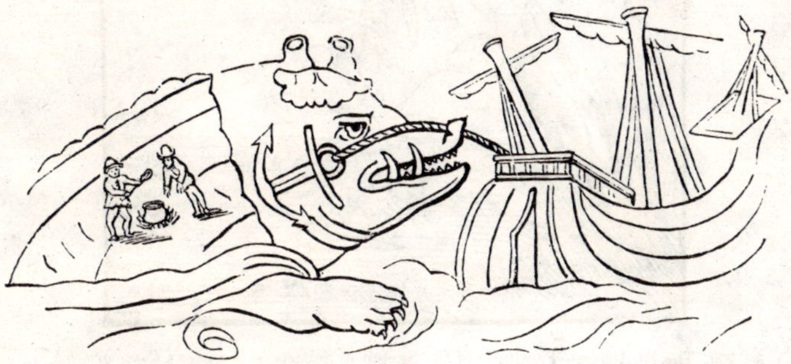

268. Marine Monster.—Facsimile from the Work of Olaus Magnus: *De Gent. Sept.*

Trees themselves and plants, notwithstanding their calm and peaceful life passed in the broad light of day, have still their legendary history and their superstitious traditions. Some have become celebrated on account of the strange animated progeny which has been attributed to their leafy tops; others for their medical or cabalistic power. Rousseau complained that plants had been defiled by transforming them into disgusting remedies. We should be more correct in accusing those who attribute ridiculous virtues to them.

Several water-birds were long considered to be the produce of certain trees which grow in the marshes or borders of the sea. Our credulous forefathers were persuaded that there was one of these growing in Scotland or the Orkneys, the fruits of which, as large as eggs and having the same shape, opened at maturity and allowed each a little duck to escape.

The vulgar would not have dared to doubt such a fact, for it was quoted by the most renowned scholars. Sebastian Munster attests the truth of it in his great work on *Cosmography*.

"We find," he says, "trees in Scotland which produce a fruit enveloped in leaves, and when it drops into the water at a suitable time, it takes life and is turned into a live bird, which they call a *tree-bird*." In order to produce a still fuller proof, the writer himself gives a drawing

269. The Bird-tree.—Facsimile of the Sketch in Sebastian Munster's *Cosmography*.

of it! We see the young ducks opening the fruits in order to escape, whilst the newly-hatched ones swim in the water near at hand!

But the case becomes still more serious when we see the most learned ornithologist of the Renaissance, Aldrovandus, propagate such ridiculous fables in his great work. He there maintains that sea-ducks are the product of certain trees, and he even represents these with the fruits which they bear. But by an unpardonable error for a naturalist, these pretended fruits from which the birds are issuing are only barnacles (*Lepas anatifera*), crustaceans which live at the bottom of the sea, and with which he nevertheless overloads the miraculous boughs!

After this one may well ask, Which is the most censurable—the savant who transcribes such absurdities, or the public who believe in them?

Some plants have also become celebrated in the annals of charlatanism. There were plants that warded off evil, plants that caused injury, and magical plants. Antiquity possessed a long list of these, and we have not fallen behind it.

On one side we find a venerated plant, the *Artemisia vulgaris* or St. John's-wort, which, gathered at the moment pointed out by the legend and hung over the outer door, preserved the house from lightning. On the other was a long list of cabalistic plants, among which the thorn-apple, *Datura Stramonium*, ought to be mentioned in the first rank. This was the frightful poison which sorcerers made use of to intoxicate their senses, and procure for themselves the spectacle of the Sabbath.

But no magical herb ever enjoyed more celebrity than the mandrake, an indispensable ingredient in all the philtres employed by the old sorcerers. Antiquity had already conducted us to this dark road, by

270. Mandragora Roots Carved; used for Enchantment.

maintaining that the roots of this plant were of a human form, a fact pointed out by the name *anthropomorphos* which Theophrastus gave it, whilst Columella called it *semihomo*.

To speak the truth, they in no way resemble a man, but the credulity of the learned and the astuteness of charlatanism have supplied what was requisite to give the appearance of truth to the opinions of the ancients. It was after they had rudely shaped them into human likeness that the magicians employed them in their incantations, and it was also under this form that the vulgar thought they were found at the foot of gibbets, where, after having fed on the remains of those who had suffered punishment, they had taken on their shape. The tenants of a place so sinister and so dreaded could not be removed without great danger. The learned themselves did not attempt to destroy so many absurdities, for in their works they sometimes represent mandrakes which resembled men and women, for there were some of both sexes.

They possessed the same power as the enchanted philtres of Circe, to which Pliny and Dioscorides had given this name. One thing is certain, the mandrake is one of the most fatal poisons we possess.

A charming little plant, all covered with hairs, which abounds on the slopes of Mount Ida, the dictamnus of Crete (*Origanum Dictamnus*) was formerly considered the most marvellous vulnerary that nature ever presented to man. The gods themselves had revealed its omnipotence to him, and animals instinctively made use of it. It was with this dictamnus that Venus dressed the wounds of Æneas. Aristotle tells us that the goats scattered over the celebrated mountain, so soon as the hunter has pierced them with an arrow, seek out the plant and eat it in order to make the arrow drop out and so to heal the wound. Half a century ago, who would have dared to deny such a wonderful property, when at that time a noble work on Greece contained a long chapter on the virtues of the divine vulnerary, and when, in addition to this, the reader might see an engraving representing a goat pierced with arrows and browsing upon the salutary herb?

In this way, unfortunately, did the authority of the learned retard and fetter the progress of truth.

INDEX.

B.

D

E.

F.

G.

H.

I.

J.

K.

L.

M.

N.

O.

P.

T.

U.